W9-ACD-722

The Ideologies of African American Literature

From the Harlem Renaissance to the Black Nationalist Revolt

A Sociology of Literature Perspective

Robert E. Washington

ROWMAN & LITTLEFIELD PUBLISHERS, INC.
Lanham • Boulder • New York • Oxford

ROWMAN & LITTLEFIELD PUBLISHERS, INC.

Published in the United States of America
by Rowman & Littlefield Publishers, Inc.
4720 Boston Way, Lanham, Maryland 20706
www.rowmanlittlefield.com

12 Hid's Copse Road, Cumnor Hill, Oxford OX2 9JJ, England

British Library Cataloguing-in-Publication Information Available

Library of Congress Cataloging-in-Publication Data

Washington, Robert E., 1941–
  The ideologies of African American literature : from the Harlem Renaissance to the Black nationalist revolt / Robert E. Washington.
    p. cm.
  Includes bibliographical references and index.
  ISBN 0-7425-0949-4 (alk. paper)—ISBN 0-7425-0950-8 (pbk. : alk. paper)
    1. American literature—African American authors—History and criticism. 2. Politics and literature—United States—History—20th century. 3. African Americans—Politics and government. 4. African Americans in literature. 5. Black nationalism in literature. 6. Harlem renaissance. 7. Black nationalism. I. Title.

PS153.N5 W35 2001
810.9'8960730904—dc21
                                                            2001019743

Printed in the United States of America

⊗™ The paper used in this publication meets the minimum requirements of American National Standard for Information Sciences—Permanence of Paper for Printed Library Materials, ANSI/NISO Z.3948-1992.

Contents

Contents

Acknowledgments

This study grew out of the resuscitated spirit of the Chicago School of Sociology in the late 1960s, at the University of Chicago, under the leadership of Morris Janowitz. I owe much gratitude to him for encouraging me to embrace a broad intellectual vision of sociology that took me into uncharted terrain and for helping me to obtain a fellowship to launch this study. I have never met anyone who cared about sociology's civic responsibilities as much as Morris Janowitz. I am also grateful to the late Benjamin Nelson and Edward Shils who taught me during the formative years of my development, and exemplified the highest standards of intellectual seriousness and integrity. Victor Lidz is someone who deserves a special acknowledgment, although I suspect he will be surprised to hear this. He played a large role in helping me to sustain my commitment to this study, with his encouraging and constructive critical comments, during the earlier phase of the study, when it was far from possessing a coherent theoretical argument.

I would also like to acknowledge several friends and colleagues: Elijah Anderson, with whom I have often discussed the ironic and baffling developments in American race relations; Xavier Nicholas, with whom I have shared and received both opinions and exciting discoveries about individual black writers; and Ernest Washington Jr. (my big brother), with whom I have been engaged in what now seems a lifelong, fascinating conversation about being black in America.

Finally, I would like to express my gratitude to Gretchen Hanisch at Rowman & Littlefield, who guided the manuscript through the varied phases of its production, and to Anna Cannavan and Lorraine Kirschner at Bryn Mawr College for their able secretarial assistance.

Introduction

Black American Literature in Sociological Perspective

Systems of culture are open to downward and upward mobility as are occupations and persons. Yesterday's moral virtue is today's ridiculed fanaticism.

—Gusfield, *Symbolic Crusade*

It is indeed the extremism of literary theory, its obstinate, perverse, endlessly resourceful refusal to countenance social and historical realities, which most strikes a student of its documents.

—Eagleton, *Literary Theory*

Contrary to what some literary scholars claim, literary works consist of more than aesthetically pleasing configurations of language or linguistic form. While the artistry of literary works is certainly important, it is hardly the reason they matter sociologically. That is, as cultural discourse, literary works matter because they depict social worlds. By projecting perspectives on human experiences that expand the horizons of our awareness, they shape our perceptions of social reality. From this sociological standpoint, we can liken literary works to movies, newspaper reports, magazine articles, political cartoons, historical chronicles, and sundry other modes of cultural discourse, because all project ideological constructions of human experiences that convey normative messages about social behavior.

ANALYTICAL OBJECTIVES OF THE STUDY

Embracing this sociological view of literature, this study investigates the ideological constructions of black American life produced by five dominant black American literary schools that prevailed in the American public arena at different times between 1920 and the early 1970s, and thereby helped to shape the changing public perceptions of black Americans. More precisely stated, this study has three distinct but related objectives. First, it seeks to explain the social and political forces that fostered each of these dominant black literary schools and its particular ideological construction of black American experiences. In pursuit of this objective, it attempts to answer such questions as: How did political developments and the climate of race relations in the black community affect the school's formation? How did social changes such as urban migration, proletarization, and structural alterations in the black community influence the way the literary school depicted black American experiences? To what extent was the school's development influenced by external forces, such as wars, social conflicts, political movements, and intellectual fashions emanating from the surrounding white American society?

Second, this study aims to explain each of these literary schools' social functions—the normative messages it conveyed through its ideological constructions—that shaped public perceptions of black American life. In short, what was the literary school's sociological significance? Did its normative messages encourage black American cultural solidarity? Or, conversely, did its normative messages communicate an assimilationist conception of black American life? Were those normative messages designed to arouse white American compassion or anxiety in reference to racial injustices suffered by blacks? Or were they designed to entertain and reassure its audience by presenting happy-go-lucky and carefree images of black American life? Which sector of the black American population did those normative messages highlight and which did they ignore? (E.g., The black lower class? The black middle class? Southern blacks? Northern blacks? Black women? Black men? Black family life? Black religion? Black politics?) Did the literary works that make up the school depict white Americans, and if so, from which sector of the white community were those characters drawn? What type of tensions or conflicts did the school's ideological perspective highlight—for example, racial, political, family, economic, interpersonal, psychological? How were those tensions resolved, and what normative messages—and expectations—did that resolution convey in reference to the future direction of both black community life and American race relations?

Third, shifting from these concerns with textual depictions of black American life, this study addresses the central problematic issue underlying the ideological production of these black literary works: What was the role of the white American cultural establishment in facilitating the dominance of these particular black literary schools over their rivals in the public arena? Rejecting the simplistic, though widely accepted, view that American culture constitutes a "free marketplace of ideas," this study maintains that ideological conceptions of reality do not emerge and gain dominance within a sociological vacuum. As Dick Hebdige has noted in *Subculture: The Meaning of Style:* "When we come to look beneath the level of 'ideology-in-general' at the way in which specific ideologies work, how some gain dominance and others remain marginal, we can see that in advanced Western democracies the ideological field is by no means neutral" (Hebdige 1979, 14–15).

Why one ideology enjoys dominance while competing ideologies are marginalized or ignored is seldom the consequence of its greater truth or rationality. Did slavery ideology gain acceptance in Western societies because it was based on a more truthful conception of Africans than antislavery ideology? Did Nazi ideology ultimately prevail over liberal democratic ideology in Weimar Germany because it possessed a more truthful or rational conception of Germany's problems? Did new criticism reign in literary studies during the 1950s because of its greater veracity? Did structural functionalism prevail from the mid-1940s to the mid-1960s in American sociology because it presented a more accurate conception of social life than did the Chicago school of sociology? To understand how certain ideologies gain dominance, we must recognize that modern cultural process consists of ongoing struggles among groups promoting ideas through which they seek to gain power or influence. Whether within the esoteric domains of leading academic journals in economics, philosophy, or history, or within the mass culture domains of movies, television, or popular music, ideologies operate as instruments of cultural combat, seeking either to reinforce or to alter the prevailing cultural hegemony.

Though never addressed in these terms, black American literature needs sociological scrutiny because it has been dependent—throughout much of its history—on the hegemonic influence of a white American cultural establishment. To understand that hegemonic cultural process we must examine not just the lives of black American writers but also the roles played by white Americans, often hidden from view, in the formation and ascendance of certain black literary schools in the mainstream public arena. Who were the key white American players behind the emergence of those schools? How were they involved in promoting or steering those literary schools? Did the cast of white American players involved in black literary life change from one dominant black literary school to another? What concerns drew these white Americans to black American literary works? What was the nature of their relationships to black

American writers? How did those relationships change from one school to the another? Were the black writers conscious of being dependent on a white American cultural establishment? And finally, what is for this study most important: How did that white American cultural establishment influence the normative content of the dominant black literary constructions of black American life?

These analytical questions will no doubt strike some literary scholars as irrelevant—if not to say offensive—to their concerns with black literary works as aesthetic products. This would be hardly surprising. Sociologists are no more likely to share the literary scholars' take on literature than they are the religious scholars' take on religion. Such are the realities of the intellectual division of labor. No intellectual discipline monopolizes the study of any human activity. Be it sex, sports, religion, family life, literature, or humor, specializations—embodying divergent angles of vision—abound. In recognition of that fact, this study proffers no claim to expert or unique insights into the aesthetic dimensions of black literary works. There exists a large and growing body of impressive scholarly writings that deal with the aesthetic features of black literary works. What this study does claim to provide, departing from those studies, is a sociological reading of black literary works as ideological forces in the cultural process of race relations. Focusing on the social and political dynamics that lay behind the emergence of the dominant black literary schools, this study explains how those schools both developed their ideological images of black American life and subsequently influenced public perceptions of black America during roughly five decades, from the 1920s through the 1960s.

Beginning during the black mass migration to northern cities shortly after World War I and ending with the demise of the civil rights revolution in the late 1960s, that half century witnessed black America's most dynamic historical period. Setting in motion the black community's modernization, the social forces of that period altered every sphere of black American life as black America increasingly was transformed from a rural peasantry into a diverse and energetic urban community. It is hardly coincidental that the emergence of that urban black community, which effected profound changes in black America's cultural and political landscape, corresponded to black American literature's ascent in the public arena. As tens of thousands of black Americans flooded into northern cities, creating a new and rich urban black ethnic culture, black American literature became the most visible and influential mode of black American intellectual discourse. That was because it fulfilled a vital sociological need. By transmitting insider information about urban black life to a curious white American public, forging a communication channel between the segregated black and white social worlds, black literary works bridged the chasm of the racial caste system.

Yet in acknowledging this momentous development, I must hasten to add that the functions of these dominant black literary schools were seldom what they seemed. As demonstrated throughout this study, though these literary schools were affected by changes within the black community, their perspectives on black American life seldom resonated the black community's social consciousness. Rather they functioned, for the most part, as a hegemonic discourse, which refracted black American experiences through ideological perspectives that emanated from the liberal white American intellectual community.

This thesis no doubt will provoke controversy. Even though some scholars have noted white American influence on black American literature, no study has theorized this dependency as a sociological process (Kramer 1987; Singh 1989; Cruse 1967). Other features of this study, while less likely to be controversial, set it apart from previous analyses of black American literature. To the best of my knowledge, black American literature has never been conceptualized in terms of the development of its dominant ideological schools, an analytical focus derived from the sociology of knowledge that allows us to view this literature in terms of its major normative trends. Also, in contrast to previous analyses of black American literature, this study traces the shifts in that literature's ideological constructions of black American life over a broad historical span of time, which allows us to contrast the different social environments that shaped the dominant schools. Finally, viewed from the standpoint of its larger theoretical objective, this study aims not just to chronicle the ideologies of these dominant black literary schools, but also to explain their cultural dependency, their attachment to the liberal white intellectual community, as by-products of the social and cultural dynamics of American racial stratification.

SITUATING THIS STUDY WITHIN THE SOCIOLOGY OF CULTURE

This study should be viewed not as an isolated intellectual venture but rather as part of the expanding body of sociological explorations of cultural process, ranging from studies of movies, music, art, architecture, and literature to advertising and clothing fashions. The sociology of culture has emerged, over the past several decades, as a major, multifaceted field of sociological inquiry. My aim here is not to review the large array of studies linked to this field which, aside from the daunting scale of the task, would divert us from the business at hand. Rather I aim for the more modest objective: to indicate the relationship of this study—as an analysis of a minority group's literary culture in a racially stratified society—to some of the major sociological approaches to studying cultural process and, thereby, denote its points of convergence or divergence from those approaches. To facilitate clarity, I will divide the sociological approaches to studying cultural process into four categories and discuss each in turn. (Readers who are uninterested in this scholarly context can skip this discussion and proceed to the next section, which describes this study's organization.)

The first of these approaches focuses on culture as symbolic codes. Describing and analyzing cultural classification systems, these studies seek to determine how the symbols are organized into systems and how they communicate meaning. In pursuit of these objectives they encompass a broad range of topics: myths, public rhetoric, religious beliefs, political ideology, penal codes, advertisements, plot structures in novels, and music (Bourdieu 1984; DiMaggio 1987; Foucault 1977; Goffman 1976; Griswold 1983, 1986, 1987; Gusfield 1981; Habermas 1984, 1987; Levi–Strauss 1963; Luker 1984; Meyer and Rowan 1977; Popcock 1987; Swidler 1986; Wuthnow 1987). While the current study views the ideologies of the dominant black literary schools as symbolic constructions, it does not attempt to analyze the "deep structure" of those ideologies. Which is to say, this study does not focus on the internal organization of those ideologies as symbol systems. Rather it focuses on the linkages of those ideologies, as normative messages, to the sociopolitical climates of race relations in which they prevailed.

The second of these approaches highlights the reader's interpretations of the text. After being ignored for many years, this focus on textual interpretations over the past several decades has been undertaken by scholars, resulting in an impressive group of reader-response studies examining such subjects as romance novels, religious texts, best-selling novels, children's books, reviews of novels, and science fiction (Ammermann 1987; DeVault 1990; Fiske 1989; Gottdiener 1985; Howard and Allen 1990; Iser 1974; Modleski 1982; Radway 1984; Rodgers 1991). While this study does not analyze readers' responses to the texts of the dominant black literary schools, it does incorporate an indirect version of the reader-response approach by presenting the responses of book reviewers to leading black literary works, which provides valuable insights into the meanings that literary opinion leaders attached to those texts. Book reviews are not, of course, representative of ordinary reader responses. But in studies of noncontemporaneous literary texts, where reader surveys are infeasible, a proxy methodology such as analysis of book reviews provide a reasonable alternative. Future studies of black literary works using the reader-response approach no doubt will provide significant insights into the different normative preconceptions black and white readers bring to those texts.

The third major approach focuses on the production of culture, which analyzes the status, organizational, and marketing constraints involved in creating cultural products. Emphasizing both the division of tasks and the decision making in cultural production, this approach has characterized a diverse group of studies. For example, an exemplary work embracing this orientation, Becker's *Art Worlds*, demonstrated that artistic production, contrary to conventional wisdom about art, constituted a collective rather than an individual endeavor (Becker 1982). Highlighting a different but no less significant aspect of the production of culture, Hirsch (1972) focused on the network of functionaries and gatekeepers who determined the nature of the artists' access to the public arena. Long's study of best-sellers demonstrated how the publishers' shift to capture a new reading public changed the thematic content of novels from a pro-capitalist to an anti-capitalist outlook (Long 1985). Coser, Kadushin, and Powell studied decision making in publishing (1982). These are just a few of the many studies that have used the production-of-culture approach (Cantor 1980; Crane 1987; Drass and Kisers 1988; Griswold 1992a, 1992b; Kiser 1983; Kiser and Drass 1987; Peterson 1976; Powell 1985; Schudson 1984; Tuchman 1978; White and White 1965). The current study converges with this approach as it problematizes the role of white Americans (i.e., mentors, patrons, publishers, editors, critics, and reviewers) in the ideological production of the dominant black literary schools. By focusing on the racial constraints circumscribing black literary production, the production-of-culture approach helps to illuminate the problems black American writers faced in launching their literary works. But this perspective does not go far enough. Specifically, it provides little insight into the normative consequences of those constraints—namely, the particular ideological meanings projected by the dominant black literary schools and their implications for public perceptions of black American life—which are this study's chief concerns.

This brings me to the fourth and final approach to the sociology of culture being considered, which focuses on the relationship among culture, inequality, and power. Though this approach derives from the writings of Karl Marx and Frederick Engels, it has undergone many revisions by twentieth-century theorists who have rejected Marxism's rigid reductionist view of cultural process for a more flexible analytical perspective that emphasized the interdependence between culture and social power. One example of this revisionist approach was formulated by the German Frankfurt School, which suggested that modern capitalist culture had neutralized class conflict by corrupting working-class consciousness with cheap and escapist mass entertainment (Horkheimer and Adorno 1944). Many of these revisionist perspectives, eschewing attempts to predict the actual content of culture, emphasized the limits imposed on the society's cultural discourse (i.e., the ideologies it excludes). Gitlin's pioneering study of the media's coverage of the student antiwar movement, *The Whole World Is Watching* (1980), demonstrated the variety of techniques the dominant culture used to distort and marginalize an oppositional ideology. Recent revisions of the Marxist perspective in the writings of such European cultural theorists as Pierre Bourdieu and Michel Foucault view culture as "having the power to frame alternatives and contain opportunities, to win and shape consent, so that the granting of legitimacy to the dominant classes appears not only spontaneous but natural and normal" (Hall 1984). Seen from this perspective, culture not only shapes the way individuals perceive social reality; it also has a large hand in determining their class position (Lamont and Wuthnow 1990, 295).

While these and other revisions of the Marxist perspective have contributed sharp insights into ideological forces sustaining modern capitalist societies, they have failed to problematize cultural production, particularly the roles of intellectuals. This issue has special relevance for the current study, because a major part of my analysis of the dominant black literary ideologies entails explaining the roles of the leading black writers who adapted and transmitted those ideologies.

In reference to this problem of explaining the roles of black writers, Karl Mannheim's writings provided useful leads (Mannheim 1936, 1952, 1953, 1956). An early practitioner of the sociology of knowledge, Mannheim sought to explain the social conditions that lay behind divergent intellectual conceptions of reality. Rejecting the conventional wisdom of Western intellectual tradition, he argued that it was not the intellectual's individual creativity but rather her social location, her position in the social structure, subjecting her to a certain pattern of life experiences, that most affected her conception of reality. Mannheim's concept of social location unfortunately had little influence because it presented abstract theoretical arguments when what was needed were concrete empirical studies that demonstrated the viability of the sociology of knowledge as a research field. Despite those shortcomings, Mannheim's theoretical arguments marked a refreshing departure by highlighting the effects of social influences on intellectual thought. It was through reading Mannheim's essays that I became interested in studying the social forces that shaped the ideological outlooks of the leading black American writers.

However, the more I explored the black literary scene the more I realized that I needed an analytical framework that focused on not only the black writers but also the larger culture of race relations, namely, the ideological climate within which the black writers operated. This became the key concern of this study's theoretical perspective. Derived from the writings of Antonio Gramsci, the brilliant Italian social theorist, this theoretical perspective, in contrast to the narrow Marxian theory, developed a more complex account of the interactions between culture and structures of social domination (Hoare and Smith 1971). This Gramsci set forth in his theory of cultural hegemony, which explains the way one class achieves dominance over other classes by cultural rather than coercive means. As will be evidenced in the last chapter, I have reformulated and extended Gramsci's theory to racial relations to account for the ideological outlooks of the dominant black literary schools between 1920 and the mid-1960s.

ORGANIZATION OF THIS STUDY

Now a few words about the organization of this study. Beginning with the 1920s and culminating with the 1960s, this study is presented in six chapters. The first five chapters recount each school's formation and ascent by delineating its sociohistorical setting, its leading figures and literary works, its ideological constructions, and its cultural functions. Chapter 1 concentrates on the 1920s and examines black American literature's most sociologically misunderstood development—the so-called Harlem Renaissance. Bracketing that label and its dubious connotations of a black literary revolution, this chapter analyzes the social forces of the 1920s that generated the dominant primitivist black literary school and its crude images of blacks as exotic primitives. In addition to removing the obfuscating misconceptions fostered by the Harlem Renaissance doctrine, this chapter explains why the 1920s marked the beginning of black American literature's unique public role as the preeminent vehicle of black American intellectual discourse, a position it retained for the next half century.

Chapter 2 shifts to the politically volatile social climate of the 1930s, and analyzes the Depression-era naturalistic protest school. Focusing largely on the role of Richard Wright, this chapter traces the development and influence of his explosive novel *Native Son*, which—through its depictions of black Americans as alienated and enraged victims of white racial oppression—launched the first dominant black American literary school that was rooted in a radical political ideology. If the 1920s primitivist school initiated black literature's role as the leading mode of black intellectual discourse in the public arena, the naturalistic protest school expanded and consolidated that role as black American literature operated, for the first time, as a major ideological force in the cultural politics of race relations.

Chapter 3 turns away from the politically volatile years of the Great Depression to the quiescent Cold War era, and focuses on the social conditions that generated the black existentialist literary school, spearheaded by Ralph Ellison's highly acclaimed *Invisible Man*. This chapter examines how the Cold War political climate and the structural changes in the black community set in motion an unprecedented, if brief, conservative ideological trajectory in the dominant black literary discourse. Though not then apparent, that novel's existentialist ideology would help to foster within the black American intellectual community an individualistic modernist ideological legacy, which would become the rallying cry of many culturally conservative black intellectuals.

Departing from the Cold War environment of political retreat, chapter 4 moves to a new period of activist social change as it charts yet another shift in black American literature's ideological direction, with the emergence in the late 1950s of the moral suasion school under the leadership of James Baldwin. In addition to recounting Baldwin's unusual social background and intellectual development, this chapter traces the origins of that school's ascendant integrationist ideology in the liberal political climate of the period and, in particular, the civil rights movement. The demise of the moral suasion school marked the end of liberal ideological dominance in not just black American literature but post–World War II American political culture, as a new and more racially alienated black American ideological movement challenged white liberal cultural influence.

This brings us to the fifth chapter, which focuses on the transformed ideological production of the dominant black literary discourse that was launched by the militant black cultural nationalist literary school. Inspired and mobilized by the angry, militant, and visionary leadership of Amiri Baraka during the mid-1960s, following the collapse of the civil rights movement, this cultural nationalist school marked a new historical moment, a critical watershed in black American intellectual culture, as it ended black American literature's ideological dependence and helped to galvanize a new radical black American ethnic consciousness. It was that new black ethnic consciousness, in large part broadcast by the cultural nationalist literary school, that shifted many black Americans from concerns with racial integration to concerns with black ethnic identity.

BLACK AMERICAN LITERATURE AS A CULTURAL INSTITUTION

Despite the outpouring of books and articles and the convening of numerous conferences and workshops devoted to analyzing black American literature during the past several decades, its role as a cultural institution remains opaque and unexplored. Most scholars writing about black literary works simply assume those works have been socially consequential but fail to explain how they operate—sociologically speaking—in cultural space. Also, and equally significant, they have failed to examine that literature's functions in relationship to the functions of other black American cultural institutions, such as black religion, black newspapers, black popular music, black dance, and black cinema. I address these matters in the last chapter where I set forth a theoretical model that illustrates the peculiar social functions of the first four dominant black literary schools.

In conclusion, I should say a few words about this study's limitations. Despite its broad historical scope, this study constitutes only a beginning. Much more work in the sociology of black American literature needs to be done, if we are to understand how black literary works have operated as vehicles of ideological discourse. This study's focus has been restricted to the implications of the ideologies of the dominant black literary schools for public perceptions of black American life and American race relations. Many questions remain to be explored. For example, did minor black literary works project more reflexive constructions of black American life (i.e., perspectives grounded in black community consciousness) than did the dominant black literary schools? Did their ideological reflexivity hamper their access to notoriety? Did they exhibit a different audience orientation? Were their authors more integrated into black community life? What type of sexual, religious, and family ideologies have black literary works projected? Why were black women writers, who now are the leading black American authors, largely absent in the dominant black literary schools until the 1970s? Did the ideological preoccupations of black female writers differ from those of black male writers? To what extent was the earlier prevalence of black male writers influenced by patriarchal values of the white American cultural establishment? Moving beyond gender perspectives to a more global concern, future studies should also ask: Do similarities exist between the dominant ideological trajectory of black American literature and the literatures of colonial and post colonial African and Caribbean societies? Did the latter also evidence white Western cultural hegemony? Were they confronted by the same type of organizational and marketing constraints? These are only a few of the many questions that must be answered. If we are to achieve a comprehensive sociological account of the ideological functions of black American literary discourse, other sociological analyses must follow. I hope this study constitutes a fruitful beginning.

1

✳

The Era of the Primitivist School

The Beginning of Black American Literature's Public Role

We younger Negro artists who create intend to express our individual dark skinned selves without fear of shame. If white people are pleased we are glad. If they are not, it doesn't matter. We know we are beautiful. And ugly too. The tom-tom cries and the tom-tom laughs. If colored people are pleased we are glad. If they are not, their displeasure doesn't matter either. We build our temples for tomorrow, strong as we know how, and we stand on top of the mountain, free within ourselves.

—Hughes 1926a, 694

By any standard of comparison, the 1920s set in motion a most extraordinary period in American cultural history. Marking the nation's transformation from a rural and small-town way of life into a predominately urban and industrial society, the decade produced a dizzying array of changes in both the mainstream white society and the black American community. In fact, in virtually every sphere of life—from the pedestrian worlds of work, religion, and recreation to the high cultures of science, art, and literature—the surging waves of new cultural developments swept a still-provincial and straitlaced nation into the uncharted, turbulent sea of modernity.

Within the black community, the signs of that modernity appeared most dramatically in black American literature. In the confused, helter-skelter ideological outlook of the first dominant black literary school, the leading writers were rebelling against what they saw as the lies and distorted beliefs about black American life that earlier literary works had fostered. As seen in the above brash declaration by Langston Hughes, one of the key figures in the new black literary school, these young black writers sought to celebrate blackness, and dismissed the objections of both blacks and whites who felt embarrassed or offended by what they wrote.

Nurtured in the bohemian interracial haunts of the Jazz Age and enchanted by the flattering inducements of the Harlem Renaissance doctrine, these young black writers reveled in a defiant and freewheeling spirit of adventure, which grew out of their exaggerated—if not to say delusional—expectations of social reform. Odd though it may seem now in retrospect, they saw themselves not simply as a new generation of black writers but as the juggernaut of a race relations revolution.

After what had seemed an interminable night of racial oppression extending from the brutal ordeal of slavery to the bitter frustrations of the postreconstruction period, many black American intellectuals, in the early 1920s, thought they were witnessing the dawn of racial equality on the horizon. That perception was shaped largely by the new opportunities that were opening to talented young black Americans, which aroused unprecedented excitement and optimism and unleashed a flood of black intellectual and artistic energy. Nowhere were those new developments more visible than in the surge of black American literary works printed by mainstream white American publishers.

Resonating the Jazz Age spirit of exploration and rebellion, mainstream publishers printed an impressive array of black literary works, including Jean Toomer's *Cane* (1923); Jessie Fausett's *There Is Confusion* and Walter White's *Fire in the Flint* (1924); Eric Walrond's *Tropic Death* and Walter White's *Flight* (1926); W. E. B. DuBois's *Dark Princess,* Nella Larsen's *Quicksand,* Rudolph Fischer's *Walls of Jericho,* and Claude McKay's *Home to Harlem* (1928); Nella Larsen's *Passing,* Wallace Thurman's *Blacker the Berry,* and Jessie Fausett's *Plum Tree* (1929); Langston Hughes's *Not Without Laughter* (1930); Arna Bontemp's *God Sends Sunday,* Jessie Fausett's *The Chinaberry Tree,* and George Schuyler's *Slaves No More* (1931); Claude McKay's *Gingertown,* Countee Cullen's *One Way to Heaven,* and Rudolph Fischer's *The Conjure Man Dies* (1932); Claude McKay's *Banana Bottom* and Jessie Fausett's *Comedy: American Style* (1933). Though not all of these books projected the dominant school's ideological outlook, this sharp upsurge of black literary works printed by mainstream publishers reflected a momentous development in American race relations: educated white Americans' growing curiosity about black American life. Aroused as much by the black community's dramatic social and political changes as by a search for the exotic, this increased white American curiosity had a large hand in transforming the black American literary landscape.

As Arna Bontemps, a young black writer of the era, later recalled: "When acceptances from Harpers, Harcourt, Brace, Viking, Boni and Liveright, Knopf, and other front-line publishers began coming through in quick succession, the excitement among those of us who were writing was almost unbearable. The walls of Jericho were toppling" (Emmanuel and Gross 1968, 64). Indeed, the barriers of racial exclusion were declining, and this was producing important and far reaching repercussions. Particularly for such talented black writers of the era as Langston Hughes, Claude McKay, and Jean Toomer, the 1920s seemed to be opening an age of limitless opportunity.

But this view, which made them optimistic about white America's proclivity for racial reform, turned out to be mistaken. Believing that black literary works revealing the cultural richness and uninhibited sensuality of lower-class black American ethnic life would liberalize white American culture, they fell prey to a controversial hedonist ideology. That dubious ideological strategy for racial enlightenment soon ran into opposition from several astute political black activists, who denounced its salacious literary images of blacks as degrading racial insults that would set back black America's struggle for citizenship rights. But those criticisms fell on deaf ears. These young black writers, swayed by their optimistic anticipation of racial reform, believed they had a nobler literary mission than that of promoting political propaganda.

To understand how this odd literary development came about, we must examine the changing culture of the American racial system, specifically the social forces that fostered this dominant black literary school and its controversial ideological perspective on black American life. But before turning to that task, we will briefly examine, from a sociological viewpoint, the cultural process that fostered the dominant literary/ideological images of black American life prior to the 1920s. Those earlier literary images, as we will see, were not produced by black American writers.

THE DEMISE OF PATERNALISTIC CULTURAL HEGEMONY

Got one mind for white folks to see,
Another for what I know is me;
He don't know, he don't know my mind.

—An old black American folk song

There is considerable risk and not a little arrogance in any white writer's attempt to describe black life and culture.

—Silberman 1978, 136

Typically, accounts of black American literature's historical development have lacked an analytical perspective that explained its relationship to the surrounding society. Consequently, more by default than by design, those discussions conveyed the impression that black literary works developed in a sociological vacuum, as the outcomes of an autonomous and mysterious process manifested through the creative imaginations of individual writers. That approach was flawed not because it emphasized the importance of the individual writers' creativity, but rather because it attributed far too much influence to the latter—while ignoring the social forces that shaped their ideological worldview. The ideological worldview expressed by a literary work is almost never the product of the writer's creative imagination. Rather it usually emanates from the writer's social world— that is, the interpersonal relations and culture from which he derives his values and conception of social reality. The German sociologist of knowledge, Karl Mannheim, articulated this point quite well:

> Just as it would be incorrect to attempt to derive a language merely from observing a single individual, who speaks not a language of his own but rather that of his contemporaries and predecessors who have prepared the way for him, so it is incorrect to explain the totality of an outlook only with reference to its genesis in the mind of the individual. (Mannheim 1936, 2–3)

Because they ignored this sociological context, studies of black American literature failed to explain not only the origins but also the alterations of its ideological constructions of black American experiences from one historical period to another. More specifically, they failed to explain those ideological constructions as manifestations of a cultural process that was embedded in the historical dynamics of American race relations. To comprehend the historical dynamics behind that cultural process, we must view black American literature's development from a sociological perspective.

When we look at black American literature in preindustrial America, the one glaring sociological fact that confronts us is its extreme marginalization, which resulted from the mainstream society's disregard of literary works by black writers. Because it is simply untrue that no talented black American writers existed prior to the 1920s, we must explain this situation by taking into account the structures of domination, the deeply rooted patterns of extreme social inequality, that characterize preindustrial societies. In contrast to industrial societies, preindustrial social structures are typically based on rigid structures of domination (e.g., slavery, colonialism, feudalism, serfdom, or caste subjugation) through which ruling groups control and exploit low-status groups. As James Scott put it in *Domination and the Arts of Resistance:*

> As a formal matter, subordinate groups in these forms of domination have no political or civil rights, and their status is fixed by birth. Social mobility, in

principle, if not in practice, is precluded. The ideologies justifying domination of this kind include formal assumptions about inferiority and superiority which, in turn, find expression in certain rituals or etiquette regulating public contact between strata. (Scott 1990, x–xi)

To understand black American literature's extreme marginalization, we must go one step further, and take into account the effects of those structures of domination on the society's cultural process. That is because in preindustrial structures of domination the ruling group typically controls not only the subordinate group's economic and political life, but also its cultural representations—namely, the ideas and images inscribing its social identity in the public arena. In effect, the dominant literary, artistic, journalistic, and historical representations of subordinate groups in these societies emanate from a cultural system of paternalistic hegemony, which, in contrast to other types of hegemonic cultural systems, is distinguished by two features: the agents (the producers) and the agency (the ideological perspectives) of the representations derive from the ruling group. Thus writers and intellectuals from the ruling group in this paternalistic cultural system—through propagating ideas and images in the public arena that deny or devalue the subordinate group's humanity—have a large hand in legitimating the prevailing structure of extreme social inequality.

It was under this type of paternalistic cultural system that the dominant literary images of black American life were produced in preindustrial America, prior to the 1920s. Though black Americans wrote novels and poems during this era, black American literature was relegated to a feeble social role. Within the mainstream public arena controlled by major white American book publishers, newspapers, and magazines, white American writers produced the dominant images of black American life and, thereby, largely defined black America's social identity. Effected through direct, transparent, and often crude practices of ideological construction, the hegemonic process of the pre-1920s American racial system was distinguished by three features: its authors were white Americans; its images of black American life emanated from white American ideological perspectives; and its credibility was supported by the prevailing white racial stereotypes about blacks.

This is not to say white American culture was monolithic. Various white literary schools, expressing divergent ideological perspectives on black American life, gained notoriety for periods of varying duration. During the high point of slavery, the dominant literary/ideological images of black Americans were, without exception, racially degrading (McDowell 1966, 71–83). In contrast, the images of blacks that prevailed during the second half of the nineteenth century diverged sharply, the products of contrasting sociopolitical climates that fostered two very different white literary schools.

The first of these two schools, the Abolitionist literary school, emerged during the social climate of mounting political conflict, initiated by the stern antislavery ideology of Harriet Beecher Stowe's *Uncle Tom's Cabin* (1851). This literary school dominated during the mid-nineteenth century, constructing ideological images of blacks as abused victims of enslavement. The school, and especially Stowe's novel, helped to arouse the northern white opposition to slavery that led to the Civil War.

Several decades after the war, however, a different white literary school assumed dominance. This was the Plantation literary school that prevailed during postreconstruction. Initiated by the literary works of the white southern writer Thomas Dixon (the author of the novel on which D. W. Griffith later based the racist movie *Birth of a Nation*), this literary school projected images of blacks as amoral, uncivilized, and dangerous brutes, who were unfit to exercise their recently acquired citizenship rights. In disseminating these images of blacks, the Plantation school helped to foster and legitimate the reactionary climate of antiblack hatred and lynchings that swept across the South from the 1880s to World War I, and demolished the race-relations reforms of reconstruction.

Despite their very different strategic objectives and images of blacks, both literary schools shared one striking similarity: the representation of black American life through white ideological perspectives rooted in assumptions of black racial inferiority. This hegemonic paternalism was manifest even when blacks were depicted sympathetically, as in the case of the Abolitionist school. White racial superiority remained the core cultural assumption undergirding the preindustrial American racial system, with the result that white writers and white ideological perspectives dominated literary depictions of black America in the public arena.

In contrast, the literary depictions of black American life by black writers had a far different fate. In fact, only two black American writers—Paul Lawrence Dunbar (1872–1908) and Charles Chestnutt (1858–1932)—managed to sustain literary careers of some duration before the 1920s. And both paid a heavy price. To find outlets for their literary works, which appeared around the turn of the century, they were obliged to appropriate the racially derogatory perspective of the dominant white Plantation school. As Robert Bone, in *The Negro Novel in America,* has observed: "Both launched their literary careers by exploiting the Plantation tradition; both brought them to fruition with the help of white patrons" (Bone 1958, 35). More bluntly stated, we might say, both writers had to ideologically accommodate the racist cultural climate to sustain their literary careers.

Frustrated by this situation, Chestnutt later departed from the Plantation school perspective and began to write novels that depicted black American life from a more reflexive ideological perspective. But he encountered resistance. The prevailing racist social climate in American society was not ready for such literary works, and Chestnutt soon abandoned his literary career to practice law. Dunbar, however, acquiesced to the degrading black racial stereotypes, and "continued to write in the Plantation tradition, or avoided controversy by making his main characters white" (Bone 1958, 36).

We can see another example of the repression black writers faced under the regimen of paternalistic hegemony in the experiences of poet Claude McKay. During the early years of his literary career in the United States, about the time of World War I, McKay concealed his racial identity and avoided expressing a black point of view in his writings. He did this to get his poetry published in white literary magazines. A few years later, when he decided to use his name and express a black viewpoint, he encountered resistance. One surprising source of resistance came from the black American editor of a Boston literary magazine (a man assimilated into the dominant white culture's European-centered conception of literature), who rejected McKay's poems and instructed him to send only those that did not betray his racial identity. McKay reacted with outraged astonishment, but there was nothing he could do (McKay 1963, 28).

Formidable racial barriers confronted all black Americans who attempted to pursue literary careers under the cultural system of paternalistic hegemony. Summarizing the pathetic predicament of the black literary enterprise from the turn of the century to the early 1920s, one historian has noted that, "with the exception of the fiction of Charles Chestnutt and Paul Lawrence Dunbar, which were printed by major publishers between 1898 and 1905, Negro novels and short stories between the latter year and 1923 were almost invariably presented by small firms that were unable to give their authors a national hearing" (Gloster 1948, 110–11). Thus, to restate the key sociological point: black American literature, prior to the 1920s, existed in a state of extreme marginalization.

Hardly the random outcome of historical accident, this paternalistic hegemony was an integral feature of the preindustrial racial caste system. Implemented as a social structure for exploiting black agricultural labor, that preindustrial caste system's survival was based on the black community's economic, political, and cultural subjugation, a reality that could be readily observed in the dismal conditions of black American life. Backbreaking toil, abject poverty, rural shacks, illiteracy, and powerlessness prevailed as common conditions of the preindustrial racial caste system designed to produce an obedient, socially inferior, and cheap supply of labor. Given this degraded state of black American life, it is scarcely surprising that whites living in this preindustrial environment of American race relations thought blacks lacked a genuine culture—ideas and feelings, subjective experiences, and values—that were worthy of white

American respect. White America's distorted perceptions of black American culture thus formed an essential part of the prevailing structure of racial oppression.

Buttressing and legitimizing the repressive racial caste system, white writers and intellectuals, in effect, invented a spurious black American culture in the public arena, consisting of crude and venomous stereotypes, suggesting that the racial caste system was a natural outgrowth of innate differences between the races. Blacks were not alone, of course, in being subjected to such venomous stereotypes. Other American racial minorities also experienced cultural dehumanization in the public arena. Images of American Indians as evil savages, Mexican Americans as slow-witted, lazy malingerers, and Chinese Americans as inscrutable and devious aliens—to cite only a few examples—were also deeply inscribed in American public culture, operating as commonplace rationalizations of the preindustrial structure of white racial domination (Takaki 1993). But if black images were featured more prominently in the paternalistic cultural hegemony, it was because black labor in the American economy occupied a more important role.

Significantly, the degrading images of black Americans in literary works were paralleled in minstrel shows, a major form of nineteenth-century popular entertainment, in which white comedians, painted in black face, acted out ludicrous and demeaning black stereotypes, for the entertainment of white audiences (Osofsky 1968, 196). In fact, throughout American public culture, in white literary works, minstrel shows, newspaper cartoons, advertisements, folk humor, and figures of speech, crude racial images of blacks functioned like inverted mirrors, transmuting repressed white American sexual and aggressive impulses into caricatures of pathological black American personality.

But even more important, images of blacks emanating from this paternalistic hegemony nurtured and reinforced white racial arrogance, the attitudes of white racial superiority that allowed whites both to embrace Christianity and to monopolize political and economic privileges without feeling moral guilt. It was that racial arrogance that encouraged most white Americans to accept, without questioning, the view that blacks constituted a lower species. As Digby Baltzell has noted in reference to nineteenth-century white racial attitudes toward blacks: "The Negro, it was almost universally agreed even among the most educated people, was definitely an inferior breed and situated at the very base of the evolutionary tree" (Baltzell 1967, xxi).

Wrote the editor of the Charleston *News and Courier* in 1898: "Everybody knows that when freed from the compelling influence of the white man he reverts by a law of nature to the natural barbarism in which he was created in the jungles of Africa" (Gutman 1977, 344). This view of blacks as an uncivilized people of the jungle was widespread in white American culture.

Actually, as Herbert Gutman points out, "The real world inhabited by poor rural and urban southern ex-slaves and their children between 1880 and the start of the vast northward migration after 1900 was invisible to nearly all observers" (Gutman 1977, 531). This ignorance about black American life conduced to the needs of the preindustrial racial caste system. Hence the existence of paternalistic hegemony.

But in the 1920s that situation changed. With the nation's increasing industrial and urban expansion that brought black American migrants flooding into northern cities, the rigidly repressive preindustrial racial caste system, along with its cultural regimen of paternalistic hegemony, began to break down.

The rapidly expanding urban black American community changed race relations. The effects of that change were revealed nowhere more clearly than in the new literary images of black American life and the dramatic ascent of black writers in American public culture. Black literary works were at last emerging from the shadows of marginalization and shedding the yoke of paternalistic hegemony. But to what end? That is the critical question: What supplanted paternalistic hegemony?

THE BLACK COMMUNITY'S TRANSFORMATION AND BLACK AMERICAN LITERATURE'S NEW PUBLIC ROLE

> The Negro of nineteenth-century literature was a comic, essentially idealistic Negro associated with the fiction of the Southern Plantation; few writers conceived of a Negro who differed from the humorous or pathetic type. The New Negro, in contrast, is frenetic, pugnacious, curious, and at times violent.
>
> —Emmanuel and Gross 1968, 62

> The American mind must reckon with a fundamentally changed Negro.
>
> —Locke 1925, 11

Without question, the single most important development behind black American literature's new public role was the beginning of black mass migration to northern cities. "From 1910 to 1920, the black population of Chicago increased by 148.2 percent (65,355 to 109,458), of Pittsburgh by 117.1 percent (9,190 to 20,355), of New York by 66.3 percent (60,758 to 152,467), of Philadelphia by 58.9 percent (25,894 to 69,854), and of St. Louis by 58.9 percent (25,894 to 69,854). Similar gains were shown in almost all the second-line northern industrial cities, such as Indianapolis, Kansas City, and Columbus" (Wilson 1978, 67).

Impelled by both the "push" of the South's economic devastation and the "pull" of the North's economic opportunities, large streams of black Americans began to flow into northern cities, setting in motion the black community's social and cultural modernization. That modernization was revealed partly in new patterns of social organization—fraternal groups, charities, hospitals, insurance companies, retail stores, labor unions, and professional associations—that expanded the black community's social service and economic functions. It was also revealed in the increased complexity of the black community's social stratification, as evidenced in its expanded middle class and its new cosmopolitan elite. Furthermore, and perhaps most significant, black urbanization fostered a new dynamic urban black ethnic culture, which was manifested in distinct forms of speech, clothing, musical forms, dance styles, leisure activities, and religious life—as well as in a new restive and assertive urban black political consciousness. Developing in response to the rampant racial discrimination blacks encountered in housing, jobs, and recreational facilities as they settled in northern cities, this assertive political consciousness propelled blacks into open racial conflicts with working-class whites, who inhabited the neighborhoods in which blacks sought to settle.

These conflicts were exacerbated by competition for employment. Excluded from union membership, blacks often accepted jobs as strikebreakers, undercutting the wage demands of white workers. As William Julius Wilson points out in *The Declining Significance of Race,* "The significance of black strikebreaking is not that it provided an early opportunity for Negroes to enter northern industries . . . , but that it created incidents that dramatically revealed and directly contributed to the racially charged atmosphere. Indeed, whether blacks were used as strikebreakers or whether they were simply hired on a regular basis, their movement into industry sharply exacerbated not only the economic and social anxieties of the white working class but also their racial antagonism" (Wilson 1978, 72–73).

Sparked by that antagonism, race riots erupted in northern cities shortly after World War I. In cities such as Chicago; Philadelphia; Chester, Pennsylvania; and East St. Louis, Illinois, violent clashes between black and whites resulted in hundreds of injuries and deaths. These riots grew out of the tensions aroused by changing race relations. But unlike earlier episodes of racial violence in the South, where blacks usually found themselves unarmed and outnumbered by white mobs, the post–World War I racial violence in the North took a different turn. Blacks now fought back as they exhibited a spirit of defiance, emboldened by the new political consciousness, which some observers hailed as the black community's new revolutionary spirit.

Though this characterization of the black community, driven by a revolutionary spirit, was exaggerated, one thing was indisputably clear: many black Americans were gravitating toward a more radical political outlook. Inspired by Marcus Garvey's black nationalist United Negro Improvement Association, the first black mass political movement, these blacks viewed racial nationalism as the black community's only hope for political progress. The specter of this radical black nationalist movement , surfacing in the unsettling period of mass black migration, not only stirred controversy within the black community; it aroused much anxiety, and trepidation, in white America (Cronon 1955).

We will return to this movement momentarily when we discuss the relationship of the major forms of social consciousness within the 1920s black community to the ideology of the dominant black primitivist literary school. But for our current purpose, most important was the effect of these black social developments on white American perceptions of the urban black community. Many whites began to see blacks—for the first time—as a strange or potentially threatening presence. Though they hardly foresaw the complex repercussions the rapidly expanding northern black community would have for race relations, one thing was clear: white Americans could no longer afford to ignore the new black voices rumbling on the urban landscape. It was in this social and historical environment of changing race relations that many educated whites turned to literary works by black writers, seeking to understand the social realities and aspirations of this emerging, and restive, urban black community.

This dramatically changing terrain of race relations in the urban North, particularly in New York City, eroded the cultural regimen of paternalistic hegemony, and fostered black American literature's new public role. This was what Arna Bontemps was referring to when he declared, "The walls of Jericho were toppling." But neither he nor any other young black writers of the era understood the complex social conditions that had brought about that development and, in consequence, they succumbed to delusions—sincere but grossly misguided fantasies—about the role they would play in shaping the future direction of American race relations.

Why did this changing climate of race relations prompt these leading young black writers to embrace an ideological perspective that, in the view of many observers, undermined the black community's struggle for civil rights? During a period when many black Americans were developing a more radical political consciousness, why did these writers—newly liberated from the harness of paternalistic hegemony—construct literary images of black American life that seemed to promote a retrograde racial ideology? Did they intend this? To answer these questions, we must move beyond the macro structural changes in black American life, and focus on the specific social influences that distorted these young black writers' perceptions of the American racial scene.

Misguided Optimism and the Embrace: A Retrograde Racial Ideology

It seems that the interest in the cultural expression of Negro life . . . heralds an almost revolutionary revaluation of the Negro.

—Locke 1925, 8

If any characteristic distinguished the leading young black writers of the 1920s from those who would participate in later dominant black American literary schools, it was their naiveté, their vulnerability to the lure and the illusion of literary celebrity. As young black writers coming of age during the 1920s, they felt that they were living in a time of "fresh beginnings." But they possessed neither the intellectual disposition nor historical perspective needed to comprehend the changes that were transforming American society. It was primarily because of this innocence that they misunderstood both their new opportunities for recognition and the changing American racial scene in the 1920s, and ended up embracing a racially controversial ideological perspective.

To understand how their perceptions of American race relations became so distorted, we must first examine the assumptions that shaped their social consciousness as literary artists. Unless we take those assumptions into account, we are apt to conclude that these writers were merely unscrupulous opportunists, seeking to advance their literary careers and achieve public recognition by any available means. This argument has been made by critics such as Harold Cruse (Cruse 1967, 32–53).

But this argument is much too simplistic. Explaining the ideological development of this literary school in terms of the writers' personal ambitions is like accounting for German Nazi ideology by saying that its adherents were driven by material greed. While material or status interests may compose part of an ideology's appeal, they hardly explain its content, namely, the particular nature of its social consciousness. That is because reductionist psychological arguments stressing the motives of individuals ignore the social conditions underlying the ideology's development as *a form of social consciousness,* a shared set of perceptions and attitudes, that resonate specific experiences of reality.

To understand this resonance, we must examine that social consciousness in relationship to the configuration of social and historical experiences from which it emanated. Viewing the outlook of the young black writers in the 1920s from this standpoint, we will see that they were not so much unscrupulous opportunists as gullible and ambitious romantics, seized by delusions of literary celebrity and influence.

The key assumptions that shaped these writers' worldview and perceptions of the American racial scene derived from their experiences in the heady environment of the 1920s. Those assumptions were (1) that American society was moving toward liberal racial reforms, (2) that their literary works would play a major part in effecting those racial reforms, and (3) that the chief effect of their literary works would be to emotionally liberate white America. We will examine each of these curious assumptions in turn.

The first assumption, that American society was moving toward liberal racial reform, appeared to be confirmed not only by the growing white American interests in black American life, as noted earlier, but also, and more important, by the attraction of many younger white American writers to black American culture. The young black writers, of course, realized that American society had hardly achieved racial equality. Nevertheless, they believed they saw unmistakable signs, particularly in the attitudes of these young white writers, that the nation was beginning to repudiate its conservative Anglo-Saxon traditions and appreciate the cultures of its ethnic and racial minorities. Noting that trend among the young white writers, one critic has observed:

> In the works of novelists like Willa Cather, Theodore Dreiser and Sherwood Anderson, and poets like Vachel Lindsay and Carl Sandburg we no longer see Anglo-Saxon writers bemoan the misfortunes of the poor and the foreigners . . . . (But rather) writers still Anglo-Saxon by birth or thoroughly assimilated to Anglo-Saxon attitudes of temperament were beginning to find in the foreign stock qualities superior to their own. (Burgum 1970, 111)

Though conservative white American intellectuals saw this trend as alarming evidence of white America's cultural decline, the young black writers saw it as a sign that the nation was at last opening to progressive racial reform.

Second, their assumption that their literary works would accelerate this racial reform was based on their belief that those works were creating respect and appreciation of black American culture. To comprehend the origin of this assumption, it is important to understand that they viewed their literary works not simply as artistic products but also—indeed most important—as social documents that would enlighten white American racial attitudes. Because they believed it was the richness and vitality of black American culture that was attracting the white cultural elite to black Harlem nightclubs and after-hours joints, they figured that their literary works, by depicting this black ethnic life for a broader audience, would expand the white society's understanding and acceptance of black American culture. To achieve that objective, they believed black American writers had to reject the legacy of special pleading and propaganda that had plagued earlier black literary works, and commit themselves to writing honest and truthful depictions of black America. This commitment to what they regarded as "literary realism" emanated from their optimistic faith in prospective racial reforms.

The most forceful and eloquent proponent of this new black literary realism was without question Alain Locke. A Harvard- and Oxford-educated philosophy professor and cultural critic, Locke belonged to the small group of cosmopolitan black Americans in the urban North, the vanguard of the emerging generation he termed "the New Negro," who detested the legacy of racist propaganda and patronizing indulgence that had suffused earlier literary depictions of black America. "The intelligent Negro today is resolved to not make discrimination an extenuation of his short comings in performance . . . ," Locke declared in his famous essay heralding the New Negro. "He is trying to hold himself on par. . . . He must know himself and be known for precisely what he is, and for that reason he welcomes the scientific rather than old sentimental interests" (Locke 1925, 12).

Though he operated as the leading spokesman for black literary realism, Locke hardly led the ascendant black literary school in the sense of fostering its ideological perspective or producing literary works that exemplified its style. Rather his importance derived from his activities as a publicist, the chief propagandist and missionary of black aesthetic works, who cultivated the dubious Harlem Renaissance doctrine (a matter I will have more to say about later). Through those activities Locke influenced the young black writers' conception of their social roles as literary rebels. "The day of 'aunties,' 'uncles,' and 'mammies' is . . . gone," proclaimed Locke in reference to this new direction of black literary expression. "Uncle Tom and Sambo have passed on. . . . The popular melodrama has about played itself out, and it is time to scrap the fictions, garret the bogeys and settle down to a realistic facing of facts" (Locke 1925, 12).

It was this Lockean sentiment Langston Hughes was echoing in his defiant pronouncement—"We build our temples for tomorrow, strong as we know how, . . . free within ourselves"—that appeared in the liberal white *Nation* magazine shortly after the publication of Locke's New Negro essay. Embracing this insurgent and optimistic conception of their social role, Hughes and the other leading young black literary artists saw themselves as not simply writers but cultural emissaries, carrying the tidings of black America's rich ethnic life to the alien terrain of a misinformed but curious white society.

Finally, and most surprising, was their third assumption, that their literary depictions of black American ethnic life would change white American culture. This assumption operated as the hidden sociological agenda—the pivotal faith—that energized their social consciousness by enlarging their conception of their social role and impact as literary artists. This went beyond simply promoting ethnic pluralism. Though gaining acceptance of American ethnic cultures certainly constituted part of their objectives, their hidden sociological agenda envisioned something far more radical than increased cultural tolerance. Rather it envisioned their literary images of black American ethnic culture emotionally liberating white Americans. By helping white Americans to overcome their inhibitions, to unleash their impulses, and to discover their capacity for sensual pleasures—in short, by awakening white American society to the passionate side of human nature that had been repressed by its puritanical heritage—these black literary works would psychologically emancipate white America. And in doing so, they would humanize mainstream white American culture and make it conducive to racial reform. It was the convoluted logic of this hidden sociological agenda that caused them to feel justified in representing black Americans in terms of a hedonistic primitivist ideology.

To be sure, American society in the 1920s was undergoing dramatic changes. But neither those changes nor the increased white American interests in black American life they stimulated portended the enlightened and tolerant white racial attitudes that these young black writers anticipated. Put simply, they grossly underestimated the depth and resilience of white American racism. And in consequence, they fell prey to a white primitivist literary movement whose potentially damaging implications, it seems accurate to say, they never understood. Noted one critic in reference to this odd image of black Americans projected by this white primitivist ideology:

> The figure who emerged from their pages is a Negro synchronized to a savage rhythm, living a life of ecstasy, superinduced by jazz (repetition of the tom-tom, awakening vestigial memories of Africa) and gin. A kinship exists between this stereotype and that of the contented slave; one is merely a "jazzed up" version of the other, with cabarets supplanting cabins, and Harlemized blues instead of the spirituals and slave reels. (Brown 1968, 164)

To explain how this peculiar development came about in the wake of the paternalistic cultural system, we must shift to the national social scene, and examine the historical and cultural setting of the 1920s that spawned the primitivist ideology.

THE SOCIOHISTORICAL SETTING AND THE ORIGINS OF THE PRIMITIVIST IDEOLOGY

> What American literature decidedly needs at the moment is color, music, gusto. . . . If the Negroes are not in a position to contribute these items, I do not know what Americans are.
>
> —Van Doren 1924, 93–94

The most significant sociological change in the new climate of American race relations, evidenced in increased white American interests in black literary works, was not the unprecedented opportunities it provided black writers. Though important, those opportunities hardly constituted the most crucial change. Rather it was the tendency of black writers to overestimate their autonomy and potential influence. Feeling free of social and political constraints, they believed they were helping to spearhead a new era of racial enlightenment and reform. This delusion caused them to misperceive the extent to which their perspective on black American life was being influenced by white American writers. What they and proponents of the Harlem Renaissance doctrine promoted and defended as ethnic realism—a literature committed to expressing the unvarnished truth about black American life, a literature that aimed to be, as Langston Hughes had put it, "without fear of shame"—turned out to be a vehicle for a romantic primitivist ideology.

As a cultural outlook, this primitivist ideology suggested that the defining features of black American ethnic life consisted of its emotional vitality, its proclivity for earthiness and sensual pleasure, which set it apart from white America's emotional sterility. This hedonistic view of black American ethnic life originated not in the black community, but in Europe where artistic and literary celebrations of primitivism, especially in reference to people of African ancestry, had become an intellectual fashion of the age. The young black American writers, through their associations with bohemian white American writers, were simply lured into this primitivist vogue, thinking that they were pioneering new, defiant black American literary works that would engender public respect and appreciation of black American ethnic culture. But, as we will see, the facts of the situation suggest a far different conclusion.

The National Cultural Scene: Conflict and Fragmentation

Civilization is at its lowest mark in the United States precisely in those areas where the Anglo Saxon still presumes to rule. He runs the whole South—and in the whole South there are not as many first-rate men as in many a single city of the mongrel North. Wherever he is still firmly in the saddle, there we look for such pathological phenomena as Fundamentalism, Prohibition and Ku Kluxery, and there they flourish.

—Mencken 1955, 130

The 1920s set in motion one of the most turbulent periods in American cultural history. The old verities of the Protestant ethic and small business culture no longer occupied positions of undisputed dominance. Challenged by the expansive new lifestyles and values emanating from the ethnic subcultures and the young generation of white Protestant intellectuals, mainstream American culture underwent unsettling pressures toward liberalization. It was in this volatile milieu of cultural conflict that the young black writers formed both their perceptions of the American racial scene and their ideas about black American literature's mission.

To understand the origins of the primitivist ideology and the formation of the black primitivist literary school, we must not only focus on the tensions and antagonisms that rent the national culture. We must also focus on the influence of the rebellious white American intellectuals, who attacked American mainstream culture, and launched a movement to reform its values. In pursuit of cultural reform, one sector of that intellectual movement, which was attracted to the black American ethnic world, fashioned an unconventional perspective on black American life.

Ironically this movement for cultural liberalization initiated a new, more subtle, regimen of cultural hegemony over black literary discourse. Adapted to the less rigidly authoritarian racial caste system in the urban North, this new regimen of cultural hegemony gave rise to ideological perspectives that transformed the dominant literary images of black America in American public culture. We will return to examine the distinctive features of this new regimen of cultural hegemony momentarily, but first we must place it in historical perspective and explain its linkage to the primitivist movement.

As earlier noted, many young white writers in the 1920s became attracted to the black American community—particularly New York's Harlem—because they believed that black ethnic culture possessed uninhibited emotional vitality that white American culture lacked. To understand why they arrived at this peculiar conception of black American ethnicity and how it, in turn, was transmitted to black American writers, we must begin with the conflicts that shook the foundations of American culture in the 1920s.

Perhaps the most important development behind those conflicts was the nation's rapid modernization, transforming the United States from a predominately rural and small-town way of life into a complex urban industrial society. This modernization was driven primarily by the nation's steadily accelerating industrial expansion, which resulted in the rapid growth of large cities and mechanical modes of transportation. All of this spelled the doom of the small town and rural way of life as dominant influences in American culture. But the transition was hardly smooth. The small-town and rural white Protestant provincials mounted vigorous resistance to what they regarded as the morally dissolute culture of the nation's big cities, which were populated, in large part, by recent immigrants from Europe, particularly European Catholic countries, and increasingly by black migrants from the rural South. These emerging urban

ethnic cultures, in the eyes of the white Protestant provincials, posed a serious threat to the United States' Anglo–Saxon traditions of thrift, sobri-
ety, and self-reliance which had to be defended if the nation was going to
preserve its democratic way of life.

A bitter cultural war soon erupted. Pitting small-town inhabitants
against city dwellers, native-born against foreign-born, and religionists
against secularists, that cultural war soon surfaced in political strife over
such issues as alcohol consumption, big-city political machines, labor
unions, and immigration, as provincial white America sought to suppress
the rising tide of urban cultural influences in American society (Gusfield
1966).

Running parallel to this conflict in American mass culture was a similarly bruising conflict in the nation's intellectual culture. Though having
many facets, that conflict arose primarily between conservative and cosmopolitan intellectuals. The cosmopolitans consisted primarily of New
York–based, young white Protestant intellectuals, who had been educated
in elite Ivy League colleges, where they had learned to revere European
culture and to regard American culture with disdain. Viewing small-town
Americans as stupid, narrow-minded, and emotionally stunted, these cosmopolitan intellectuals launched a ferocious assault on the provincial
American way of life. A typical example of this assault was exhibited in
the remarks of a character in Sinclair Lewis's critically acclaimed novel
Main Street who describes small-town American life as "a negation can-
onized as the one positive virtue. It is the prohibition of happiness. It is
slavery self-sought and self-defended. It is dullness made God" (Lewis
1920, 265). Not content to stop there, he plunges the dagger of invective
even deeper, ridiculing provincial Americans as "a savorless people,
gulping tasteless food, and sitting afterward, coatless and thoughtless, in
rocking chairs prickly with inane decorations, listening to mechanical music, saying mechanical things about the excellence of Ford automobiles,
and viewing themselves as the greatest race in the world."

While these intellectuals targeted their scorn particularly at small-town
American social mores and the puritanical sexual code, they also denounced such mainstream institutions as American religion, American
business, American politics, American education, and American newspapers. Virtually no aspect of the old cultural order escaped their contempt
(Stearns 1922).

This oppositional intellectual movement was unified not by a single
ideology but by feelings of contempt, alienation from what they regarded
as banal and hypocritical American values, the legacy of rigid puritan traditions, that pervaded American life. Coming of age in the transitional
world of 1920s America where modern secular and scientific values were
gaining increasing influence, these cosmopolitan intellectuals dismissed

sentiments like patriotism and religious piety as relics of ignorance and superstition. Religion had lost its place of centrality in the nation's intellectual culture, and many of these young white American intellectuals, feeling spiritually adrift and disoriented, were attracted to exotic and deviant lifestyles. In their quests to locate values on which to re-center their lives, they regarded the old culture as being worthless. We can see this sense of cultural desolation clearly evidenced in the observations of Van Wyck Brooks, one of their most influential spokesmen, who noted:

> Thought is nourished by the soil it feeds on, and in America to-day that soil is choked with the feckless weeds of correctness. Our sanitary perfection, our material organization of goods, our muffling of emotion, our deprecation of curiosity, our fear of idle adventure, our horror of disease and death, our denial of suffering. . . . Small wonder our intellectual plants wither in this carefully aseptic sunlight. (Brooks 1922, 148)

Brooks, however, noted that all was not lost as he saw the prospect of change in the younger generation. "The most hopeful thing of intellectual promise in America today is the contempt of the younger people for their elders; they are restless, uneasy, disaffected. . . . It is a genuine and moving attempt to create a way of life free from the bondage of authority that has lost all meaning, even to those who wield it" (Brooks 1922, 149).

Reflecting this mood of disaffection, rootless and alienated lifestyles surfaced among not just the young cosmopolitan white intelligentsia but also other groups in urban America, spawning such varied expressions of cultural rebellion as the proliferation of speakeasies, the hedonistic nightlife of the Jazz Age cabarets, the new rhythms of swing music and sexually risqué dance styles, the antics of Greenwich Village's bohemia, the expatriation of many talented young white writers to Europe, labor strife, radical political activity, intellectual denunciations of the Palmer raids and the Sacco-Vanzetti trial, H. L. Mencken's satirical assaults on national pieties in the *American Mercury* magazine, T. S. Eliot's *Wasteland*, F. Scott Fitzgerald's *The Great Gatsby*, Sinclair Lewis's *Babbitt,* and Ernest Hemingway's *The Sun Also Rises*. All attested to the era's deep discontents, the pervasive feelings of cultural alienation, which one historian eloquently summarized in his description of a character in *The Sun Also Rises:*

> There were not, to be sure, many Brett Ashleys in the United States. Yet there were millions to whom in some degree came for a time the same disillusionment and with it the same unhappiness. They could not endure a life without values, and the only values they had been trained to understand were being undermined. Everything seemed meaningless and unimportant. Well, at least one could toss off a few drinks and get a kick out of physical passion

and forget that the world was crumbling. . . . And so the saxophones wailed
and the gin-flask went its rounds and the dancers made their treadmill circuit with half closed eyes, and the outside world, so merciless and so insane,
was shut away for a restless night. (Allen 1969, 266)

The Great War and the Primitivist Vogue

If any one event can be said to have marked the break with the old cultural order, as the watershed in American cultural history, it was World
War I. In the eyes of many European and American intellectuals, that war
revealed the spiritual bankruptcy of Western civilization. The war for democracy, as it came to be known, the war to end all wars, turned out to
be—in their view—yet another cynical maneuver of big-power politics.

One momentous outcome of the growing disillusionment with Western
civilization was a primitivist vogue, which emerged initially among writers and artists in Europe. Believing the purest embodiments of emotional
and sexual freedom—that is, the essence of human happiness—existed
only among primitive peoples, these writers and artists turned toward
those peoples who presumably had avoided the corruptions of civilization. South Sea Islanders, American Indians, bullfighters, criminals, and
even the insane would be painted with the crude brushstrokes of primitivist identity. But it was black Africa, the infamous "dark continent," that
emerged as the quintessential symbol of primitivism.

As one historian has observed in reference to this primitivist vogue, it
began in Europe with the "rediscovery of primitive African painting and
sculpture by French artists. During this period, painters (Picasso, Derain,
Matisse, and Vlanick), composers (Satie, Auric, Honneger, Milhaud,
Poulenc, and Tallia Ferro), and writers (Guillaume Apollinaire, Jean
Cocteau, Max Jacob, Blaise Cendras, and Reverdy) were inspired by primitive Negro art" (Gloster 1948, 104–05). And like most of that era's European cultural fashions, it soon crossed the Atlantic Ocean and arrived in
New York—albeit in an altered form. Whereas in Europe, Africans were
viewed as the exemplars of primitivism, in the United States the doctrine
focused on black Americans. As one critic perceptively noted: "This
stereotype grew up with America's postwar revolt against Puritanism and
Babbitry. Literary critics urged a return to spontaneity, to unrestrained
emotions, American literature had been too long conventional, drab
without music and color. Human nature had been viewed with too great
a reticence" (Brown 1968, 164).

This primitivist vogue attracted young white American writers to black
American ethnic life, with the objective of producing literary works that
displayed black America's primitive qualities. Among the literary works
by white writers of the era that reflected that primitivist vogue were: Sher-

wood Anderson's *Dark Laughter*, William Seabrook's *Magic Island* and *Jungle Ways*, Harvey Wickham's *The Impuritans*, DuBose Heyward's *Porgy*, Eugene O'Neill's *The Emperor Jones* and *All God's Chillun Got Wings*, Waldo Frank's *Holiday* and, most important of all, Carl Van Vechten's *Nigger Heaven*. We will return to Van Vechten's novel momentarily, because it exerted major influence on several key black writers.

While both the black community's rapid expansion in the northern cities and the white middle class's increased curiosity about urban black life had a large hand in fostering black literature's new public role, it was the primitivist vogue, specifically the white literary movement portraying blacks as exotic primitives, that shaped the ideological perspective and images of that literature's first dominant school.

The older cultural regimen of paternalistic hegemony was fading over the horizon, but it had by no means disappeared. In fact, the 1920s marked a transitional phase. White literary works portraying black American life continued to have a large hand in shaping perceptions of black American identity in American public culture. Now, however, there was one important difference: they shared that function with literary works by black writers.

This dominant black literary school emerged from an odd new interracial alliance, under the leadership of white writers. Because the primitivist ideology extolled black America's alleged emotional freedom and sensuality, the white writers needed to gather materials firsthand that revealed those black primitivist qualities. They thus fostered friendships with black American writers, who helped them gain access to segregated black ghetto communities and provided testimonials defending these primitivist images of black Americans.

But why were the black writers attracted to those friendships? The answer is quite simple. Those friendships provided opportunities to advance their literary careers, to acquire support networks and access to publishers. It is important to recall, as I noted earlier, that the black writers regarded themselves as tough minded ethnic realists, rebelling against the legacy of using black literary works for political propaganda. They thus viewed the white writers as kindred spirits with a similar rebellious mission. Also, there is the further point that these black writers, in contrast to the more skeptical black political activists, failed to perceive potential harm from their associations with the white primitivist writers. Quite the contrary, they regarded their white counterparts as being racially enlightened, whites who not only rejected the racist values of the old America but also exhibited sensitivity and respect for black American ethnic culture. But most important, the black writers were oblivious to any alleged sinister influences from white writers because they believed they had attained artistic freedom. It was this belief, celebrated and reinforced by the rhetoric of the Harlem Renaissance doctrine, that convinced them they were artistic pioneers, destined to inscribe a new black American identity in American public culture. If anything, their friendships with white writers reinforced their delusions about their social role.

The delusions of the young black writers notwithstanding, another question remains: How does one explain the outlook of the white writers, who had presumably rejected the old culture's racism? Why did they embrace an ideological perspective on black American ethnic life that so easily could be construed as reviving and fortifying racially degrading stereotypes? To answer this question, we must understand the outlook of the larger white literary movement, including the group who expatriated to France, in the 1920s. They were privileged and alienated intellectuals, who exhibited an obtuse sociological sensibility. This was evidenced in their naive assumption that their modernist literary works engaged spiritual values that transcended the mundane world of politics, which they regarded as little more than sleazy backroom deal-making and demagogic pandering to public whims. Being educated in Europe-centered humanities and living apart from ordinary working-class Americans, they remained largely ignorant of the political and sociological realities that characterized early twentieth-century American society. This is not to say they were indifferent to social reform, but that they based their hopes for such reform in literature, which they saw as the only credible force for social enlightenment. In short, they believed only literature had the prospect of effecting social reform, even though they scarcely understood the people they aimed to reform.

For the white primitivist writers in particular, this quest to reform American society meant creating literary works that highlighted the emotional vitality of black American ethnic life—to psychologically liberate mainstream white America. Odd though this formula may now seem, they honestly believed these exotic images of blacks, by displaying an uninhibited and sensuous way of life, would transform American culture. It was this dubious sentiment that was being echoed by the white literary critic Mark Van Doren, quoted earlier, when he declared: "What American literature decidedly needs at the moment is color, music, gusto. . . . If the Negroes are not in a position to *contribute these items* (emphasis added), I do not know what Americans are." Put simply, these white writers were prescribing black emotional vitality for white America's spiritual anemia. In this sense, they were radically departing from the practices of the old racist culture, because they aimed to use black Americans not to buttress white supremacy—but to purge white American emotional inhibitions.

Some observers might argue that black American music actually served this function beginning in the 1960s, with the development of rock 'n' roll and the proliferation of a less-inhibited, white American youth culture.

But the 1920s was hardly the time for such cultural diffusion, nor was the dubious white primitivist ideology of black culture an appropriate vehicle through which to effect it.

The white writers' elitist arrogance toward mainstream American culture hardly went unchallenged. The literary critic Bernard DeVoto stepped forward in defense of American culture as he subjected the lost generation writers to perhaps the harshest rebuke they were to encounter. Characterizing their exalted notions about literature's redemptive powers as the literary fallacy, DeVoto wrote:

> Reduced to general terms, the literary fallacy assumes that a culture may be understood and judged solely by means of its literature, that literature embodies truly and completely both the values and content of a culture, that literature is the highest expression of a culture, that literature is the measure of life, and finally that life is subordinate to literature. (DeVoto 1944, 43)

This literary fallacy, DeVoto suggested, led an entire generation of young American writers astray. "Building houses of thought with Mr. Brooks's bricks, innumerable playwrights and novelists were told that we were a puritanical, materialistic, acquisitive people, without personality, of base ideals, unlovely in our private and public life, inhibited in emotion, uniform in thought, mediocre, dull, dreary, and base" (DeVoto 1944, 45).

DeVoto regarded the alienated modernist outlook of these literary works as a corruption of literature's true functions:

> Is there any one respect in which the literature of our time . . . differs from the literature of previous ages? . . . I think it has one trait, and one that is striking in a perspective now of twenty-five years; and this is that writers have ceased to be voices of the people. . . . Preponderantly, our literature . . . has been the expression of self-conscious intellectuals who do not even wish to be voices of the people; a way of saying that the literary mind of our time is sick. It has lost its roots in the soil of mankind. (DeVoto 1944, 25–26)

In effect, DeVoto believed the lost generation writers had turned away from the problems and conflicts of ordinary people, and chose instead to venerate deviant lifestyles and values that offended ordinary Americans. DeVoto's bitter attacks, however, proved futile. The white primitivist writers, ignoring his remonstrations, plunged headlong into the swirling vortex of the literary fallacy and—what for us is most important—pulled in with them the most gifted young black American writers of the era: Jean Toomer, Claude McKay, Langston Hughes, and Countee Cullen, who would follow later, toward the end of the primitivist vogue.

Echoing the sentiments of their white literary cohorts, the black writers also argued that literature transcended politics; that it served a higher, more noble mission than that of appealing to popular sentiments. This was the implication of Hughes's arrogant declaration that it did not matter if white or black people were displeased with their literary works: "We build our temples for tomorrow, strong as we know how."

We thus see how the complex array of social changes that swept across American society in the 1920s—the growing ethnic diversity, the beginning mass settlement of blacks in northern cities, the increasing white American curiosity about urban black life, the cultural conflicts between small-town and big-city residents, the rebellion of the young white American intellectual elite, and, finally, the interests one sector of the latter developed in black ethnic life—produced not only unprecedented opportunities for black American writers, but also an ideologically muddled dominant black literary school.

This development marked the beginning shift in the ideological production of literary works representing black American life in American public culture. But contrary to claims of the young black writers and Harlem Renaissance propagandists, this shift hardly heralded black literary freedom. Rather, it marked a transition of that literature's ideological production from the old regimen of paternalistic hegemony to a new—and still fledgling—regimen of co-optive hegemony. In short, black writers were becoming major players, for the first time, in producing the dominant literary images of black America in American public culture. But the ideology shaping those literary images still derived from white Americans. Which is to say, black American literature's cultural marginality was replaced by an insidious, though more rewarding, cultural dependency.

THE PRIMITIVIST IDEOLOGY
AND THE BLACK AMERICAN COMMUNITY

The Harlem Renaissance propagandists never comprehended the cultural regimen of co-optive hegemony. In fact, they thought the rebellious black literary outlook of the 1920s emanated from social forces within the black American community, particularly the new assertive racial consciousness of the black masses. We can see an expression of this belief in Alain Locke's confident declaration: "The young generation is vibrant with a new psychology; the new spirit is awake in the masses, and under the eyes of the professional observer is transforming what has been a perennial problem into progressive phases of contemporary life" (Locke 1925, 3).

A new spirit was awakening among the black masses—but it was hardly driven by the primitivist ideology. As noted earlier, the primitivist ideology of the dominant black literary school did not derive from the black community. Black Americans never thought of themselves as uninhibited primitives. In fact, a huge void yawned between primitivist ideology and black American social consciousness. To understand the nature of that void and the resulting literary distortions of black American life inscribed by the dominant black literary school, we must first examine the social conditions and preoccupations that characterized the black community.

The Social Climate within the Black Community

The mood within the black American community during the 1920s can be described perhaps best as cautiously optimistic. This generation of urban blacks perceived a sharp contrast between their memories of the grim ordeal of postreconstruction racial repression in the South and the new personal freedoms and economic opportunities they were experiencing in northern cities. What one observer noted about blacks in Chicago during the 1920s reflected the general outlook of blacks in the urban North:

> The Industrial Department of the Urban League places about 1,000 (black workers) a month. Many of the industrial plants endeavor to maintain a ratio of one Negro to every three white workmen, although the population ratio in Chicago is one Negro to thirty whites. The outlook for retention of this labor is excellent, according to all reports.

He went on to add:

> Negroes are rapidly adjusting themselves to the new industrial and social environment; they are saving money, which is evidenced by the large number of depositors in banks located in the (Second and Third Worlds, where most of the colored population live); they are conducting an increasing number of business enterprises, and real estate dealers are reaping a rich harvest in selling homes to Negroes. (White, 3)

As we noted earlier, the mass black migration to northern cities stimulated the black community's social development. "There were evidences on every hand," observed Horace Cayton and Sinclair Drake in *Black Metropolis,* "'that the Race was progressing'. Here were colored policemen, firemen, aldermen, and precinct captains, state representatives, doctors, lawyers, and teachers. Colored children were attending the public schools and the city's junior colleges. There were fine churches in Negro areas, and beautiful boulevards. It seemed reasonable to assume that this development would continue with more and more Negroes getting ahead and becoming educated. There were prophets of doom in the Twenties, but a general air of optimism pervaded the Black belt, as it did the whole city" (Cayton and Drake 1945, 80).

Though in absolute numbers still small, the nascent urban black bourgeoisie seemed to portend even greater advances, leading many to believe that the black community's social and economic development was destined to parallel that of the mainstream white society. After all, they reasoned, the mass black northern migration had begun only a decade ago. Who could deny what these urban black communities had already accomplished? In business, the professions, theater, music, art, and literature—in fact, in every sphere of modern culture—black Americans were producing impressive achievements. It seemed that only cranks and chronic malcontents could deny the prospect of future prosperity.

That optimism, however, remained restricted to the conditions of the racial caste system: the anticipation that this social and economic prosperity would take place *within a segregated black community*. Concerning the prospects of racial integration and social equality, most black Americans remained more guarded and skeptical—and for good reason. As I noted earlier, the beginning of the black migration to the North, following the war, had sparked race riots, the worst of which was the Chicago race riot of 1919.

> The tensions of the Riot period gradually subsided, but the migration left a residue of antagonism toward Negroes. There were definite restrictions on the activities of Negroes. . . . There were stores and restaurants that didn't like to serve Negroes. To walk into certain downtown hot-spots was unthinkable. To run for any state office higher than Senator from the Black Belt just wasn't done. . . . To hope for a managerial or highly skilled job in industry was ridiculous. To buy or rent a house out of the black Belt precipitated a storm. (Cayton and Drake 1945, 80)

Much the same could be said about the climate of race relations in other northern cities as the mass migration precipitated increased racial discrimination and tensions. Though less brutally repressive than in the South, racial injustices in the northern cities comprised a significant part of the northern black community's social concerns. Hence its guarded optimism. This stood in stark contrast to the young black writers' optimistic anticipation of racial enlightenment, an attitude undergirding their primitivist ideological agenda, which made them largely oblivious to persisting racial injustices.

MAJOR IDEOLOGICAL FORCES
WITHIN THE BLACK COMMUNITY

While most urban black Americans shared the mood of guarded optimism, they hardly embraced a single, overarching ideology. Urbanization created a more complex black American social structure, with widening divisions in occupational and social class levels, which was reflected in an increased diversity of lifestyles and ideological perspectives. Yet despite the black community's broad spectrum of ideological perspectives, none approximated even remotely the primitivist ideology. We can discern more clearly the hegemonic origin of the 1920s black primitivist literary ideology by first contrasting that ideology to the ideological forces that formed the major modes of social consciousness within the black community. Those ideological forces are noted in typology presented in figure 1.1.

The typology in figure 1.1 classifies the social bases of the black community's major ideological forces by aligning them along two axes: (1) their approach to racial reform (activist versus nonactivist); and (2) their constituency orientation (elite versus mass). The first axis distinguishes activist ideological forces that protested racial injustices from nonactivist ideological forces, which lacked political concerns and ignored racial injustices. Conversely, the second axis distinguishes those ideological forces that appealed to a narrowly based elite constituency from those that appealed to a broadly based mass constituency. The aim of this typology is not to account for the ideological perspectives of every individual black American intellectual, but rather to classify the social bases of the main ideological forces—the most prevalent modes of social consciousness—that characterized the 1920s black community.

While most black intellectuals (I use this term broadly to include all black Americans involved in producing ideas or symbols that interpreted black American experiences) were attached to only one of these social bases, several straddled social bases. For example, James Weldon Johnson, the civil rights leader and writer, was attached to both the political intelligentsia and the local cultural intelligentsia, a situation that made him more sensitive to the aesthetic dimensions of black American literature. By contrast, members of the political intelligentsia, such as W. E. B. DuBois, Walter White, and other civil rights activists, who were attached only to a political social base, tended to view black literary works as instruments to advance black political aspirations. Aesthetic considerations were at best secondary.

Like Johnson, Alain Locke also straddled two social bases. But in Locke's case, these social bases consisted of the local black cultural intelligentsia and the cosmopolitan white cultural intelligentsia. In fact, as we will see, Locke's attachment to these two social bases placed him in a strategically important position, which he used to propagate the Harlem Renaissance doctrine. While there were other black intellectuals who straddled social bases, Johnson and Locke were by far the most important black literary intellectuals to do so. Their experiences of straddling social bases broadened their outlooks and gave them more critical detachment

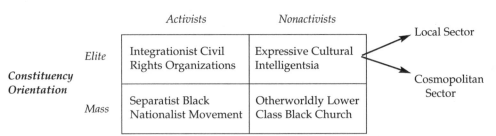

Figure 1.1.   Social Bases of Major Black American Ideological Forces during the 1920s

than the political black intellectuals, whose identities and social roles were anchored in a single social base. Now let's turn to a closer examination of these major ideological forces.

First, there was the civil rights integrationist ideology, which was located primarily in the NAACP and the Urban League. Operating under the leadership of black intellectuals such as DuBois, White, and Johnson and the control of a small group of liberal white philanthropists and social activists, these race relations groups constituted black America's political establishment. Presenting themselves as black community spokesmen, they were recognized as such by many people, though they lacked a significant black working-class following (Huggins 1971, 34–35). In fact, their effort to operate as black community spokesmen while being socially distant from the black masses jaundiced their relations with the black primitivist writers, who regarded themselves as authentic spokesmen of the black masses, a view the civil rights intellectuals firmly rejected.

These civil rights intellectuals, whose social base was situated in the small black middle class, took quite seriously their leadership charge, to combat racial injustices and promote the integration of blacks into mainstream American society. They exhibited little interest in black American literature as aesthetic objects. With the notable exception of James Weldon Johnson, mentioned earlier, they regarded the functions of black American literary works as essentially political. Actually several of these civil rights intellectuals wrote political protest novels during the 1920s, novels that constituted a minor politically oriented black literary school, which failed to gain significant recognition in the public arena. Nevertheless, DuBois, that school's leading practitioner, left no doubt about his view of literature, which we can see in his defense of art as propaganda.

> All art is propaganda and ever must be, despite the wailing of the purists. I stand in utter shamelessness and say that whatever art I have for writing has been used always for propaganda. . . . I do not care a damn for any art that is not used for propaganda. But I do care when propaganda is confined to one side while the other is stripped and silent. (Tuttle 1973, 54)

Though DuBois failed to achieve much influence as a novelist, he prevailed as one of the primitivist school's most dogged and pugnacious critics, becoming a virtual pit bull in efforts to protect the terrain of civil rights ideology. Like the other black civil rights intellectuals, he took a dim view of literary works that celebrated the black lower class's putative emotional freedom and sensuality. Rather he and his colleagues in the NAACP and Urban League saw lower-class black lifestyles as the center of the black community's most aggravating social problems, the problems such as crime, juvenile delinquency, alcoholism, and family instability, which, in their view, reflected not just that group's low levels of education and income, but the tragic legacy of slavery, the psychological devastation of racial oppression, which had to be overcome. If the black community was going to succeed in destroying racial stereotypes and gaining mainstream white America's respect and acceptance, they believed, the black lower class would have to be uplifted and rehabilitated, not sensationalized and celebrated as exotic primitives. In short, the civil rights intellectuals' perspective clashed with the perspective of dominant black literary school.

In contrast to the civil rights integrationist ideology, the second major ideological force circulating in the black community emanated from the lower-class black church. Oriented to a constituency drawn from the black American masses, which was its main base of support, the lower-class black church exerted pervasive influence. "In the cities of the North and even in the cities of the South," observed the black sociologist E. Franklin Frazier, "these 'storefront' churches are constantly being organized by all kinds of so-called preachers in order to attract lower-class Negroes."

> During the 1920s when southern Negroes were flocking to Harlem in New York City, it was found that only 54 out of 140 churches in Harlem were housed in regular church structures. The remainder were the "storefront" type which had been organized by preachers, many of whom were exploiters and charlatans. (Frazier 1964, 59)

These lower-class black churches were led by semiliterate preachers who possessed neither the disposition nor the ability to meld their fundamentalist theology with a social and political perspective highlighting the black community's problems. As Frazier noted, "They based their appeal on the Negro's desire to find salvation in the next world and to escape from the sickness and insecurities of this world" (1964, 59). Put simply, they embraced an ideology of other worldly salvation. Though the congregations of these black churches displayed uninhibited emotions in such worship activities as singing, dancing, and shouting, they did not attract the interests of the black primitivist writers. Their spiritually driven emotional expression and conservative lifestyles hardly fit the primitivist conception of uninhibited black sensuality, and in consequence their social consciousness was conspicuously absent in black primitivist literary depictions of black American life.

A similar pattern of dissociation existed between the primitivist perspective and black nationalism, the third major ideological force in the black community, which also occupied a black lower-class social base. Despite the handicap of being a relatively new development that was confronted by formidable black middle-class hostility, the black nationalist movement exploded onto the landscape of northern cities shortly after World War I, forming the black community's most unusual and dynamic ideological force. Galvanized by the flamboyant and rhetorically gifted Marcus Garvey, that movement's meteoric rise in influence was nothing short of startling. In the words of one witness of Garvey's influence: "Let it be observed that no man can stand in one of those teeming Liberty Hall audiences, see one of Garvey's ostentatious parades, hear Garvey's magnetic voice, read his Negro world, watch the sweep of his ideas, and then say there is nothing to it" (Quarles 1969, 197).

There was indeed much to it. Operating through the United Negro Improvement Association (UNIA), Garvey launched the first black American mass-based social movement (as earlier noted), a radical political sect that challenged the influence of both the civil rights intelligentsia and the lower-class black church. By encouraging black Americans to feel racial pride in their physical appearance as blacks and in their African cultural heritage, Garvey's UNIA promoted a vision that, despite having been ignored by both the integrationist civil rights ideology and the fundamentalist ideology of black religion, resonated powerfully among lower-class blacks. So too did Garvey's equally important effort to create autonomous black American economic and political institutions by advocating a doctrine of racial self-reliance and separatism, ideas that struck like daggers in the heart of the integration agenda of the civil rights intellectuals.

Though the Garvey movement had subsided by the time the primitivist literary vogue crystallized, it left a rich and intricate residue of beliefs and symbols highlighting black ethnic consciousness, which some scholars have mistakenly identified as the ideology that inspired the leading black literary works in the 1920s (Bone 1958, 62). Though they shared a superficial resemblance as outlooks that celebrated black racial pride, the Garvey and primitivist ideologies had virtually nothing in common. Not only would Garvey have condemned depictions of lower-class blacks as exotic primitives, for his conception of black culture ironically embraced many traditional Western values that the primitivists scorned; but he also would have despised the black primitivist writers' lifestyles, as he had the lifestyles of other black American intellectuals, who fraternized in white American social circles, and were socially distant from the black masses.

We must forgo a more detailed consideration of the Garvey movement, which would take us beyond the objectives of this study, and conclude our observations on that movement by noting several key points about its impact. Without question, it operated as black America's most momentous cultural development in the 1920s, posing the greatest threat the civil rights ideology had ever faced within the black community: namely, the threat of being displaced by an antiwhite ideological movement. But that threat never materialized. The Garvey movement ultimately failed as an ideological force not because its appeal faded, but rather because its inexperience and marginal political status rendered it vulnerable to powerful foes. Several years after the movement emerged, Garvey ran into formidable opposition as Federal government officials and civil rights leaders worked in close collaboration to undermine him. They ultimately succeeded in getting him convicted, imprisoned and, finally, deported to his native Jamaica on a dubious charge of mail fraud (Cronon 1955). However, it is what became of the Garvey movement, specifically its legacy of racial pride, that concerns us here. As is often the fate of suppressed popular movements, its symbolism was adopted by some of its detractors, the proponents of a more moderate ideology, who sought to appropriate its appeal. This brings us to the Harlem Renaissance doctrine—the fourth and, in many ways, the most misrepresented major black ideological force in the 1920s. The Harlem Renaissance doctrine was located within the social base of the black cultural intelligentsia.

As indicated in figure 1.1, the black American cultural intelligentsia was divided into two sectors: a local sector comprising writers, musicians, dancers, and artists whose social location was restricted to the segregated black community; and a cosmopolitan sector, the social base of the primitivist literary school, whose social location and professional relationships were located outside the black community in the newly forming, predominately white Jazz Age social milieu in downtown Manhattan. It was the local cultural intelligentsia that became the chief bearer of the Harlem Renaissance doctrine.

To comprehend that doctrine's origins and subsequent appeal during the 1920s, it is necessary to recognize that the black middle class faced a cultural predicament. Encountering the popularity of both black racial consciousness aroused by the Garvey movement and exotic black images being propagated by the black primitivist literary works, the black middle class needed a cultural ideology that would allow it to profit from these developments by affirming its aspirations and identity as the driving forces behind black American culture. This it did by appropriating the new public symbols of black ethnic identity, a feat that the narrowly focused and defensive civil rights ideology, rooted in assimilationist assumptions, lacked the flexibility and scope to accomplish.

This task of ideological appropriation began when Alain Locke moved onto the black cultural stage as a significant player. In response to the exciting social and cultural developments stirring in black Harlem and the curiosity these developments were arousing among educated whites, *Survey Graphic*—a cosmopolitan white literary magazine—commissioned Locke to edit an issue of the magazine featuring recent black American creative works (Long 1976, 14–20). Locke hardly hesitated to comply. Ever eager to occupy the role of spokesman for the black American creative community, he seized the opportunity like a fox circling a fresh prey and crafted a unique black cultural ideology (Locke 1925, 3–18). With the appearance of his essay, which represented the decade's black artistic and literary ferment in the terminology of black middle-class aspirations, the dubious Harlem Renaissance doctrine was born.[1] On the surface, the publication of this inaugural essay celebrating the recent black cultural awakening in a white literary periodical might seem paradoxical—that is, if we ignore the social dynamics that brought about that awakening. Once we recognize, however, that it was white American interests that sparked and supported the 1920s black American literary ferment, the venue of that inaugural essay seems perfectly reasonable. Favorable recognition by white American elites was the yardstick most middle-class blacks used to determine whether blacks were making racial progress.

Thus what initially surfaced as conflicting ideological forces, namely, racial nationalism and bohemian celebrations of black exoticism, were cleverly pruned and grafted by Locke into the cultural ethos of the "New Negro." In effect, Locke suggested that the eruption of both the black political militancy and the black literary rebellion flowed from the same stream: the aspirations of the new generation for democratic freedom. Pitched as the foundation of a new black aesthetic, this doctrine amounted to little more than slick propaganda. As one historian has aptly observed:

> The vogue of the New Negro . . . had all the character of a public relations promotion. The Negro had to be "sold" to the public in terms they could understand. Not the least important target in the campaign was the Negro himself; he had to be convinced of his worth. It is important to understand this, because much of the art and letters that were the substance on which the New Negro was built and made up the so-called Harlem Renaissance was serving this promotional end. (Huggins 1971, 125)

The "New Negro" referred to in this passage was actually the nascent black middle class, the educated blacks who appropriated black artistic and literary achievements as symbols of racial esteem. In light of this fact, it should hardly be surprising that the Harlem Renaissance doctrine lacked a black aesthetic philosophy, or even an interpretive rationale for explaining the new black literary sensibility. The doctrine constituted not a critical theory but an opportunistic cultural ideology, which was revealed by the odd assortment of black literary works Locke drew under the Renaissance tent.

Oblivious to the varied, often conflicting, messages these works projected about black American life and the complex social changes that produced their sudden notoriety, Locke—whose words soon would be echoed by other Renaissance propagandists—hailed the appearance of these black literary works as a milestone in black America's social advancement. This was sociologically analogous to the way the larger black community had celebrated Jack Johnson's boxing exploits, as triumphs in the status politics of race, as evidence of the black community's advance. Which is to say, the Renaissance propagandists thought these black literary achievements would help to destroy white American stereotypes of black inferiority, and enhance black esteem in American public culture. It was this middle-class preoccupation with converting black literary achievements into black middle-class status gains that lay behind the doctrine's popularity.

If middle-class blacks had been able to look beyond their status anxieties, they no doubt would have found reasons not to celebrate, but to protest the 1920s black literary scene. Unbeknownst to most of them, they became targets of much black literary ridicule and scorn. The black primitivist literary school, the most acclaimed black literary works of the decade, subjected the black middle class to the most acid abuse. Contrary to the blandishments of Locke's New Negro essay, suggesting a new cultural spirit emanating from a solidified black community, the black primitivist writers despised middle-class blacks. In fact, just as their white counterparts used the primitivist ideology to berate provincial white Americans, they used that ideology to flog the black middle class, mocking, deriding, and parodying their lifestyle and values, with a level of rancor and meanness that went beyond any previous public criticism of the group.

It was W. E. B. DuBois, then presiding as editor of the NAACP's *Crisis* magazine, who first sounded the alarm, and tried to arouse black public opposition to the primitivist vogue. Seeing the sensationalist direction these literary works were taking, he launched bitter attacks against their primitivist images of blacks. But to little avail. As a powerless black intellectual possessing neither a mass black constituency nor access to the mainstream public arena, DuBois failed to derail the primitivist vogue.

If working-class blacks were untouched by that vogue, most middle-class blacks, basking in the euphoria induced by the Harlem Renaissance doctrine, misunderstood its social implications.

As is illustrated in figure 1.2, the Harlem Renaissance doctrine was constructed from a confluence of forces. While the renaissance propagandists advocated racial integration, they differed from the civil rights intellectuals in one crucial aspect: their assumptions about how black creative works could help to achieve that goal. Because they viewed white American acclaim as the yardstick for measuring black achievement, the renaissance propagandists believed virtually any black American literary or intellectual work that gained notoriety in the white public arena would

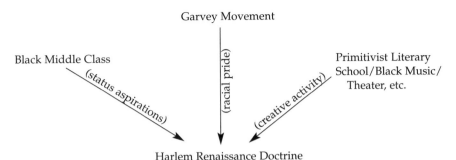

Figure 1.2.   Ideological Origins of the Harlem Renaissance Doctrine

advance racial reforms. All blacks, in their view, should take pride in such works because they enlightened white racial attitudes by demonstrating black American creative talents.

In contrast, the civil rights intellectuals embraced a more constricted view, seeing that literature's social role in political terms. They believed only literary works projecting favorable images of blacks could advance racial reform. Based on their less sanguine reading of the American racial scene, they believed that most white Americans regarded blacks as racially inferior. Hence, in their view, it was not enough to demonstrate black American creative talents; whites had to be shown that blacks and whites possessed similar human qualities of morality, feeling, and intelligence. Any images of blacks that projected a contrary view, namely images suggesting that blacks in matters of morality, feeling, or intelligence differed from whites because of dissimilar biological endowments, they believed, would only fortify white racial prejudice and impede racial reform. This was precisely what they thought the black primitivist literary works were doing.

In concluding this overview on the primitivist school's relationship to the black community, I should reiterate its central point: primitivism resonated none of that community's major ideological forces.

Emanating from a sector of the white American literati, the primitivist movement not only detached the most talented black writers from the social consciousness of the black community. It induced them to project oddly distorted images of black Americans as a frivolous and licentious people. To understand more concretely how this came to pass, we must turn to the social relations that spawned the primitivist school.

The Harlem Social Scene: The Social Relations That Spawned the Primitivist School

But it is the zest that the Negroes put in, and the enjoyment they get out of things that causes one more envy in the ofay (white). Notice how many whites are unreal in America: they are dim. But the Negro is very real; he is there. And the ofays know it. That's why they come to Harlem—out of curiosity and jealousy and don't know why.

—Cunard 1976, 125

Willingly would I be an outsider in this if I could know that I read it aright—that out of this change in the old familiar ways some finer thing may come. Is this interest akin to that of the Virginians on the verandah of a plantation's big house—sitting genuinely spellbound as they hear the lugubrious strains floating up from the Negro quarters? Is it akin to that of the African explorer, Stanley, leaving a village far behind, but halting in spite of himself to catch the boom of its distant drum? Is it significant of basic human responses, the effect of which, once admitted, will extend far beyond cabarets? Maybe these Nordics at last have tuned in our wavelength. Maybe they are at last learning to speak our language.

—Fischer 1976, 82

The social process that gave birth to the primitivist vogue of the 1920s was manifested particularly in the interests whites exhibited in Harlem nightlife. As a result of those interests that attracted affluent white patrons to Harlem, Harlem nightclubs became major showcases of black entertainment. For the first time, talented black Americans such as Duke Ellington, Bessie Smith, Louis Armstrong, Paul Robeson, Josephine Baker, Roland Hayes, Florence Mills, Gladys Bentley, and Bert Williams were featured in the theater and on the musical stage, and launched into the spotlight of national celebrity. Though still obliged to operate within the constraints of the racial caste system, black performers now found more opportunities to advance their careers because of the increased interests of affluent white tourists in Harlem.

Harlem acquired a unique status during the 1920s. In much the same way that New York City emerged as the nation's cultural capital, Harlem became the mecca of black America's intellectual and artistic life, as talented young blacks, aspiring to careers in music, literature, journalism, and race-relations organizations, flocked to that black Manhattan community like pilgrims converging on a holy shrine. From the red clay farmland of the rural South, the dusty plains of the Southwest, the flat prairie of the Midwest, and the sun drenched tropical islands of the Caribbean, these young blacks arrived in Harlem, often with little more than the clothing they carried in their suitcases, seeking their fortunes in the epicenter of black American culture. It is noteworthy that these artistically ambitious young blacks rarely felt attracted to black colleges, because those colleges, located primarily in the provincial South, were rooted in conservative values that seemed antiquated and obsolete to these restless young blacks.

In contrast to the black colleges, New York City existed as not only the nation's intellectual and artistic hub, but also its most racially liberal environment. This strongly influenced Harlem's emergence as the center of black American creative activities, because in New York's more tolerant racial environment, where whites and blacks associated with fewer constraints of racial caste, black writers and performers found it easier to establish contacts with the cosmopolitan white American intelligentsia. This is hardly to say that New York lacked racial discrimination—the boundaries of its neighborhoods, schools, occupations, wealth, and political power followed the familiar pattern of American racial segregation—only that it provided black and white intellectuals and artists more opportunities to develop interracial friendships and informal social networks than did southern black colleges, or even such cities as Chicago, Philadelphia, and Detroit, where racial segregation pervaded virtually every sphere of life. Indeed, most white Americans living outside New York would have perceived its cosmopolitan interracial scene as being peculiar, if not deviant.

Though most white tourists who invaded Harlem night spots shared this aversion to associating with blacks, this hardly deterred them from seeking entertainment in uptown Manhattan. Observed the British writer Nancy Cunard:

> The mass of whites . . . treat Harlem in the same way that English toffs used to talk about 'going slumming'. The class I'm thinking of is the 'club-man.' They want entertainment. Go to Harlem, it's sharper there. And it doesn't upset their conception of the Negro's social status. From all time the Negro has entertained the whites, but never been thought of by this type as possibly a social equal. (Cunard 1976, 126)

In the eyes of these white tourists, Harlem occupied "the other side of the tracks": the place where they could "let down their hair" and explore risqué pleasures, beyond the withering gaze of white middle-class morality. For this reason, they descended on Harlem in large numbers, in fact, so much so that many Harlem nightclubs began to exclude black customers. As Langston Hughes observed in his biography, places such as the Cotton Club were only "cordial to the patronage of Negro celebrities." All other blacks were turned away. Rudolph Fischer, another young black writer, recalled his surprise at how much Harlem nightlife had changed after he had been away to college. "Time and again, since I've returned to live in Harlem, I've been one of a party of four Negroes who went to this or that Harlem cabaret, and on each occasion we've been the only Negro guests in the place. The managers don't hesitate to say that it is upon these predominately white patrons that they depend for success" (Fischer 1976, 78).

Informal socializing between blacks and whites in these nightclubs was infrequent. Even among the interracial vanguard of black and white intellectuals and artists, contacts were restricted, for the most part, to a few Harlem night spots and private parties. This turned out to have crucial significance for the leading literary images of black American life projected during the decade. As the only view many white writers ever got—or sought—of the urban black social world, these entertainment settings largely shaped their perceptions of black Americans as exotic, happy-go-lucky revelers. Virtually nothing was seen of the day-to-day lives of the countless thousands of blacks who worked, worshipped, supported families, and went about their affairs as did members of white American ethnic communities.

The young black writers of course knew about this more pedestrian side of black American life, but their bohemian-primitivist proclivities hardly disposed them to write about conventional black working-class experiences. Black life was thus transmuted from ordinary experiences into exotic spectacles. With a delightful twist of irony, Langston Hughes later recalled that many nightclubs catering to whites soon closed because they barred blacks, whom the whites had come to see.

Private parties were by far the major settings where black intellectuals and liberal whites associated informally, because the social mores still discouraged interracial fraternization in public. As Claude McKay observed: "Ned's was one place of amusement in Harlem in which white people were not allowed. It was a fixed rule with him, and often he turned away white slummers. This wasn't entirely from pride-of-race feeling, but because of the white unwritten law which prohibits free social intercourse between colored and white" (McKay 1937, 132).

The main party givers were Carl Van Vechten, Alelia Walker, and the civil rights intellectuals. Van Vechten gave bohemian parties that included a variety of white literary and artistic celebrities as well as his circle of black intellectual associates. "Because his acquaintance was wide and undiscriminating, he became one of the most successful party givers of the 1920s simply by indulging his taste for strange combinations," observes Van Vechten biographer Edward Leuders (1965, 37). Alelia Walker, who inherited the fortune her mother had earned from selling hairdressing products, was renowned for the extravagance of her Harlem parties. These were open affairs which—according to Langston Hughes—included every social type from the numbers runners to downtown (white) poets (Hughes 1940, 227). A fun-loving woman without social pretensions, Walker owned a country mansion at Irving-on-the-Hudson and a townhouse in Harlem, where she gave her famous parties. Often the number of her guests swelled beyond the capacity of the townhouse. As a close friend of Walker, Carl Van Vechten turned up frequently at her parties, which doubtless left strong impressions on him, as would be later revealed by his depictions of Harlem parties in his novel. In contrast to Walker's parties, Van Vechten's parties were not Harlem parties as such, since he had no contacts outside his small circle of black intellectual associates. Nevertheless, his parties were reported regularly by the black press, which saw them as evidence of important advances in race relations. This response was characteristic of the black middle class's preoccupation with gaining recognition in the white public arena. Van Vechten was an influential celebrity in New York's cultural life.

The other sources of parties were the black civil right intellectuals: Walter White, James Weldon Johnson, and Jessie Fausett. These parties were considerably more subdued, reflecting this group's more conservative lifestyle. The activities consisted mostly of literary and intellectual discussions. Among the young black writers, Langston Hughes and Countee Cullen were the only ones who frequently attended these parties. Although James Weldon Johnson gave a going away party for Claude McKay in 1923, shortly before the young writer departed for a long stay in Europe and also, significantly, before he published his major primitivist novel, McKay remained marginal to the social life of the civil rights intellectuals. He associated mostly with the politically oriented white writers of the *Masses*. Jean Toomer's relationship to the black civil rights intellectuals was even more tenuous; his primary social circle consisted of white literary bohemians in Greenwich Village.

Hughes referred to the parties given by the black civil rights intellectuals as "upper-class parties." In contrast to the "every-class parties" of Alelia Walker, these upper-crust parties included white celebrities among their guests. Recalling these parties, Walter White (the NAACP official) noted that "sometimes there would be parties at my home or the homes of one or another of those I met at Jim's (James Weldon Johnson). Heywood Broun, Claude McKay, Fania and Carl Van Vechten . . . Langston Hughes, Eva and Newman Levy, Ruth Hale, Countee Cullen, Carl and Irita Van Doren, Marie Dora, Edna St. Vincent Millay, Sinclair Lewis, George Gershwin, Mary Ellis, Willa Cather, Blanche and Alfred Knopf, Walter Wanger, Juan Bennet and many others" (White 1955, 37). Jessie Fausett, literary editor of *Crisis* and author of fiction that depicted the genteel black middle class, gave what were characterized as literary parties, with poetry readings, discussions of literature and art, and occasional conversations in French (Hughes 1940, 241). This was the world of the "genteel" black middle class. Only the most distinguished whites were included among their guests. At the publisher Alfred Knopf's New Year's

Eve party, recalled Hughes, he met Ethel Barrymore and Jascha Heifetz; and at Van Vechten's parties such people as Somerset Maugham, Hugh Walpole, Fannie Hurst, Witter Brynner, Isa Glenn, Emily Clark, William Seabrook, Arthur Davison Ficke, Louis Untermeyer, George Sylvester Viereck, Waldo Frank, Salvador Dali, Helena Rubenstein, and Horace Liveright (Hughes 1940, 252). Though most of these contacts were superficial, they contributed importantly to fostering a cosmopolitan and assimilated black American cultural intelligentsia.

It is useful to recall that this was precisely the time when blacks were allegedly awakening to an appreciation of their ethnic culture, which was not as contradictory as it may seem. Once we realize that it was white Americans—specifically the liberal white American cultural intelligentsia, who had a large hand in shaping the direction of that cultural awakening and in giving the writers access to the public arena—the white American role in that "black cultural awakening" ceases to be surprising.

Carl Van Vechten is often mentioned as the vital link, but the social relations that fostered the dominant black primitivist literary school actually consisted of several white American intellectual networks, which formed intersecting circles. Van Vechten was without question the most important of those white Americans, because he occupied a position of major influence within the New York cultural establishment. But there were others such as Waldo Frank, Gorham Munson, and Hart Crane, close associates of Jean Toomer's; Frank Harris and Max Eastman, close associates of Claude McKay; Alfred Knopf, one of the most important publishers of black writers during the 1920s and a close friend of James Weldon Johnson. Then, there was the liberal civil rights circle that included Joel Spingarn, Mary Ovington, Julius Rosenwald, Clarence Darrow, Arthur Spingarn, and numerous others. Also, there was influence and support from wealthy white donors, such as Charlotte Osgood Mason, who financially assisted Langston Hughes and Zora Neale Hurston, but chose to remain anonymous.

It is usually impossible to attribute an ideological movement to a single individual. Such developments tend to emanate from a confluence of social forces, as indicated earlier in reference to the origins of the primitivist ideology. Nevertheless, it is often possible to identify those individuals who figure importantly in giving that ideological movement a particular direction and tone. Carl Van Vechten was undeniably the key figure in shaping the ideological direction and promoting the ascent of the dominant black primitivist literary school.

Walter White wrongly credited James Weldon Johnson with developing the so-called Harlem Renaissance as he noted that Johnson's apartment was the "frequent gathering place of writers, poets, singers, and men and women of the theater. . . . The color line was never drawn at Jim's. It was there that many who were to do much in wiping out the color line learned to know each other as fellow human beings and fellow artists without consciousness of race" (White 1955, 39). It is certainly true that Johnson appreciated and encouraged the young black writers. But to say that he fostered the Harlem Renaissance amounted to sincere but misguided flattery. There was no Harlem Renaissance *literary movement*. As we noted earlier, black literary works of the 1920s projected no single overarching aesthetic or ideological perspective. While the dominant primitivist school did project such a perspective, it hardly derived from Johnson's inspiration or direction. A talented and versatile writer, Johnson never produced a primitivist literary work. In fact, as we will see, Johnson was among those black intellectuals who later objected to some of the exotic and sensational images of blacks projected by the primitivist literary school.

The fact that neither Johnson nor Alain Locke assumed leadership of this literary school, and gave it an ideological direction that more faithfully resonated with black American ethnic culture, is easy to explain. Neither man possessed a reputation outside the black community. Neither had produced a literary work that defined or exemplified a paradigm for a truly ethnic black American literature. To lead the dominant literary school one needed a social network within the white literary world. Neither man had such a network. In short, neither man possessed the cultural capital needed to gain recognition for black literary works in the public arena. Whites controlled the publishing facilities, the marketing outlets, and the rewards for literary work in American public culture. That was the reality of literary life in the United States. If black literary works were to gain significance, white Americans would have to be involved.

The only 1920s black cultural movement that derived financial support from the black community was Garvey's black nationalist movement. But it lacked a literary school as it failed to attract the young black American writers because they loathed racial nationalism. Moreover, it is doubtful that Garvey's largely working-class followers would have become consumers of black literary works.

In summary, the new interracial intellectual milieu of the 1920s created a more cosmopolitan and assimilated group of black writers. But even more important, it was through those networks, particularly their associations with the liberal, bohemian white American literati, that the young black writers assimilated an exotic primitivist perspective on black American life. Carl Van Vechten was without question the chief white American figure who influenced that ideological development. We will now turn to consideration of his role.

THE WRITERS AND LITERARY WORKS OF THE DOMINANT
PRIMITIVIST SCHOOL

Carl Van Vechten (1880–1964): The White American Impresario of the Black Primitivist Literary School

Despite its caste restrictions, the American racial system has shown a peculiar capacity to produce what might be termed white race-relations brokers: individual white Americans with an uncanny ability to traverse the chasm of racial segregation. Usually coming from privileged social backgrounds and with a penchant for the unconventional, these individuals have felt attracted to black American life, with the result that they exerted significant influence in promoting some aspect of black American cultural development. The fields they embarked on covered virtually the entire terrain of black American creative endeavors, fields blacks themselves were unable to promote in the mainstream public culture. Thus white race-relations brokers were needed to navigate around the racial caste system's constraints. Exercising their influence behind the scene, they typically faded into historical oblivion after effecting major changes in some area of black American culture. Carl Van Vechten was such a man. As the white American who played the central role in nurturing the dominant black primitivist literary school, Van Vechten was one of the first in what has become a long line of white race-relations brokers in black American cultural endeavors.

Born in 1880 into the family of a wealthy manufacturer, Van Vechten grew up in Cedar Rapids, Iowa, and later attended the University of Chicago (Leuders 1965, 21). After graduating from college, he worked as a reporter for a Hearst newspaper in Chicago. But his life soon changed when he received a letter from a hometown girlfriend urging him to abandon the windy city for the more exciting cultural fare of New York City. Heeding that advice, Van Vechten moved to New York where, shortly after arriving, he landed a job as the *New York Times* music critic. This event marked the beginning of his long and remarkable career as a celebrity in New York's cultural life. His emergence as a New York celebrity journalist did not, however, occur immediately. Soon after he joined the *Times*, he was assigned to Paris as the paper's foreign correspondent in the early 1920s. Moving about in the heady Parisian cultural life, Van Vechten befriended many prominent writers and artists. But perhaps most important for the subsequent direction of his energies was his encounter with the primitivist vogue, the cultural movement that highlighted the alleged uninhibited emotionality of black Africans. Almost immediately, primitivism captured his imagination.

He returned to New York in 1924 still enchanted by this primitivist vogue, which prompted his first contacts with black Harlem. Through his close friend, the publisher Alfred Knopf, he met Walter White, the NAACP official. White had just written the civil rights protest novel *The Fire in the Flint*, which Knopf had published. Soon after their initial meeting, White introduced Van Vechten to James Weldon Johnson. Through these two black civil rights leaders Van Vechten quickly expanded his contacts to other black intellectuals. He met Langston Hughes and Countee Cullen, as well as other young Harlem writers, at an NAACP cabaret party. Sustained by his engaging personality and deft social skills, Van Vechten moved through Harlem intellectual circles like a politician working a church picnic, and found almost immediate acceptance. By the end of 1924, he was said to have known every important black person in Harlem.

From the NAACP and black intellectual social circles, he moved to Harlem nightclubs and parties. Becoming one of the most prominent white publicists of Harlem nightlife entertainment, he was soon recognized as a familiar figure on the Harlem nightlife scene, as he frequently visited the famous Small's cafe, where he took many of his white literary friends, helping to popularize the risqué image of Harlem's cabaret world. Because of his celebrity status in New York's cultural life, Van Vechten's activities attracted the attention of trendy high-brow periodicals such as *Vanity Fair*, which at one point informed its readers, with obvious reference to his Harlem escapades, that he was "getting a heavy tan." Little did they or anyone else then suspect, but Van Vechten was doing more than indulging his penchant for offbeat recreation. He was preparing to launch a black American literary movement. Moreover, paralleling that venture, he was busily engaged in other promotional projects, helping to create opportunities for black writers and performing artists in New York's cultural life. It is noteworthy that many members of the black middle class felt flattered by Van Vechten's interests in Harlem, seeing his presence as a sign of racial advancement.

Van Vechten's influence on black ethnic literature during the 1920s derived primarily from his many contacts throughout the New York publishing community, which he used to assist black writers in getting their works published. For example, he introduced both Langston Hughes and Countee Cullen to the editors of *Vanity Fair*. He gave a set of poems written by Hughes to his friend Alfred Knopf, who later published them under the title *The Weary Blues* (Hughes 1926b), launching Hughes's first book. Van Vechten wrote the introduction to that book. He also persuaded the editors of *Vanity Fair* to publish Hughes's *Spirit of Negro Folklore*. Several months later he favorably reviewed James Weldon Johnson's *Book of American Negro Spirituals*. In short, he was doing nothing less than opening mainstream publishing outlets, and helping to cultivate a white

American audience for black American literary works. But his promotion of black creative artists was by no means restricted to writers. As the *Times* music critic, he wielded considerable clout, which he used often on behalf of black performers. In the field of music, for instance, he introduced both Paul Robeson and Lawrence Brown to larger audiences, resulting in their being recognized as outstanding musical talents. He also put considerable effort into popularizing black theatrical performances on Broadway such as *Emperor Jones* and *Shuffle Along*.

But Van Vechten's many and varied activities on behalf of black writers and performers were hardly motivated by altruism. He sought and received much in return. Most important, he gained privileged access to areas of Harlem's community life that were routinely off-limits to whites. Because his black middle-class associates regarded him as a trusted friend, they talked openly in his presence, revealing racial anxieties and frustrations they usually concealed in the presence of whites. From this privileged access, Van Vechten gained considerable advantages that advanced his own career. Nevertheless, despite his more intimate view of black community life, his understanding of black American experiences remained surprisingly shallow.

In light of his position as an outsider and his shallow understanding of black ethnic culture, Van Vechten's role in shaping the ideological direction of a dominant black literary school was ironic. It is doubtful that emphasis on the exotic and sensational features of black Harlem life would have gained momentum without his influence. Yet on the other hand, it is also doubtful that the leading black writers of the era would have achieved recognition in the public arena without his assistance. Critics of his involvement with black writers often ignored his positive contributions. The considerable access black writers gained to mainstream New York publishing outlets in the 1920s, as earlier noted, was simply unprecedented; and Van Vechten deserved much of the credit for bringing it about.

This is hardly to say these writers became American literary celebrities. Their notoriety was at best modest compared with that of such major white writers of the decade as Sinclair Lewis, Ernest Hemingway, and F. Scott Fitzgerald. Nevertheless, it marked a historic watershed. Black American literary works were being taken seriously as discourse depicting black American life in American public culture, thanks, in large part, to Van Vechten's role in brokering their access.

On the negative side, Van Vechten did not represent the kind of serious literary artist from whom black writers could have learned or refined their craft as had many expatriate white American writers under the influence of such mentors as Gertrude Stein and Ezra Pound. As a newspaper journalist who lacked both the literary sensibility and intelligence of a Stein or Pound, Van Vechten cut a pathetic figure as a literary mentor. By imitating the crude, sensational style of his commercially successful black novel, the black primitivist writings were doomed to the inglorious fate of a passing fad.

Even so, it would be too simplistic to say that Van Vechten led these black writers astray. It was the American racial caste system that brought that about. They had no better alternative for reaching a public and sustaining their literary careers in the 1920s. Van Vechten simply exploited their naive conception of their social role as ethnic realists; but he was not the source of the problem, merely a symptom. The problem stemmed from the cultural process of co-optive hegemony fostered by the new urban racial caste system. While that hegemonic cultural process afforded black writers a narrow spectrum of opportunities, it also obliged them to cultivate white patrons and to submit to white cultural conceptions of black reality—if they aimed to gain public recognition. That was the reality of American cultural life in the 1920s.

Notwithstanding his motive of personal gain, Van Vechten sincerely attempted to generate more public support for black American literature, and to improve white America's understanding of black American life. The irony is that his understanding of Harlem and the American racial scene was so cursory that he failed to realize the damage that could result from depicting black Americans as primitives. Virtually all the subsequent controversy concerning his role ignored his many efforts on behalf of black writers and performers, and centered on his novel, and particularly its noxious title, *Nigger Heaven* (Van Vechten, 1971). How could a man who valued and respected black Americans give his book this title? Most black American critics regarded the title as a colossal insult, which— if anything—Van Vechten had compounded by saturating the text with inane black stereotypes. Let's now examine some of the novel's images of black American life that provoked that controversy and initiated the development of the black primitivist literary school.

Nigger Heaven: *The Paradigmatic Novel of the Primitivist Literary School*

What better evidence is there of black American literature's immaturity as a cultural institution in the 1920s than the fact that the novel that operated as the prototype of its dominant school was written by a white American journalist? Van Vechten's *Nigger Heaven* (Van Vechten 1971) was by far the most popular novel depicting black American life published in the 1920s, greatly outselling the literary works of black writers. It instantly made the best-seller lists, serving as a "sort of guide book for visitors who went uptown seeking a re-creation of the primitive African jungle in the heart of New York City" (Gloster 1948, 158). Van Vechten sought this result.

"Doing research for the novel, he spent most of the first half of 1925 in the company of Negroes. . . . The extensive notes he took during the book's gestation were wide-ranging and curious" (Leuders 1965, 97). He kept a notebook in which he recorded black idioms and slang expressions. In fact, he approached the writing of the novel like an anthropologist undertaking an ethnographic exploration of a remote tribe. Because he aimed to make the publication of the novel a major cultural happening, he spared no effort in seeking to provide it with fashionable artistic embellishment. "The element of 'modern primitivism' in the novel was important to its author. At one point in the history of the book he sent a cable to Gertrude Stein in Paris: 'If not too expensive we want Picasso to illustrate *Nigger Heaven*. Could you help persuade him. Love Carlo'" (Leuders 1965, 105).

Shortly before the book's publication, he wrote a letter to his publisher stating:

> Ordinarily . . . books should not be advertised so long in advance, but this book is different. It is necessary to prepare the mind not only of my own public, but of the new public which this book may possibly reach, particularly that public which lies outside New York. If they see the title, they will ask questions, or read The New Negro or something, so that the kind of life I am writing about will not come as an actual shock. (Leuders 1965, 102)

Aside from selfish motives, Van Vechten definitely intended to nurture a primitivist vogue and, thereby, a new direction in black American ethnic literature. So eager was he to see this black primitivist literature created that at one point he wondered, as he put it in one of his letters, if black writers were going to exploit those materials while they were still "fresh." This faddist penchant was revealed most clearly in the novel's pseudo-ethnographic format, which even included a glossary of black vernacular, listing fifty black slang expressions that were explained for the white reading public. The following are examples:

Arnchy: A person who puts on airs
August Ham: A watermelon
Blue Vein Circle: After the Civil War the mulattos organized themselves
    in a guild from which those who were black were excluded. This is a
    form of color snobbishness.
Bolito: See *numbers*
C.P.T.: Colored People's Time
Daddy: Husband or lover
Eastman: A man who lives on women
Fagingy-fagade: A white person. This word and the corresponding word
    for Negro are theatrical hog Latin.

High Yellow: Mulatto or lighter

Jig: A Negro

Jig Chaser: A white person who seeks the company of Negroes.

Miss Annie: A white girl.

Monkey Chaser: A Negro from British West Indies.

Numbers: A gambling game highly popular in contemporary Harlem. The winning numbers each day are derived from the New York Clearing House Bank exchanges and balances as they are published in the newspapers, the seventh and eight digits, reading from the right, of the exchanges, and the seventh of the balances. In Bolito, one wagers on two figures only.

Snow: Cocaine (Van Vechten 1971, 285–86)

The terms of this glossary suggested black America's exoticism, a message hardly designed to please the black civil rights intellectuals, who were striving to persuade white America that there existed no fundamental differences between the races. The thought that these images might reinforce racist stereotypes of blacks, however, apparently never entered Van Vechten's mind.

He aimed to serve his white audience as a seasoned white explorer of the urban black jungle, who possessed more intimate knowledge about its exotic and primitive customs than did any other white person. It was by means of this ethnographic content, rather than literary invention, that he sought to arouse public interest in the novel. It would not be an exaggeration to say that *Nigger Heaven* constituted a pathetic excuse for a novel. The novel's protagonist, Byron Kasson, a young middle-class black man who aspires to be a writer, serves as merely a prop for its chief preoccupation: depictions of Harlem street life and nightclubs as embodiments of primitivist culture.

Byron falls in love with a vivacious woman-about-town, Lasca Sartoris, who soon abandons him for a prominent local racketeer, Randolph Pettijohn. Encountering the racketeer later, Byron in a fit of jealous rage fires several shots into Pettijohn's prostrate body. Not knowing Pettijohn was already dead as a result of wounds inflicted by another assailant, Byron thinks he has killed him, and surrenders to the police. This feeble plot, which comprises only a small fraction of the actions depicted in the novel, fails to reveal or illuminate a central theme. In the words of one critic, "Byron is a sorry figure of confusion" (Arden 1966, 111). The melodramatic plot seeks to secure the book's claim to being a novel rather than a jumble of exotic vignettes, which is what it amounts to. Let's take a closer look at an example of its primitivist imagery.

The book opens as Anatole Longfellow, a sporting-life type character, ambles down a Harlem street. We learn that Longfellow is alias the

Scarlet Creeper; and if we bother to refer to the glossary, we discover that a "creeper" is a man who invades another's marital rights—an adulterer. The existence of this black slang expression thus is used to suggest that adulterers in black Harlem possess an esteemed social status. This clearly implies, from the standpoint of mainstream white American morality, that black Americans possess bizarre social norms. This view is reinforced by the fact that the Scarlet Creeper, like other characters Van Vechten describes in Harlem street and nightclub life, is a rootless figure, emerging from a decontextualized void. Nothing is revealed about his past, his family, his education, his occupation, or even serious thoughts that he might have. The nature of his social existence remains a mystery. There is only a description of his preoccupation with seducing women.

The novel thus opens with this rootless character strolling along Seventh Avenue, flirting with young women as he proceeds. His rootlessness sets him up as an ideal primitivist stereotype: a creature driven by hedonistic instinct. He reaches the corner of 137th Street where other blacks are dancing on the sidewalk—"a crowd of urchins executed the Charleston"—is Van Vechten's lame description. "Apparently *without intent* (emphasis added), Anatole joined these *pleasure seekers* (emphasis added). His eyes, however, quickly shifted from the dancers and stole around the ring of onlookers, in hasty but accurate inspection. Suddenly he found that for which he had been searching" (Van Vechten 1971, 9).

The phrase "without intent" suggests an instinctual response to pleasure. We see throughout the novel similar depictions of mindless impulse that are dictated by Van Vechten's primitivist view of black American life, which, in this instance, we see even more clearly revealed when he describes the object of the Scarlet Creeper's attention: "She was a golden-brown and her skin was clear, as soft as velvet. *As pretty a piece* (emphasis added), he reflected, as he had seen around these parts for sometime, and he had not happened to see her before" (Van Vechten 1971, 9).

Van Vechten is faking familiarity with behavior that is essentially foreign to him. He had not come to know blacks such as the Scarlet Creeper well enough to create a plausible fictional character; nor did he have any notion about what such a man would be thinking when he encounters a young woman. About all Van Vechten had to guide him were primitivist suppositions and socially distant observations of Harlem nightlife. We see the shallowness of Van Vechten's understanding of lower-class black ethnic culture again revealed in the ludicrous conversation he describes between the Scarlet Creeper and the woman who attracted his attention. "'Ah been jes' nacherly crazy to meet you.' The Creeper was stern. 'Waht fo?' he shot back. 'You know, Mr. Toly. I guess you knows.' He drew her a little apart from the ring" (Van Vechten 1971, 11).

What transpires next suggests that Harlem constituted an alien moral universe, for the young woman sexually propositions the man. He momentarily considers her offer, and then asks:

> "How much you got?"
> "Oh, ah been full o' prosperity dis evening.
> Ah met an ofay wanted to change his luck.
> He gimme a tenner." (Van Vechten 1971, 11)

Hence we learn she is a prostitute who just had sex with a white patron for ten dollars; this she apparently is willing to give the Scarlet Creeper to have sex with him. Van Vechten apparently intends to portray the social interactions between a pimp and a prostitute, but he failed to realize that prostitutes don't pay pimps for the sake of having sexual relations; nor, exploitative as pimp/prostitute bonds may be, that they are not the result of momentary passions, but of a gradually unfolding sequence of stages that culminate in relationships, rooted in reciprocal obligations. Van Vechten thinks it is the woman's desire for sex that is the basis of the pimp's financial gain.

> The Creeper appeared to be taking the matter under consideration. "Ah met a gal las' night dat offer me fifteen," he muttered. Nevertheless, it would be seen that he was weakening. "Ah got anunder five in mah lef' stokin, an' Ah'll show you lovin' such as you never seen." The Creeper became affable. "Ah do seem to remember you' face, Miss Silver," he averred. "Will you do me duh favor to cling to mah arm?" (Van Vechten 1971, 11)

Almost everything depicted in this encounter violates mainstream white American morality. The man is a predatory drifter, not an employed, respectable member of a community. The woman, not the man, takes the sexual initiative. The physical intimacy results from a casual encounter, not an ongoing affectionate relationship. These are plausible images only if one assumes that black Americans belong to an alien world of uninhibited instinct, devoid of a community life and cultural morality that constrain and sanction social behavior. This is not to say, of course, that pimps and prostitutes were nonexistent in Harlem, but they were hardly so prevalent as to warrant being placed in the novel's opening pages, describing a "typical" Harlem street scene. One would never suspect from Van Vechten's account that pimping and prostitution also violated the black community's morality.

Van Vechten, however, aims to highlight Harlem as a place pervaded by licentious sexuality. This we can see in the closing passage of the scene, where he underscores the primacy of eroticism among blacks in his description of the couple walking slowly along the sidewalk, anticipating the sexual intimacy they will soon experience. "Their bodies touching . . . his hand freely explored her flesh, soft and warm under the thin covering of coral silk" (Van Vechten 1971, 11).

In contrast to these exotic images of lower-class black Americans, Van Vechten presents images of middle-class blacks, who are portrayed as being emotionally repressed and neurotic, the psychological casualties of a confused racial identity. Though materially better off than their working-class compatriots, these middle-class blacks possess a melancholic and depressed spirit, because they had abandoned their rich African heritage for the emotional sterility of white American culture. We see an example of this outlook expressed in the introspection of a young middle-class black woman, who muses about her lost primitive heritage.

> Savages! Savages at heart! And she had lost or forfeited her birthright, this primitive birthright which was so valuable and important an asset, a birthright that all civilized races were struggling to get back to. . . . this fact explained the art of Picasso or Stravinsky. To be sure, she, too, felt this African beat . . . it completely aroused her emotionally . . . but she was conscious of feeling it. This love of drums, of exciting rhythms, this naïve delight in glowing colour . . . the colour that exists only in cloudless, tropical climes . . . this warm sexual emotion, all these were hers only through mental understanding. . . . We are all savages, she repeated to herself, all, apparently, but me! (Van Vechten 1971, 89–90)

We thus encounter the image of the black middle class's cultural ambivalence, projected as a subsidiary message, which is contrasted with the novel's primary message: lower-class blacks possess a healthy primitivist lifestyle. Though Van Vechten was aware of America's race problems, his bohemian proclivities made him oblivious to the negative political repercussions that could result from primitivist depictions of black ethnic life. As one critic correctly observed about *Nigger Heaven:* "While it is clear that the author cares about his characters, he does not preach in the book. . . . It is not a sociological study, it is not a sermon, it is not a plea for the downtrodden" (Leuders 1965, 98).

Though these remarks were expressed as a compliment to Van Vechten for his detachment from the black community's social problems, they also can be read as evidence that *Nigger Heaven* comforted conservative defenders of the racial caste system. Whites could read the novel without feeling discomforted about the plight of blacks in American society.

Let's now turn to a closer examination of the book's primitivist message. Given the prevailing racist attitudes of whites toward blacks, there was only one way Van Vechten could have framed primitivist images of black Americans to project a positive message. This demanded using those images to attack white American culture. The novel thus would have contrasted the black primitive culture it favored with the mainstream white American culture it scorned and hoped to change. This dialectical formula was hardly farfetched. American intellectuals during this period routinely denounced white Western civilization; incorporating such denunciations in a novel celebrating primitivism would have made a more plausible case for its acceptance.

> The Negro's proximity to his native instincts . . . his ability to drop the trappings of false civilization and to reveal a rapport with elemental emotions shared by all men . . . is, of course, presented in many portions of the novel. And this "primitivism" is one of the things that should have recommended the book to believers in basic instincts, such as D. H. Lawrence. . . . The novel gained the helpful notoriety of being banned in Boston. More importantly though, Van Vechten shrewdly equates the "savage" Negro with the inhibited white—or at least the white society to which the Negro is "supposed" to adapt in the ambivalence of the highly "civilized" Mary Love (a black middle-class female character). (Leuders 1965, 105)

But Van Vechten avoids attacking white American culture—which is to say, he failed to use the primitivist ideology to critique flawed mainstream American values. The novel envelops only a black American social world; and, in this sense, sociologically it was a "black" novel. Whites remained in the background, obliquely implicated by proxy, through the "white" values exhibited by the assimilated black middle class. Yet white readers easily could have viewed the resulting problems middle-class blacks experienced as evidence of black American racial inferiority (i.e., their inability to adjust to a "respectable way of life"), rather than as indications of white America's cultural sterility. Like the conservative critic quoted above, most white American critics failed to see any normative implications in the novel for white American culture. And this is noteworthy. In a cultural climate buzzing with Freudian ideas about the psychological perils of civilization, none of these critics saw a connection between Van Vechten's primitivist novel and the alleged malaise of Western culture.

There were novels written during the era that effectively mounted such critiques. D. H. Lawrence's *Lady Chatterly's Lover*, for example, successfully employed a Freudian perspective to promote an instinctual conception of healthy human sexuality. Similarly, though not oriented to a primitivist ideology, the novels by white American writers such as Sinclair Lewis's *Babbitt*; Sherwood Anderson's *Winesburg, Ohio*; and Thomas Wolfe's *Look Homeward Angel* attacked mainstream white American culture by highlighting its corrupt values and hollow lifestyles. This Van Vechten's *Nigger Heaven* failed to do. Instead it depicted black American life as an isolated moral universe, a social world divorced from Western culture. Though Van Vechten may have felt primitivism constituted a more desirable way of life than did the Protestant ethic that undergirded mainstream white American society, he depicts no white American antagonists to primitivist values in the novel. This suggests that he aimed not to critically engage and challenge his white readers' values but rather to titillate their appetites for exotic adventure.

The young black primitivist writers followed Van Vechten's path. Despite the fact that blacks lived in a social world suffused by white American political, economic, and cultural influences, these black writers, for the most part, ignored race relations. Depicting the black social world as an isolated universe sustained by happy-go-lucky hedonism, they inadvertently reinforced the white public's tendency to perceive black Americans as aliens. As a result, their depictions of black American life neglected to give white Americans any insight into the effects of their (i.e., white American) attitudes and behavior on the lives of black Americans; the toll of racial oppression was simply ignored. This, it is important to note, would be the only dominant black literary school between 1920 and 1970 that failed to link white Americans to black American experiences.

Nigger Heaven provoked a barrage of critical reactions, which revealed not only the different criteria used to assess the novel but also, what was even more significant, the deeply fractured culture of race relations in 1920s America.

Critical Responses to Nigger Heaven

Nigger Heaven struck the American literary landscape like a meteorite, arousing more interest than was customary for literary works depicting black Americans. It provoked strong favorable and unfavorable responses. The two most salient categories of unfavorable responses were literary and political. Among the responses based on literary criteria, it is noteworthy that no critic regarded the book as a significant literary achievement. D. H. Lawrence's reaction constitutes an example of an unfavorable review, based on literary criteria, that embraced a derogatory primitivist conception of blacks.

> Mr. Van Vechten's book is a nigger book, and not much of one. It opens and closes with nigger cabaret scenes in feeble imitation of Cocteau and Morand, second hand attempts to be wildly lurid, with back-ground effects of black and vermilion velvet. . . . Altogether the usual old bones of hot stuff, warmed up with all the fervor the author can command—which isn't much. (Leuders 1965, 103)

The most strident negative reviews by far came from politically engaged critics, who viewed the novel in terms of the cultural politics of race. Mike Gold, the white editor of the leftist *New Masses* magazine, leveled a brutal political attack on Van Vechten.

> We believe Carl Van Vechten the worst friend the Negro ever had. This night club rounder and white literary sophisticate was one of the first to take an interest in Negro writers in this country. He has been the most evil influence . . . gin, jazz, and sex. . . . This is all that stirs him in our world, and he has imparted his tastes to the young Negro litterateurs. He is a white literary bum, who has created a brood of Negro literary bums. So many of them are wasting their splendid talents on the gutter life of Harlem. (Gold 1930, 1)

Gold later launched a similar attack on Claude McKay, which helped to sour McKay's relationship with the leftist political subculture of the *New Masses* magazine. Also leftist in perspective was the response of Nancy Cunard, a radical British writer, who assailed primitivism as:

> A bourgeois ideology with no horizon, no philosophical link to life. And out of all this, need it be said, such writers as Van Vechten and Co. have made a revolting and cheap lithograph, so that Harlem, to a large idle-minded public, has come to mean nothing more what-so-ever than a round of hooch-filled night-clubs after a round of "snow" (cocaine) filled bodies. Van Vechten, the spirit of vulgarity, has depicted Harlem as a grimace. (Cunard 1976, 130)

Striking an even more caustic tone, W. E. B. DuBois, then editor of *Crisis*, was outraged by *Nigger Heaven*, which he described as "a blow in the face, an affront to the hospitality of the black folk and the intelligence of the white. . . . A caricature of half-truths . . . an astonishing and wearisome hodge-podge of laboriously stated facts, quotations and expressions illuminated here and there with something that come near to being nothing but cheap melodrama" (DuBois 1926, 10).

Reflecting the responses of reviewers committed to leftist political perspectives on black American life, these critics regarded *Nigger Heaven* as a threat to the struggle for racial justice in American society. They were especially disturbed by the prospect that the novel's primitivist images of blacks as contented and carefree and amoral hedonists would further legitimize racial discrimination. This accounted for their abrasive tone.

Yet there was by no means a consensus of unfavorable responses. The two categories of favorable responses emanated from, on the one hand, white critics who shared Van Vechten's primitivist conception of blacks and, on the other hand, black writers who valued Van Vechten's friendship. The response of Ellen Glasgow, a white Virginian novelist, illustrates the pattern of white reviewers who accepted the novel's primitivist depictions as accurate.

The roots of this book cling below the shallow surface of sophistication in some rich primitive soil of humanity. . . . That the book attempts to prove nothing, that it does not masquerade as ethnology in the fancy dress of a novel, that it points no moral and preaches no doctrine of equality—this absence of prophetic gesture makes *Nigger Heaven* only the more impressive as a sincere interpretation of life. A thrilling, a remarkable book. There is fire at the heart of it. (Leuders 1965, 106)

In contrast, the black writers with close personal ties to Van Vechten revealed a different approach. More than one black writer had assisted Van Vechten during the writing of the book—which was indicative of the collaborative relationships between white and black writers that developed under the new cultural regimen of co-optive hegemony. In their favorable commentary, it is important to understand, these black writers were defending not only the novel's primitivist perspective on Harlem life but also their roles in assisting Van Vechten. The novel opens with a poem by Countee Cullen. Both James Weldon Johnson and Walter White had read the novel in galley proofs; Rudolph Fisher gave it a last check for authenticity. As close personal friends and beneficiaries of Van Vechten's support, they denied that he was a racist. Instead they tried to place the controversy in a broader interpretive context, as a manifestation of the struggle to free literary works depicting blacks from politics. This followed from the young black writers' inclinations toward what they conceived as uncompromising ethnic realism—pitched in Langston Hughes's declaration—"We . . . intend to express our individual dark skinned selves without fear of shame"—which we noted earlier. *Nigger Heaven* was defended in that light.

James Weldon Johnson, for instance, submitted a strong testimonial on behalf of the white author: "Carl Van Vechten had a warm interest in colored people before he ever was in Harlem. In the early days of the Negro literary and artistic movement, no one in the country did more to forward it than he accomplished in frequent magazine articles and by his many personal efforts in behalf of individual Negro writers and artists" (Johnson 1937, 33).

Johnson went on to attest to their close friendship. "Indeed, his regard for Negroes as a race is so close to being an affectionate one, that he is constantly joked about it by his most intimate friends. . . . Mr. Van Vechten's birthday, that of young Alfred Knopf and mine fall on the same day of the same month. For four or five years we have been celebrating them jointly, together with a small group of friends" (Johnson 1937, 33).

Johnson concluded by endorsing the book—"from the first, my belief has held that *Nigger Heaven* is a fine novel"—while dismissing the political criticisms. "As the race progresses it will become less and less susceptible to hurts from such causes. . . . Their objections were really based upon chagrin and resentment at the disclosures to a white public." Perhaps unwisely, Johnson was not content to stop there, but went on to claim that Van Vechten's novel exemplified a genuine black American ethnic novel because it enveloped "nearly every phase of (black American) life."

This oddly inflated assessment should be understood in terms of Johnson's close friendship with Van Vechten. As a black intellectual who straddled two often contradictory roles as a civil rights leader and a literary artist, Johnson often held his political opinions in check when commenting on literary and artistic work. However, in praising Van Vechten's novel he apparently suspended both literary and political judgment. For as we will see momentarily, he would later admonish Claude McKay for producing a novel in much the same primitivist mold. Johnson's positive response to *Nigger Heaven* illustrates the constraints imposed on black writers by the collaborative relationships with white writers. If Van Vechten needed their testimonials to establish the book's credibility in the eyes of his white American audience; they needed Van Vechten's assistance to gain access to the white publishers and the mainstream public culture.

Langston Hughes, who would soon emerge as one of the leading black primitivist writers during the 1920s, also defended Van Vechten. While most blacks regarded the book's title as odious, Hughes articulated a very different opinion. He argued that the book's meaning had been misunderstood and that it was intended as a reference to the segregated upper balcony of Broadway theaters, not as a racial insult. Given his close personal relationship to Van Vechten, Hughes refused to believe the book's title was motivated by racism.

> To Mr. Van Vechten, Harlem was like . . . a segregated gallery in the theater, the only place where Negroes could see or stage their own show, and not a very satisfactory place at that, for in this novel Mr. Van Vechten presents many of the problems of Negroes of Harlem, and he writes of the culture as well as the people of the night clubs. (Hughes 1940, 8)

Actually Van Vechten had intended to suggest that Harlem was a hedonistic paradise. "You can laugh all you want," declares one character in the novel. "Harlem is a sort of Mecca." Or note another example from the novel in the following passage.

> "Ah sho' will show you some lovin, daddy," she promised. The Creeper grunted his approval. "Does you know what Ah calls dis?" she continued rapturously. "Calls what?" "Dis place, where Ah met you—Harlem. Ah call et, specerly tonight. Ah calls it Nigger Heaven! I jes' nacherly think dis heah

is Nigger Heaven!" On the floor a scrawny yellow girl in pink silk embroidered with bronze sequins in floral designs began to sing. "Mah daddy rocks me with one steady roll; Der ain't no slippin when he takes hol'. . . ." The Creeper sipped his gin meditatively. (Van Vechten 1971, 15–16)

It is doubtful that Langston Hughes misunderstood the actual meaning of the book's title; he used similar crude racial images of Harlem in his own works. Though aiming to defend Van Vechten against the charge of racism, he knew enough about the sensibility of black civil rights intellectuals like DuBois to avoid arguing that the novel's primitivist images of blacks were true. That would never wash with these politically oriented blacks. Instead he opted for a different strategy, arguing that Van Vechten's intentions had been misunderstood. Like Johnson, Hughes pointed to Van Vechten's generous support of blacks:

> Many other of the Negroes in the arts, from Paul Robeson to Ethel Waters, Walter White to Richard Barthe, will offer the same testimony as to the interest Van Vechten has displayed toward Negro creators in the fields of writing, plastic arts, and popular entertainment. To say that Carl Van Vechten harmed Negro creative activities is sheer poppycock. The bad Negro writers were bad long before *Nigger Heaven* appeared on the scene. And would have been bad anyway, had Van Vechten never been born. (Hughes 1940, 8)

Carl Van Vechten's black associates also knew that his father had long been involved in philanthropic activities assisting blacks in rural Mississippi, where he had founded a vocational school for blacks. Actually the elder Van Vechten had also reacted to the book's title with dismay, which he revealed in a letter to his son, where he stated his objections to the word *nigger*.

It is no doubt true that most who attacked the book never got beyond its title. Yet Carl Van Vechten was hardly naive; he knew that most blacks objected to the word *nigger*, as he observed in a footnote: "While this informal epithet is freely used by Negroes among themselves, not only as a term of opprobrium, but as also actually a term of endearment, its employment by a white person is always fiercely resented" (Van Vechten 1971, 26). But he never said why he used it. In view of his knowledge of the stigma surrounding the word, it seems plausible to conclude that he was pandering to interests in sensationalism.

As the author of the first systematic empirical sociological study of an urban black American community—*The Philadelphia Negro* (DuBois, 1967)—W. E. B. DuBois was especially sensitive to the possibility that this novel would be taken as sociological fact. "The overwhelming majority of black folk there (in Harlem) never go to cabarets," DuBois declared. "The average colored man in Harlem is an everyday laborer, attending church, lodges and movies and is conservative and as conventional as ordinary working people everywhere" (DuBois 1926, viii–ix).

This was the voice of the civil rights integrationist ideology, which sought to encourage politically engaged and mainstream American images of black American life. The point DuBois should have made, however, was not that ethnic blacks were similar to working-class whites, who were themselves characterized by ethnic differences. Rather he should have noted that black American ethnic life was something other than what Van Vechten had constructed.

Let's now turn to the major black writers and literary works of the primitivist literary school.

THE BLACK PRIMITIVIST WRITERS

Like most ideologies, the primitivist ideology consisted of a set of assumptions or precepts. Many black American literary works during the 1920s evidenced, in varying degrees, these primitivist ideological precepts, which can be delineated in the following ideal-type construct:

1. A biological conception of black American ethnic culture which was seen as derived from their African ancestry.
2. Equation of African ancestry with primitive instinctualism.
3. Depiction of lower-class blacks as the chief bearers of primitive instinctualism, the defining feature of black ethnic culture, which is manifested in their carefree and hedonistic lifestyles.
4. Depiction of middle-class blacks as social misfits, alienated from the emotional vitality of black ethnic culture.
5. Depiction of white Western culture as being emotionally repressed and sterile.

Conspicuously absent in their primitivist depictions of black America were images of racial problems, environmental influences (e.g., family, neighborhood, school, church), poverty, black nationalism, and the white American social world.

The literary works of the dominant primitivist school highlighted the above ideological precepts. Many black literary works published in the 1920s, as noted, exhibited primitivist influences, but the extent to which they projected that ideology as their worldview varied from what we might term "the core works" that were centered on primitivist ideology to "the peripheral works" that simply echoed some of its elements. It is the core works and their authors that concern us here.

Major Writers and Literary Works of the Dominant Black Primitivist School

Claude McKay, Langston Hughes, and Jean Toomer emerged as the authors of the core primitivist works. It is hardly coincidental that each of these writers was weakly attached to the black community's institutional life; their social marginality in the black community was directly linked to their cosmopolitan lifestyles, which brought them into white American social networks that benefited their literary careers. And therein lay the central paradox posed by elite racial integration. As talented black American intellectuals gained entry into previously segregated cosmopolitan domains, they were obliged to absorb white American cultural preoccupations.

Stated somewhat differently, this racial integration, which proceeded on terms dictated by whites, resulted not in cultural amalgamation but in cultural co-optation. As we noted earlier, the regimen of paternalistic hegemony was being supplanted by a new and more subtle regimen of co-optive hegemony. The black primitivist writers mistook this new development for artistic independence.

Many facts about the backgrounds of the major black primitivist writers were remarkably similar. They were born around the turn of the century. McKay, the oldest, was born in 1889; Toomer in 1894; and Hughes in 1902. Their childhoods preceded World War I and were thus free of the racial strife that characterized the childhoods of the major black American writers who emerged in the 1930s. In fact, perhaps the most notable characteristic about their childhoods was the cordiality of their contacts with whites. McKay enjoyed a close friendship as a youth with a British folklorist who had come to Jamaica to do research and subsequently spent a considerable amount of time tutoring him. Toomer's family lived in a predominately white neighborhood in Washington, D.C.; and most of his early childhood friends were white. Hughes attended predominately white schools and his closest friends, particularly while he was in high school, were children of recent immigrants from Europe. As a consequence of these early interracial relationships, these writers felt favorably disposed toward whites, a fact that no doubt contributed to their later misreading of the American racial scene.

It is also significant that none of these writers was born in the big northern industrial cities which became the centers of the nation's economic life and its most violent racial clashes, shortly after the turn of the century. McKay was born in Jamaica, where he remained until he was an adult. Although Toomer's family came from Louisiana, he was born in Washington, D. C., where his family later settled. Hughes was born in Missouri but spent his childhood in various places, including Mexico. Also, each of these writers came from unconventional family circumstances, backgrounds characterized by marital discord or early childhood separation from their parents. Though their families encountered various economic hardships, these writers grew up in households that embraced middle-class values, which strongly emphasized the importance of education. The effects of those educational influences were evidenced by the fact that each enrolled in college before turning to a literary career. But each also became a college dropout, a development that resulted from both their weak family support networks and their adventurous dispositions. Each had to make his way without the benefit of professional credentials. It should be noted that such credentials were an essential requirement for intellectual work within the small black middle-class intelligentsia, which regarded college degrees as important markers of racial advancement. Given the black intelligentsia's strict formal educational criteria in its hiring practices, these young black writers had no possibility of locating employment within the NAACP, the Urban League, or other middle-class black organizations.

Repulsed by the black middle class's status preoccupations and lacking alternative channels of access to professional employment, these writers gravitated to rebellious, bohemian lifestyles. In fact, it was in large part those rebellious bohemian proclivities, manifested in their wanderlusts, erratic work experiences, and unstable personal lives, that predisposed them to the sensationalist primitivist ideology.

Countee Cullen also became linked to the primitivist perspective, but he shifted to that ideology later, when the literary school was in decline. Cullen shared few of the social background characteristics of the above writers. As a college graduate with a conventional lifestyle, he was rooted firmly in Harlem's black middle class. His later attraction to primitivism, as we will see, resulted more from the popularity of primitivist literary works than from an intellectual predisposition to rebellion. Nevertheless, the primitivist phase of his literary career is noteworthy, because it reveals the impact of that ideology's notoriety in attracting writers seeking a wider audience. In short, for more conservative black writers like Cullen, the attraction to primitivism was motivated by pragmatic considerations. We will briefly examine Cullen's primitivist phase, after discussing the major primitivist writers and literary works.

Claude McKay: A Black Writer Seeking Cosmopolitan Literary Acclaim

Throughout the 1920s, Claude McKay was a young man in a hurry, seized by ambition for international literary fame. More than any other black writer of the era, he aspired to achieve eminence in white Western literary culture, an aspiration, defining his literary identity, that persistently eluded his grasp. As one of the era's leading black writers, McKay was important not only because he wrote *Home to Harlem* (McKay 1987), which, following *Nigger Heaven*, was the second most popular primitivist literary work; but also because he had such varied and unusual personal experiences. No other black writer, except perhaps Langston Hughes, left a more vivid autobiographical account of his experiences (McKay 1937). McKay's recount of those experiences revealed the workings of the emerging cultural process of co-optive hegemony, and particularly the way it absorbed black writers in the liberal white intellectual community's ideological preoccupations.

We will first briefly retrace the web of relationships and experiences that shaped McKay's literary career and then examine the primitivist images of black American life he projected through *Home to Harlem*.

McKay's experiences in his native Jamaica, where he lived until early adulthood, largely molded his intellectual identity. Jamaica existed then as a British colony, where McKay, despite being born into a poor family, had the good fortune to receive an excellent education in the humanities. Initially guided by his brother, a lay minister in the Anglican church, his education was later supervised by a British anthropologist, who had befriended McKay after coming to Jamaica to study Jamaican folklore. This British-oriented education nurtured McKay's lifelong allegiance to Western intellectual culture, which shaped his literary ambitions.

> He did not feel it necessary to cut himself off from the great artistic and philosophical traditions of Europe and America. Tolstoy, D. H. Lawrence, and Hemingway constituted a legacy he could not, and would not, repudiate . . . . Throughout his life and writing, McKay struggled to believe that such separation from the best in white Western culture was not necessary for the black man. (Giles 1972, 21)

Among other things, his Jamaican background and Europe-centered intellectual identity caused him to feel ambivalence toward the black American community, particularly the black American intelligentsia.

McKay began his writing career in colonial Jamaica, and by the age of twenty-two he had authored two books of poetry published in England. Despite these early achievements, he felt frustrated with his life under British colonialism, which offered him no opportunities to become a professional writer. Professional jobs for blacks in Jamaica were almost nonexistent. He worked brief periods as a cabinetmaker and a constable, but, after a short time, found these jobs unsuited to his aspirations, and decided to migrate to the United States. He aimed to attend Tuskegee Institute in Alabama. However, after reaching the United States and enrolling in that conservative black institution, which was then operating under the imperious control of Booker T. Washington, he realized he had made a mistake. He soon left Tuskegee, and headed to Kansas State School of Agriculture, where, still dissatisfied, he abandoned his quest for a college education and moved to Harlem.

McKay arrived in Harlem before the mass black migration from the South and the post–World War I race riots. Struggling to earn a living at a variety of menial jobs (railroad porter, hotel waiter, bartender, and short-order cook), he continued to write poetry and submit his work to publishers. This was before the primitivist literary vogue; black writers were still marginalized under paternalistic hegemony, which denied them a significant public role.

As a young black aspiring to pursue a literary career, McKay became entwined in liberal white intellectual networks soon after his arrival in New York, networks that forecast the emerging cultural regimen of co-optive hegemony. In the words of one McKay biographer: "The awakening of Negro American Art was supposed to come from within the racial group itself and was to be as free as possible of white control. . . . Because of having worked at a series of menial jobs, (McKay) had deep associations and sympathies with the black masses. But from the beginning his career was guided and influenced by whites" (Giles 1972, 21).

In fact, McKay, who had only fragile attachments to the black community, actively sought and cultivated white patrons from the beginning of his residence in the United States. Before the primitivist vogue, his two most important white literary patrons were Frank Harris and Max Eastman. Harris, then working as editor of the iconoclastic, avant garde *Pearson's* magazine, exerted a strong, though brief, influence on McKay's literary career. Starting with their first meeting shortly after McKay arrived in New York, Harris assumed the role of his mentor and began to alter his literary work, urging him, among other things, to turn away from poetry, and to concentrate on prose. Harris also advised McKay to change the perspective of his writing, which then consisted of a bland and ethereal universalism, by encouraging him to identify with black America's political struggle, and to assert a more militant outlook.

This occurred during the immediate postwar period, when masses of blacks were moving to northern cities and encountering racial strife, as we noted earlier. White mobs often assaulted black pedestrians on the streets while white policeman, in obvious sympathy with the mobs, stood idly watching. It was this acceleration of racial violence, along with the accompanying feelings of fear and insecurity, that attracted many blacks to the nascent Garvey movement.

Frank Harris quickly perceived the new possibilities for black literary expression created by white America's racial injustices, and implored

McKay to protest the black community's plight. As a native of Ireland who had experienced British oppression, Harris felt he could empathize with black American writers living in a racist white society. "You have to wrench it out of your guts on man's inhumanity to man," he advised McKay. Heeding his advice, McKay shifted to a more political focus and shortly afterwards wrote his most celebrated work, the militant protest poem *If We Must Die*. The poem exhorted blacks to mobilize and to fight in self-defense against white mob violence:

> If we must die, let it not be like hogs
> Hunted and penned in an inglorious spot,
> While round us bark the mad and hungry dogs,
> Making their mock at our accursed lot.
> If we must die, O let us noble die,
> So that our precious blood may not be shed
> In vain: then even the monsters we defy
> Shall be constrained to honor us though dead!
> O kinsmen! we must meet the common foe!
> Though far outnumbered let us show us brave,
> And for their thousand blows deal one death-blow!
> What though before us lies the open grave?
> Like men we'll face the murderous, cowardly pack,
> Pressed to the wall, dying, but fighting back! (McKay 1937, 21)

Despite the benefits McKay garnered from Harris's advice, their relationship cooled when the Irish editor voiced intemperate racist remarks, suggesting that West Africans possessed an innately coarse sensibility. After seeing this bigoted side of Harris's personality, McKay lost his earlier enthusiasm for their friendship. Nevertheless, despite this disaffection, he continued to publish his poems in Harris's magazine, a rare opportunity he was unwilling to sacrifice. McKay was then the only black writer who was being published regularly in such cosmopolitan white literary magazines as *Pearson's* and *Seven Arts*.

Shortly after the Harris incident, he gravitated to Max Eastman, the editor of the Marxist oriented *Liberator* magazine.[1] Eastman had agreed to publish *If We Must Die* in the *Liberator*, and almost immediately replaced Harris as McKay's mentor. In contrast to the libertarian and caustic Frank Harris who relished violating conventional morality, Eastman exhibited a more temperate, urbane, and courtly demeanor. McKay was immediately impressed by Eastman's intellectual seriousness. Through his friendship with Eastman, he was drawn into a white Marxist intellectual network, which gave him opportunities to publish in leftist periodicals. In fact, prior to the primitivist vogue, most of the support McKay received for his literary career came from this leftist intellectual network, support that reached a high point when Max Eastman appointed him associate editor of the *Liberator*, making him the first black writer to acquire a position of such importance within the liberal-leftist white intellectual community.

Similar to its impact on other socially marginal minority group intellectuals, Marxism provided McKay not only a universalistic intellectual perspective, but also, though much less obvious, a rationale for his estrangement from black ethnic culture. Frowning on ethnic chauvinism as an obstacle to working-class solidarity, the Marxist movement often attracted minority-group intellectuals who felt alienated from their ethnic or racial ancestry.

McKay, however, never exhibited more than a vague ideological commitment to Marxism during this political phase of his literary career. Followers of Marxism were then subjected to little discipline by the movement, which consisted of a loose coalition of socialist intellectuals who advocated workers' rights, interracialism, and opposition to bourgeois values, without an explicit program of political action for writers and intellectuals. That would come later, after Stalin took over the Soviet Union and attempted to subject all Marxist intellectuals to communist party control. As we will see later in the case of Richard Wright, during the totalitarian phase of the Marxist movement, the American communist party attempted to harness Depression-era American communist writers to its rigid hierarchical control. But McKay experienced no such heavy-handed interference. In fact, as a black writer seeking to advance his literary career prior to the primitivist vogue, he found the Marxist movement a far more attractive proposition than either the civil rights or the black nationalist movements.

As for the nascent black nationalist movement, McKay detested its racialist ideology. McKay's attitude toward that movement was actually ironic, because much of his poetry during this phase of his literary career resonated black anger. Yet *If We Must Die* was the only one of his militant poems that he read to a black audience. That occurred when he was employed as a railroad porter. He read it to his fellow black railroad workers. One of these workers, a Garvey follower, was deeply moved by the poem's militant spirit, and urged McKay to take the poem to Garvey's headquarters. But McKay dismissed the suggestion, saying he "had no desire to harangue a crowd" (McKay 1937, 32). His fellow black workers enthusiastic response to *If We Must Die* failed to impress him because he believed their interests were motivated by racial chauvinism rather than genuine appreciation of his poetry. As he cynically put it, "that one great outburst was their sole standard of appraising my poetry."

His attitude toward his Jamaican compatriot Marcus Garvey was—if anything—even more contemptuous. "A West Indian charlatan who came to this country full of antiquated social ideas," was the way McKay described him. Though some people thought McKay's militant poems were inspired by black nationalism, he wrote those poems to protest racial injustices, not to celebrate racial pride or promote racial separatism. As we noted earlier, McKay's intellectual identity and aspirations remained committed to European cosmopolitan culture. "He was trained to believe that culture and art were essentially what England and Europe declared them to be. . . . His belief that the great ideas of the West transcended racial concerns would always . . . (keep) him from adopting a position of total cultural separatism" (Giles 1972, 21–22).

Marxism, as one of those great Western ideas that transcended race, hardly reflected the black community's social consciousness. Except for a few socialist black intellectuals around the *Messenger* magazine, such as A. Philip Randolph and Chandler Owen, virtually all major black leaders opposed Marxism. Marcus Garvey, in particular, viewed the Marxist advocacy of working-class interracialism with a jaundiced eye. "I am advising the Negro working man and laborer against the present brand of Communism . . . as taught in America, and to be careful of the traps and pitfalls of white trade unionism in affiliation with the American Federation of white workers or laborers" (Garvey 1963, 95).

Though McKay came into close contact with working-class blacks while he worked at various menial jobs, no deep or lasting relationships resulted. Perhaps the most important of those contacts—at least from the standpoint of subsequent influences on his literary works—were those that occurred when he worked as a porter on a passenger train, traveling weekly between New York and Pittsburgh. He had ample opportunity to observe the behavior of his fellow black railroad workers during layovers in Pittsburgh and was disturbed by what he perceived as their frivolous lifestyles, exhibited in their leisure-time preoccupations with drinking, gambling, and pursuing women. Strikingly similar negative attitudes toward lower-class blacks would be voiced, approximately a decade later, by Richard Wright. Both McKay and Wright wrote about lower-class blacks without feeling personally identified with their social world.

However, in his literary depictions of lower-class black lifestyles, McKay expressed greater ambivalence than did Wright. Due chiefly to influences from the primitivist ideology, McKay tended to depict those black lower-class lifestyles as mindless and gratifying. In contrast, he depicted a black intellectual, a character apparently modeled on himself, as being a refined but psychologically tormented individual, rootless and estranged from both the black community and the mainstream white society. This contrast between lower-class blacks and the black intellectual constituted the central tension in McKay's *Home to Harlem*.

But what about McKay's relationship to the black civil rights intellectuals? As we noted earlier in reference to the major ideological forces in the black community, relations between the civil rights intellectuals and the black primitivist writers were strained. Those strains surfaced when *Crisis*, the NAACP magazine then edited by W. E. B. DuBois, rejected one of McKay's militant protest poems for publication. McKay was incensed to discover that the periodical of the flagship black civil rights organization refused to publish his poems protesting racial injustices. In fact, after he shifted his orientation from the British poetic tradition, McKay encountered persistent difficulties trying to publish his work in black periodicals, and those difficulties only worsened when he become involved in the primitivist vogue. Observed McKay biographer James Giles: "It is a comment on the limitations of the Renaissance movement rather than upon McKay's work that his poetry, which was always hampered by conscious imitation of traditional British models, was infinitely more acceptable to the contemporary Negro cultural establishment than his fiction" (Giles 1972, 22).

Actually, McKay's problem emanated not from the black cultural establishment but from the black political establishment, the civil rights intelligentsia, who controlled the two major black periodicals that published black literary works: *Crisis* (NAACP) and *Opportunity* (Urban League). The editors of these two periodicals detested both black nationalism and black primitivism. His encounters with these ideological obstacles reinforced McKay's contempt for middle-class blacks and their conservative intellectual standards that denied him access to their educated black readers. Though he had written those militant poems for a black audience, he ended up publishing them in liberal white publications, such as the *Liberator* and *Pearson's*, where few blacks were likely to read them.

McKay's dissociation from the black middle-class intelligentsia was revealed even more emphatically by the way he initially met the civil rights intellectuals. This occurred at a conference organized by the *Liberator* magazine to bring white and black radicals together. Though McKay had been living in Harlem for some time, he was a stranger to members of the black intellectual establishment. Attending the conference as a representative of the white leftist *Liberator* magazine, he recalled meeting DuBois (whom he described as having "a cold, acid hauteur of spirit"), Walter White, the novelist Jesse Fausett, and James Weldon Johnson (Cruise 1967, 47). But no close associations resulted. Except for the blossoming of a brief friendship with James Weldon Johnson, which soon withered after the appearance of McKay's primitivist novel, McKay remained distant from the civil rights intellectuals.

As for Alain Locke, the leader of the local black cultural intelligentsia, their relationship began cordially but eventually soured. McKay became offended when Locke, in a book of black poetry he edited in 1927, changed the title of one of McKay's poems without asking his permission.

Still smoldering from that arrogant gesture, McKay offered his assessment of Locke: "As an individual, Locke was autocratic and 'high handed'; his taste in the arts was severely limited; and, most importantly, he was never a man to lead a black literary renaissance" (Giles 1972, 17–18). Though McKay, like the other young black writers, shared Locke's optimistic belief that black American literary works were assuming a vanguard role, his writings were never influenced by Locke. McKay's relations to his fellow black writers also evidenced strains. In commenting on those relations, James Giles notes that they

> were not always smooth. . . . At one point in the 1930s, McKay attempted to work with Cullen on a new magazine of Negro art, but, in a June 28, 1933, letter to Eastman, he refers to Cullen with icy contempt. . . . The Jamaican admired Langston Hughes as a poet; the two apparently never had any meaningful personal contact, but McKay's admiration for Hughes's art is, however, significant. (Giles 1972, 18)

Hughes had admired McKay since high school when he read McKay's poem *If We Must Die* in the *Liberator* magazine. The two writers, during the 1920s, maintained a lively correspondence which revealed not only their mutual attraction to primitivism but also their shared belief that black writers should chronicle lower-class black ethnic culture (Rampersad 1986, 158). Having been exposed to McKay's writings while just a teenager, Hughes regarded McKay as a role model. Let's now turn to McKay's major primitivist novel.

Home to Harlem: *A Black Writer's Primitivist View of Black America*

Published in 1928, *Home to Harlem* achieved the distinction of being the most popular black novel of the primitivist era. As one McKay biographer has noted: "It has often been called the first Afro–American 'best seller,' because of the brief vogue it enjoyed in New York City. . . . Not until the publication of Richard Wright's *Native Son* in 1940 did another Afro–American novel enjoy such popular success" (Cooper 1987, ix–x). *Home to Harlem*'s ideological message was also the most bluntly anti-assimilationist of the black primitivist literary works. This was revealed in its depictions of primitivist black ethnic culture as a psychologically healthy alternative to white Western culture. Like Van Vechten's *Nigger Heaven*, the novel depicts the adventures of a working-class black character (Jake Brown), its footloose and picaresque protagonist, personifying black American primitivism. Jake starts out in the U.S. Army but soon becomes frustrated, because he has been assigned to menial labor rather than combat duty; and, in consequence, he deserts the Army and returns to the United States—specifically, Harlem. Soon after his arrival in Harlem, he falls in love with a beautiful woman but unwittingly loses her address. A clumsy melodramatic contrivance of the sort that frequently set the characters in motion in the poorly crafted primitivist novels, this accident allowed McKay to focus on the novel's chief objective: an exploration of Harlem's seamy side.

By setting up Jake's search to locate his girlfriend, McKay gains the freedom to reveal the underside of Harlem life as Jake ventures into the twilight world of nightclubs, after-hours joints, rent parties, and other off-beat settings. The novel depicts black community life as a world of hedonistic indulgence as Jake winds through a series of experiences that make the Lost Generation novels of Ernest Hemingway, Floyd Dell, and F. Scott Fitzgerald seem like adolescent antics. Finally, Jake locates his girlfriend, emerges from Harlem's twilight world, and departs for the Midwest and a more conventional life (which, significantly, is not depicted).

In McKay's novel, as in *Nigger Heaven*, there is a black intellectual (Ray, a young Haitian immigrant aspiring to be a writer), who—in contrast to the robust, impulsive pleasures of his black lower-class environment—is depicted as a morose and repressed neurotic. In the words of Robert Bone, "Ray embodies the dilemma of the inhibited, over-civilized intellectual. A misfit in the white man's civilization" (Bone 1958, 68). In this character, McKay presents a black individual whose predicament registers the frustrations of being a black intellectual living in but apart from Western society, and estranged him from his African heritage. "Upset in his thinking by World War I and the Russian Revolution, (Ray) stands as a confused black man in a social order dominated by whites." As one commentator put it:

> In his wide reading, which ranges from Sappho to Sherwood Anderson, he discovers no solution to his dilemma. He shrinks from marriage because he does not want to become one of the contented hogs in the pigpen of Harlem, getting ready to litter little black pigmies. Finding slight meaning in human existence, he cynically considers himself a "misfit" and sometimes wonders if he can abandon his education and lose himself "in some savage culture in the jungles of Africa." (Gloster 1948, 164–65)

This novel's primitivist depictions of Harlem's black ethnic life came as close as the Eurocentric McKay ever got to losing himself "in some savage culture in the jungles of Africa." In contrast to those primitivist pretensions, his depiction of Ray, the frustrated black intellectual, actually reflected the psychological reality of cosmopolitan black intellectuals like himself and Jean Toomer, estranged from both the black community and the mainstream white society.

Ray, however, serves as merely a foil, whereas Jake embodies its ideological message. As Robert Bone has astutely noted, it was "through Jake that McKay strikes at the heart of the Protestant Ethic. . . . Jake is a typical McKay protagonist—the primitivist Negro, untouched by the decay of Occidental civilization" (Bone 1958, 69). This was the paradigmatic formula of the black primitivist literary school.

Mesmerized by the Jazz Age primitivist vogue, McKay and his fellow black primitivist writers believed their literary constructions of a hedonistic Harlem, depicting uninhibited characters like Jake, would enlighten and liberalize an uptight white society.

To see what McKay actually produced, let's examine in more detail some of his novel's primitivist images. These include images of Harlem; Harlem nightclubs; sensuous black music and dance; Africa; black sexuality; black drug use; middle-class blacks; and alienated black intellectuals.

Images of Harlem

Following the primitivist ideological formula, McKay depicts Harlem as an exotic African oasis, transcending the drab, joyless desert of white American culture.

> Oh, to be in Harlem again after two years away. The deep-dyed color, the thickness, the closeness of it. The noises of Harlem. The sugared laughter. The homey-talk on its streets. And all night long, ragtime and "blues" playing somewhere, . . . sing-in somewhere, dancing somewhere! Oh, the contagging fever of Harlem. Burning everywhere in dark-eyed Harlem. . . . Burning now in Jake's sweet blood. (McKay 1987, 15)

Images of Harlem Nightclubs

While Harlem symbolized the geographical locale of this black exotic existence, the nightclubs, cabarets, and house parties—the "get down" arenas of Harlem recreation and entertainment—represent the vortex of its hedonistic life. We thus encounter this description of a Harlem nightclub scene:

> But the Congo remained in spite of formidable opposition and foreign exploitation. The Congo was real throbbing little Africa in New York. It was an amusement place entirely for the unwashed of the Black Belt. Or, if they were washed, smells lingering telling the nature of their occupation. Pot-wrestlers, third cooks, W.C. attendants, scrub maids, dishwashers, stevedores. Girls coming from the South to try their fortune in New York always reached the Congo first. The Congo was African in spirit and color. No white persons

were admitted there. The proprietor knew his market. He did not cater to the fast trade. "High Yallers" were scarce there. Except for such sweetmeat that lived off the low-down trade. (McKay 1987, 29)

Here as in other passages intended to reveal Harlem nightlife to the un-tutored white world, McKay's writing resembles more an ethnography than a novel. Like Van Vechten, he aimed not so much to develop a nar-rative as to provide a guidebook to Harlem. Note the following account of the racial mores in nightclubs catering to white patrons: "There were one or two cabarets in the Belt that were distinguished for their impolite attitude toward the average Negro customer, who could not afford to swill expensive drinks. He was pushed off into a corner and neglected, while the best seats were reserved for notorious little gangs of white champagne-guzzlers from downtown" (McKay 1987, 316).

Images of Sensuous Black Music and Dance

Black music and dance, which many Jazz Age bohemians regarded as the quintessence of black primitivism, is given special emphasis. This can seen in the following passages where music is used to evoke a nightclub's primitive ambiance:

Lean, smart fingers beating barbaric beauty out of a white frame. (McKay 1987, 94)

The women, carried away by the sheer rhythm delight, had risen above their commercial instincts (a common trait of Negroes in emotional states) and abandoned themselves to pure voluptuous jazzing. They were gorgeous an-imals swaying through the dance, punctuating it with marks of warm phys-ical excitement. (McKay 1987, 108)

Images of Africa

Nowhere is *Home to Harlem*'s hegemonic consciousness revealed more clearly than in its conception of Africa, which resembles the lurid Holly-wood images later popularized in Tarzan movies (the only thing missing was the white Ubermensch) that would shape perceptions of Africa throughout American popular culture. Although McKay does not place his characters in "African jungles," his depictions of their dancing and musical performances achieve much the same effect, reproducing crude stereotypes of Africa as a throwback to primordial, savage instincts, rooted in black American personality:

The piano-player had wandered off into dim far-away, ancestral source of music. Far, far away from music-hall syncopation and jazz, he was lost in some sensual dream of his own. No tortures, banal shrieks and agonies. Tum . . . tum-tum . . . tum-tum. . . . The notes were naked in the bush. Love in the deep heart of the jungle. . . . The sharp spring of a leopard from a leafy limb, the snarl of a jackal, green lizards in amorous play, the flight of a plumed bird, and the sudden laughter of mischievous monkeys in their homes. Tum-tum . . . tum-tum . . . tum-tum. . . . Simple-clear and quivering. Like a primitive dance of war or of love . . . the marshaling of spears or the sacred frenzy of a phallic celebration.

Black lovers of life caught up in their own free native rhythm, threaded to a remote scarce-remembered past, celebrating the midnight hour in themselves. (McKay 1987, 196–97)

The black players grinned and swayed and let the music go with all their might. The yellow in the music must have stood out in their imagination like a challenge, conveying a sense of that primitive, ancient, eternal, inexplicable antagonism in the color taboo of sex and society. (McKay 1987, 296–97)

Here we have a truly ironic spectacle: a black writer depicting black America's African heritage by evoking European images of Africa. What some black observers found surprising, if not shocking, in light of the prevailing white racist stereotypes of blacks, were the ways in which McKay's novel seemed to embrace those stereotypes, melding images of exotic settings and animalistic sexuality: "A jungle atmosphere pervaded the room, and, like shameless wild animals hungry for raw meat, the females savagely searched the eyes of the males" (McKay 1987, 68).

Images of Black Sexuality

McKay's emphasis on black American preoccupations with carnal pleasures is hardly restrained, as is revealed, for example, in a jocular conversation about sex that transpires between Jake (recently returned from Europe) and another male character in the novel.

"Take it from me, buddy, there ain't no honey lak to that theah comes out of our belonging-to-us honey-comb."

"Man, what you telling me?" cried Jake. "Don't I knows it. What else you think made me leave over the other side? And dog mah doggone ef I didn't find it just as I landed."

"K-hhhhhhh! K-hhhhhhh!" Zeddy laughed. "Dog mah cats! You done tasted the real life a'ready?" (McKay 1987, 23–24)

"The real life"—this curious phrase—means sex with a black woman. Although McKay avoids graphic depictions of sexual acts—this is after all the 1920s—there can be no question that he intends to convey the message: blacks are obsessed with sex.

Further reinforcing this amoral and sensational image of black American ethnic life is his depiction of a pimp. While McKay's depiction is more plausible than that of Van Vechten's Scarlet Creeper, it nevertheless implies that within the black community pimping was an accepted way of life:

> Formerly he had always been envious when any of his pals pointed out an extravagantly dressed dark dandy and remarked, "He was living sweet." There was something so romantic about the sweet life. To be the admired of a Negro lady of means, or a pseudo grass-widow whose husband worked on the railroad, or of a hardworking laundress or cook. *It was much more respectable and enviable to be sweet—to belong to the exotic aristocracy of sweet men* than to be just a common tout [emphasis added]. (McKay 1987, 82)

Although the character goes on to express misgivings about "living sweet" because of the personal jealousy it arouses, this image suggests that black men preferred pimping to a conventional job—that pimping, in short, was an esteemed occupation.

Images of Black Drug Use

Further reinforcing those images of Harlem amorality, McKay depicts blacks attracted to cocaine, one of the earliest literary accounts of drug use among blacks.

> "Bowers cabaret was some place for the teasing-brown pick-me-up-then, brother—and the snow. The stuff was cheap then. You sniff boh?" Strawberry Lips asked Jake and Zeddy.
> "I wouldn't know before I sees it," Jake laughed.
> "I ain't no habitual prisoner," said Zeddy, "but I does any little thing for a change. Keep going and active with anything, says I." (McKay 1987, 64–65)

Cocaine use in Harlem during the 1920s was, at most, a peripheral rather than a pervasive activity. But McKay's depictions of drug indulgence suggests it is commonplace, like his depictions of pimping and sexual escapades. All derive from his primitivist ideological aim to represent the sensational and aberrant as ordinary behavior in black ethnic life.

Lest *Home to Harlem*'s readers assume that it is unrelated to Van Vechten's novel, McKay leaves no room for doubt. He simply has a character repeat the controversial phrase in his novel: "'I should think the nigger heaven of a theater downtown is better than anything in this heah Harlem,' said Suzy" (McKay 1987, 98).

Through these exotic, hedonistic images of the lower-class black American social world, readers are encouraged to believe that the emergence of

Harlem and other urban black communities emancipated black instinctual life. But McKay hardly relies on these primitivist images to deliver
the full thrust of the novel's ideological message. To achieve this, he contrasts primitivist images of robust lower-class blacks to negative images
of the dispossessed black middle class, the alienated black intellectual,
and the repressed white culture—all symbolizing psychologically noxious ways of life. In drawing these contrasts to fortify the novel's primitivist message, he also invokes then fashionable Freudian ideas delineating the malaise of modern civilization.

Images of Black Middle Class

Attacks on the educated black middle class appeared as standard tactics
in the black primitivist battle plan. In alluding to black bourgeoisie
hypocrisy, *Home to Harlem* mocks the group with contemptuous humor:

> Jake's life had never before touched any of the educated of the ten dark mil-
> lions. He had, however, a vague idea of who they were. He knew that the
> "big niggers" that were gossiped about in the saloons and the types he had
> met at Madame Adelina Suarez's were not the educated ones. The educated
> "dick-tee," in Jake's circles were often subjects of raw and funny sallies. He
> had once heard Miss Curdy putting them in their place while Susy's star eyes
> gleamed warm approval. "Honey, I lived in Washington and I knowed inside
> and naked out the stuck-up bush-whackers of the race. They all talks and act
> as if loving was sin, but I tell you straight, I wouldn't trust any of them after
> dark with a preacher. . . . Don't ask me, honey. I seen and knows them all."
>   "I guess you does, sistah," Susy had agreed. "Nobody kaint hand me no
> fairy tales about niggers. Wese all much of a muchness when you git down
> to the real stuff." (McKay 1987, 164)

This reflects McKay's low regard for middle-class blacks, who he believed possessed neither the culture nor the economic power of a genuine
bourgeoisie class.

Image of the Alienated Black Intellectual

More complexly drawn is the alienated black intellectual. Through Ray,
the Haitian immigrant writer, McKay registers the black intellectual's resentment at being lumped together with lower-class blacks just because
he and they have a shared racial ancestry.

> These men claimed kinship with him. They were black like him. Man and na-
> ture had put them in the same race. He ought to love them and feel them (if
> he felt anything). He ought to if he had a shred of social morality in him.

They were all chain-ganged together. And was counted as one link. Yet he loathed every soul in that great barrack-room, except Jake. Race. . . . Why should he love a race? (McKay 1987, 153)

The black lower-class workers, displaying their primitivism, respond to Ray's aloofness with derisive anti-intellectual humor: "Better leave that theah nigger professor alone and come on 'long to the dinning car with us. That theah nigger is dopey from the books of a' hisn. I done told him befoh thm books would git him yet" (McKay 1987, 159).

This image of the black intellectual as a misfit is reinforced by Ray's own self-doubts and envy of his co-workers' emotional freedom: "Ray felt alone and a little sorry for himself. Now that he was there, he would like to be touched by the spirit of the atmosphere and, like Jake, fall naturally into its rhythms. He also envied Jake. Just for this one night only he would like to be like him" (McKay 1987, 194).

Underscoring this primitivist message, Ray confesses to Jake his frustration being a black intellectual in a white culture:

"The fact is, Jake," Ray said, "I don't know what I'll do with my little education. I wonder sometimes if I could get rid of it and go and lose myself in some savage jungles of Africa. I am a misfit—as the doctors who dole out newspaper advice to the well-fit might say—a misfit with my little education and constant dreaming, when I should be getting the nightmare habit to hog in a whole lot of dough like everybody else in this country. Would you like to be educated like me?"

"If I had your education I wouldn't be slinging no hash on the white man's chu'chu," Jake responded.

"Nobody knows, Jake. Anyway, you're happier than I as you are. The more I learn the less I understand and love life." (McKay 1987, 274)

This expresses a harsh conclusion about the effects of Western education. But McKay is not satisfied to leave the matter there. Echoing the white primitivists' complaints about modern society, he voices many of the era's fashionable clichés bemoaning the emotional sterility of Western civilization. In a transparent imitation of Ernest Hemingway's astringent style, McKay expresses these clichés through Ray, who is tutoring the primitive Jake about the predicament of modern life:

You and I were born in the midst of the illness of this age and have lived through its agony. . . . Keep your fine feelings, indeed, but don't try to make a virtue of them. You'll lose them. You'll lose them, then. They'll become all hollow inside, false and dry as civilization itself. And civilization is rotten. We are all rotten who are touched by it. (McKay 1987, 243)

Finally, through Ray, McKay arrives at the novel's central sociological theme: the notion that black American ethnic culture possessed emotional vitality that white America desperately needed. "No wonder the whites, after five centuries of contact could not understand his race. How could they when the instinct of comprehension had been cultivated out of them? No wonder they hated them, when out of their melancholy environment the blacks could create mad, contagious music and high laughter" (McKay 1987, 267).

Here we encounter the primitivist writers' assumption, noted earlier, that whites, as a consequence of being exposed to primitivist images of black American life, would not only come to appreciate black ethnic culture and develop more tolerant racial attitudes. But also, and even more important, they would overcome their psychological inhibitions, and live emotionally liberated lives. This was the hidden agenda—this notion that primitivist art was therapeutic—that led McKay and other black writers to embrace a hedonistic conception of black ethnic culture.

Critical Responses to Home to Harlem

Home to Harlem, like *Nigger Heaven,* reached a large audience. James Weldon Johnson in his biography noted that "the two books about Harlem that were most widely read and discussed were Carl Van Vechten's *Nigger Heaven* and Claude McKay's *Home to Harlem.*" But between the two books he drew a curious distinction, which indicated more about his relationship to Van Vechten than about the books' relative merits. Invoking a tone of critical detachment, Johnson praised *Nigger Heaven* as a "fine novel" that enveloped "nearly every phase of life," but then went on to denounce *Home to Harlem* for dealing with low levels of life "entirely unrelieved by any brighter lights" (Johnson 1933, 73).

What actually disturbed Johnson was McKay's depiction of the black American middle class. Instead of presenting a middle-class black American intellectual as a contrast to the primitive images of black ethnic life, McKay had substituted a West Indian intellectual, a man from the Caribbean, as the model of a cultured black. Even more important, Johnson was displeased to see that the protagonist of McKay's novel was not a refined member of the black middle class, but rather a carefree working-class black. "Mr. McKay made no attempt to hold in check or disguise his abiding contempt for the Negro bourgeoisie or 'upper class,'" Johnson complained. In fact, McKay detested the black American middle class who—in his eyes—constituted a pathetic imitation of a genuine bourgeoisie. Stating this position in response to Johnson's review, he wrote:

In comparing it (*Nigger Heaven*) to *Home to Harlem* James W. Johnson said that I had shown contempt for the Negro bourgeoisie. But I could not be contemptuous of a Negro bourgeoisie which simply does not exist as a class or group in America. Because I made the protagonist of my novel a lusty black worker, it does not follow that I am unsympathetic to a refined or wealthy Negro. (McKay 1987, 110)

McKay was being disingenuous. While it was logically true, his choice of Jake as the novel's protagonist did not prove that he lacked respect for middle-class black Americans. But in actuality he did.

Johnson was hardly alone in denouncing the novel. A reviewer for *The Chicago Defender* (a black newspaper) wrote "*Home to Harlem* is *Nigger Heaven* in a larger dose. Where Mr. Van Vechten hesitated to delve too deeply into the morass of filth with which we all know Harlem abounds, Mr. McKay comes 'full steam ahead' and 'shoots the works'" (McKay 1987, 111). Even more acidic was DuBois' response: The book "for the most part nauseates me, and after the dirtier parts of its filth I feel distinctly like taking a bath" (DuBois 1928, 202).

McKay rejected these critics' conceptions of the black writer's social role. Seeing himself as a modernist writer, he "disliked the idea that the Negro artist should 'uplift' the masses, and he believed that the black common man was more in tune with his racial culture than were the 'Talented Tenth'"(Giles 1972, 19).

As noted earlier, none of these writers regarded the civil rights intellectuals as the black community's legitimate spokesmen. But that did not stop DuBois from venting his anger. As a concerned black political activist, he thought the novel's primitivist message was scandalous:

DuBois was outraged by *Home to Harlem* since it expressed these (primitivist) views. Its descriptions of cabarets, rent parties, and lovely "brownskins" collectively form images of the validity of this culture. DuBois' objection to the novel rested upon one challenge—how can the blacks progress if they are happy with the way of life described in *Home to Harlem*? (Giles 1972, 19)

This was a question the obstinately romantic McKay failed to answer. As a writer with strong bohemian proclivities, he was hardly convinced that the black masses should be integrated into white American society. Elaborating his side of the debate, Robert Bone has argued that a central theme in his writings suggests "that Negroes are still capable of unstructured emotional behavior, especially when it is appropriate. Not only is that capacity a positive thing in the three novels (by McKay), it is what enables the Afro–American to resist dehumanization by the white power structure" (Giles, 20–21).

But what precisely is meant by "unstructured emotional behavior?" That is the critical question. If it means the retention of a culture that allowed blacks an emotional release from the harsh realities of racial oppression, it is certainly true that black American ethnic culture, for the most part, sustained a rich reservoir of rituals that permitted blacks to affirm their humanity, particularly through humor, music, dance, and religious worship. But this is a far cry from McKay's primitivist images of licentious black American sexuality. It is difficult to see how pimping and adultery could have been defended as behaviors that enabled blacks "to resist dehumanization by the white power structure." In fact, a plausible argument could have arrived at the opposite conclusion, namely, that primitivist images of blacks, by depicting them as creatures of animalistic instinct, posed a greater threat of dehumanizing them, given the racial attitudes that prevailed in mainstream white American society; those images unwittingly reinforced the racist stereotypes whites used to justify racial discrimination.

More a bohemian adventurer than a race man or political rebel, McKay dropped out of the black American literary scene during the Depression era. In fact, during the ferment stirred by the black Marxist literary school in the late 1930s and early 1940s, his voice would be conspicuously absent. The only other writing he produced during this later phase of his literary career, except his sociological essay on Harlem (McKay 1940), were religious essays and pamphlets. Disillusioned with radical politics and primitivism, McKay was exhausted both intellectually and spiritually after roughly two decades of struggling to make his mark as a writer. He never achieved his goal of achieving acclaim in the cosmopolitan literary world. Claude McKay died in 1948, in virtual obscurity, following a long illness, at the relatively young age of fifty-nine.

Langston Hughes: A Derailed Folk Sensibility

Langston Hughes was born in 1902 and appeared on the Harlem scene in the early 1920s. But unlike most black writers of that era, whose literary ambitions were spent by the late 1930s, Hughes produced literary works through the next three decades until his death, in 1967. This remarkable achievement reflected not only Hughes's extraordinary stamina, but also his passionate commitment, his virtual religious devotion, to his calling as a black writer. Writing did not, however, always afford him a means of livelihood.

Hughes's 1920s literary career, like Claude McKay's, was fostered by the emerging cultural regimen of co-optive hegemony, evidenced in his dependence on white American patronage and influence, which drew him into the primitivist movement. But before examining his 1920s literary activity, we must take into account his early formative experiences that predisposed his romantic view of black ethnic culture.

Among Langston Hughes's most lasting formative experiences was an unstable family life (Hughes 1940). Rent by his parents' marital discord, his early family life left him emotionally scarred and insecure, with psychological wounds for which he later attempted to compensate by developing a strong familial attachment to the black American masses. His parents, who were well educated by the standards of the day, separated when he was a young child, with the result that he never experienced the emotional and financial support of conventional middle-class family life. After the separation, his father moved to Mexico, leaving him and his mother in virtual poverty. His father later persuaded his mother to attempt a reconciliation, which resulted in Hughes and his mother moving to Mexico, but the reconciliation failed.

After he and his mother returned to the United States, she moved to Chicago in search of employment and sent him to live with his grandmother, Mary Langston, who was to become the most crucial influence in Hughes's childhood. As the first black woman to attend Oberlin College and the widow of one of the five men (Larry Sheridan Leary) who accompanied John Brown to Harper's Ferry, Mary Langston not only regarded herself as a proud widow of that failed revolt; she also maintained a lifelong commitment to the struggle for black American rights. This was reflected in her choice of a second husband, James Charles Langston, Langston Hughes's maternal grandfather, who had worked in the Oberlin Underground Railway to assist escaped black slaves.

During the five years that Langston was under her care, his politically astute grandmother played a key role in shaping his racial consciousness. Informing him about the history of slavery, teaching him about freedom fighters such as John Brown, Frederick Douglass, Nat Turner, and Harriet Tubman, and exposing him to black publications such as *Crisis* magazine and W. E. B. DuBois' *Souls of Black Folk,* which Hughes read while he was still quite young, Mary Langston expanded his awareness of past and current black American political struggles. The effects of her tutelage left a lasting imprint on Langston Hughes's character, giving him a clear, proud, and unwavering feeling of black identity.

Following his grandmother's death when he was twelve, Langston Hughes went to live with his mother, who had remarried. He now experienced the difficult economic situation faced by working-class blacks as his family moved from one city to another seeking employment. They finally settled in Cleveland where, due to the wartime demand for labor, his stepfather landed a job in a steel mill, and his mother found a job as a maid.

Though he lived in a slum neighborhood, his Cleveland years constituted some his most pleasant and memorable youthful experiences, particularly in race relations. Attending a racially integrated high school, which was composed primarily of children from Jewish and Catholic immigrant families, he developed his first interracial friendships during after-school activities with his white schoolmates, and also often visited their homes. It was through those friendships in Cleveland that he got his first glimpse of radical political ideas from reading the leftist *Liberator* magazine and hearing such radical speakers as the socialist leader Eugene Debs. Hughes was surprised to discover that these immigrant whites were different—more democratic and racially tolerant—than the American-born whites he had known in Kansas. Ironically, those positive interracial experiences in Cleveland—which taught him to appreciate America's ethnic diversity—had a large hand in shaping his optimistic outlook on race relations that lay behind his attraction to the primitivist ideology in the 1920s.

Hughes attributes the greatest influence on his early intellectual development to a Jewish high school teacher, Ethel Weiner, who introduced him to the works of Shakespeare, Carl Sandburg, Vachel Lindsay, Edgar Lee Masters, Amy Lowell, Robert Frost, and other major writers. His early intellectual socialization, much like that of McKay and Toomer, took place in a friendly and supportive interracial environment, which left him with a feeling of trust and good will toward most whites.

Langston Hughes's positive interracial experiences should not, however, be overstated. He encountered racial hostility outside his personal network of white friends and teachers in Cleveland. One of his most traumatic youthful experiences occurred one summer in Chicago, where he had gone to visit his mother and stepfather, who had moved there from Cleveland to secure better employment. "The first Sunday I was in town," Hughes later recalled, "I went out walking alone to see what the city looked like. I wandered too far outside the Negro district, over beyond Wentworth, and was set upon and beaten by a group of white boys, who said they didn't allow niggers in that neighborhood. I came home with both eyes blackened and a swollen jaw. That was the summer of the Chicago riot" (Hughes 1940, 85). Despite that ugly encounter, Hughes avoided becoming embittered, because he knew from his Cleveland experiences that all whites were not racists.

Another development that was to leave lasting repercussions on his life occurred in 1918, when he was sixteen. He received a letter from his father asking him to come to Mexico in the summer. Langston had not heard from his father since he was five, but felt an urge to make the trip, infuriating his mother, who wanted him to stay home and help out by working. His mother finally consented to let him go. But soon after Langston arrived in Mexico, he realized he had made a mistake. His father was a major disappointment. Arrogant, embittered, and crassly materialistic, the elder Hughes, who had prospered financially as a lawyer and rancher in Mexico, frequently made bigoted comments about poor people of color, particularly Indians, Mexicans, and American blacks, whom he berated for having tolerated racism in the United States. The strains in their relationship worsened when his father tried to force him to learn bookkeeping, an experience that depressed Langston so badly he contemplated suicide. Shortly afterward, he returned to Cleveland.

The social climate in the United States to which he returned during the summer of 1919 had changed. Mounting postwar racial tensions in northern cities had erupted in race riots, marking the onset of a period of racial violence that came to be known as the Red Summer. It was during this period of racial strife that McKay wrote his militant poem *If We Must Die*, which Hughes happened to read in the *Liberator* magazine, an experience that deeply impressed him.

Though Hughes was disturbed by the worsening climate of race relations, his personal life was not directly affected. Following his summer in Mexico, he returned for his senior year in high school, and was elected editor of the yearbook. He graduated with a solid B grade-average, but had little prospect of going to college, until he received a letter from his father, who hinted that he would pay the expenses if Langston agreed both to attend school in Europe and to return to visit him in Mexico the following summer. Langston's heart was set on attending Columbia University, but he went to visit his father nevertheless.

That journey to Mexico turned out to be a momentous occasion in his literary career. While he was riding on the train, with the racial tensions of the United States receding in the background, he wrote his first major poem, *The Negro Speaks of Rivers*:

I've known rivers;
I've known rivers ancient as the world and older than the flow of human blood in human veins
My soul has grown deep like the rivers.
I bathed in the Euphrates when dawns were young.
I built my hut near the Congo and it lulled me to sleep.
I heard the singing of the Mississippi when Abe Lincoln went down to New
    Orleans, and I've seen its muddy bosom turn all golden in the sunset.
I've known rivers: Ancient, dusky rivers.
My soul has grown deep like the rivers. (Rampersad 1994, 23)

Inspired by the folk art conception of DuBois' *Souls of Black Folk*, that poem echoed the latter's lyrical style as it evoked a collective black "spirit." Significantly, in evoking that black folk spirit, it exhibited no primitivist connotations. Rather it attributed black folk spirit to an African heritage, an ancient repository of human wisdom, not a legacy of licentious sexuality. This poem of course preceded Van Vechten's influence, being written when Hughes was free of concerns about whether to pursue a literary career or a social mission.

The poem impressed DuBois, who published it in *Crisis*. No doubt it also impressed Langston's father, because he agreed to send him to Columbia University, despite his desire to have Langston study in Europe. However, it was a revealing feature of the elder Hughes's character that he ceased to be impressed by news of the poem's publication when he learned that Langston had received no money for it. Nevertheless, contrary to his father's crude criteria of evaluation, that poem's publication marked an important milestone in Langston Hughes's life by launching his literary career in Harlem's black intellectual culture.

At the end of the summer of 1921, shortly after his nineteenth birthday, Langston Hughes moved to New York, or rather—black Harlem, which, in spirit, he would never leave. Harlem was undergoing dramatic changes brought about by its rapid population growth. From 1921—when Hughes moved into the Harlem YMCA—to 1931, Harlem's population soared an astonishing 300 percent. This was also the decade when Marcus Garvey was stirring black nationalist sentiments in Harlem, W. E. B. DuBois and Arthur Schomberg were calling attention to Africa, and Harlem nightlife became the showcase of great black American musical artists. Small wonder that Hughes thought black America was undergoing a social revolution, for it was during this time of Harlem's transformation that white American artists and writers gravitated to black American ethnic life.

After spending a brief and miserable time as a student at Columbia University, which permanently soured him on white universities, Hughes dropped out of school, and plunged into black Harlem. His first notable Harlem experience occurred shortly after he left Columbia, when he met the civil rights intellectuals. The meeting resulted from the modest notoriety he had gained as the author of *The Negro Speaks of Rivers*. The editors of the NAACP's *Crisis* magazine, which had published the poem, heard he was in town and invited him to lunch. As he later recalled, "Jesse Fausett, the managing editor (of *Crisis*) invited me to a luncheon at the Civic Club. I was panic stricken." He went on to describe the place where they had lunch. "The Civic Club was one of the few clubs in New York admitting both Negro and white members, and the leaders of the National Association for the Advancement of Colored People, the organization that published the *Crisis*. The club being near their office they usually lunched there" (Hughes 1940, 93).

Although his works now appeared regularly in *Crisis*, Hughes lacked money to support himself. This problem of poverty persistently dogged black writers, because their notoriety was restricted to black publications, which had a small audience. This is not to say that such financial problems were peculiar to black writers (most white writers also faced financial problems), but only that their financial problems were more severe. They had almost no potential commercial appeal prior to Van Vechten's appearance on the scene, as was evidenced by Hughes's threadbare existence.

To support himself during his early years in Harlem, he held a variety of menial jobs, culminating with his employment as a ship steward on a freighter. This job, which opened his life to a new, adventurous phase of personal discovery and growth, resulted in another momentous experience: his first visit to Africa. "Along the West Coast of Africa," he recalled visiting "some thirty-two ports, from Dakar in Senegal to Loanda (Luanda) in the South. The Ivory Coast, the Gold Coast, Lagos, the Niger, the Bight of Benin, and the slave coast, Calabar, the Kameroon, Boma up the Congo, where we moored to a gigantic tree, and our last port, San Paolo de Leanda in Portuguese Angola" (Hughes 1940, 106). While at sea he wrote an essay, "Ships, Sea and Africa," which appeared in *Crisis*.

This was a time when many black Americans were awakening to an awareness of Africa. DuBois was challenging stereotyped images of Africa, Schomberg was exhibiting African art in Harlem, and Garvey was highlighting the glories of Africa in speeches to his followers. Traveling about Africa, Hughes was particularly struck by Garvey's influence. As he observed:

> At that time, 1923, the name Marcus Garvey was known the length and breadth of the West Coast of Africa. And the Africans did not laugh at Marcus, as so many people laughed in New York. They hoped what they heard about him was true—that he really would unify the black world, and free and exalt Africa. They did not understand the terrific complications of the Colonial Problem. They only knew the white man was there in Africa, heavy and oppressive on their backs. (Hughes 1940, 102)

Though Langston Hughes never embraced black nationalism, his African experiences deepened his sensitivity and appreciation of African culture. Reinforcing his feelings of racial identity that had been cultivated by his grandmother, the experience of visiting Africa made him more aware than ever of his ancestral roots as a black American.

After losing his ship job in December 1923, he had what he euphemistically termed "a series of memorable European experiences." Two jobs in Paris nightclubs, the second as a dishwasher at the famous Grand Duc on the Rue Pigalle, brought him nightly familiarity with blues and jazz played by top Negro musicians. In Italy during his final four months abroad, he almost starved as a beachcomber in Genoa, his wallet having been stolen during a train ride from Venice (Emmanuel and Gross 1968, 193). Despite these mishaps, he continued to write and publish poetry, though this hardly alleviated his financial predicament. For example, three poems he published in *Vanity Fair* yielded only $24.50.

While living in Paris, he was visited by Alain Locke, who took him to the opera and arranged a visit to a private collection of African art. A man of genteel temperament, Locke had no interest in visiting the coarser haunts of Hughes's Parisian life. Significantly, it was during their encounter in Paris that Locke told Hughes about the forthcoming issue of *Survey Graphic*, which would be devoted to black art. Locke got Hughes's permission to include some of his poems in that issue. The Harlem Renaissance doctrine was then in the state of gestation.

Hughes's involvement in the primitivist movement began when he returned to the United States. Shortly after his arrival in New York, he ran into Countee Cullen who told him about an upcoming NAACP benefit party, which he attended. That evening turned out to be one of the most consequential of Hughes's literary career. As he later recalled: "At the door I met Walter White and he introduced me to Mary Ovington, James Weldon Johnson, and Carl Van Vechten." Meeting Van Vechten marked a turning point in his life. From the moment they met, he and Van Vechten felt a strong mutual attraction, which blossomed into a close friendship. In fact, according to Hughes biographer, Arnold Rampersad, "Van Vechten would be one of the most important people in Hughes' life" (Rampersad 1986, 97).

For the next three years, Van Vechten nurtured Langston Hughes's primitivist literary career, using his influence to gain the young black writer a wider audience in the mainstream public arena. For example, shortly after their first meeting, "Van Vechten began to pave the way for *The Weary Blues*" (Rampersad 1986, 111). Van Vechten chose the title for that book and probably also *Fine Clothes to the Jew*, Hughes's second collection of poetry. This second book by Hughes was dedicated to Van Vechten, who not only collaborated closely with Hughes in putting it together, but also got his friend Alfred Knopf to publish it.

But their relationship was by no means asymmetrical. Hughes, in turn, did valuable favors for Van Vechten. To show his gratitude for Van Vechten's assistance in getting *The Weary Blues* published, Hughes wanted to know:

What could he possibly do for Van Vechten in return? Well, there was something; Langston could help Carl prepare a series of articles for Vanity Fair on black subjects, including one about the blues, the form that had supplanted Ragtime and now under girded modern jazz, but was unknown to Northern whites. Hurrying to oblige, Hughes brushed aside the fact that Van Vechten, a white man, most likely would make a great deal of money from essays on a black subject about which, by his own admission, he knew nothing. (Rampersad 1986, 111)

This revealed the lingering vestiges of paternalistic hegemony, with whites functioning as authorities on black Americans in the public arena. This paternalistic cultural process was receding as black writers were being granted visible roles through the regimen of co-optive hegemony.

On another occasion, Hughes came to Van Vechten's assistance when the latter was threatened with a lawsuit for using some copyrighted songs in *Nigger Heaven* without permission. Hughes wrote songs to replace the copyrighted songs, for which Van Vechten apparently paid him only one hundred dollars (Rampersad 1986, 137). These are only a few of the many favors Langston Hughes, the black insider, did for Carl Van Vechten, the white outsider, as the latter sought to establish his credibility as an informed observer of Harlem life. Hughes's testimonial in defense of *Nigger Heaven*, noted earlier, was probably the most important, if not to say the riskiest, favor he did for Van Vechten.

Some observers took a dim view of that friendship, seeing it as exploitative and demeaning. For instance, Hughes's close friend and fellow black poet Countee Cullen expressed that view "disapproving of Langston's close link to Van Vechten ('I know Carl is coining money out of the niggers') and detesting the title *The Weary Blues* as catering to whites 'who want us to do only Negro things'" (Rampersad 1986, 113). Ironically, as we will see, Cullen would later climb aboard the primitivist bandwagon. Hughes rejected the charge that he was being misguided by Van Vechten and, in this opinion, not surprisingly, he got support from his idol and fellow black primitivist writer Claude McKay (Rampersad 1986).

The other important white patron who encouraged Hughes's primitivist literary works was Charlotte Osgood Mason. A wealthy widow who lived in New York, Mason's interests in primitivism derived from an idiosyncratic philosophical predilection—the type of pet project to "improve the world" that only the rich can afford to indulge—totally divorced from any desire for financial gain or personal notoriety. In fact, Mason, who insisted on remaining anonymous, was not a recent convert to the primitivist ideology. As Arnold Rampersad points out, "There was nothing faddish about her interest in primitivism. Having spent time among Indians of the Great Plains, she later financed research that resulted in 1907 in Natalie Curtis's famous *The Indians' Book*. In her sudden enthusiasm for Africa," Rampersad adds, "Charlotte Mason was an ancient volcano erupting again. She believed in cosmic energy and the intuitive powers of primitive life, from which came her drive to nourish those races still keenly in tune with spectral harmonies lost to the ear of overcivilized whites" (Rampersad 1986, 148).

Hughes met Charlotte Mason through Alain Locke, that indefatigable wooer of wealthy white patrons, after Locke had delivered a public lecture on African art. Mason at the time was seeking ways to promote interests in black primitivism. In the words of Rampersad, "she had committed herself to nothing less than a personally directed and financed project to elevate African culture to its rightful place of honor against its historic adversary, which she unhesitatingly identified as the white race" (Rampersad 1986, 147).

Hughes and Mason soon developed a close relationship, which seemed less a friendship than a familial bond, with Hughes taking the role of the dependent child—he came to address Mason as "Godmother"—and Mason taking the role of guiding parent. She soon became the sole source of Hughes's financial support, providing him money for clothing, theater tickets, and a monthly stipend, which was intended to give him time to concentrate on his primitivist literary work. She was seriously committed to promoting the primitivist mission. As Hughes later recalled:

> Concerning Negroes, she felt that they were America's great link with the primitive, and that they had something very precious to give the Western world. She felt that there was mystery and mysticism and spontaneous harmony in their souls, but that many of them had let the white world pollute and contaminate that mystery and harmony, and make it something cheap and ugly, commercial and, as she said, "white." She felt that we had a deep well of the spirit within us and that we should keep it deep and pure. (Hughes 1940, 228)

Significantly, Mason also supported Zora Neale Hurston, setting her up in an apartment on the west side of Manhattan and paying her living expenses. While Hughes managed his dependency with a measure of decorum, Hurston displayed little concern about her dignity, as she sought to flatter Mason by playing into the worst "Sambo" stereotypes. In Mason's presence, for example, she characteristically referred to herself as "Godmother's primitive child" and "dumb darky" (Berry 1983, 103). With Mason's financial assistance, Hurston collected black folk materials in Florida that fit into the older woman's conception of primitivist black culture.

Langston Hughes, however, was Mason's prized client, the recipient of her most generous financial assistance. Although it surpassed the contributions other white patrons gave to black writers during the 1920s, Mason's support of Hughes's work illustrates the inducements that helped to co-opt black writers into the primitivist ideological movement. Whites, like Mason, advocated this ideology because they sincerely believed the primitivist influences of black American culture would counteract the cold and dehumanizing rationalism of Western culture.

Let's now examine some of the primitivist images of black American life that Langston Hughes produced in the 1920s.

Primitivist Images in Langston Hughes's Literary Works

Hughes's first book, a collection of poems published in 1926, situated him solidly in the primitivist camp. This resulted from his meeting Carl Van Vechten, who assisted him in getting the collection of his poems published by Alfred Knopf, one of Van Vechten's close friends. Knopf published the poems under the seductive title *The Weary Blues*. The book's primitivist message is revealed in the coarse language and lewd images projected in poems such as *Mulatto*, which obviously was addressed to a white public.

> I am your son, white man!
> . . . .
> You are my son!
> Like Hell!
> . . . .
> Great big yellow stars.
> What's a body but a toy?
> Juicy bodies
> of nigger wenches
> Blue black
> Against back fences.
> O, you little bastard boy,
> What's a body but a toy?
> . . . .
> What's the body of your mother?
> Sharp pine scent in the evening air.
> A nigger night,
> A nigger joy,
> A little yellow
> Bastard boy. (Rampersad and Roessel 1994, 100)

In contrast to Hughes's earlier poem *The Negro Speaks of Rivers*, this poem projected a crude, degraded black sensibility, which paradoxically resonated white racist stereotypes of blacks as vulgar and brutish, bereft of the moral restraints demanded by civilized society. The frequent usage here of the epithet "nigger" expressed not simply a colloquial figure of speech. Rather it expressed a racist worldview, in which promiscuous black women have sex with white men and give birth to mulatto offspring, who are portrayed as children with a tainted ancestry.

In the poem *The Weary Blues*, Hughes shifts from primitivist vulgarity and exhibits his superb talents as the creator of the blues poetic style, which he uses here to evoke a familiar, but nonetheless primitivist, stereotype of black musical instinct.

Droning a drowsy syncopated tune
Rocking back and forth to a mellow croon,
I heard a Negro play.
Down on Lenox Avenue the other night
By the pale dull pallor of an old gas light
He did a lazy sway . . .
He did a lazy sway . . .
To the tune o' those Weary Blues.
With his ebony hands on each ivory key
He made that poor piano moan with melody.
O Blues!
Swaying to and fro on his rickety stool
He played that sad raggedy tune like a musical fool.
Sweet Blues
Coming from a black man's soul. (Rampersad and Roessel 1994, 50)

Hughes, reflecting the influence of Van Vechten and McKay, contrasted black America's primitive African ancestry to (white) civilization, as can be seen in one of his later poems.

All the tom-toms of the jungle beat in my blood
And all the wild hot moons of the jungles shine in my soul.
I am afraid of this civilization. (Rampersad and Roessel 1994, 32)

This suggested that black Americans were displaced aliens in a Western culture, precisely the situation that white aficionados of primitivism, like Charlotte Mason, not only perceived, but sought to preserve.

In the following year, Hughes published *Fine Clothes to the Jew,* his second book of poetry, whose title ignited controversy. Hughes's account of this controversy is noteworthy because it revealed his dependence on the advice and opinions of his white publisher. Recalling the controversy roughly a decade later, Hughes noted that it was "a bad title, because it was confusing and many Jewish people did not like it. I do not know why the Knopfs let me use it, since they were very helpful in their advice about sorting out the bad poems from the good, but they said nothing about the title" (Hughes 1940, 270). Hughes's remorse for having maligned Jews, while admirable, was never paralleled by a similar display of remorse for having degraded black Americans in his primitivist literary works. This second book exhibited primitivist images that were, if anything, even coarser than those in his first book, as its poems placed greater emphasis on black sexuality. In *Listen Here Blues,* we see a playful, risqué treatment of this theme.

Sweet girls, sweet girls,
Listen here to me All you sweet girls,

Listen here to me:
Gin an' whiskey
Kin make you lose yo' 'ginity. (Rampersad and Roessel 1994, 69)

In contrast to this poem's light, jocular tone, we encounter an odd, vulgar exhortation to black prostitutes in *Red Silk Stockings:*

Put on yo' red silk stockings,
Black gal.
Go out an' let de white boys
Look at yo' legs,
Ain't nothin' to do for you, nohow,
Round this town,—
You's too pretty
Put on yo' red silk stockings, gal,
An' tomorrow's chile'll
Be a high yaller.
Go out an' let de white boys
Look at yo' legs. (Rampersad and Roessel 1994, 122)

In light of the long history of sexual racism in the United States, evidenced in the sexual exploitation of black women by white men, this poem evoked images of black racial degradation. Its crude normative implications, in the eyes of sensitive liberal political observers, aroused both shock and puzzlement. How could a leading black writer under the banner of artistic freedom celebrate that ugly legacy? How was it possible to construe such images as advancing the cause of racial enlightenment and cultural liberalization? Even more paradoxical were the pronouncements of black literary critics like Alain Locke who promoted such literary works as evidence of a black renaissance, emancipation from the legacy of racial propaganda. Were not such primitivist images egregious expressions of propaganda that reinforced retrograde racist beliefs about blacks?

Finally, turning to yet another example of Hughes's primitivist poetry, we encounter a different but no less odious stereotype of black sexuality in the poem *Ma Man.*

When ma man look at me
He knocks me off ma feet.
When ma man look at me
He knocks me off ma feet.
He's got those 'lectric-shockin' eyes an'
De way he shocks me sho is sweet.
He kin play a banjo.
Lordy, he kin plunk, plunk, plunk.
He kin play a banjo.

> I mean plunk, plunk . . . plunk, plunk.
> He plays good when he's sober
> An' better, better, better when he's drunk.
> Eagle-rockin',
> Come and eagle-rock with me.
> Honey baby,
> Eagle-rockish as I kin be! (Rampersad and Roessel 1994, 66)

This poem, in contrast to the others, actually referred to sexual inter-course, albeit encoded in the black slang term *eagle-rockin*, which gave the poem an even stronger flavor of exotic vulgarity. Had these poems been produced for black audiences as were similarly salacious black blues lyrics of the time, such as the songs of Bessie Smith and Ma' Rainey, they no doubt would have provoked little negative criticism. But black writers were not producing for black audiences. They were producing for white audiences, who were often ignorant about black American community life. That was why Hughes's poems aroused so much controversy.

Reactions to Hughes's Primitivist Poetry

Responding to these images of black American ethnic life, most black critics denounced Hughes for being oblivious to the sociological implications of his poetry. Hughes, for his part, defended the images as truthful reflections of black American life. The case for the other side was well stated by a critic in *The Philadelphia Tribune*, a black newspaper, who in reaction to Hughes's first book, *The Weary Blues*, wrote: "It does not matter to me whether every poem in the book is true to life. Why should it be paraded before the American public by a Negro author as being typical or representative of the Negro?"

Reflecting black middle-class status anxieties, this critic went on to observe: "Bad enough to have white authors holding up our imperfections to public gaze. Our aim ought to be to present to the general public, already misinformed both by well-meaning and malicious writers, our higher aims and aspirations, and our better selves" (Hughes 1940, 267).

Yet another critic labeled Hughes as the "poet-lowrate of Harlem." Black critics' responses to his second book were even more vitriolic:

Under a headline proclaiming Hughes a "SEWER DWELLER," William Kel-ley of the *New York Amsterdam News*, who once had sought to publish his work, denounced *Fine Clothes to the Jew* as "about 100 pages of trash. . . . It reeks of the gutter and sewer." . . . In the *Pittsburgh Courier*, historian J. A. Rogers called it "piffling trash" that left him "positively sick." The *Chicago Whip* sneered at the dedication to Van Vechten, "a literary gutter-rat" who perhaps alone "will revel in the lecherous, lust-reeking characters that Hughes finds time to poeticize about." (Rampersad 1986, 140)

Especially offensive to these black critics were Hughes's depictions of uninhibited black sexuality. In the words of Arnold Rampersad: "To these and other black critics, Hughes had allowed the 'secret shame of their culture, especially its apparent unspeakable or unpardonable sexual mores, to be bruited abroad by thick-lipped black whores and roustabouts. How could he have dared publish *Red Silk Stockings*?" (Rampersad 1986, 141). The problem was less the "secret shame" of black culture than the way it was exhibited. Erskine Caldwell's *Tobacco Road* some years later represented a similar "secret shame" of white American culture, but no one assumed that it depicted typical features of white American community life. That was because *Tobacco Road* was never treated as a leading white American literary work. By contrast, Hughes's depictions of the deviant fringe of black American community life did become a leading black literary work, because it was white rather than black Americans who determined its status.

To fully understand Hughes's penchant for producing crude primitivist poetry, we must take into account his attitude toward middle-class blacks. It is important to remember that Hughes, who was quite young in the 1920s, deliberately flaunted the cruder aspects of primitivism to offend the black middle class. These primitivist poems reflected his disdain for what he saw as their status pretension and hypocrisy. His problems with middle-class blacks began shortly after he returned to the United States from Europe, when he lived for a short period in Washington, D.C.

He learned about black middle-class status pretensions from a particularly bitter personal experience. Shortly after his poetry appeared in the special issue of *Survey Graphic* edited by Locke, he and Countee Cullen were invited to Washington black society's annual dinner. Believing that his mother would enjoy the occasion, he asked permission to bring her along. He also informed them he himself had no formal attire. All appeared well until that fateful day. Hughes recalled:

> On the evening of the dinner . . . I came home from work to find my mother in tears. She had left her job early to get ready to go with me. But about five o'clock one of the ladies of the committee had telephoned her to say that, after all, she didn't feel it wise for her to come—since it was to be a formal dinner, and perhaps my mother did not possess an evening gown. (Hughes 1940, 210)

Encounters like this one jaundiced Hughes's attitude toward the black middle class. As can be seen from his description of the Washington group, he loathed their lifestyle: "They were on the whole as unbearable and snobbish a group of people as I have ever come into contact with anywhere. They lived in comfortable homes, had fine cars, played bridge, drank

Scotch, gave exclusive 'formal' parties, and dressed well, but seemed to me altogether lacking in real culture, kindness, or common sense."

He went on to complain about their practices of class and color discrimination against other blacks:

> To me it did not seem good, for the "better class" Washington colored people, as they called themselves, drew rigid class and color lines within the race against Negroes who worked with their hands, or who were dark in complexion and had no degrees from college. These upper class colored people consisted largely of government workers, professors and teachers, doctors, lawyers, and resident politicians. (Hughes 1940, 208)

Other black intellectuals in subsequent decades would express similar sentiments about middle-class blacks. In the works of the naturalistic protest writers Richard Wright and Chester Himes and in the works of the black sociologist E. Franklin Frazier (Frazier 1957), for example, we will see harsh criticisms of the status-conscious black middle class. However, it was not just the status pretensions of the black middle class that offended Hughes and these other black intellectuals. It was also, and equally important, the black middle class's failure to appreciate and support black American literary and intellectual products. In the view of these black intellectuals, the black middle class departed from their boorish indifference only when black literary or artistic works gained notoriety in white American public culture.

Given Hughes's low opinion of the black middle class, he hardly felt inclined to apologize for any embarrassments his writings caused them. Rampersad relates Hughes's response to his black middle-class critics, in a very revealing defense of his primitivist writings. It is worth quoting at length:

> When the *Pittsburgh Courier* invited Hughes to defend himself against his critics, he did not hesitate. In "These Bad New Negroes: A Critique on Critics," he identified four reasons for the attacks: the low self-esteem of the "best" blacks; their obsession with white opinion; their nouveau riche snobbery; and the lack of artistic and cultural training "from which to view either their own or the white man's books or pictures." As for the "ill-mannered onslaught" on Van Vechten: the man's "sincere, friendly, and helpful interest in things Negro" should have brought "serious, rather than vulgar, reviews of his book." A nine-point defense of his own views and practices ended in praise of the young writers, including Toomer, Fisher, Thurman, Cullen, Hurston, and the Lincoln poet Edward Silvera.

And then Hughes turned to his own writings:

> "My poems are indelicate. But so is life," he pointed out. He wrote about "harlots and gin-bibers. But they are human. Solomon, Homer, Shakespeare,

and Walt Whitman were not afraid or ashamed to include them." (Van Vechten thought the situation easy to explain; "you and I," he joked to Hughes while making an important distinction, "are the only colored who really love niggers"). (Rampersad 1986, 144–45)

It is quite obvious from this statement that Hughes saw his primitivist stance as a healthy rebellion against black middle-class cultural hypocrisy and denial.

Not all of the black critical responses to Hughes's poetry were negative. Not surprising, among defenders of the *Fine Clothes to the Jew* stood Alain Locke and Claude McKay. Hughes also received complimentary reviews from many eminent white critics, including Howard Mumford Jones, V. F. Calverton, Margaret Larkin, Arthur Davison Ficke, Hunter Stagg, Abbe Niles, Julia Peterkin, and Babette Deutsch, reviews that reflected not only their recognition of Hughes's exceptional talent for writing black vernacular poetry but also, and most telling, their appetites for his primitivist images of black America.

The Culmination of Hughes's Primitivist Literary Career

By 1930, Hughes's primitivist proclivities had waned. Abandoning his bohemian rebellion against middle-class conventions, the novel he published that year, *Not Without Laughter* (Hughes 1930), shifted focus to this familiar world of his childhood experiences, and explored the serious theme of a black youth's struggle to come of age in American society. Highlighting the problem of racial injustice, the novel suggested that blacks needed a defensive response of "ironic laughter." But the novel fell short of being a major literary achievement because it lacked coherence. As Robert Bone has perceptively observed: "The novel and its main character simply part company. Instead of supporting the defense-of-laughter theme, Sandy (the protagonist) emerges as a symbol of racial advancement, which is hardly a laughing matter" (Bone 1958, 76).

Its flaws notwithstanding, several critics hailed it as an example of the realism and complexity that were needed if black writers were to succeed in producing a truly ethnic black American literature. In the words of the ever-glib Alain Locke: "If this book were a trilogy, and carried its young hero, Sandy, through a typical black boy's journey from the cradle to the grave, we might perhaps have the all-too-long-prayed-for Negro novel" (Locke 1931, 49).

Nevertheless, that novel's appearance made one thing indisputably clear: Langston Hughes had become a different type of writer. This can be discerned in the statement he made in *Amsterdam News* in 1930 outlining his aims in *Not Without Laughter*. "In this book I have attempted to depict what I believe to be more or less typical small-town life in any town out-side the South. I am interested primarily in life, not local color, so I have chosen as a setting . . . what I feel is more truly American—the average main street town" (Gloster 1948, 185).

This hardly resembled his earlier brash declaration ("We . . . intend to express our individual dark skinned selves without fear of shame") that became the black primitivist school's literary manifesto. Gone were his re-bellious bohemian proclivities, his infatuations with Harlem's deviant fringe, and perhaps most important, his illusions of a primitivist black culture liberalizing white America. The Depression, which struck Harlem in the late 1920s, caused him to recast his ideological outlook as he ob-served the black community's descent into economic desperation; he em-braced a radical political perspective.

We can see the effects of this new political consciousness on his writing in the poem *Pride* which he wrote in 1931:

> Let all who will
> Eat quietly the bread of shame.
> I cannot,
> Without complaining loud and long,
> Tasting its bitterness in my throat,
> And feeling to my very soul
> Its wrong.
> For honest work
> You proffer me poor pay.
> For honest dreams
> Your spit is in my face,
> And so my fist is clenched
> Today—
> To strike your face.

His changed ideological outlook soon led to problems with Mason, who objected to the new political focus of his writings (Rampersad 1986, 175). "It was Charlotte Mason's view that the expression of political opin-ions should be left to white people, like herself. . . . The 'advancement' she was most interested in for Afro-Americans was limited to her belief in an image of cultural exoticism and in supporting black artists whom she thought would foster it, not in encouraging their political consciousness" (Berry 1983, 106).

In fact, Mason even went so far as to insist that "she see everything that he wrote," a demand that further strained an already troubled relationship. Hughes's displeasure with this demand prompted him to write an irate poem criticizing her interference. Though he never showed her the poem and did not publish it until nine years later, it clearly reveals his anger.

Poet to Patron
What right has anyone to say
That I
Must throw out pieces of my heart
For pay?
For bread that helps to make
My heart beat true,
I must sell myself
To you?
A factory shift's better,
A week's meager pay,
Than a perfumed not asking
What poems today?

Although the break in their relationship was gradual (in part because he needed her financial support), Hughes eventually realized the relationship was beyond repair. The event precipitating the break occurred when he published a poem criticizing rich white capitalists (*Advertisements for the Waldorf Astoria*) in the Marxist *New Masses* magazine, a development that infuriated Mason. But it was now clear to Hughes that he could never be the feral black primitivist writer Mason sought to cultivate. As he pointed out:

> She wanted me to be primitive and know and feel the intuitions of the primitive. But, unfortunately, I did not feel the rhythms of the primitive soaring through me, and so I could not live and write as though I did. I was only an American Negro—who had loved the surface of Africa and the rhythms of Africa—but I was not Africa. I was Chicago and Kansas City and Broadway. (Hughes 1940, 325)

The strains generated by his ideological transformation and estrangement from Mason plunged Hughes into a nervous breakdown, with the result that he was obliged to withdraw from the Harlem literary scene for several years. After his recovery, he returned to college to finish his undergraduate education at Lincoln University, a black institution in Pennsylvania, before he resumed his literary career. Though he never again became a leading figure in a dominant black literary school, he continued to be an active and significant presence in black literary life for many years.

Jean Toomer: The Alienated Mystic of the Black Primitivist School

The oddest black writer of the 1920s, Jean Toomer had the distinction of preceding the high point of the primitivist school. His novel *Cane* (Toomer 1969)—like such literary works as Vachel Lindsay's *The Congo: A Study of the Negro Race* (1914); Eugene O'Neill's *The Moon of the Caribees* (1919); and

DuBose Heyward's *Porgy* and Sherwood Anderson's *Dark Laughter* (1925)—were published before Van Vechten's *Nigger Heaven* and were influenced by the broader primitivist vogue emanating from Europe via New York's Greenwich Village. Although Toomer must be counted as a major figure of the black primitivist literary school, his writings differed in significant respects from those of later black primitivist authors.

Toomer was not only the most enigmatic and gifted black writer of the decade, he was also the most alienated from both black community life and black racial identity. Much of his motivation to become a writer apparently derived from his intellectual quest for a new identity, for a conception of himself that transcended conventional American racial categories. Although he expressed this alienated quest for racial transcendence as *weltschmerz*, it emanated in large part from the peculiar and painful circumstances of his family life.

Toomer was the grandson of P. B. S. Pinchback, the black former reconstruction governor of Louisiana. After the Republicans were swept from power by the racist white reaction to reconstruction, Pinchback and his family moved to Washington, D.C., where he bought a large house in a white neighborhood, and lived a life of social elegance. Jean Toomer, who was the child of Pinchback's daughter, Nina, was born in Washington, D.C. in 1894, the offspring of an interracial marriage, which his grandfather had opposed. Toomer's father, a white Southerner, disappeared after the first year of marriage, leaving his mother to struggle financially as a single parent. His family situation became even worse when his mother died several years later. This marked the beginning of Jean's greatest family difficulties, because he had to spend the remainder of his childhood in his grandfather's household. Bitter conflicts soon erupted between him and his grandfather, who, having detested Jean's father, soon displaced those hostile feelings onto Jean. The tension was further exacerbated by Pinchback's declining social status, due to his dwindling financial resources. The family was forced to move from the upper-class white neighborhood to an affluent, but less prestigious black neighborhood. "For the first time," Toomer recalled, "I existed in a colored world."

Toomer responded to the stresses in his personal life by becoming reclusive and introspective, and later, after leaving his grandfather's house and striking out on his own, by falling into a lifestyle of restless wandering, which was reflected in his erratic occupational experiences (selling mutual funds in Chicago, teaching physical education in Milwaukee, teaching public school in rural Georgia, and working briefly in ship construction in New Jersey) and in his attendance at some half-dozen colleges without attaining a degree.

Moving to New York in the early 1920s, he became associated with an avant garde social network of white literary intellectuals which included

Hart Crane, Kenneth Burke, Gorham Munson, and Waldo Frank. Significantly, none of Toomer's intellectual influences derived from his associations with black intellectuals which were, at best, sparse.

Toomer developed his primitivist perspective on lower-class blacks through the influence of his white literary associates. Among those associates, Waldo Frank was the one he credited as the greatest influence on his literary career (Benson and Dillard 1980, 27). In the words of one critic, "The two were intimate friends and this was possibly because they shared a common artistic vision" (Hebling 1988, 69). Together Toomer and Frank traveled to rural Georgia to observe black southern life, which was, in Toomer's words, "more dense and primitive" than black life in the North. This was an unusual and dangerous venture for a black man and a white man from the North to undertake, traveling in the South as companions. The trip bonded the two writers in a deep and lasting friendship.

But beyond being a close friend, Frank also operated as Toomer's chief literary patron, having a large hand in getting *Cane* published. He sent the manuscript to his publisher Horace Liveright and wrote its preface. In short, Frank, more than any other individual, advanced and promoted Toomer's literary career.

However, the benefits from that relationship were reciprocal. As I noted earlier in reference to the relationships between the white and black writers, the white writers typically gained something in return. In Frank's case, he gained access to a rural black social world, which, under the ordinary rules of racial caste, would have been inaccessible to a white northerner. Frank's novel *Holiday* was inspired by the experience of traveling to rural Georgia with Toomer. Acknowledging that experience, Frank later expressed his gratitude to Toomer. "In his *Rediscovering America,* Frank . . . attributed his real knowledge of America to the materials he found on the trip with Toomer." In Frank's words: "Then America came to my weariness: the America of beauty and splendor. . . . The Negro South, where with my friend Jean Toomer and I had lived within the veil, drinking the warm life that rises and blows within the cane and the other South" (Benson and Dillard 1980, 30).

Despite having firsthand experience of the lower-class black social world, Frank produced a novel that suffered from many of the flaws of other primitivist literary works. As Michael Ogorzaly has noted in his biography of Frank: "Whites conceived of blacks as 'sensual and passionate, high-spirited and exotic.' Waldo Frank was no exception, as is evidenced by his novel *Holiday* (1923). . . . Frank failed to grasp (perhaps because as a white man he could never really know) what it really was to be black in America" (Ogorzaly 1994, 41). Although Frank possessed more talent and a more serious commitment to literature than did Carl Van Vechten, his superficial depictions of black American ethnic life were reminiscent of the latter's novel. Noted one critic, "The characters (in his novel) are either stereotypes or abstractions" (Ogorzaly 1994, 41).

Sherwood Anderson was another important white writer who associated with Toomer, operating as his literary mentor; Anderson advised and assisted the young black writer. Though Anderson recognized Toomer's exceptional talents, he was drawn to him out of fascination with the black primitivist myth.

> As one who wrote poetically of rural Georgia, Toomer perfectly captured the spiritual and aesthetic qualities which Anderson saw most threatened by the emergent industrial order of the twentieth century. . . . Toomer became in Anderson's eyes the very embodiment of what was most "fine" in the American black . . . expressed by one who had succeeded in realizing through art the primitive depth of his, and his people's, racial soul. (Hebling 1988, 130)

In light of Toomer's alienation from black racial identity, Anderson's belief that he embodied black primitivism was indeed ironic. As one critic has put it, "Anderson's encouragement and offer to help . . . was part of a deeper need to remind (perhaps convince) Toomer that he was, after all, black and that somehow this constituted the inner source of his unique vision" (Hebling 1988, 115). Toomer never accepted that proposition.

Toomer was enmeshed in a white associational network, and resented being defined as black. At one point when asked permission to include his writings in an anthology of black writers, he declined the request, declaring: "I am of no particular race. I am of the human race, a man at large in the human world, preparing a new race" (Emmanuel and Gross 1968, 95). But his alienation from black racial identity did not hamper his attraction to a primitivist perspective on black American ethnic life.

That primitivist outlook, which he acquired during his literary apprenticeship in New York, crystallized while he worked three months as a vocational school superintendent in rural Georgia. It was this experience, along with his later trip to Georgia with Frank, that provided the background from which he wrote about the rural black South in *Cane*. At the time he wrote that book, he identified with southern black ethnic culture, as was evidenced in an article he wrote, in 1922, for the *Liberator* magazine. "Within the last two or three years . . . my growing need for artistic expression has pulled me deeper and deeper into the Negro group. . . . I found myself loving it in a way I could never love the other" (Fullinwider 1969, 135).

But as the tone of those comments suggests, Toomer hardly felt that he belonged to that social world. Instead, he saw himself as an outsider, whose attachment to that world derived from intellectual, not personal identification. Which is to say his attitude toward this black social world resembled that of white primitivists, who also expressed intellectual affection for the alleged emotional richness and spontaneity of lower-class black life. They, too, felt they had found a culture they could admire more than Western white culture. Toomer was simply expressing this romanticized view of black ethnic culture.

Toomer's perspective was also revealed in his romantic attitude toward black spirituals, and his surprise at the reactions of black town dwellers to their demise. "But I learned that Negroes of the town objected to them. . . . The folk spirit walked in to die on the modern desert. That spirit was so beautiful. Its death so tragic" (Fullinwider 1969, 141).

This was reminiscent of Hughes's writings about the common people of Seventh Street, but with one significant difference: Hughes felt he belonged to that world; Toomer did not.

Cane: *An Early Manifestation of the Black Primitivist Literary School*

Without question, *Cane* (1923) was the least conventional and most artistically engaging black American literary work of the 1920s. As one critic has noted: "If we are to take the word and trust of those who participated in the Harlem Renaissance in the 1920s, the most exciting single work produced by the movement was *Cane*, by Jean Toomer" (Davis 1987, 185). Presenting a melange of stories and poems, melding realistic and mystical images, *Cane* poetically evokes the sensuality of black American life:

> Her skin is like dusk on the eastern horizon,
> O can't you see it, O can't you see it,
> Her skin like dusk on the eastern horizon
> . . . When the sun goes down. (Toomer 1969, 1)
>
> * * *
>
> Wind is in the cane. Come along.
> Cane leaves swaying, rusty with talk,
> Scratching choruses above the guinea's squawk,
> Wind is in the cane. Come along. (Toomer 1969, 16)

Not all of *Cane* is written in such elevated language, as we can see in the following passage where the language is racially crude, if not insulting: "Houses are shy girls whose eyes shine reticently upon the dusky body of the street. Upon the gleaming limbs and asphalt torso of a dreaming nigger. Shake your curled wool-blossoms, nigger. Open your liver lips to the lean, white spring. Stir the rootlife of withered people. Call them from their houses, and teach them to dream" (Toomer 1969, 104).

The book is pervaded by primitivist images of black sexuality. The following passage, for example, could easily have been written by Van

Vechten, McKay, or Hughes: "Funny how some women can do those things. Muriel dancing like that! Hell. She rolled and wabbled. Her buttocks rocked. She pulled up her dress and showed her pink drawers. Baby! And then she caught my eyes. Don't know what my eyes had in them. Yes I do. God, don't I though!" (Toomer 1969, 123).

In saying that *Cane* is in the primitivist mold, I do not mean to imply the artless wallowing in sensationalism that characterized Van Vechten's novel. If anything, *Cane*'s literary objectives often bordered on the abstruse, doubtless an influence of Toomer's avant garde circle. Some of the book's images defy the conventional reader's comprehension:

> African Guardians of Souls,
> Drunk with rum,
> Feasting on a strange cassava,
> Yielding to new words and a weak palabra
> Of a white-faced sardonic god—
> Grins, cries
> Amen
> Shouts hosanna. (Toomer 1969, 49)

Such passages were no doubt influenced by Toomer's mystical studies, which encouraged him to strive for the appropriate literary form and diction, sometimes with dubious results.

As to his primitivist outlook, it differed in several significant aspects from that of the later black primitivist writers. Having preceded Van Vechten's novel, Toomer's romanticized conception of black ethnic life evidenced none of the gratuitous exoticism that pervaded the later primitivist writings, images inserted for the purpose of provoking psychological shock. Also, Toomer's most powerful primitivist images focused on southern black life, a simpler and more rustic way of life than that found in Harlem. Hence *Cane* does not feature such exotic vices as gambling and pimping that appear in *Nigger Heaven* and *Home to Harlem*. Finally, and perhaps most important, *Cane* projects a more tragic view of that culture's fate, as the black folk culture of the rural South that Toomer observed was dying, being uprooted and transformed by the boll weevil, agricultural machinery, and mass black migration to the north.

In expressing this tragic view of southern black cultural change, Toomer exhibited no corresponding sensitivity to the black community's social problems. In this regard his outlook, like that of other primitivist writers, was apolitical. As Waldo Frank put it:

> For Toomer, the Southland is not a problem to be solved; it is a field of loveliness to be sung; the Georgia Negro is not a downtrodden soul to be uplifted; he is material for gorgeous painting; the segregated self-conscious

brown belt of Washington is not a topic to be discussed and exposed; it is a subject of beauty and drama, worthy of creation in literary form. (Frank 1923)

If Frank seemed sympathetic to Toomer's apolitical perspective, it was because his primitivist novel, *Holiday*, published the same year as *Cane*, shared that view.

It is noteworthy that *Cane* aroused no public outcries. This was apparently due to several reasons. First, although primitivist, the book was not sensational. Second, much of its content focused on the rural black South. Third, and most significant, it was published when black American literary works were still marginalized. The new regimen of co-optive hegemony was still in its infancy, which explains why *Cane* attracted little attention. As Langston Hughes recalled: "The colored people did not praise it. The white people did not buy it. Most of the colored people who did read *Cane* hated it. Although the critics gave it good reviews, the public remained indifferent" (Hughes 1940).

This simply underscores the crucial importance of Van Vechten's role. In launching the black primitivist vogue in the public arena, he had a major hand in transforming the black American literary landscape. His job at the *New York Times*, as noted earlier, placed him in an ideal position for galvanizing support for that movement.

Though Toomer continued to publish widely during the 1920s— in such periodicals as *Broom, Opportunity, Crisis, The Little Review, The Double-Dealer*, and *Secession*—he published no work of fiction after *Cane*.

Cane's poor commercial performance no doubt influenced his decision to turn away from his literary career. Gurdjieff mysticism replaced fictional writing as his primary concern as he traveled to the Gurdjieff Institute in Fontainbleau, France, where he studied for a short time.

He later turned up in Harlem as a teacher of psychological mysticism to a group of young black writers—Wallace Thurman, Dorothy Peterson, Aaron Douglas, and Nella Larsen—who apparently believed that *Cane's* extraordinary eloquence derived from Toomer's mystical studies. Reputed to have been quite handsome, Toomer soon attracted a cult of devoted followers. This class allowed Toomer to earn his livelihood for a short time by teaching. But the classes did not last, because they demanded too much time from the young writers who also had full-time jobs.

Toomer's alienation from the black American community stemmed from his identity problems as a man of biracial ancestry. In fact, there is ample evidence indicating that, at sometime in the late 1920s, he ceased to regard himself as a black American. In 1930, in response to James Weldon Johnson's letter asking his permission to publish several poems from *Cane* in *The Book of American Negro Poetry*, an anthology Johnson was editing, Toomer sent the following chilling reply:

> My poems are not Negro poems, nor are they Anglo-Saxon or white or English poems. My prose likewise. They are, first, mine. And, second, in so far as a general race or stock is concerned, they stem from the result of racial blendings here in America which has produced a new race or stock. We may call this stock the American stock or race. My energies are devoted and directed towards the building of a life which will include all creative people or corresponding type. (Fullinwider 1969, 137)

Although both racial groups accepted him, it is clear from the above statement that he identified with neither. But this racial ambivalence soon dissolved. According to Langston Hughes, the next thing they heard of Toomer after the Harlem classes was that he had married a white novelist, Margery Latimer, in August 1932. Toomer and his wife lived in Chicago until she died during childbirth. His second wife was also white. Toomer's racial identity no longer seemed confused, as was clear from his response to a question about whether he was black:

> I would consider it libelous for anyone to refer to me as a colored man, I have not lived as one, nor do I really know whether there is colored blood in me or not. My maternal grandfather, Pinkney Bentor Pinchback, was the "carpet-bag" governor of Louisiana. In order to gain colored votes, he referred to himself as having colored blood. His two brothers never did so, however, so the fact is, I do not know whether colored blood flows through my veins. (Emmanuel and Gross 1968, 96)

This marked the end of whatever attraction Toomer may have had to black American life. To say Toomer was a more talented writer than Van Vechten would be like saying Paris was more interesting than Peoria. Toomer's importance derives from not only his early attachment to the white primitivist ideology, but also his extraordinary ability to poetically evoke the textures and rhythms of black American ethnic life. He gave the primitivist school it most eloquent voice.

Like McKay, Toomer eventually took refuge in religion. Joining the Society of Friends in Philadelphia, he disappeared into that Quaker environment, where he apparently found a stable and supportive community. Little is known about Toomer after this conversion, except that he died in 1967 at the age of seventy-three.

Countee Cullen: A Reluctant Latecomer to Primitivism

Though the primitivist vogue exerted its impact chiefly on black writers who were dissociated from the black community life, Countee Cullen was an exception. A black writer who was anchored firmly in Harlem's black middle class, he exhibited none of the rebellious bohemian proclivities of the other writers, as he had different motives for becoming affiliated with the primitivist movement. As a latecomer, he turned to primitivism when both the movement and his literary career were in decline.

Cullen had an unusual family background. But unlike the other primitivist writers, his formative adolescent years were characterized by a stable middle-class family life. Born in Kentucky, he was adopted at the age of eleven by the Reverend Frederick Cullen, who was the pastor of a large church as well as a prominent leader in Harlem community life. Countee Cullen thus had the good fortune of growing up in the comfort and security of an upper-middle-class lifestyle, which included, among other things, vacations at the family summer home and several trips to Europe with his father. He grew up free of the problems of poverty or family instability that plagued the childhoods of Claude McKay and Langston Hughes.

Countee Cullen was recognized early as being intellectually gifted, an estimation that was subsequently validated by his outstanding scholastic achievements, beginning with his attendance at New York City's DeWitt Clinton high school (the school that James Baldwin later would attend) and proceeding through his undergraduate study at New York University, where he majored in literature and graduated Phi Beta Kappa. His schooling culminated with a master's degree in French at Harvard and two years of study at the Sorbonne in Paris on a Guggenheim fellowship. Cullen adapted easily to the discipline of academic work; again in contrast to McKay and Hughes, he had no experiences of working at menial jobs that would have drawn him into the social world of black lower-class lifestyles.

The effect of his education was perhaps nowhere revealed more clearly than in his orientation to literature. Deeply immersed in the European literary canon, Cullen embraced a traditional Europe-oriented conception of his role as a writer, and felt uncomfortable with ethnic-racial definitions of literature. Writing in metered verse and poetic diction, he sought to imitate his idol, John Keats, and the other English Romantic poets, as he crafted abstract lyrical images that transcended the pedestrian realities of Harlem life. These images can be seen in the following examples:

This wistful angel down in hell
Will smile to see my face.
And understand, because they fell
From that all-perfect place.

* * *

Not writ in water, nor in mist,

Sweet lyric throat, the name;
Thy singing lips that cold death kissed
Have seared his own with flame. (Emmanuel and Gross 1968, 180)

Expressing his paradoxical identity as an outcast black and a poet in a white society, Cullen wrote the now famous lines:

Yet do I marvel at this curious thing:
To make a poet black, and bid him sing! (Emmanuel and Gross 1968, 176)

Not surprisingly, Cullen's relationship with Carl Van Vechten was circumspect and wary; he hardly fit Van Vechten's conception of an ethnic black writer, an impression Van Vechten conveyed when they met for the first time at an NAACP ball at the Rockland Palace. "The Iowan did not immediately warm to him. He had already seen some of Cullen's poetry and considered it good in spite of what he called its derivative quality. *He frowned on Cullen's affinity with the classics and the English poets.* (emphasis added) On the other hand, he found Langston Hughes natural and original, deriving from no sources other than the blues" (Ferguson 1966, 47–48).

Given Cullen's more conventional middle-class lifestyle and his extensive training in European literary tradition, he was a poor candidate for being co-opted into the primitivist vogue. Nevertheless, Van Vechten offered to help both Cullen and Hughes get their work published. Cullen failed to pursue Van Vechten's offer, displaying an obstinate pride that apparently irritated Van Vechten (Ferguson 1966, 48).

Van Vechten was not the only race-relations broker available to black writers; he was simply the most important. Cullen eventually found a publisher through Frederick Lewis Allen, then a literary scout for Harpers and Brothers, whom Cullen met at an Urban League–sponsored dinner. This contact resulted in the publication of Cullen's first book, *Color.*

Cullen's academic credentials gave him access to employment in the professional, black middle-class community. After graduating from Harvard, he worked as assistant editor of *Opportunity*, the Urban League's periodical, where initially he screened and processed manuscripts, and later reviewed books and wrote literary commentary. These scarce jobs within the black middle-class intellectual community were restricted to blacks with stellar academic credentials. For "uncredentialed" blacks like McKay, Hughes, and Toomer, such jobs were out of reach. This made all the more the ironic the editorial position McKay occupied at the *New Masses*, the white leftist publication. No such opportunity was open to him in the black middle-class intellectual community.

Cullen, like McKay, Hughes, and Toomer, spent time in Europe during the 1920s, but under far different circumstances. Cullen spent two years in Paris studying at the Sorbonne on a prestigious Guggenheim fellowship. Though his European sojourn evidenced none of the bohemian pursuits of his peers, it marked a turning point in his literary career, because it brought him into contact with writers who had a large hand in changing his conception of literature and his social role as a writer.

Cullen was invited to visit the Irish American poet, Patric Colum, who was then living in Paris. Meeting with Colum, along with several other Irish poets, Countee Cullen soon found himself deeply engrossed in a discussion about the functions of literature.

> Countee listened with lively interest as they talked of the Irish Literary Revival and the responsibilities of Irish authors. He agreed with those who believed that poetry is essentially fine art and that it should not be used merely as propaganda. He knew that in Colum's poetry dealing with the Irish peasant there had been no compromise. He also found here a basis of comparison between the Irish writer's relationship to Britain and the Negro writer's place in American literature. Countee found no apathy among these Irishmen. (Ferguson 1966, 119)

In fact, this meeting prompted Cullen to reexamine his thinking about literature and his role as a black writer. As a traditionalist, Cullen had long opposed the notions of ethnic literature he encountered in the United States, particularly among black writers. Believing "there was no such thing as Negro poetry" he had preferred the term "verse by Negro Poets" (Ferguson 1966, 92). In a comment at a symposium that later appeared in *Crisis*, Cullen had argued that "Negro authors should not be bound to respect the 'implied conditions' of publishers restricting them to racial material." Although Cullen detested the noose of racial categorization, he hardly avoided the pitfalls of hegemony. Rather he had merely managed to resist the new co-optive hegemony of primitivism, while embracing—albeit unwittingly—the more conservative hegemony of Eurocentrism.

But his conversation with the Irish writers helped to convince him of the legitimacy of ethnic literature. That encouragement to change his conception of his social role was reinforced by his dissatisfaction with the current state of his literary career. He had lost his inspiration to write traditional verse. In the words of his biographer, "he . . . (had) produced a shamefully small amount of poetry in the past year" (Ferguson 1966, 93). The poems that he did manage to produce attracted little interest, because there existed no public demand for the works of traditionally oriented black poets. What publishers wanted from black writers were exotic depictions of urban black life, like those produced by Van Vechten, McKay, and Hughes, which Cullen scorned. But now he found a justification to change. If Irish writers he respected could produce an ethnic literature that sustained its artistic integrity, why couldn't he?

The result of his reorientation was his novel *One Way to Heaven*, which reflected Van Vechten's influence. Though the novel diverged in certain aspects from the earlier primitivist works by presenting a more balanced focus on the disorganized and stable sectors of the black community, its satirical depiction of the Harlem black bourgeoisie was hardly flattering. In the words of one critic, Cullen took

> keen pleasure . . . in ridiculing the Harlem social register, the "New Negro" coterie, colored reactionaries to whom all Negro literature after Dunbar and Chestnutt is anathema, . . . inquisitive white writers mingling with colored people in order to get material for their books, scholarly white researchers on Negro life and culture, advocates of the Back-to-Africa Movement, and pseudo-scholars who deprecate darker folk as indolent, untrustworthy, unintelligent, unclean, immoral, and cursed of heaven. (Gloster 1948, 85)

In short, Cullen's primitivist perspective on black Harlem life stung with venom of satire.

This was Cullen's last significant literary work. Despite his extraordinary talent and potential for higher literary achievements, his literary career ended in the mid-1930s. Without the possibility of earning a living as a writer, he settled into a career of school teaching, becoming a French instructor in a New York junior high school in 1934, a job he held for eleven years until his untimely death on 10 January 1946, at the age of forty-three.

THE END OF DELUSION: THE DEMISE OF THE DOMINANT BLACK PRIMITIVIST LITERARY SCHOOL

Now to recapitulate the main points of this chapter. The 1920s ushered black literary life into an era of social change and social delusions. Stimulated by new opportunities to publish and gain recognition in the mainstream society, the leading young black writers fell prey to a racially retrograde primitivist ideology, which became the guiding vision of their writings, forming the first dominant black literary school. The appearance of those primitivist literary works, which were mistaken as evidence of black American literature's new-found cultural independence, marked a change in the cultural process of American race relations, a change that neither the black writers nor their white associates understood. While whites continued to fashion the ideology of literary works depicting black Americans in the public arena, blacks were now supplanting whites as the authors of those literary works. This evidenced a shift in the cultural process from the old regimen of paternalistic hegemony to the new—and more subtle—regimen of co-optive hegemony, which occurred as the racial caste system adapted to the changed social and political realities of black America's mass urbanization.

Though nonprimitivist black literary works were also published in the 1920s, it was the primitivist writings that achieved the greatest notoriety and influence in the American public culture. Only by taking into account this changed cultural process of black literary production can we under-stand how black writers succumbed to delusions of racial reform and came to embrace a racially retrograde primitivist ideology.

Langston Hughes summed up that odd experience perhaps best when he later recalled:

> I was there. I had a swell time while it lasted. But I thought it wouldn't last long. . . . They thought the race problem would be solved through art plus Gladys Bentley. . . . I don't know what made many Negroes think that—except that they were mostly intellectuals doing the thinking. The ordinary Negroes hadn't heard of the Negro Renaissance. And if they had, it hadn't raised their wages any. (Cruse 1967, 33)

Never again would a dominant black literary school succumb to such naive delusions about the obstacles to race relations reform.

NOTE

1. *Liberator* would be renamed *New Masses* in 1926.

2

The Era of the
Naturalistic Protest School

The Politicization of
Black American Literature

In the lives of Negro writers must be found those materials and experiences which will create a meaningful picture of the world today. Many young writers have grown to believe that a Marxist analysis of society presents such a picture.

—Richard Wright 1978, 44

The 1930s Great Depression transformed the social and cultural climate of American society. Gone were the frivolous jazz-age and primitivist celebrations of the black American lower class. No longer did black American writers comfortably depict the social milieu of the black American masses as a hedonistic paradise. No longer did they assume that American society was evolving inexorably toward racial enlightenment. No longer did they think that their peculiar version of "literary realism" was liberalizing white America. Finally, and perhaps most crucial, no longer did the white American literati, publishers, and reading public exhibit an appetite for exotic depictions of black ethnic life. The bohemian indulgences of the 1920s had come to an end.

In this new atmosphere of crisis and desperation, a number of leading black writers gravitated to the white American Marxist movement, marking the formation and ascent of the naturalistic protest school. With the appearance of this literary school, the dominant ideological tendency in black American literature for the first time embraced a radical political ideology. Spearheaded by Richard Wright's *Native Son* (Wright 1940), this new ideology launched a fierce assault on the American racial caste

system, signaling a new era in the cultural dynamics of American race relations. In the words of the literary critic Irving Howe:

> The day *Native Son* appeared, American culture changed forever. No matter
> how much qualifying the book might later need, it made impossible a repe-
> tition of the old lies. In all its crudeness, melodrama and claustrophobia of vi-
> sion, Richard Wright's novel brought out into the open, as no one ever had
> before, the hatred, fear and violence that have crippled so many and may yet
> destroy our culture. (Howe 1963, 256)

In tracing the development of this controversial literary school, this
chapter has four objectives. First, we will determine the origins of Marxist influence on the naturalistic protest school by providing a brief account
of both the early white leftist political initiatives toward black Americans
and the later impact of the Great Depression on the black community's
political consciousness. Second, we will examine Richard Wright's social
background and intellectual development, which culminated in the creation of *Native Son*, the literary work that launched the naturalistic protest
school. Third, we will analyze that literary school's major images and implications, its normative messages, for public perceptions of black American life. Finally, shifting to a different terrain, we will examine the critical
responses to *Native Son* and other naturalistic protest literary works, and
conclude by assessing that school's sociological significance as a product
of co-optive hegemony.

THE DEPRESSION YEARS: THE SOCIOHISTORICAL SETTING

The Great Depression hit the black community like a major earthquake. In
particular, it devastated the lives of working-class blacks who, having occupied jobs on the bottom rung of the labor market, found themselves ex-
truded from the economy en masse. In the words of Gunnar Myrdal, author of *An American Dilemma*: "The Great Depression struck the Negroes
even harder than it did whites. Not only did they lose jobs in the cities
in greater numbers than did whites, but many of those who retained
employment—especially in agriculture—were driven down to starvation
wages" (Myrdal 1964, 754).

Myrdal further noted that "unemployed Negroes, unlike many unemployed whites, had no savings upon which they could fall back in crisis. . . .
Between 1930 and 1933 there was utter distress and pessimism among Negroes." But he concluded with a curious observation: "Practically the only
ones with hope were the few who turned to communism."

The importance of the Depression for our purposes revolves around
this critical question: To what extent did that economic crisis radicalize

the black community? We must answer this question to determine both the effects of that crisis in generating the naturalistic protest school and the relationship of that school's ideological perspective to the black community's social consciousness. But before answering that question, we should briefly review the early history of socialist influence in the black community, to illuminate the background of the peculiar conditions that fostered a Marxist-oriented, dominant black literary school in the 1930s.

Socialist Parties and the Black Community

During the early years of their formation in the United States, socialists parties were composed primarily of immigrant laborers from Germany, who exhibited no special interest in black Americans. Adhering to the socialist ideological line that stressed universalist principles of working-class solidarity, they viewed the situation of blacks as simply a manifestation of the class struggle. Hence they formulated no special policies in reference to blacks. As the leader of the Social Democratic Party, Eugene Debs proclaimed, "We have nothing special to offer the Negro, and we cannot make separate appeals to all the races. The Socialist Party is the party of the working class—the whole working class of the whole world" (Spero and Harris 1969, 26). However, in paying homage to this universalistic principle, the socialists ignored the realities of ethnic-racial divisions within the American working class, for the typical American worker—contrary to what the early socialists leaders assumed—regarded his Irish, Italian, German, or Polish ethnic community as being more important than his social class. Moreover, and perhaps most damaging, the socialist leaders failed to perceive their own ethnocentrism. While articulating a rhetoric of socialist universalism, they naively subsumed European values as the basis of its normative order. It was largely this bogus universalism, specifically its ignoring of black American culture, that doomed the early socialist initiatives in the black community.

Later, around the period of World War I, socialist ideology surfaced among a handful of black intellectuals, who attempted to attract black workers to the socialist movement. Those efforts, however, encountered formidable opposition from the black community leaders. Urging black Americans to steer clear of socialism, this opposition, led initially by Booker T. Washington and later by NAACP officials, reflected the black political elite's financial dependence on wealthy white patrons closely tied to corporate capitalism. Attempting to overcome those obstacles, two black proponents of socialist ideology—A. Philip Randolph and Chandler Owens, who edited *The Messenger* magazine—ran for political office in New York on the socialist party ticket in 1917, Randolph for state controller and Owens for state assemblyman, but to no avail. They failed to

attract significant support within the black community because they encountered opposition from the black political elite and indifference from
the black masses, who remained committed to the Republican party, the
party of Abraham Lincoln.

COMMUNIST PARTY INITIATIVES IN THE BLACK COMMUNITY

World War I and the Russian Revolution altered the landscape of leftist
politics in the United States. By forging a split in the socialist movement,
those events marked a significant turning point in leftist political initiatives toward black Americans. On one side of the division emerged the
revolutionary American Communist Party. Operating as an instrument
of Soviet policy, the Communist Party was oriented to the new
Marxist-Leninist variant of socialism, which viewed minority populations
as cultural nationalities oppressed by imperialist capitalist states. For the
first time, black Americans were viewed by a leftist political party as a
unique and strategically important sector of the American working class.
Implementing this new policy, the party assigned the task of politically
mobilizing the black community to a newly converted group of black
communists that included former members of the Socialist Party, such as
Otto Huiswood, Lovett F. Whiteman, Richard B. Moore, Cyril Briggs, and
Otto Hall, who had been affiliated with *The Messenger* magazine (Cruse
1967, 141–42).

But in this postwar social climate, when widespread racial violence was
erupting in northern cities, the communist efforts encountered formidable
resistance from both the Garvey movement and the NAACP, which
warned blacks against involvement with the communists. Though the
party tried to infiltrate these two organizations and counteract their opposition, it had little success. By 1927, out of an estimated 9,600 members,
the Communist Party had attracted only fifty blacks into its ranks (Record
1964, 5).

Disappointed by this feeble response, the party changed its strategy on
the black question in 1928, on the eve of the Great Depression. At the Sixth
International Conference, party leaders decided to promote the black
community's self-determination; specifically a black republic to be established in the South. With this policy, which sought to appropriate and
rechannel the Garvey-inspired black nationalist sentiments, the party set
forth several tactical objectives: "Link all short-term demands in behalf of
Negroes with the ultimate goal; bring 'wide masses of Negroes' into the
struggle alongside the C.P.; select issues that could be joined readily with
the self-determination struggle; place communists in the forefront of the
Negro liberation movement; develop a revolutionary trade union move-

ment among Negroes and whites in the South; 'expose' bourgeois Negro leaders who rejected self-determination for the race, and co-ordinate the struggle for Negro rights in the North with the separate nation move in the South" (Record 1964, 56). Though pursued with greater tenacity than the earlier policy, this Stalinist strategy of subterfuge and subversion also failed to attract the black masses to the communist movement.

In fact, the party's activities in the black community remained pathetically ineffectual until the economic crisis of the 1930s, which proved to be something of a windfall. As Herbert Gosnell observed in *Negro Politics,* "the world wide economic crisis which started in 1929 afforded the Communist Party in the United States some special opportunities" (Gosnell 1967, 323). Recounting the party's activities in the Chicago black community, Gosnell offered several examples of the ways it sought to exploit those opportunities.

> The literature of the party was widely circulated, frequent meetings were held, elaborate demonstrations were staged, interracial dances were frequent, and strikes among Negro and white workers were fostered. To carry out this elaborate program the communists created a large number of subsidiary organizations like the Unemployed Councils, League of Struggle for Negro Rights, The United Front Scottsboro Defense, the Young Communist League, the Pioneers, and the Trade Union Unity League. . . . All were controlled by party members. The party proper was composed of shop nuclei and street units of at least three members each. (Gosnell 1967, 325)

Engaging in protest activities with high visibility, the party aimed to dramatize the black community's racial and economic oppression. For instance, the Unemployed Councils typically moved into action on the street to return evicted families to their homes, attracting large crowds of sympathetic onlookers, which often led to clashes with the police. On one such occasion in Chicago during August 1931, a communist-led confrontation escalated into a riot, resulting in injuries to three white policemen and the death of three blacks. The incident was reported by Horace Cayton and Sinclair Drake in *Black Metropolis*:

> Through the Spring of 1931 small groups of Negroes under communist leadership skirmished with the police at the scenes of eviction. Then, one August day, several thousand people decided to march en masse to a home in a poverty stricken neighborhood to replace some furniture. When the police arrived there were at least five thousand people on the spot. The crowd refused to "break it up"; there was some scuffling, and then shooting. Three Negroes lay dead on the pavement when it was over and scores were wounded. Three policemen were badly injured. By nightfall fifty thousand leaflets had been distributed throughout Black Metropolis, bearing the slogan: DEMAND DEATH PENALTY FOR THE MURDERS OF THE WORKERS. (Cayton and Drake 1945, 87)

In an alternative line of action, the party attacked moderate black organizations such as the NAACP and Urban League by publicly berating their leaders. As Wilson Record pointed out in his study of the conflict between NAACP and the Communist Party, "unsympathetic leaders of indigenous groups were subjected to continuous, merciless attack which would brand them as 'social fascists,' 'misleaders of labor,' and 'betrayers of the Negro people'" (Record 1964, 53–54).

Equally important, the party sought to capitalize on any event that could provide national or international publicity for the communist cause. The event that yielded the most dramatic favorable publicity for the party in the 1930s was the Scottsboro trial. In rural Alabama, a group of nine young black males had been arrested for raping two white girls. The charge, based on the girls' testimony, was not supported by the medical findings. Powerfully symbolizing persisting racial oppression in the American South, the trial gained extensive publicity not only in the United States, but also in Europe. Because of its enormous potential influence on public opinion, the Scottsboro case soon led to antagonism between the NAACP and the Communist Party, as both groups vied for the job of defending the nine accused black males in court. Mindful of the growing menace of Nazism that was stirring in Germany, the party saw the trial as a rare opportunity to highlight what it regarded as the latent fascist tendencies in capitalist America. Much to the disappointment of the NAACP, which persistently sought to dissociate the cause of racial justice from radical politics, the communists won permission from the families to serve as the boys' defense lawyers. This was for the Communist Party a major victory. Though historians still disagree about the party's motives in defending the Scottsboro boys, one thing is indisputably clear: its involvement in that trail enhanced its image in the eyes of many black Americans. Indeed, it would hardly be an exaggeration to say that the Scottsboro trial marked the highpoint of the party's notoriety in the black community. As we will later see, a similar Communist courtroom defense in the name of racial justice was depicted in Richard Wright's *Native Son*, where a considerable portion of the text focuses on the trial of a young black man accused of murdering a white woman.

When it came to the matter of protesting racial injustices, the Communist Party enjoyed major advantages over the NAACP. As a revolutionary movement , it could dramatize its opposition to racial injustices by using illegal tactics that the NAACP, dependent on support from white business interests, was obliged to avoid.

Nevertheless, despite being able to exploit its tactical advantages, as well as the economic distress of the period, the Communist Party's influence in the black community remained shallow. Few black Americans were attracted to the party, a fact that makes all the more curious the ascent of a dominant black literary school, whose ideological constructions of black American life derived from communist influences. To gain insight into how this happened, we must focus on those blacks who became involved in the party.

Blacks Attracted to the Communist Party

Those few blacks who gravitated to the Communist Party were hardly representative of the average working-class black American. As Herbert Gosnell indicated in his brief biographical sketches of black communists, most shared the following characteristics: direct experiences of racial abuse; frustrated ambitions for middle-class status; and feelings of estrangement from American society (Gosnell 1967, 342–48).

One man who typified this pattern was James Ford, the son of a southern sharecropper (as was Richard Wright), who became the party's vice-presidential candidate. Ford had grown up in a southern environment steeped in racial brutality; his grandfather was lynched following an argument with a white man over the ownership of a pig. The family later moved to another southern town where he and his father worked for a coal company. Ford's strong ambitions were revealed in his having worked his way through Fisk University for three years, and then, after dropping out due to financial difficulties, joining the Army where he hoped to find an alternative to the bleak job prospects for blacks in the domestic economy. But the racially segregated U.S. Army proved to be a dead end. After being discharged, he settled in Chicago, where he got a job with the postal service, the refuge of many ambitious blacks, and shortly thereafter he became involved in the postal union. This marked a crucial turning point in Ford's life, because it exposed him to a radical political perspective for understanding his frustrating personal predicament. In the words of Gosnell, Ford personified "the grievances of the Negroes in the United States, lynching, the cropping system, discrimination, exploitation in southern industries, limited vocational opportunities in the North, and lack of recognition."

Another man who typified the pattern was Comrade X, one of the first blacks to join the party in Chicago. He was married to a white woman and was reputedly one of the most knowledgeable black Americans on matters of communist doctrine. "In conversation he showed great familiarity with the Soviet leaders and with the more important works of theory on the communist state." A northern black by birth, Comrade X had grown up in a lower middle-class family. His alienation from conventional black American life was reflected in his description of his parents: "a meek Baptist mother and a discontented father who had to turn to waiting tables in a hotel because of his inability to find a job in his trade, house-painting."

He came from a family of four children, which included a sister who taught in the Boston school system, and had been trained as a printer. However, his frustrated ambitions began to surface soon after he graduated from high school; he spent several years wandering around the country and ended up in Chicago in 1925. "I knew something was wrong. I had been groping ever since I finished school. I couldn't seem to fit. I was an agnostic. . . . After looking vainly for work, I joined the Communist Party in 1926. . . . I turned atheist after joining the party." The party sent Comrade X for eighteen months of training in the Soviet Union. Counteracting his feelings of aimlessness and despair, the party gave him—as it did Richard Wright—intellectual direction and self-esteem.

Still another example of the pattern was Comrade Y—a street organizer—who had been "in the thick of most of the riots and fights between the Communists and the police on the South Side of Chicago." In fact, his behavior had been so fearless and reckless "that he was sent as an example of militant leadership" to several other cities of the Middle West. Born in Tennessee, the son of a farmer, Comrade Y was another example of a man who could find no satisfactory outlet for his ambitions. After spending two years at Fisk University , he wandered around the country for several years, working at a variety of jobs which included Pullman porter, packing-house laborer in the stockyards, and steel mill worker. "I worked in Gary for a year-and-a-half, a good Baptist just like my folks, worrying not about the revolution but about my pay and an occasional spree." But the Depression changed all that. "Soon after I joined the party I lost what little deep religious feelings I had." As was true of the others, his rejection of black religion reflected not just a loss of faith. It also reflected the party's influence in detaching its black members from the institutional life of the black community.

We can abstract from Gosnell's sketches the following general profile of Chicago's black communists:

1. young men and women in their 20s and 30s
2. former Garveyites
3. a few activists from the riots of 1919
4. World War I veterans
5. disillusionment with religion
6. unemployed
7. educationally well above the average for the black community, but lacking professional credentials for black middle-class occupations. (Gosnell 1967)

It was from this socially estranged group of black Americans that the writers of the naturalistic protest school emerged. More ambitious and better educated, as well as more religiously alienated, than the typical working-class black American, they found themselves in a distressful situation during the Depression, a situation for which only the Communist Party—with its commitment to social justice and interracial solidarity—appeared to provide a solution.

Like the other blacks who had gravitated to the white leftist political movement, these writers were hardly representative of working-class blacks. In fact, when we examine the relationship of the naturalistic protest school's ideological perspective to the major patterns of social consciousness that characterized the black community, one thing becomes indisputably clear: that literary school's ideological perspective on black American life failed to reflect black American culture.

Like its predecessor in the 1920s, the ideological perspective of the naturalistic protest school derived from the white American intelligentsia, in this case, the social network of the Communist Party and the leftist political movement, which operated as the primary conduits of co-optive hegemony in the 1930s.

Let's now turn to these writers and the development of this literary school.

RICHARD WRIGHT AND THE DEVELOPMENT OF THE NATURALISTIC PROTEST SCHOOL

> It was not the economics of Communism, nor the great power of trade unions, nor the excitement of underground politics that claimed me; my attention was caught by the similarity of the experiences of workers in other lands, by the possibility of uniting scattered but kindred peoples into a whole. It seemed to me that here at last, in the realm of revolutionary expression, Negro experience could find a home, a functioning value and role.
>
> —Richard Wright 1944, 106

The naturalistic protest school was the product of a small but energetic group of socially marginal black American writers. Their marginality was highly significant. Because they lacked professional status and middle-class support networks, they had no jobs or reputations to protect and, thus, were free to embrace a radical ideological perspective as they sought to unravel the causes of their frustrations.

The writers who gravitated to the Communist Party and its Marxian ideological perspective were Richard Wright, Ralph Ellison, Langston Hughes, and Chester Himes, along with several minor writers. In addition, a peripheral stream of black writers, including Ann Petry, Willard Motley, and Frank Yerby, were influenced by leftist political ideology but remained outside the party.

If the emergence of this literary school marked a critical milestone in black American literature's development, it was not simply because it was the first dominant black literary school to project a radical political ideology. It was also—and equally important—because its writers constituted the first truly professional group of black literary artists, evidenced in both their enhanced mastery of their craft and relatively long literary careers. In contrast to Claude McKay, Jean Toomer, and Countee Cullen, as well as less accomplished 1920s black writers whose careers flamed out when the Jazz Age faded, the leading naturalistic protest writers would continue writing as a lifelong occupation, beyond the Depression era.

The leader of the naturalistic protest school was without question Richard Wright, the first internationally renowned black American writer. Richard Wright had a literary career that extended from the 1930s to the early 1960s, resulting in the publication of seven works of fiction and a total of eleven books: *Uncle Tom's Children* (1938), *Native Son* (1940), *12 Million Black Voices* (1941), *Black Boy* (1945a), *The Outsider* (1953), *Savage Holiday* (1954b), *Black Power* (1954a), *The Color Curtain* (1956), *Pagan Spain* (1957a), *White Man, Listen!* (1957b), *The Long Dream* (1958), *Eight Men* (1961), and *Lawd Today* (1963). Other black writers who began their literary careers in the naturalistic protest school would produce similarly long lists of publications.

When we examine the social profile of the leading naturalistic protest writers, we discover that it resembled that of other blacks—noted by Gosnell—who gravitated to the Communist Party. Born during the period from 1902 to 1914, just before the beginning of the northern black migration, they experienced the crisis of the Great Depression while still in their formative years, when they were seeking to settle into adulthood and acquire stable employment. Langston Hughes was the only exception. Having participated in the dominant primitivist literary school of the 1920s, he had already established a professional identity and reputation. Though he interrupted his literary career to recover from a nervous breakdown and to complete his college education, he returned to writing after he graduated from college. In contrast to Hughes, the other naturalistic protest writers were young men still in the process of forming their personal and occupational identities on the eve of the Great Depression: Wright was 21; Himes, 20; Attaway, 17; and Ellison, 16.

Though their family circumstances varied, most of these writers came from working-class backgrounds. Wright, Hughes, and Himes grew up in broken homes and experienced childhood poverty; whereas Ellison, the youngest of the group, came from a more stable and conventional home life. Significantly, unlike their white Marxist intellectual peers, these black writers had experienced firsthand the poverty, hardships, and frustrations of working-class life. In fact, one of them—Chester Himes—had spent seven years in prison for armed robbery. Richard Wright had worked at a series of menial jobs and undergone the unpleasant ordeal of living in an impoverished black ghetto and subsisting on welfare, experiences that alienated him from black working-class life.

Equally important, these writers shifted the geographic focus of black American literary works away from Harlem, particularly during the early years of the school's development, to the ghettos of Chicago and other less celebrated black communities. Coming north in the later stream of black migration, they encountered ghetto environments, which—in sharp contrast to those of the 1920s—were suffused with pessimism and despair. No doubt most of them would have continued their educations and entered middle-class professions, in fields such as education, medicine, or law, if they had come of age in a more prosperous and stable era. Unlike the primitivist writers of the 1920s, they were not bohemian adventurers but working-class strivers, bright and ambitious individuals, seeking professional status and a better quality of life. But under the conditions of the Depression, those aspirations led them into a commitment to radical political change. The Communist Party succeeded in gaining their allegiance, in part, because they refused to relinquish their personal ambitions for upward social mobility. In this ironic sense, the Communist Party became for them an alternative avenue to the American Dream.

Though the naturalistic protest school's ideological perspective developed from Marxism, it would be a mistake to view it as simply a mechanical translation of Marxist theory. While retaining the latter's broad philosophical perspective, that school adapted and altered Marxist precepts into a literary form that incorporated significant phenomenological features of black ghetto life. Going beyond the proletarian-bourgeois typology and opening a new racialized terrain of Marxist discourse, this ideological-phenomenological synthesis constituted the naturalistic protest school's most notable intellectual achievement.

Though this development proceeded as part of the process of co-optive hegemony, that process was now manifest in a more mature and complex form, evidenced by the naturalistic protest school's emergence under the leadership of a black American writer. White American influence was now less transparent, more muted. No Carl Van Vechten paraded onto the stage and orchestrated the development of the naturalistic protest school. Its adaptation of the Marxian paradigm to black American ghetto experience was effected by Richard Wright. Because Wright's personal experiences in both the black community and the Communist Party played such a crucial part in shaping that school's literary orientation, we must begin our discussion of the naturalistic protest school with a brief examination of his personal background and development.

RICHARD WRIGHT: THE EARLY YEARS

Richard Wright, the son of an illiterate sharecropper, was born on a plantation near Natchez, Mississippi, in 1908. This was a time when some 90 percent of the black American population lived in the South, subsisting as cheap laborers. Lynchings, along with other brutal acts of racial violence, were used frequently against blacks as means of social control. To escape the harsh conditions of Mississippi life, the Wright family, like tens of thousands of other blacks during that period, left the plantation and sought their fortunes in a city. Memphis, the metropolitan hub of the deep South, was their destination. But the good fortune they were seeking eluded them. After reaching Memphis, Wright's father—aptly described by one author as a man of "casual affections"—deserted the family. Richard Wright, who was only nine years old at the time, later recalled: "When I awakened one morning my mother told me that we were going to see a judge who would make my father support me and my brother."

But to no avail. His father simply pleaded to the judge that he could do no better. And typical of the racist criminal justice system that provided little legal support for black family life, the judge simply dismissed Wright's father. "Back at home," Wright recalled, "my mother wept again and talked complainingly about the unfairness of the judge who had accepted my father's word. After the court scene I tried to forget my father" (Wright 1945a, 35).

Economic privation was a central reality of Wright's childhood. Even before his father deserted the family, hunger was a frequent menace in the Wright household. As Wright later recollected, it "stole upon me so slowly that at first I was not aware of what hunger really meant. Hunger had always been more or less at my elbow when I played" (Wright 1945a, 21). The situation worsened after his father's departure. "Often when we were so hungry," Wright recalled, "my mother would beg me to go to my father's job and ask him for a dollar, a dime, a nickel. . . . But I would never consent to go. I did not want to see him." These family hardships toughened Richard Wright's sensibility. For he was to become one of the coldest, and least sentimental, black writers of his generation, constructing black characters who exhibited unemotional, benumbed detachment from their social surroundings.

Leaving his father behind in Memphis, the family returned to Mississippi; this time to Jackson, where they stayed with Wright's grandmother. Never again did Wright live with his father, who eventually went back to the plantation and the life of sharecropping. After visiting his father many years later, in 1940, Wright with characteristic emotional detachment reflected on his father's life as a metaphor for the tragic black American encounters with the temptations and perils of the urban world. "From far beyond the horizons that bound this black plantation there had come to me through my living the knowledge that my father was a black peasant who had gone to the city seeking life, but who failed in the city; a black peasant whose life had been hopelessly snarled in the city, and who had at last fled the city" (Wright 1945a, 43).

Richard Wright came to view his childhood as having been shaped by the disintegrating southern plantation economy and the subsequent turmoil of migration and urban settlement. As we will see, his view of the transformation in black American life wrought by urbanization was strongly influenced by writings of the University of Chicago school of sociology.

Another childhood experience that would significantly affect his sensibility as a writer was his rejection of religion. "After my father's desertion, my mother's ardently religious disposition dominated the household and I was often taken to Sunday School where I met God's representative in the guise of a tall, black preacher" (Wright 1945a, 33). This religious fervor of his childhood environment intensified when they lived with his grandmother in Jackson. "Granny was an ardent member of the Seventh-Day Adventist Church and I was compelled to make a pretense of worshipping her God, which was her exaction for my keep." The failure of his mother's and grandmother's efforts to spiritually engage his personality turned out to be consequential, for he grew up alienated from the black American religious worldview, the spiritual foundation of working-class black American culture. Religion played no role in the ideological perspective through which Wright would later represent black American experiences. Nor did it figure in the works of other naturalistic protest writers, who turned deaf ears to black religious consciousness.

Wright's estrangement from his childhood environment was further evidenced in his relations to his schoolmates, whom he characterized as "a docile lot . . . will-less, their speech flat, their gestures vague, their personalities devoid of anger, hope, laughter, enthusiasm, passion or despair." These students' conventional black working-class lifestyles failed to impress or engage Wright's imagination. He was far more intrigued by those blacks who lived beyond conventional morality. Even at this young age, Wright recalled, he saw himself as different from his fellow students. As he put it,

> They were claimed by their environment and could imagine no other, whereas I had come from another plane of living, from the swinging doors of saloons, the railroad yard, the roundhouse, the streetgangs, the river levees, an orphan home; had shifted from town to town and home to home; had mingled with grown-ups more perhaps than was good for me. I had to curb my habit of cursing, but not before I had shocked more than half of them. (Wright 1945a, 116)

Though he found stability and order in his grandmother's house, it came too late to curb his rebellious disposition.

Exacerbating his alienating childhood experiences, the aspect of his early life that turned out to be most consequential for his development as a writer was his experience growing up under the southern racial caste system. Nothing was to preoccupy his mind and shape his sensibility more than the cruel manifestations of white racism, the most bitter legacy of his southern childhood. Wright's first significant contacts with whites occurred in his early teens, after he found a job, which obliged him to move about outside the black community. We see an example of the racial abuses he encountered in an incident he recounted in his book *Black Boy*. While he was employed as a delivery boy in Memphis, he recalled, one day his bicycle broke down while he was on the road. As he walked back, a car filled with young whites pulled alongside of him and they inquired about his problem. Wright told them what had happened. Expressing sympathy, they offered to take him back to town. Wright accepted and stepped on the running board. While under way, Wright recalled:

> They were drinking. I watched the flask pass from mouth to mouth.
> "Wanna drink, boy?" one asked.
> The memory of my six-year-old drinking came back and filled me with caution. But I laughed, the wind whipping my face.
> "Oh, no," I said.
> The words were barely out of my mouth before I felt something hard and cold smash me between the eyes. It was an empty whiskey bottle. I saw stars, and fell backwards from the speeding car into the dust of the road, my feet becoming entangled in the steel spokes of the bicycle. The car stopped and the white men piled out and stood over me. "Nigger, ain't you learned no better sense'n that yet?" asked the man who hit me. "Ain't you learned to say sir to a white man yet?" (Wright 1945a, 199)

After being reprimanded for violating southern racial etiquette, Wright declined to ride further, and walked back to town.

It is impossible to say if this incident as reported by Wright actually happened. What is significant is that such incidents *could* happen in the South. Countless thousands of southern blacks had experienced similar racial abuse, which they usually suffered in silence. Richard Wright internalized these experiences of black victimization, storing these arbitrary and degrading acts in his memory, as his sensitivity to the potential dangers of interactions with whites steadily increased. He later recollected: "I was learning rapidly to watch white people, to observe their every move, every fleeting expression, how to interpret what was said and left unsaid." But it was not until he encountered the Communist Party that he found a perspective through which he believed he could effectively represent those racial abuses. By interpreting black racial oppression from the standpoint of this broader worldview, he would transform the social role of black American literary discourse.

Despite creating this new black literary discourse which drew heavily on his experiences as a lower-class black American, Richard Wright was not simply the product of a ghetto environment. In striking contrast to the lives of the lower-class black characters he constructed in his literary works, his life evidenced progressive upward social mobility. Moving from a world of poverty and provincialism to a world of affluence and cosmopolitan sophistication, Wright—never content to merely acquiesce to racial barriers—persistently transcended the limits of his environment. We see evidence of this tendency early in his life, for example, in his account of his experience of discovering the writings of H. L. Mencken, the social critic and satirist. Wright became aware of Mencken's writings while living in Memphis. Because Mencken was being attacked in a Memphis newspaper, Wright, feeling alienated from Memphis's conservative white culture, figured Mencken must be worth reading. But getting access to Mencken's writings turned out to be difficult; blacks were denied admission to the public library. So to borrow books written by Mencken, Wright forged a note to librarian. "Dear Madam: will you let this nigger boy have some books by H. L. Mencken?" (Wright 1945a, 270). By thus cleverly eluding the racial barriers of the Memphis library, he got to read Mencken's writings, which he found to be refreshing breezes of heresy in the stifling atmosphere of southern white conservatism. It was through reading antinomian writers like Mencken that Wright became aware that another world existed beyond the South, a more enlightened and tolerant world, that offered freedom and opportunity to blacks. This world he yearned to join.

Chicago Years

At the age of nineteen, Richard Wright moved to Chicago, later to be joined by his mother and younger brother, where he was to experience his most significant intellectual development while enduring terrible personal hardships. Arriving in Chicago in 1927, like most poor black migrants who lacked education and skills, Wright began his new life in dire economic straits. With scarcely any resources except his labor, he and his family settled in Chicago's South Side black ghetto, which similar to other city residential areas inhabited by poor migrants, was plagued by varied forms of social disorder and deviance—broken homes, abandoned children, prostitution, alcoholism, teenage gangs, robberies, and homicides—which deeply disturbed Wright. A proud and ambitious young man who detested being poor, Wright never felt at home in Chicago's ghetto. As his friend the writer Nelson Algren, reflecting on Wright's discomfort in Chicago, later recalled, "Richard Wright came to Chicago because there was no other place for him to go. He came as a stranger, lived as a stranger, and he left without looking back. 'Whenever I leave that town I feel as though I had been in a three-day nightmare,' he wrote from Mexico in 1940" (Algren 1961, 85).

In addition to the disorder and deviance of Chicago ghetto life, another major source of Wright's discontents derived from his work experiences, which began with his job as a porter in a Jewish delicatessen, where his reflexive distrust of whites resulted in an embarrassing incident, causing him to quit this first job without notifying his employers. Wright, who was ambitious and confident of his abilities, wanted cleaner work and better pay. Merely a job was not enough. So he signed up for a postal exam but neglected to tell his employer he would be absent. In the eyes of a southern white employer, a black worker who attempted to locate a better job would have been regarded as disloyal. Conditioned by his southern experiences, Wright feared being fired if he told the delicatessen owner the true reason that he needed time off. So he said nothing. When he returned to work he chose to lie, inventing the excuse that his mother had died suddenly in Memphis, to explain his absence. The delicatessen owner refused to believe him, and then went on to emphasize that he and his wife were not southerners. They would have given him time off, the man said, there was no reason to lie. Wright reacted in embarrassed astonishment. "Their attitudes had proved utterly amazing. They were taking out time from their duties to talk to me, and I had never encountered anything like that from whites before. . . . It dawned upon me that they were trying to treat me as an equal, which made it even more impossible for me to ever tell them I had lied, why I had lied" (Wright 1969, 177).

Demoralized by feelings of guilt, he simply left one day without telling them he would not return. Later he located a job as a cook in a Northside restaurant, where he was shocked to discover the Finnish cook spitting in the food. Again he hesitated to respond forthrightly. Fear motivated his silence. As a black he believed his word would have little credibility with a white person, especially if he was accusing another white of wrongdoing. He finally told a young black woman co-worker, and together they brought the matter to the owner's attention.

The pathological behavior he encountered in his lower-class environment caused Wright to feel displaced and alienated. Though the post office finally called him to work, the job lasted only a few months, and once again he found himself unemployed. The impact of the Depression was now widespread. Black unemployment rates soared. Jobs of any kind were scarce. But Wright eventually managed to get another job, through a distant cousin, with a black insurance agency on Chicago's South Side.

This white-collar job satisfied Wright's desire for status, but it too soon began to disturb him, when he discovered that the agents routinely defrauded their poor, illiterate black clients.

The poverty of the Chicago ghetto life encouraged such class predation, which deeply offended Wright's sense of decency and helped to jaundice his attitude toward middle-class blacks. "Each day now I saw how the Negro in Chicago lived, for I visited hundreds of dingy flats filled with rickety furniture and ill-clad children. Most of the policy holders were illiterate and did not know that their policies carried clauses restricting their benefit payments, and, as an insurance agent, it was not my duty to tell them" (Wright 1969, 185).

He recounted the ways in which black agents would exploit black women sexually—as inducements to paying off claims. Wright himself had participated in a swindle, diverting the attention of an illiterate client while a fellow agent switched policies. He later recalled, "It was dirty work and I wondered how I could stop it. And when I could think of no safe way I would curse myself and the victims and forget about it." He was also becoming increasingly cynical about Chicago's racial order as he observed that whites respected the black owners of the insurance companies as leaders of the black community.

Though he acquired extensive knowledge about the people and customs of the Chicago black ghetto, he never became involved in its community life, choosing to remain aloof. He belonged to no clubs or associations; neither, apparently, did he form any supportive or lasting friendships. But even more curious, he felt little respect for black ethnic culture. In contrast to the leading black writers of the 1920s, he largely disregarded black ethnic culture in his literary depictions of black American life. He simply ignored characteristic features of black culture such as music, dance, religious worship, food, humor, and verbal play. And interpersonal relationships, insofar as he depicted them, were fractured, uncaring, and combative encounters, fated, for the most part, to recede into the background of the protagonist's life. As we will see in *Native Son*, black American ghetto life is personified by an angry, distrustful loner, a man who lacks the bonds of family, friends, and religion as well as other black communal supports. That is, a lifestyle that reflected—in many respects— Wright's estranged Chicago existence.

A particularly revealing illustration of Wright's estrangement from intimate social bonds in the Chicago ghetto can be seen in his account of a brief relationship he had with a young black woman, while employed by the insurance company. He candidly admitted that this relationship—like those of the other agents with their female clients—was sexually exploitative. He paid the woman's ten cents insurance premium in exchange for sexual favors. Wright recalled that the woman, who seldom made demands, eventually became irritated by his habit of sitting and reading for long stretches of time. He soon discovered why:

> "Can't you really read?" I asked. "Naw," she giggled. "You know I can't read." "You can read some," I said. "Naw," she said. I stared at her and wondered just what a life like hers meant in the scheme of things, and I came to the conclusion it meant absolutely nothing. And neither did my life mean anything. . . . Sex relations were the only relations she ever had; no others were possible with her, so limited was her intelligence. (Wright 1969, 186)

Experiences such as this helped to shape the images of black ghetto life he projected in *Native Son,* whose protagonist reveals a similarly stunted intellectual development. But how did Wright come to translate those bleak ghetto experiences into a politically radical ideological perspective? To answer this question, we must examine Wright's involvement in the American Communist Party.

THE COMMUNIST INFLUENCES IN THE WHITE AMERICAN LITERARY COMMUNITY

Many white American writers came under the Communist Party's influence after the stock market crash of 1929, because they felt convinced that Marx's theory, and particularly its prediction of capitalism's collapse, was coming to fruition. As Daniel Aaron observed in *Writers on the Left:* "With such writers as Theodore Dreiser, Sherwood Anderson, Waldo Frank, Granville Hicks, Newton Arvin, Malcolm Cowley, Clifton Fadiman, Lionel Trilling, Edmund Wilson, Edwin Seever, and many others swinging leftward, literary radicalism had become a 'mainstream affair'" (Aaron 1961, 207).

The center of this new leftist literary movement was *New Masses,* the party's flagship periodical. In September 1932, Edmund Wilson and fifty-two other artists, belonging to the League of Professional Writers, published an open letter in *New Masses* that "denounced the two major parties as 'hopelessly corrupt,' rejected the Socialists as a do-nothing party, and declared their support for the Communist Party," because it was a party that "sought to defend the dispossessed classes and establish an equitable society" (Aaron 1961, 207). Also in 1932, in another *New Masses* article, the writers Waldo Frank, Clifton Fadiman, Granville Hicks, Sherwood Anderson, Edmund Wilson, and Michael Gold explained why they had joined the party. These and other public testimonials by eminent white literary figures reflected the rising tide of communist ideological influence among American writers (Aaron 1961, 209).

In contrast to its earlier policies, the Communist Party now sought not only to solicit these writers' sympathy for the plight of the working class, but to involve them directly in the revolutionary struggle, as can be seen in the no-nonsense guidelines for "proletarian realism" set forth in 1930 by Mike Gold, the hard-line editor of *New Masses:*

1. Workers, because they are skilled technicians, must write with the technical proficiency of a Hemingway, but not for the purpose of engendering cheap and purposeless thrills.
2. Proletarian realism deals with the real conflicts of men and women. It spurns the sickly, sentimental subtleties of Bohemians, best illustrated by "the spectacle of Proust, master-masturbator of bourgeois literature." The suffering of the hungry, persecuted and heroic millions precludes the inventing of "precious silly little agonies."
3. Proletarian realism is functional; it serves a purpose. "Every poem every novel and drama, must have a social theme, or it is merely confectionery."
4. It eschews verbal acrobatics; "this is only another form for bourgeois idleness."
5. Proletarians should write about what they know best. "Let the bourgeois writers tell us about their spiritual drunkards and super refined Parisian émigrés . . . that is their world; we must write about our own mud puddle."
6. "Swift action, clear form, the direct line, cinema in words; this seems to be one of the principles of proletarian realism."
7. "Away with drabness, the bourgeois notion that the Worker's life is sordid, the slummer's disgust and feeling of futility. There is horror and drabness in the Worker's life; and we will portray it; but we know this is not the last word; we know that the manure heap is the hope of the future; we know that not pessimism, but revolutionary élan will sweep this mess out of the world forever."
8. "Away with all lies about human nature. We are scientists; we know what a man thinks and feels. Everyone is a mixture of motives; we do not have to lie about our hero in order to win our case."
9. "No straining or melodrama or other affects; life itself is the supreme melodrama. Feel this intensely, and everything becomes poetry—the new poetry of materials, of the so-called common man, the Worker molding his real world." (Aaron 1961, 225–26)

Gold's brass-knuckles approach to literature derived from the Soviet doctrine of socialist realism, which suggested that literature, as well as other areas of human endeavor, must be subordinated to the ultimate political objective of socialist revolution. Following this totalitarian view of literature, fostered by the Stalin regime, the American Communist Party set out to mobilize American writers. But "not all of the writers with revolutionary inclinations were good enough to be published in the *New Masses,* . . . (So) as part of the magazine's program to develop promising artists of the proletariat, it founded the John Reed Club of New York shortly after the stock market crash of 1929" (Aaron 1961, 230). This turned out to be a fortunate development for Richard Wright.

Founded in 1932, the John Reed Club expanded to thirty chapters by 1934. Dispersed throughout the United States, in such places as—New York City (*Partisan Review*); Moberly, Missouri (*The Anvil*); Boston (*Leftward*); Grand Rapids, Michigan (*Cauldron*); Hollywood (*Partisan*); Philadelphia (*Left Review*); Detroit (*New Force*); and Hartford, Connecticut (*The Hammer*), the chapters produced their own literary periodicals, which provided unique opportunities for young writers to hone their writing skills and launch their literary careers. In addition to publishing leftist literary writings, the John Reed chapters, during the crisis years of the Depression, engaged in various other political activities: composing leaflets, improvising skits for mass rallies, writing group chants against capitalism, and lecturing on art and propaganda, poetry and revolution, intellectuals and the crisis. But more important than these political initiatives, each chapter "provided a place where sensitive and socially declasse would-be writers were sympathetically received and warmly encouraged" (Aaron 1961, 230). In effect, these clubs constituted training grounds for aspiring young leftist writers. Among those responding to the opportunities for literary training, there was a small group of socially alienated black Americans, who would in several years drastically alter the dominant ideological direction of black American literary discourse.

THE COMMUNIST PARTY'S INTEREST IN BLACK WRITERS

As a fledging enterprise struggling to gain a foothold in American society, the Communist Party sought to recruit blacks for reasons that were both strategic and ideological. Blacks, being the most oppressed group in American society, symbolized American capitalism's most glaring failures. And in this the party saw an especially attractive opportunity.

So in 1930, shortly after the Depression began, serious Communist Party initiatives toward black writers began. At the Kharhov conference in the Soviet Union, American communists were encouraged to use the John Reed Club to develop cultural activities among "the Negro masses." Actually, this was not the first time the party had exhibited interests in black writers. In the 1920s, several years prior to the Depression, both Langston Hughes and Claude McKay had traveled to the Soviet Union, where they were honored and feted as representatives of the black American masses. But no new efforts to reach blacks resulted from those contacts. Even though the Soviet Communists had long believed that black Americans, because of their unique experiences of racial and economic injustices in the United States, were ideally suited to operate as a revolutionary force, they did not develop a concrete strategy for recruiting black intellectuals until the crisis years of the Depression.

Hughes was the first black American writer to become involved in the leftist political movement. He was among the delegates at a 1932 national meeting of the John Reed clubs, which was called because the party believed the clubs had become too literary, and lacked sufficient involvement in the political struggle. Hughes was elected, along with John Dos Passos and Maxim Gorky, as an honorary member of the conferences' presidium, an honor apparently bestowed primarily because they wanted to symbolize the party's commitment to interracial solidarity. Hughes was the only major black writer then associated with the party.

RICHARD WRIGHT'S INVOLVEMENT WITH THE COMMUNIST PARTY

Richard Wright's first contacts with the party occurred in 1932, while he was working for the U.S. Post Office in Chicago. Wright recalled, "One Thursday I received an invitation from a group of white boys I had known when I was working in the post office to meet in one of Chicago's South Side hotels and argue the state of the world" (Wright 1952, 103). Though he said nothing about why he was attracted to those associations, it is possible to infer their importance from statements he later made about this period of his life. He existed in isolation and loneliness, and had no intellectual companions prior to his association with white leftists. As noted earlier, he detested living in the South Side ghetto. Except for his family, he had no significant social relationships up to that Thursday evening in 1932, when he and a small group of his fellow postal workers gathered to drink beer and talk. Wright learned during the conversation that some in the group belonged to the Communist Party, a fact that surprised him. He had felt repelled by the Communists he had observed in the South Side black ghetto. Nevertheless, he continued to attend the Thursday night gatherings. It was at one of these subsequent meetings that one fellow in the group announced that he had gotten a short story published in *Anvil*, a John Reed Club publication, and then went on to recount how he had joined the John Reed Club. Knowing of Wright's interest in writing, he invited him to join the club, but Wright responded with skepticism. "I felt that communists could not possibly have a sincere interest in Negroes. I was cynical and I would rather have had a white man say that he hated Negroes, which I could have readily believed, than to have heard them say that they respected Negroes, which would have made me doubt him" (Wright 1952, 104).

This statement, which was written after Wright renounced his party membership, was undoubtedly exaggerated. For despite his initial misgivings about Communists, whom he viewed as political fanatics who engaged in agitation and bizarre street demonstrations, he joined the Chicago John Reed Club. His reservations about Communists dissolved when he was told that the club would assist him in getting published. As an ambitious, proud young black man who detested his ghetto existence, Richard Wright wanted very much to find an alternative to his current way of life.

Little did anyone then realize it but the evening Wright attended his first club meeting in a run-down building in Chicago's Loop marked a momentous turning point in the history of black American literature. As Wright discovered a supportive intellectual network in the leftist John Reed Club, the seeds of the first dominant, politically radical black literary school began to be sown. "I was meeting men and women whom I would know for decades to come, who were to form the first sustained relationships in my life," Wright later recalled. In fact, he was surprised to learn that other members of the club were educated middle-class whites. Mindful of his own humble social background—having migrated from the South only five years ago—he noted, "I had once worked as a servant for people like this and I was skeptical." Though he was reluctant to admit it, he was also impressed, as is evident from his description of his new associates' social backgrounds. Noting that one was a school teacher, another an advertising writer, another a social worker, and another the wife of a well-known university professor, he seemed dazzled by their social status, as he recalled being introduced to "a Jewish boy who was to become one of the nation's leading painters, to a chap who was to become one of the eminent composers of his day, to a writer who was to create some of the best novels of his generation, to a young Jewish boy who was destined to film the Nazi occupation of Czechoslovakia" (Wright 1952, 105).

It is important to recognize that Richard Wright, along with other aspiring black literary artists of the era, viewed writing as not simply a means of personal expression, but also as an avenue of escape from his ghetto existence.

Wright thus found in this white leftist network a social world where he felt he belonged, a social world that respected his intelligence, a social world that was interested in what he had to say, a social world that supported his literary ambitions, and—above all—a social world that gave him a new and compelling vision of reality. Returning home later that night after that first meeting, Wright recalled, he was so moved by the new sense of possibility awakened by the Marxist worldview that he experienced an epiphany, the sudden birth of a new identity, that left him too excited to sleep. His mind swirling in the euphoria of erupting possibilities, he got up from his bed, and scribbled a poem. "Feeling for the first time that I could speak to listening ears, I wrote a wild, crude poem in free verse, coining images of black hands playing, working, holding bayonets, stiffening finally in death. I felt in a clumsy way it linked white life with black, merged two streams of common experience" (Wright 1952, 106).

This last sentence should be underscored, for in its allusion to interracial solidarity, it expressed the critically important subtext of Wright's subsequent intellectual orientation: a belief in racial integration. This belief, though covert, became a key supposition in the naturalistic protest school's ideological perspective, encouraging black writers to regard white leftist intellectual culture as the model for a new, and just, interracial society. Equally important, it also encouraged them to turn away from black American ethnic culture. Though the party's commitment to racial unity later would be questioned, it figured importantly—during these early years—in transforming Richard Wright's identity and in creating the integrationist suppositions that lay behind the naturalistic protest school's ideological perspective on black American life.

Almost immediately after Wright joined the John Reed Club, his writings began to be published. *Left Front* brought out two of his poems, which Wright later characterized as crude. Although he suspected *Left Front*'s editor was patronizing him by sending the poems to the more prestigious *Anvil* and *New Masses*, he consented when the editor told him those publications needed "Negro stuff." Recognizing the feeble state of Communist influence in the black community, party leaders encouraged the John Reed Clubs to pursue cultural contact with the black masses. The fact that the party assigned Wright to this role of putative spokesman of lower-class blacks was actually ironic, for Wright existed as an outsider in the black ghetto. As noted earlier, he had no involvement with groups or organizations within the black community. Though he had worked with lower-class blacks, he had developed no close bonds with them nor respect for their way of life. His characteristic aloofness from black community life was revealed clearly in his descriptions of the lower-class black youths he observed while working at a South Side boys club. In his words, they were

> a wild and homeless lot, culturally lost, spiritually disinherited, candidates for the clinics, morgues, prisons, reformatories, and electric chair of the state's death house. For hours I listened to their talk of planes, women, guns, politics, and crime. Their figures of speech were as forceful as any used by English speaking people. I kept paper and pencil in my pocket to jot down their word rhythms and reactions. (Wright 1952, 121)

These hardly seem to be the words of a man writing about his own social environment; rather they seem like the clinical observations of an ethnographer or social worker. In setting forth such observations about blacks in the Chicago ghetto, Wright was following the impersonal techniques of the great American naturalists, Theodore Dreiser and Frank

Norris, who painstakingly recorded factual details of the environments they depicted in their fiction. But this emotionally detached technique violated the ideological mandate of socialist realism, which aimed to produce a literature *of*—not just *about*—the masses, by insisting that the writer become involved in their political struggles. As Mike Gold had put it: "Proletarian realism deals with the real conflicts of men and women." That was the only basis, argued the socialist realists, from which working-class life could be authentically depicted. Proponents of socialist realism scorned literary professionalism because they believed it encouraged writers to see themselves as a special intellectual caste. Yet this was precisely what Wright and others of his John Reed cohorts aspired to become—professional middle-class writers.

Middle-class literary professionalism, in the view of the socialist realists, undermined the political objectives of the John Reed clubs, namely, to nurture writers who emulated the revolutionary commitment of John Reed, a Harvard-educated radical who rode with Pancho Villa in Mexico, fought in the Russian Revolution, and subsequently wrote books inspired by those experiences of political struggle.

Wright's conception of his role as a writer departed from the John Reed model, and soon led to tensions with party officials, who believed that he and the other club writers were not sufficiently involved in revolutionary activity. To alter that situation, party officials introduced reforms in the Chicago Club, which obliged Wright to become more involved in Communist political activity in the black community. This marked the beginning of Wright's problems in the party.

The problems began when he was assigned to work with black Communists in the South Side ghetto. This was Wright's first contact with black Communists who, unlike the North Side white leftist writers he had associated with, were street organizers, men accustomed to haranguing crowds and confronting police. They distrusted Wright almost immediately. After attending his first cell meeting, Wright recalled, he became an object of scrutiny. "During the following days I learned through discreet questioning that I seemed a fantastic element to the black communists. I was shocked to hear that I, who had been only to grammar school, had been classified as an intellectual" (Wright 1952, 113).

Wright's expression of surprise here was disingenuous; he certainly viewed himself as an intellectual. Though he lacked a university education, he was committed to a middle-class intellectual lifestyle, which he exhibited in his appearance and manner of speaking. "I learned to my dismay, that the black communists in my unit commented upon my shined shoes, clean shirt, and the tie I had worn, above all my manner of speech seemed an alien thing to them." Here we have an example of an assimilated black intellectual encountering hostility from ethnic blacks. "He talks like a book," Wright recalled one of the black Communists saying, "and that was enough to condemn me forever as a bourgeoisie" (Wright 1952, 114).

Wright's difficulties with the black Communists reflected a paradox underlying his party involvement. He had gravitated to the white leftist social network, in part because he felt estranged from his black ghetto community. But the party saw him as a representative of the black community. Wright realized this was a mistake, but attempted to make the best of an awkward situation. In truth, he felt more comfortable in the company of white leftist intellectuals than black leftist street organizers. He was temperamentally unsuited to working as a ghetto street organizer. The black Communists perceived his aloofness as arrogance, which was why they criticized his clothing and manner of speech and berated his character. Referring to him by such epithets as "bastard intellectual," "bourgeois degenerate," and "incipient Trotskyite," they aimed to make clear to him that intellectuals did not fit in the party. Wright, in self-defense, explained that he lacked time to engage in organizing activity, because he was writing a novel and working a full-time job. But his explanation fell on deaf ears; his party supervisor warned him that he would have "to deal with the masses."

Wright's Role as a *New Masses* Writer

Wright's ambivalent role did not prevent him from emerging as the party's leading black literary spokesman. By mid-1935, his works began to appear in the prestigious *New Masses*, the party's flagship publication, which featured some of the nation's most acclaimed white writers. Though he was unknown when he began publishing in *New Masses*—his previous writings having been published only in the club's little magazines—Wright's reputation in leftist political circles soon grew as his writings gained wider exposure.

Prompted by a blend of naive idealism and practical concerns, the party created this role of black literary spokesman, which Richard Wright gladly performed. The party leaders assumed that Wright's racial identity and Marxist perspective qualified him to operate as the black community's spokesman, an assumption they never made when dealing with white ethnic writers of Jewish, Italian, or Irish ancestry. Michael Gold was not defined as a spokesman for the Jewish American community; nor John Dos Passos for the Portuguese American community; nor James T. Farrell for the Irish American community. Those white ethnic communities were perceived as diverse and complex; whereas the black community, at least to most white Americans, was perceived as a monolith. This was primarily because the racial caste system had forged much greater social distance between the white and black American social worlds, social distance that fostered racial parochialism in both racial groups. Marxism hardly immunized white Communists from this racial parochialism. Hence their tendency to view black writers as emissaries. This was the role Wright was expected to perform.

No significant alternative literary/ideological perspectives on black American life prevailed in the public arena after the demise of the primitivist movement; there were no established black writers with national reputations. In fairness to Wright, it should be said that he sincerely embraced the role of black spokesman, even though he felt alienated from the black community; he wanted to help alleviate the black community's racial oppression. This he thought he could achieve as a writer. However, as we will see, his depictions of black American life led some to question the authenticity of his perspective.

We encounter one example of this problem of authenticity in the first important article he wrote for *New Masses*, "Joe Louis Uncovers Dynamite," which appeared in October 1935. Wright described a brief riot on the South Side that occurred after Joe Louis defeated the German boxer Max Baer in a heavyweight championship fight. Framing the riot from a Marxian perspective, Wright informed his *New Masses* audience that the riot revealed the black community's solidarity, and that this solidarity was a political force, a black dynamo, waiting to be harnessed to revolutionary ends. This no doubt expressed a message that both the editors and the readers of *New Masses* wanted to hear. Such upbeat articles about the downtrodden, which occupied much space in leftist publications, were tonic for revolutionary morale. "Two hours after the fight the area between South Parkway and Prairie Avenue on 47th Street was jammed with no less than twenty-five thousand Negroes, joy-mad and moving to they didn't know where" (Wright 1935, 18).

Wright went on to describe how the celebration got out of control, as the crowd became unruly, and the fear this aroused in whites until order was restored by a stern, but cautious, group of black policemen. Ending the article with a flourish of optimism, Wright declared:

> Say, comrade, here's the wild river that's got to be harnessed and directed. Here's that *something*, that pent-up folk consciousness. Here's a fleeting glimpse of the heart of the Negro, the heart that beats and suffers and hopes—for freedom. Here's that fluid something that's like iron. Here's the dynamite that Joe Louis uncovered. (Wright 1935, 18)

Although intellectually shallow and hardly reflective of political consciousness in the black community, such materials from black writers were welcomed by leftist publications. But significantly, in the case of this particular article, the *New Masses* editors added a cautionary comment.

The revolutionary potential Wright described, they warned, must be channeled into solidarity with white workers. Yet they, like Wright, simply misread the sentiments behind that street demonstration—the black community's latent racial nationalism. That was the actual force Louis's victory had stirred.

Wright's Experience with the Federal Writer's Project

Wright's party associations soon yielded major dividends for both his mastery of the craft of writing and his occupational mobility. His *New Masses* publications made him eligible for a job with the Federal Writer's Project (FWP). He "loved that assignment," according to Mary Wirth, the Chicago social worker who had befriended and helped him get that job (Washington 1971). His first job as a writer, this position with the Federal Writer's Project transformed his social status. Never again would he be employed as a menial laborer. Never again would he be obliged to work alongside lower-class blacks and whites. Never again would he have to pretend that he was an intellectual. This assignment with the FWP gave a major boost to his literary career as it led to the publication of his first book, a collection of short stories, published under the title *Uncle Tom's Children* (Wright 1938).

The Cause of Wright's Problems with the Party

We will probably never know the complete story pertaining to Wright's problems with the Communist Party in Chicago, because the other participants in the dispute left no published version of their side, and Wright's version, though set forth in a long essay, left open many questions of fact. Nevertheless, we can reconstruct enough of the dispute to discern the party's enormous importance in Wright's life, and particularly its influence on the ideological perspective of his fiction.

While he was affiliated with the South Side unit, Wright became interested in writing the life history of a fellow black party member—an uneducated black man from the South named Ross, who was a street organizer. Ross, who had become a political radical after migrating north, was a man who seemed to Wright to exemplify a revolutionary black proletarian. Ironically, he represented what the party had mistakenly assumed Richard Wright to be—a black political radical rooted in black ethnic culture. As we observed earlier in Gosnell's profile of black communists on Chicago's South Side, most failed to fit the Marxian conception of proletarians. But Ross was an exception. Having grown up on a southern plantation, migrated to the North, joined the party, and become a street organizer, he seemed to be a paragon of the Marxist black revolutionary worker.

Like other blacks who had grown up on plantations in the deep South, Ross had accumulated many memories of economic hardships and racial brutality. Although Richard Wright also had been born on a plantation, he had never lived as a southern black peasant. But he recognized that stories of southern black plantation life had enormous power because they evoked the worst horrors of white racial oppression. Hence his interests in acquiring information about those experiences for his literary work.

But he soon encountered obstacles. The black Communists distrusted his intentions. Because Ross had been arrested several weeks earlier in a fracas with the police and was scheduled to appear in court, the black Communists feared that Wright might be gathering material for the police. That, at least, was what Wright was told when they ordered him to stop interviewing Ross. By now Wright's standing in the party was precarious, and he had been warned by party members that he was being watched. Shortly after his aborted effort to interview Ross, he was summoned by the party leaders to a meeting where Ross—now fallen from favor—was being tried by his party unit. Wright watched as the unit leaders subjected Ross to merciless personal attacks. Though Wright found the spectacle repulsive, he did not withdraw from the party. He merely remained in limbo, ostracized by the Chicago party members but still functioning as a Communist writer.

Because the party had been the center of his life, Wright felt lonely during this period of isolation and tried to re-establish contact with party members—despite the hostility he had encountered. He decided to attend the Chicago May Day Parade, a major annual leftist celebration of working-class unity. As the parade passed along the street, Wright, who was standing among spectators on the sidewalk, was recognized by a friend in the parade and beckoned to join the procession. But when he stepped into the parade, he was physically attacked by several white party members, and thrown out of the line. This was one of the most humiliating and painful experiences of his life. As he later recalled, that incident had a significant impact in changing his political outlook: "I knew in my heart that I should never be able to write that way again, should never be able to feel with that simple sharpness of life, should never again express such passionate hope, should never again make so total a commitment of faith" (Wright 1952, 145).

Actually this describes Richard Wright's feelings about the party in 1944, when he wrote those words, some seven or so years *after* the parade incident. That incident had to have happened before 1937, because that was the year he left Chicago. Wright actually remained in the party until 1944, which was after he had moved to New York and achieved literary celebrity. The above denouncement, though expressing Wright's retrospective view of his party affiliation, also revealed his deep commitment to the party's ideological perspective in the late 1930s and early 1940s, the period when he initiated the naturalistic protest school. This was without question his most creative period, when his writings evidenced "that simple sharpness of life," "that passionate hope," and "that commitment of faith" that projected black American experiences through a Marxist ideological perspective.

It was while he lived in New York, affiliated with the more intellectually oriented New York section of the party, that Wright at last achieved recognition and acclaim as the nation's leading black writer. But before focusing on that development, we must consider his influence on other black writers.

Wright's Association with Black Writers

During this period of his party involvement, Wright also had contacts with black writers. Arna Bontemps and Langston Hughes were apparently the first of these. Bontemps, who moved from California to Chicago in 1934, was asked by Hughes to find out who were the new black writers after the breakup of the Harlem school. Hughes, just returned from a year in the Soviet Union, was then resting at the home of a wealthy friend in Carmel, California. Following up on Hughes's suggestion, Bontemps circulated among Chicago black circles making contacts with various black writers, but he failed to encounter Richard Wright. Wright's only literary associates at the time were white writers in the John Reed Club. No serious effort to locate Wright was made until Hughes visited Chicago. Having been impressed by Wright's *New Masses* article, Hughes told Bontemps that they should try to locate the young writer. After failing to find his name in the Chicago telephone directory, they finally succeeded in meeting Wright at a party. Wright—Bontemps recalled—was then a "flaming young communist," who talked mostly about politics and writing, and could not dance (Hill et al. 1966, 199). Neither Bontemps nor Hughes developed a close relationship with Wright at that time, as his social network remained centered on the John Reed Club.

The first black writer with whom Wright developed a close personal relationship was Margaret Walker, a fellow Mississippian he met in February 1936, when he was covering the first conference of the Negro National Congress for *New Masses* (Walker 1971). Walker attended the conference because she hoped to see Langston Hughes, who had become something of a literary mentor to young black writers. Walker was one of Hughes's proteges. She had met him when she was a child. Hughes, who was traveling through the South on a lecture tour, had recognized Walker's considerable literary potential, and urged her parents to send her to the North when she was ready to attend college. Walker's parents heeded

Hughes's advice, and she was now living with relatives in Chicago and studying at Northwestern University. It was during this period that Hughes visited the city to attend the Negro National Conference and introduced her to a number of writers, including Arna Bontemps, Nelson Algren, Frank Yerby, Willard Motley, and Richard Wright.

Soon after that meeting, Walker and Wright developed a close friendship—which was to last three years. A major attraction behind that friendship, in addition to their mutual interests in writing, was their shared background as black Mississippians. Largely because of Wright, Walker decided to stay in Chicago after she graduated from college in 1936. With Wright's assistance—he was then a supervisor on the Federal Writers Project—she got a job with the project as a junior writer.

Margaret Walker recalled being ignorant about Communism at the time they met (Walker 1971). Only gradually did its meaning—along with the realization that Richard Wright was a Communist—sink in. An English major in college, Walker had little knowledge of political ideas, but remembered Wright as being intensely political. During the course of their relationship, he urged her to read such politically oriented books as John Reed's *Ten Days that Shook the World,* Marx's *Das Kapital,* the works of Maxim Gorky, and Adam Smith's *Wealth of Nations.* Walker recalled that she was determined not to be left behind, and stayed up late into the night reading. Beyond these political books, she and Wright explored and discussed a wide range of literary and intellectual interests—T. S. Eliot, Andre Gide, James Farrell (whose *Studs Lonigan* she read at Wright's request), John Dos Passos, Fyodor Dostoyevsky, Thomas Mann, D. H. Lawrence, and Marcel Proust, as well as the works of such controversial thinkers as Freud, Jung, Nietzche, and Schopenhauer.

She recalled that Wright found Joseph Conrad's works especially appealing; but he also read avidly more popular works, such as those of Poe, London, and Doyle, as well as pulp fiction and detective stories, which nurtured his penchant for suspense. Though Wright tried to explain dialectical materialism to her, Walker recalled that she never understood that doctrine. It is unclear how much of Marxism's intricate theoretical arguments Wright himself actually understood, for his writings resonated its ethical and political themes, its more prosaic discussions of injustices, that highlighted capitalism's dehumanizing exploitation of workers.

While Richard Wright boosted Margaret Walker's political education, she edited and improved his prose. Throughout the period when Wright produced his most creative naturalistic protest works, which included *Lawd Today, Uncle Tom's Children,* and *Native Son,* Walker proofread his manuscripts and corrected his poor grammar, a deficiency that derived from his limited formal education.

During this latter phase of his Chicago years as his relationship to party members frayed, Wright increased his contacts with black writers, which was most strongly evidenced in his effort to steer black writers toward Marxian ideological orientation. This effort can be seen in his brief tenure as associate editor of the black literary magazine *New Challenge* (Bone 1958, 116–17).

Under the editorship of Dorothy West, *New Challenge*[1] had been started in 1934 with the initial objective of continuing the orientation of the 1920s ethnic school. It made a good start as Langston Hughes, Arna Bontemps, and Zora Neale Hurston, as well as several younger black writers—Owen Dodson, Frank Yerby, and William Attaway—were drawn into its circle of affiliated writers.

Despite that hopeful beginning, the magazine's efforts to revive the apolitical 1920s literary movement came to naught. The social forces that fostered the 1920s climate of cultural rebellion and ethnic celebrations had dissipated. Commenting on this situation, Robert Bone, in *The Negro Novel*, cites an incident which revealed the magazine's initial anti-leftist stance. A reader wrote West asking why the publication was so "pale pink," to which West replied, "Because the 'red' articles we receive were not literature." But, as Bone suggests, something must have happened to West's anti-leftist views between 1934 and 1937, because when Richard Wright signed on as associate editor in 1937, the magazine manifested a leftist perspective (Bone 1958, 116–17).

Though Wright had not yet published a book, he was well known in leftist circles because of his *New Masses* articles. By taking over the *New Challenge* editorial job in 1937 he was asserting a clear bid for leadership among black writers, marking the beginning of the naturalistic protest school (Fabre 1973). "Blueprint for Negro Writing," the Marxist manifesto Wright set forth in the magazine, sought to galvanize a new radical political consciousness for black American literature. Because this manifesto articulated the principles that defined the naturalistic protest ideology, I must quote its statement at length.

In the lives of Negro writers must be found those materials and experiences which will create a meaningful picture of the world today. Many young writers have grown to believe that a Marxist analysis of society presents such a picture. It creates a picture, which, when placed before the eyes of the writers, should unify his personality, organize his emotions, buttress him with tense and obdurate will to change the world. And in turn, this changed world will dialectically change the writer. Hence, it is through a Marxist conception of reality and society that the maximum degree of freedom in thought and feeling can be gained for the Negro writer. Further, this dramatic Marxist vision, when consciously grasped, endows the writer with a sense of dignity which no other vision can give. Ultimately, it restores to the writer his lost heritage, that is, his role as creator of the world in which he lives, and as creator of himself. (Wright 1978, 44)

In contrast to the view of the primitivist literary school of the 1920s, Wright's conception of the black writer's "lost heritage" referred not to African culture, but rather to the working class's expropriated creative power. In fact at no point in his naturalistic protest writings about black American life would Wright suggest any link between black America and Africa. Departing from the exotic, racialist depictions of black American life that characterized the 1920s literary school, Wright aimed to universalize black American experiences, to transcend racial boundaries, by depicting blacks as part of a larger human (i.e., class) struggle for social justice. It was in this spirit that he implored his fellow black writers to create literary works with a social purpose, literary works committed to liberating the masses from social oppression, informed by the ideological perspective of Marxism.

It is impossible to exaggerate that manifesto's importance. For through its vision and his editorial control of *New Challenge* magazine, Wright now functioned as a conduit through which a white leftist ideology was being transmitted into the black American literary community. Not surprisingly, Wright soon encountered resistance. The magazine's financial sponsors were upset by its new leftist turn, and forced him to resign his editorial position.

If the "Blueprint" planted the seeds of a new radical black literary perspective, those seeds did not take root and blossom until the publication of *Native Son*, the paradigmatic literary work that inspired other black writers to follow Wright's lead. We will discuss that novel momentarily.

Wright moved from Chicago to New York shortly after publishing "Blueprint." This decision was heavily influenced by his worsening relations with party members in Chicago. In New York, he would continue to be affiliated with the party as he became Harlem editor of the *Daily Worker*, the party's newspaper. His departure from Chicago marked a key turning point in his life because it ended not only the apprenticeship phase of his literary career; but also his association with Chicago's South Side black ghetto, the environment where he had undergone his most critical formative experiences. Never again would he experience such a complex, and disturbing, relationship to a black community. Never again would he live in a lower-class slum. And never again would he observe so intimately the lives of poor black rural migrants struggling to adapt to city life. What lay ahead was a professional career, celebrity, and literary acclaim.

Margaret Walker recalled the Friday afternoon on 28 May 1937, when Wright departed Chicago. It was pay day, and she remembered particularly the young white girls in the office "crowding around" to kiss Wright goodbye. He had only forty dollars, but he had found a ride with someone who was driving to New York. Ironically that same day he received a return to work notice from the post office. He tore up the notice. More than once, recalled Walker, Wright had said, "I want my life to count for something" (Walker 1971). His dream was soon to come true, as yet again he hurdled the obstacles of his environment.

RICHARD WRIGHT'S NEW YORK YEARS AND LITERARY FAME

Richard Wright's stay in New York was to be the most productive and successful period of his literary career. He continued writing under the more powerful New York branch of the party. More intellectually oriented than their Chicago counterparts, the New York party members, who had a greater appreciation of Wright's literary talent and potential influence, apparently had intervened in the Chicago dispute, and rescued him from ostracism.

Though Wright now worked in Harlem as the *Daily Worker* editor, his Chicago experiences had molded permanently his images of black ghetto life. Harlem did not figure in his naturalistic protest writings.

After arriving in New York, he found a new protégé in Ralph Ellison, a young black writer from Oklahoma by way of Tuskegee Institute, who replaced Margaret Walker as his closest black literary associate. Ellison had met Alain Locke who, in turn, introduced him to Langston Hughes. It was through Hughes, the relentless booster of black literary community, that Ellison met Richard Wright. Ellison recalled that he became interested in Wright while studying at Tuskegee, when he had read his poem *I've Seen Black Hands* in *New Masses*. Ellison had asked about Wright when he met Hughes in New York, and shortly afterward, to his surprise, he received a postcard from Wright informing him that Wright soon would be in New York. They met the day after Wright's arrival in the summer of 1937. This event, recalled Ellison, marked the beginning of a friendship that changed his life (Ellison 1971).

Wright allowed Ellison to read the manuscript of his soon to be published collection of southern short stories, *Uncle Tom's Children*, and almost immediately, Ellison remembered being fascinated by the stories and realizing that Wright possessed an exceptional talent. Although Ellison had come to New York as an aspiring musician hoping to earn some money and return to Tuskegee to finish his bachelor's degree, he soon changed his plans and decided to remain in New York, largely as a result of meeting Wright.

His life took a new direction. With Wright's help he embarked on his literary apprenticeship, beginning with a book review Wright assigned him to write and followed by a short story recounting Ellison's experiences riding freight trains in the South which Wright published in the second issue of *New Challenge* under the title "Heine's Bull."

Ellison initially lacked radical political consciousness. Though he had read some writings by Karl Marx at Tuskegee, it was not until he met Wright that he gravitated toward Marxist ideology. By 1940, he was writing articles for *New Masses*.

Meanwhile, Wright's difficulties continued. Though the New York party leaders had supported him in his dispute with the Chicago Communists, his position in the party remained precarious. He was also experiencing frustrations from both being shunned by the leading black literary magazine and having failed to make his mark as a major writer.

The publication of his first book, *Uncle Tom's Children* (Wright 1938), however, soon reversed his literary fortunes. Widely acclaimed within the liberal white literary community, the book was selected by "Lewis Gannett, Harry Scherman, and Sinclair Lewis for the $500 first prize in a contest sponsored by *Story* magazine. It was also commended as the best fiction of Southern Negro life by a colored author since Jean Toomer's *Cane* (1923), and designated, uniquely for a publication by a black writer, as "a work worthy to rank with the regional realism of T. S. Stirbling, William Faulkner, and Erskine Caldwell" (Gloster 1948, 222).

But *Uncle Tom's Children* was just the beginning of Wright's literary ascent. He was about to embark on a larger, and potentially more consequential, literary project connected to Chicago. After leaving Chicago, he continued his contact with Margaret Walker via letters. These letters, which at first consisted of short and casual notes, suddenly became longer and more serious during June 1938, when he sent her two airmail specials, seeking information about a Chicago murder case. His curiosity was aroused by a young black man named Nixon who had apparently confessed to committing five homicides. So he asked Margaret Walker to collect and mail to him all the newspaper clippings on the story she could find, and she diligently complied. The Nixon story dominated Chicago's major newspapers' headlines. With the conservative *Chicago Tribune* leading the way in presenting sensational accounts of the crimes, the trial was soon surrounded by an volatile racial climate. Noting this, Wright immediately perceived the Nixon case's rich literary potential as he informed Margaret Walker that he was using the material to write a novel.

In search of more material for his novel, he returned to Chicago in the fall of 1938 where, with Margaret Walker's assistance, he acquired a copy of the brief written by Nixon's first lawyer, which he later found very useful. He also checked out books from the Chicago Public Library on Leopold and Loeb (the two wealthy white Chicago youths who had murdered a boy) and on Clarence Darrow, the famous trial attorney. Wright would depict a defense attorney, whose arguments were modeled on Darrow's famous courtroom techniques. But Wright aimed to augment these background factual materials by inventing dramatic gestures that departed from the Nixon case. For example, though Nixon was soon arrested and incarcerated in Cook County Jail, Wright informed Walker that he would have his character escape by running across rooftops. "I like to shock people," he told her (Walker 1971).

The novel that resulted from Wright's prodigious efforts was *Native Son*. Published in 1940 in the bleak American social climate of the Depression, that novel transformed black American literary discourse. Instantly ascending to the national best-seller list, it was selected by the Book of the Month Club, and went on to achieve, what was for a black American literary work, unprecedented notoriety. Protesting white racial oppression by highlighting its brutalizing effects on black American personality, *Native Son* created black American literature's new public role as a vehicle of radical political ideology. Though some earlier black American literary works had protested American racial injustices, none achieved *Native Son*'s huge impact, nor, even more important, did any generate a literary school, which became the dominant ideological force in black American literature. *Native Son* thus marked a watershed in American culture.

Native Son was also destined to become one of the most controversial novels ever published in the United States. Depicting the life of a poor black ghetto youth who committed a brutal, racially motivated murder, that novel rocked the landscape of American race relations like an erupting volcano. Selling a quarter of a million copies within only a month of its publication, it provoked an avalanche of shocked, puzzled, enraged reactions as it shook not only mainstream America but also the leftist political community. *New Masses*, in response to the enormous response provoked by the novel, made the unprecedented decision to publish a series of reviews of the novel, which we will examine momentarily, when we discuss the ideological reactions to the naturalistic protest school's images of black American life.

Aside from its impact on both the larger culture and black American literary discourse, *Native Son* transformed Richard Wright's life. With his success as a novelist he experienced a rapid ascent in his social status, ending his years of hardship and uncertainty. He was now moving in cosmopolitan circles. Shortly after the publication of *Native Son*, he married an emigrant Russian dancer in New York, with Ralph Ellison serving as his best man, and then moved to Mexico where he planned to live permanently. But the marriage soon failed and Wright returned to New York, where he soon married again. His second wife, also white, was a relatively unknown leftist political activist of Jewish ancestry, who had grown up in Brooklyn, and participated in the New York John Reed Club. This marriage was to last as Wright would later become the father of two daughters.

Wright's Denouncement of the Communist Party

In 1944 Wright, now the nation's leading black writer, made perhaps the most difficult decision of his life: he publicly declared his break with the American Communist Party. His denouncement, which was published in the August 1944 issue of *Atlantic Monthly* under the title, "I Tried to be a Communist" (Wright 1950), marked the end of a twelve-year association, an association in which he had been changed from an anonymous and destitute black ghetto youth into an internationally renowned writer. Many factors lay behind that decision. First, there was the wave of defections from the party by many prominent white American intellectuals, which fostered an expanding intellectual climate of political disillusionment. Second, there was Wright's new celebrity status, which gave him independence. He no longer needed the party's social network and publications to advance his literary career. Third, there was his pique resulting from the attacks some party members had directed at *Native Son*, which they characterized as a flawed, defeatist book that distorted black working-class consciousness. We will probably never know all of Wright's reasons for leaving the party. The seeds of bad faith had been sown on both sides, beginning with his problems in Chicago and continuing in New York, long before his 1944 public declaration.

Wright's decision to leave the party was a momentous development that changed the direction of the naturalistic protest school, marking a brief interruption in the regimen of co-optive hegemony, which had been manifested through the Marxist ideological perspective. Those Marxist influences were evidenced most clearly in Wright's *Uncle Tom's Children* and *Native Son*. Though the school survived several years after 1944, particularly in the writings of Chester Himes, Ann Petry, and Willard Motley, it reached its pinnacle in the early 1940s shortly after the publication of *Native Son*. In later naturalistic protest works published during the school's second phase, Marxism was largely supplanted by a more direct—if less ideologically coherent—racial protest perspective. While this perspective focused on the racial injustices and poverty of urban ghetto life, it lacked a critique of American capitalism. This retreat from Marxism was hardly peculiar to black American writers, as we noted earlier; it echoed the white American intelligentsia's shift from political radicalism.

By the mid-1940s, the American social climate had changed. Discontent aroused by the Depression had receded. As the expansion of New Deal reforms and the wartime industrial activity restabilized the American economy, the Communist Party fell into disrepute. But it was not simply the economic recovery that eroded the party's appeal. It was also the Soviet Union's glaring policy contradictions—contradictions between its professed humanitarian ideals and its cynical political maneuvers (e.g., brutal purges, the Soviet-Nazi pact, and the assassination of Leon Trotsky)— that demoralized the white American leftist intelligentsia and destroyed its faith in Communism. We see an example of this intellectual disillusionment in the decision of Granville Hicks, a leading literary critic, to leave the party after the Soviet-Nazi pact. Recalled Hicks:

> I went to New York, had a talk with Earl Browder. I had given four years of my life to it. I didn't want to break. It was a very hard step to take. I went to talk with Browder to see if he had anything to say that I hadn't already read in the *Daily Worker*. He simply paralleled the *Daily Worker* line and I came home and wrote a public letter of resignation. (Bentley 1971, 206)

Wright left the party later because he lacked alternatives. In contrast to the white intellectuals who simply returned to the liberal cultural establishment, where they found jobs with magazines such as the *New Yorker, Nation, New Republic,* and *Saturday Review* or in universities, Wright had no such options.

His defection from the party left him feeling not just isolated but intellectually disoriented. Marxism had given him a vision of social reality that excited his impulses to write and create characters acting in accordance with what then appeared to be the moral and scientific imperatives of history. Like other intellectuals who had embraced Marxism, he viewed it as a science, a set of laws analogous to those of chemistry and physics. That most Marxist literary intellectuals understood almost nothing about science and scientific methodology made their leap of faith easier. What they perceived as proof of Marxism's validity had less to do with Marx's complex theoretical arguments in *Das Kapital,* which few of them grasped, than with the frustration and despair they had experienced during the Depression. It was the breakdown of the American economy, not Marx's writings on political economy, that turned them against capitalist society. It was thus hardly surprising that once that economic distress receded, they would exhibit little interest in the flaws of capitalist society. Which is to say, they—like most liberal intellectuals—were "foul-weather revolutionaries."

Richard Wright, in a very real sense, was no different. He had focused chiefly on the poverty and degradation in the black American community, whereas the white leftist intelligentsia had focused on the national paralysis, and particularly the dislocated white working class—concerns that faded as the Depression subsided. In contrast to the white mainstream society, the black community's recovery was slower and less dramatic; racial discrimination, high rates of unemployment, and abject poverty still persisted. However, Wright no longer had faith in the promise of an interracial revolutionary movement. Although he still wanted to see major reforms in race relations, he now lacked an existential base in the black community; the existential base that had prompted him to operate as the spokesman for America's dispossessed black masses had, in effect, disappeared. As leftist white intellectuals abandoned Marxism and another era of co-optive hegemony in black American literature ended, Richard Wright found himself alone and in search of a new intellectual direction.

The Influence of Chicago Sociology

Richard Wright felt the lack of a formal education. It was this, as well as his desire to fill the void left by the demise of Marxism, that caused him to seek an alternative intellectual perspective in the Chicago School of Sociology. He encountered the school through his associations with Horace Cayton and Louis Wirth. Cayton was a black graduate sociology student at the University of Chicago; and Louis Wirth, the husband of Mary Wirth, Wright's social worker and benefactor, was an eminent professor in the university's sociology department.

The Chicago sociology department, under the leadership of Robert Park and Ernest Burgess, fostered a unique intellectual perspective on the social processes of urban life. It was through being exposed to that perspective that Richard Wright gained insight into the destructive impact of urban social forces on the lives of poor southern black migrants. Naturalism had long been the literary tradition he found most compelling, as was evidenced by his attraction to the works of Theodore Dreiser and Stephen Crane, because naturalism emphasized the impact of environmental influences. Correspondingly, the Chicago school sociological perspective also derived from intellectual interests in the way environmental forces affect human behavior. In reaction to the late nineteenth-century conservative biological perspective that had been fostered by Social Darwinism, the Chicago school sought to demonstrate that environmental changes associated with urbanization caused social disorganization in certain urban neighborhoods. It was this focus on urban social disorganization that especially aroused Wright's interests in Chicago sociology as he sought an explanation for the family disintegration, the illegitimate births, the juveniles delinquency, the property crimes, and the homicides, as well as other manifestations of social disorder that plagued Chicago's black ghetto.

Marxism neglected this level of analysis, for it assigned no unique causal agency to cities as social environments. Rather Marxism emphasized the class struggle, which would intensify as workers moved from rural areas to cities, because cities were the primary settings of industrial capitalism. But beyond this, it had no sociology of city life. Family breakdowns, youth gangs, and violent crimes were regarded by Marxists as merely residual consequences of capitalist development. Hence they failed to explain matters that most concerned Richard Wright, such as, for instance, why some working-class communities experienced far worse social problems than others.

Wright's initial contact with the Chicago School of Sociology occurred largely by accident, through his relationship with Mary Wirth (the social worker assigned to his family). On one of the occasions Wright went to see Wirth for help finding a job, she sent him to the university to talk to her husband. This led to his first encounter with Horace Cayton, a young black graduate student who was assisting Louis Wirth on a research project. Cayton later recounted their meeting: "One day there came a tapping on the door of my office. I opened the door and there stood a short brown-skinned Negro, and I said, 'Hello, what do you want?' He looked like an undergraduate, so I was perhaps condescending in a polite fashion, and, of course, he *was* colored" (Hill et al. 1966, 197).

Wright explained why he had come to the office and a conversation ensued during which he informed Cayton he wanted to be a writer. To which the graduate student responded skeptically. "Who didn't want to be a writer? But who could write?" Cayton showed Wright around the office, indicating the maps on the wall, dotted with color coded pins they used to designate the various characteristics of ethnic communities in Chicago. Cayton recalled Wright's curious response: "'You've got all of your facts pointed, pinned to the wall like a collector would pin butterflies.' I looked at him. He was a poetic little Negro. I did not see Dick again for some years" (Hill et al. 1966, 197).

No friendship developed between Cayton and Wright at the time. Cayton failed to say when their friendship began, but apparently it developed before Wright left Chicago in 1937. Because several years later, when Wright returned to Chicago after the publication of *Native Son*, he telephoned the young sociologist and asked him to meet him at the airport. *Life* magazine was doing a background story on the novel.

Wright returned to Chicago again in the early 1940s to film *Native Son*, and Cayton gave a party in his honor. It was at that party that Wright met Louis Wirth, with whom he developed a warm friendship, initiating Wright's informal education in sociology. On one of his visits to Chicago, Wright asked Louis Wirth to give him a reading list of basic sociological writings, which Wirth did. After reading the books on the list, Wright discussed them with Wirth. Recalling that meeting between the two men, Mary Wirth noted that her husband had been impressed by Wright's grasp of the books (Washington 1971). Among the books on the list was

Robert Redfield's work on folk and urban societies, explaining the differences between traditional and modern cultures. This book strongly influenced Wright's post-Marxist perspective on black American experiences, as was evidenced in his interpretive essay, *12 Million Black Voices*.

While Chicago sociology gave Wright deeper and more concrete insights into the social forces affecting urban black American life than did Marxism's paradigm of class conflict, it provided him neither an intellectual community nor an ideology. He had found these in the Communist Party and felt a need to regain them. But he never did; his quest for that alternative intellectual community would continue to the end of his life.

Due to both his intellectual isolation and his interracial marriage, Wright found living in the United States increasingly uncomfortable, and he decided to move to Paris. The events culminating in that decision began after he developed a friendship with the expatriate American writer Gertrude Stein, following a favorable review he had written of her book. Stein sent a letter to Wright expressing her gratitude for the review and an exchange of letters ensued. In one of his letters to Stein, Wright expressed his desire to visit France, and Stein, who was a respected and influential figure in Parisian intellectual life, along with several French intellectuals, arranged an invitation for Wright from the French government. The invitation, signed by some of France's most eminent intellectuals, indicated that the French government would pay his expenses. This gesture deeply impressed Wright, who had never received any honor or recognition from the U.S. government.

Returning home after an exhilarating visit to Paris, Wright felt dissatisfied with New York, which now seemed dismal and depressing compared with Paris's cosmopolitan ambiance and racial tolerance. So in July 1947, as the ugly storm clouds of postwar political reaction were enveloping the United States, Richard Wright and his family expatriated to France, where the government had granted him a lifetime lease on a comfortable Paris apartment for a modest annual payment. Richard Wright thus became a Parisian resident as he once again hurdled the obstacles of his environment.

Wright's move to France marked the end of not just his life in the United States, but also of the dominant naturalistic protest school. The last book he published before leaving for France—*Black Boy* (Wright 1945a)—presented an autobiographical account of his childhood without a trace of his earlier Marxist ideology. Wright now found himself suspended in an ideological void. In Paris, where he was obliged to adapt to a new life and seek a new ideological direction, eight years would pass before he published another literary work. When that work finally did appear in the 1950s, one thing was indisputably clear—Richard Wright had become a very different type of writer.

THE NATURALISTIC PROTEST LITERARY WORKS

The sociological significance of the naturalistic protest literary works derived from their angry, raw images of black ghetto life. Those images, which contrasted starkly with the images of the primitivist literary works, resulted not simply from the more desperate plight blacks experienced during the Depression, for the naturalistic protest school's depictions of blacks as the enraged victims of a racially oppressive capitalist society were exaggerated. Blacks were staggered by the Depression, but few starved; and more important, as we have seen, few responded to their economic hardships by embracing a revolutionary ideology. Rather those images of black American rage resulted from the frustrated ambitions of a socially dislocated group of the young black writers, who were ideologically co-opted into a white leftist political movement.

Under those leftist political influences, the naturalistic protest school severed all links to the earlier primitivist and civil rights oriented literary works. Which is to say, their images of black America obliterated the lingering echoes of both exoticism and special pleading. By depicting blacks as alienated and embittered victims of white racial oppression—by thrusting black literary discourse into a radical politics of race relations—they shocked mainstream white America into an awareness of deep-seated black anger.

Let's now turn to *Native Son,* the book that launched this radical ideological construction of black American life and—in the memorable words of Irving Howe—"changed American culture forever."

NATIVE SON: THE PARADIGM OF
THE NATURALISTIC PROTEST SCHOOL

The novel opens in a slum tenement on Chicago's South Side where Bigger Thomas, the protagonist, lives with his mother, brother, and sister. Almost immediately, we realize that they live in only one room, as the mother, arising from bed, instructs Bigger to turn his head while she gets dressed. While they are still in the process of getting up, a large rat lurches out and runs behind a trunk. Reacting instantly, Bigger grabs a skillet and a contest ensues between him and the rat. After a grisly struggle in which the rat rips his pants leg, Bigger manages to kill it. The brutality of this life is conveyed by Bigger's coarse language.

> The two brothers stood over the dead rat and spoke in tones of awed admiration.
> "Gee, but he's a big bastard."
> "That sonafabitch could cut your throat."

"He's over a foot long."

"How in hell do they get so big?"

"Eating garbage and anything else they can get." (Wright 1940, 10)

The opening scenes reveal a troubled household. Bigger's relationship to his mother, a religious woman given to singing spirituals and praying, is tense and hostile. We soon learn that Bigger is unemployed and that his mother wants him to find a job, an issue that causes considerable friction between them.

"Even when the relief offers you a job you won't take it till they threaten to cut off your food and starve you! Bigger, honest, you the most no-countest man I ever seen in my life!"

"You done told me a thousand times."

"Well, I'm telling you agin! And mark my word, some of these days you going to set down and *cry*. Some of these days you going to wish you had made something out of yourself, instead of just a tramp. But it'll be too late then."

"Stop prophesizing about me."

"I prophesy much as I please! And if you don't like it, you can get out. We can get along without you. We can live in one room just like we living now, even with you gone." (Wright 1940, 12–13)

In a fit of anger Bigger leaves the house and enters the world of the street, irritated by pressures to take a menial job that he feels is beneath his dignity. It is no coincidence that his name Bigger Thomas rhymes with the phrase "Bigger Promise," for Wright informs us that "it maddened him (Bigger) to think that he did not have a wider choice of action" (Wright 1940, 16). In short, in the character Bigger Thomas, Wright paints a portrait of repressed black rage.

The first section of the novel, following closely the techniques of naturalism, presents the external forces acting on Bigger's life: his slum environment, his abject poverty, his joblessness, and his quarrelsome family life. All contribute to his feeling of being entrapped in a defeated existence of aimless drift. As he enters the world of the street, his family recedes into the background, powerless to deter his fate.

He soon encounters several cronies with whom he has planned to undertake a robbery. But Bigger is now apprehensive. An argument ensues as he attempts to hide his fear. Finally, the robbery is called off. His friends, like his family, soon recede into the background, unable to shield him from his fate.

Moving to the scene of that fate, Bigger leaves his black neighborhood and enters the nearby neighborhood of Chicago's Hyde Park, an upper middle-class white community, adjacent to Bigger's slum environment.

Responding to the information about a prospective job his mother had given him, he is on his way to the home of a Mr. Dalton. Wright immediately makes clear the strangeness of this world to Bigger's eyes. "This was a cold and distant world; a world of white secrets carefully guarded . . . only fear and emptiness filled him now" (Wright 1940, 45).

Bigger gets the job of chauffeur and, almost immediately, is instructed to drive Dalton's daughter, Mary, to the university where she is a student. The Dalton family is liberal, and hiring Bigger is a gesture demonstrating their sympathy for blacks.

> "Oh Bigger," said Mr. Dalton.
> "Yessuh."
> "I want you to know why I'm hiring you."
> "Yessuh."
> "You see, Bigger, I'm a supporter of the National Association for the Advancement of Colored People. Did you ever hear of that organization?"
> "Nawsuh."
> "Well, it doesn't matter," said Dalton. "Have you had dinner?" (Wright 1940, 54–55)

The irony here is intended. By indicating that Dalton belongs to the NAACP, Wright is suggesting not only that its wealthy white supporters are hypocrites. But also, and even more important, he is suggesting that lower-class blacks like Bigger view such organizations as irrelevant. Mary Dalton, however, is presented in a different light. As soon as she meets Bigger, she begins questioning him in front of her father about belonging to a union. Bigger responds in confusion.

> "But you wouldn't mind belonging to a union, would you?" the girl asked.
> "I don't know, mam," Bigger said.
> "Now, Mary, you can see the boy is new," said Mr. Dalton. "Leave him alone."
> The girl turned and poked out her tongue at him.
> "All right, Mr. Capitalist!" She turned again to Bigger. "Isn't he a capitalist, Bigger?"
> Bigger looked at the floor and did not answer.
> He did not know what a capitalist was. (Wright 1940, 54)

Bigger, who has only eight years of education, now reveals his ignorance, as he reflects on the girl's remarks. "The best thing he could do was leave that crazy girl alone. He had heard about unions; in his mind unions and communists were linked."

Bigger finally leaves to take Mary to the university. But once inside the car, Mary changes her plans and instructs him to take her to a different place, where they meet her Communist boyfriend, Jan Erlone. Afterward the two leftist white youths ask Bigger to take them to a black South Side night spot—which he does—and, by the time they leave the night club, both Mary and Erlone are intoxicated. They drop Erlone off at the trolley station where he can take a train home, and then Bigger drives Mary back to the Dalton residence. When they reach the house, however, he realizes there is a problem. Mary is too drunk to walk, so he has to carry her upstairs to her bedroom. Reaching her bedroom, he places her down on the bed and, then, momentarily ponders whether he should exploit the situation and have sex with her. But suddenly another complication arises. Mrs. Dalton (the mother, who is blind) enters the room after being awakened by the commotion, and calls out to her daughter. In panic, fearing that he will be discovered in Mary's bedroom, Bigger presses a pillow over Mary's face knowing that if she awakens in response to her mother's voice, he would have a problem explaining his presence. After a few moments, Mrs. Dalton leaves the room satisfied that everything is all right. Bigger meanwhile has unwittingly pressed the pillow too forcefully over Mary's face, and suddenly he realizes she has suffocated.

Following this, in a scene that can be described only as shockingly grotesque, Bigger carries Mary's body into the basement, dismembers it, and disposes of the parts in a furnace. When the girl's absence is discovered the next day, Bigger fabricates a story intended to implicate the Communist Jan Erlone, but to no avail; the fabrication falls apart. Although Bigger manages to escape with the help of his girlfriend, whom he later murders as well, he is eventually arrested by the police and placed on trial.

In this first section of the novel, titled "Fear," Wright uses primarily the techniques of naturalism. We see evidence of Bigger's frustrations early as he reflects on the racial system that imposes narrow limits on his existence.

> I know I oughtn't think about it, but I can't help it. Every time I think about it I feel like somebody's poking a red-hot iron down my throat. Goddammit, look. We live here and they live there. We black and they white. They got things and we ain't. They do things and we can't. It's just like living in jail. Half the time I feel like I'm on the outside of the world peeping through a knothole in the fence. (Wright 1940, 23)

Bigger's violence is depicted as a natural outcome of his living in this cold and uncaring social order. In short, the reader is being warned that racial oppression inevitably leads to criminal violence. This view pervaded Wright's outlook on black ghetto life. As was evidenced several years later in the introduction he wrote to *Black Metropolis,* a landmark sociological study of the Chicago black community done by Horace Cayton and Sinclair Drake, Wright leaves no doubt about the link between black ghetto life and crime.

If, in reading my novel, *Native Son*, you doubted the reality of Bigger Thomas, then examine the delinquency rates cited in this book; if in reading my book Black Boy, you doubted the picture of family life shown there, then study the figures on family disorganization given here. *Black Metropolis* describes the processes that mold Negro life as we know it today. (Wright 1945b, xx)

Significantly, as Bigger attempts to escape, he develops consciousness about his plight. But it is a consciousness informed not by class warfare but by the instinct for survival. Bigger is incapable of comprehending the political and economic forces that have shaped his life, an incapacity created by his segregated, impoverished environment.

The first section of the novel, as Bigger succumbs to the forces of his environment and his fate of violence, adheres to the naturalistic philosophy; but the second section, "Flight," when he wrests control over his life, departs from that naturalistic philosophy. In fact, his achievement of freedom here is ironic; for he gains it by committing another murder, killing his black girlfriend, which allows him for the first time to make choices in his life. The parallels between *Native Son* and Dostoyevsky's *Crime and Punishment* are hardly coincidental; Wright was strongly influenced by that great Russian novel. If Dreiser guided the construction of Bigger's predicament, Dostoyevsky guided the construction of his response, his liberation through violence. Thus after accidentally murdering Mary Dalton, Bigger murders his girlfriend Betsy, now fully conscious of the meaning of the act for his struggle to stay alive.

All along Wright has been preparing us for some larger meaning of the actions of the first two sections of *Native Son*. That meaning, which consists of an indictment of American racism, appears in the book's last section, "Fate," where we encounter the Marxian perspective. Wright, it should be noted, introduces this perspective not as a part of the novel's action but as a rhetorical argument presented in Bigger's courtroom defense. In this respect, the novel violates the canons of socialist realism. Class conflict is presented as a retrospective interpretation of Bigger's life rather than as a central part of the narrative. Bigger belongs to no union; he participates in no strikes or mass demonstrations; expresses no feelings of solidarity with other poor people. He confronts societal authority not as a revolutionary but as a criminal, as a man motivated by egocentric impulses. In short, Bigger is a lumpen proletarian, a crude, corrupted manifestation of that larger political struggle. As constructed by Wright, Bigger is incapable of revolutionary consciousness; he is too mentally stunted, too isolated from other black workers, to grasp its meaning.

The character who presents the meaning of Bigger's life in terms of that larger struggle is Max, Bigger's white communist lawyer. Using techniques of argument modeled on Clarence Darrow's famous trial defenses,

Max places moral responsibility for Bigger's crimes on white American racism. "The hate and fear which we have inspired in him, woven by our civilization into the very structure of his consciousness, into his blood and bones, into the hourly functioning of his personality, have become the justification of his existence" (Wright 1940, 366–67).

Situating Bigger's homicidal violence within a societal context, Max proceeds to articulate the ideological rationale that informed the naturalistic protest school's images of black American rage.

> It is a physiological and psychological reaction, embedded in his being. Every thought he thinks is potential murder. Excluded from, and unassimilated in our society, yet longing to gratify impulses akin to our own but denied the objects and channels evolved through long centuries for their socialized expression, every sunrise makes him guilty of subversive actions. Every movement of his body is an unconscious protest. Every desire, every dream, no matter how intimate or personal is a plot or a conspiracy. Every hope is a plan for insurrection. Every glance of the eye is a threat. His very existence is a crime against the state. (Wright 1940, 367)

Max's portrait of Bigger is far from flattering. And this points to a paradox in that novel's construction of black American life. In its efforts to highlight American racial injustices, *Native Son* depicts a dehumanized black American personality. Which is to say, Max's Marxist conception of Bigger is not Bigger's conception of himself.

By stressing the brutalizing effects of racial injustice, the novel underscored the urgent need for radical change. It could scarcely have projected that message so forcefully by focusing on the black middle class, or even the stable black working class, where the most brutalizing effects of white racism were counteracted by black communal supports, the bonds of the black family, the black church, the black neighborhood, and other associational networks, that affirmed the individual's humanity. Also, and equally important, the religious worldview and community ethos of working-class black culture attenuated mainstream white society's stress on material success as the measure of the individual's self-worth. It was precisely this nurturing and humanizing role of black ethnic culture that *Native Son*—in its depiction of Bigger's personality—ignored.

This ignoring of black ethnic culture, it is important to understand, was encouraged by that novel's subtext, namely, the quest for assimilation. Though Marxism advocated a radical transformation of capitalist race relations, its conception of social order was rooted in the cultural and intellectual traditions of European culture. Swayed by these Marxian influences, as well as his alienation from the black community, Wright never envisioned black American ethnic culture as a viable source of meaning and order in black American life. Hence, although Wright avoided saying this explicitly, the major cause of Bigger's tragic life is racial segregation. Representing Bigger as a microcosm of a culturally dispossessed black America, Max's pleas to the jury (or Wright's pleas to his white American audience) is for black America's assimilation: "Multiply Bigger Thomas twelve million times, allowing for environmental and temperamental variation, and for those Negroes who are completely under the influence of the church and you have the psychology of the Negro people" (Wright 1940, 364).

The implications of Max's argument are clear: either blacks must be absorbed into the larger white society or they will succumb to the abyss of alienation and violence. Recall Max's description of Bigger, noted above, as a man "excluded from, and unassimilated in our society. . . ." Also, in his introduction to *Black Metropolis*, we find Wright stating this viewpoint even more directly: "Do not hold a light attitude toward the slums of Chicago's South Side. Remember that Hitler came out of such a slum. Remember that Chicago could be the Vienna of American Fascism" (Wright 1945b, xx).

As we will see in the next section, this aversion to black American ethnic culture, while manifested most strongly by Wright, would be echoed in the works of other naturalistic protest writers. Let's now turn to the reactions to *Native Son*.

Reactions to *Native Son*

> I think Negroes are to blame for the reactions to *Native Son*. So few of them have ever tried to tell the truth about how they feel. They are shamed, scared, and want to save their pride. Well, in writing that book, I just threw shame, fear and pride out the window.
>
> —Richard Wright in a letter to Nelson Algren (Algren 1961, 85)

Native Son generated an enormous public response. Within one month after its publication, it sold more than a quarter million copies, made the national best-seller's list, and was selected by the Book of the Month Club, reaching a much larger audience than had any previous black American literary work. It was published in more than fifty foreign translations, and, by almost any criterion, constituted a milestone as not only one of the most important books of the Depression era, but also the most acclaimed novel ever written by a black American.

The diverse and emotionally heated reactions that novel provoked reflected the ideological divisions pervading American society. Reflecting those ideological divisions, *New Masses* published reviews of *Native Son* that appeared in the national press (Sillen 1940, 25–27). However, the *New Masses* sample was limited to negative reactions from white publications

and positive reactions from black publications, while ignoring positive reactions from white liberal publications, the party's closest ideological rivals, who viewed the book as a racial protest rather than a Communist
novel. *New Masses*, of course, had a vested interest in pro-Communist interpretations of the novel.

Publications reviewing the novel can be classified in the following categories:

1. Communist publications
2. black publications
3. northern white liberal periodicals
4. the northern white press
5. mass-circulation news magazines
6. the southern white press

Communist Publications

The Communist publications tended to interpret *Native Son* as pro-
Communist, and generally approved its content:

> The communist party joins with the Negro people in rejoicing over his
> (Wright's) magnificent artistry, as a native son of his people and America . . .
> a brilliant courageous job. (Ben Davis in *Sunday Worker*)

> After ten years of fumbling and experiment, of visions and uneven fulfill-
> ments our American realism, our American proletarian literature, or what-
> ever critics wish to name it, has finally culminated in two sure classics—
> Steinbeck's *Grapes of Wrath* and Richard Wright's *Native Son*. (Mike Gold in
> *New Masses*)

> (Into) the life of white Americans who never begin to realize what being
> black means comes a searing, scorching novel, burning indelibly an illusion
> that becomes to every reader a vital experience of a literature. (Ben Burns in
> *People's World*)

> But don't you feel the awful wrongness in a social system wherein a living
> human has to believe that he has committed a gruesome murder to ensure
> his identity as a human being? (Chester Himes in a letter to *New Masses*)

> I put the book down feeling guilty of my skin. My experiences in the
> progressive movement, however, may have made me atypical; would the
> Book-of-the-Month Club reader react similarly? (Sillen 1940, 24–25)

The leftist responses were not, however, unanimous in their enthusiasm. Some leftist reviews were negative because they found the book ideologically flawed. Moreover, a few leftist reviewers—including Ben
Davis, Samuel Sillen, and Mike Gold—warned that Bigger should not be

mistaken as a true representation of black Americans. They also criticized Wright for depicting the Communist in the book as naive and misguided. For example, Sillen—while praising Wright's achievement—cautioned against the view that Bigger symbolized the black American personality. Gold, who lavished praise on the book in his public pronouncements, expressed a totally different viewpoint in private, as was revealed by the letter he wrote to Wright assailing the book's weak Marxist position. He accused Wright of not being representative of black people, suggesting that *Native Son* was alien to past black expression, and that Wright had to depend on white writers and techniques to adapt his way of seeing black life. This last observation by Gold was both peculiar and striking, peculiar because he was attacking the very hegemony he had helped foster, and striking because he perceived clearly Wright's problematic relationship to the black community, and the way it had affected the novel's construction. For instance, he was one of the few commentators to criticize Wright for believing that the Black Belt had no traditions (Margolis 1971). Nevertheless, despite the reservations expressed by some leftist commentators, most praised *Native Son*, and saw it as a triumph for Marxism. We will have more to say about Gold's penetrating critique later, when we discuss the hegemonic functions of Marxist ideology in the naturalistic protest school.

Black Publications

In contrast to the leftist periodicals, black publications viewed the novel almost exclusively in racial terms, as a blow struck against racial oppression, and they generally believed Wright had achieved that objective. This is somewhat surprising. Ordinarily members of the black middle class, who controlled these publications, would have opposed a novel that represented black America's plight through the words of a white Communist lawyer. Also, due to the black middle class's preoccupation with fostering favorable black images for white American consumption, they typically disdained images of lower-class blacks like Bigger, who fit the prevailing white stereotype of black criminality. Yet neither of these two features of the novel repelled the black middle class. It was no doubt *Native Son*'s unparalleled notoriety that caused them to overlook these "flaws" and see it in a favorable light. For not unlike the black middle-class celebrants of the so-called Harlem Renaissance, these black reviewers perceived black literary works primarily in terms of the status-politics of race.

> While the critics are in unanimity in proclaiming Richard Wright a novelist of first magnitude, we, who belong to the world of social proscription, of frustrated hopes, of organized discrimination out of which came Bigger

Thomas . . . fervently hope that *Native Son* shall not only focus attention upon the evils which are visited upon us, but that it shall, by the very urgency of its message, transform a rotten social, economic system into a living democracy. (*Chicago Defender* editorial)

Richard Wright unquestionably has the touch of genius. He belongs to the Negro, but in a larger sense he belongs to America and the world of art and literature. (*Opportunity* editorial)

It's going to be interesting to watch the reactions of both black and white America to this masterpiece. Many of our pale brothers, blind to life among Negroes, will want to deny the cruelty of the nation's color attitude; still others, angered at the truth, will want to condemn the book in self-defense. (Frank Davis, *Association of Negro Press Review* [Sillen April 1940, 13–21])

Focusing on the novel as a sociological document, most saw *Native Son* as a strong argument for racial integration.

Northern White Liberal Publications

This group, as strong advocates of social change, stood closest to the Communists ideologically. But unlike the Communists, they sought reform rather than revolution. Many were former Communists or Communist sympathizers, as we noted earlier, who became disaffected with the party because of the 1939 Nazi-Soviet pact, and resumed their allegiance to a liberal political perspective. This liberal perspective was exhibited clearly and unequivocally in their assessment of *Native Son*. Surfacing in such publications as the *New Republic, New Yorker, The Nation,* and the *New York Times Book Review,* their reviews generally gave the novel high marks as a protest against American racial injustices.

The sullen helplessness of an oppressed race living in the midst of its oppressors. (David Daiches in *Literature and Society*)

Native Son is the most important novel I have read since the *Grapes of Wrath.* (Malcolm Cowley, *New Republic*)

Native Son does for the Negro what Theodore Dreiser in *An American Tragedy* did a decade and a half ago for the bewildered, inarticulate American white. (Clifton Fadiman, *The New Yorker*)

Certainly, *Native Son* is the finest novel yet written by a Negro. Like the *Grapes of Wrath,* it is a fully realized story of the unfortunates, uncompromisingly realistic, quite as human as it is Negro. (Henry Seidel Canby, *Book of the Month Club News*)

A ready way to show the importance of this novel is to call it the Negro "American Tragedy." (Peter Munroe Jack, *New York Times Book Review*)

It (*Native Son*) bends no knees, it asks no pity; it seeks no scourge. (Milton Rugoff, *New York Herald Tribune Book Review*)

For terror in narrative, utter and compelling, there are few pages in modern American literature which will compare with this story. (Jonathan Daniels, *The Saturday Review of Literature*)

The Harper's prize novel is this year's most compelling and trenchant. (Marguerite Wylie, *Canadian Forum*)

This is the tragedy of the black man in America. (Margaret Marshall, *The Nation* [Sillen 1940, 25–27])

One exception among liberal publications was a review in the *Atlantic Monthly* magazine written by David Cohn. A white conservative, Cohn not only doubted the feasibility of equality between the races, he also attacked Wright for displaying what he termed the "headlong" attitude of racial hatred. Why *Atlantic Monthly* chose to print the article is difficult to say, for the article reflected the outlook of southern white publications.

The Northern White Press

Reviews of *Native Son* in northern newspapers were generally unfavorable. Like the leftist publications, but for different reasons, they tended to regard the novel as pro-Communist. This is not surprising in view of the conservative Republican ideology that dominated most of these newspapers. Thus, for instance, *The St. Louis Globe Democrat* saw the book as a "distinctive story despite a suspicion of special pleading on behalf of communism and the Jewish question."

Similarly, *The New Bedford Standard Times* referred to the book's "warped ideology," noting that "its course is twisted by an attempt to make the Communist Party seem the friend of the Negro."

The injection of Communism and radical theorizing weakens the plot and the author's plea. (*Des Moines Register*)

As a novel, it is hindered by too much analysis, too much talk, too much propaganda, if we may use the term, for the cause of the Negro and of labor unions. (*The Worcester Telegram* [Sillen May 1940, 25–27])

The *Cleveland Plain Dealer* and the *San Francisco Chronicle* also attributed the novel to radical politics.

Several reviewers in these newspapers, invoking tones of condescension, simply dismissed the book. Despite feeling repelled by *Native Son*, they could hardly ignore a novel that had garnered so much attention, so they reverted to the tactic of trivializing its meaning. For example, Fanny

Butcher in the conservative *Chicago Tribune* overlooked totally the social problems dealt with in the novel, and described it as a suspense story. This tactic was also used by the reviewer in the *Washington* (D.C.) *Star*: "The story is splendid but the reviewer cannot for the life of her tell you what Mr. Wright means by it."

Perhaps the most egregious example of trivialization was exhibited by Professor Howard Mumford Jones of Harvard, who expressed dismay about Bigger's motives. "After all," he reasoned, "Bigger Thomas did get a job, so what's all the killing about?"

These newspapers, it should be noted, reflected the opinions of the privileged class of whites, who felt far more threatened by Communism than by black protest. Insofar as they wrote about black Americans at all, it was stereotypical. Black people did not inhabit the moral universe they defined as fully human. References to blacks typically appeared in their newspapers only in association with crimes. *Native Son* aptly fit this pattern.

Mass-Circulation News Magazines

Also controlled by the privileged class of whites, the mass-circulation weekly news magazines failed to embrace the novel. *Time* magazine, for instance, the nation's most popular news weekly, attacked *Native Son*, but with an odd twist: it saw the book as an anti-Communist novel. The reviewer's preoccupation with Communism was captured perhaps best in his caustic description of Mary Dalton's and Jan Erlone's behavior as "tragic-comic Negrophilious bohemianism which passes among the communists as a solution to the Negro problem."

The Southern White Press

The novel was seen differently in the South. If the conservative response of the northern white press was stimulated by its preoccupation with the threat of Communism, the southern white response was triggered by images of black violence. Interestingly, the newspapers in the border states seemed more sympathetic than did the newspapers of the deep South.

> In a year when the ideals of democracy are once more under challenge and when all Americans are deeply concerned for the plight of Europe's racial minorities, *Native Son* will serve as a reminder that the United States has a race problem that has yet to be solved. (*Kansas City Star*)

> There are those today who are daring to tell the truth, however unpleasant it may be. One cannot but think of Hugo, Zola, Tolstoy, Dostoyevsky, and Gorky, and the name of Richard Wright must be added to the list of those

who through the medium of the novel have cried out against injustice and oppression. (Louisville, Kentucky, *Courier-Journal* [Sillen May 1940, 25–27])

Sillen, the *New Masses* editor, also cited a *Louisville Times* editorial which, recalling Wright having forged a library card when he lived in Memphis, saw the novel as positive evidence of the effects of education on blacks. It "constitutes the best publicity in behalf of better educational opportunity for Negroes." These border state responses apparently reflected the gradual changes in racial attitudes that were entering the South.

But these moderate attitudes had by no means penetrated the South's deep interior, where conservative racist attitudes continued unabated. One of the most noteworthy appeared in Louisiana:

> Most Southern readers will find this material irritating, if not outright revolting; if we thought that *Native Son* was significant enough as a novel to warrant the advice, we would recommend that they shove aside their biases and read it in any case. But somehow we do not have that feeling about the book. (*New Orleans Times-Picayune*)

Some among this group of hostile southern reviewers saw *Native Son* as anti-Communist as had *Time* magazine. It was the role of the Communists, in their view, that accounted for Bigger's tragic end. When the Communists entered the novel, declared one reviewer from the deep South: "At this point the reader damns the stupidity of such idiotic, idealistic communists and wishes them all in Siberia."

Another reviewer attributed Bigger's action to "patronizing whites" (*Dallas News*), while the *Memphis Commercial Appeal*, the paper whose opposition to Mencken had inspired Wright to read his books, saw the radicals as responsible for the killings in the book.

We should note in concluding this section that while *Native Son* certainly constituted an outstanding black literary achievement, that hardly accounted for its unprecedented notoriety. Black Americans had produced better written and better constructed novels, prior to *Native Son*, that failed to provoke such interests. Nor does that novel's focus on the unfolding tragedy of a black youth's ghetto life explain the enormous interest it aroused. Other naturalistic protest literary works would highlight the hardships of urban black ghetto life without arousing so much interest. Put simply, it was not *Native Son*'s focus on the frustrations and despair of ghetto life, but rather its depictions of a black youth driven by hatred and alienation to murder a white American that riveted the nation's attention. Moving onto a new terrain of racial discourse, going beyond what black American writers had ever dared to express, that murder violated the racial caste system's most fundamental taboo. If American society changed forever the day *Native Son* was published, as Irving Howe perceptively observed, that was because it seemed to morally justify black violence against whites.

OTHER WRITERS AND LITERARY WORKS
OF THE NATURALISTIC PROTEST SCHOOL

As previously noted, *Native Son* set the standard for many black writers in the 1940s as did Van Vechten's *Nigger Heaven* for black writers during the 1920s. But with one important difference. Richard Wright was black, the first black writer to lead a dominant black literary school, as was evidenced by his enormous influence. The writers who came under Wright's influence included Ralph Ellison, Chester Himes, Frank Yerby, Roi Ottley, Willard Motley, Ann Petry, William Gardner Smith, and Carl Offord. The school's inner circle, consisting of Wright, Ellison, and Himes, had been affiliated with the Communist Party. As noted earlier, Ellison became closely linked to Wright shortly after Wright arrived in New York. "Ellison's early apprenticeship," writes Robert Bone, "was dominated by Richard Wright, and the stories of this period yield none in bitterness and stiffness. Violent, brutal, and full of mutilation fantasies which reveal an intense fear of a hostile environment" (Bone 1958, 190). Chester Himes, while serving a seven-year prison sentence in Ohio for robbery, began writing short stories, which were published in the black press and eventually in *Esquire* magazine. Himes "a product of the Great Depression, . . . the labor movement, the Federal Writer's Project, and the Communist Party . . . borrowed freely from the visceral style of Richard Wright." His first two novels, *If He Hollers Let Him Go* (1945) and *Lonely Crusade* (1947), followed Wright's paradigm. *If He Hollers Let Him Go*, for instance, exhibits a similar emphasis on the frustrations of a powerless black character who feels entrapped by a destructive racial system.

William Attaway (*Blood on the Forge*), Willard Motley (*Knock on Any Door*), Ann Petry (*The Street*), and William Gardner Smith (*Last of the Conquerors*), though not affiliated with the Communist Party, resonated the naturalistic protest orientation. In fact, it would hardly be an exaggeration to say that *Native Son* reinvented black American literary discourse.

Naturalistic Protest School Images of Black American Life

That reinvented black literary discourse was strongly evidenced in the new images of black America. In the grim, acrid, and harsh depictions of ghetto existence, unrelieved by intervals of conviviality or simple pleasures, the frustrations of poverty and racial outcast seemed omnipresent.

Images of the Black Middle Class

Both the primitivist and the naturalistic protest literary schools despised the black middle class. Probably no aspect of these two literary schools revealed more clearly their alienation from the black community's leaders than did their negative images of middle-class blacks. However, the reasons these two literary schools disliked middle-class blacks differed. The primitivist writers, as we saw in the previous chapter, despised middle-class blacks because they believed these "successful blacks" had abandoned their African cultural heritage, and, in consequence, were ashamed of their racial identity. In contrast, the naturalistic protest writers despised middle-class blacks for political reasons; bourgeois blacks, in their view, lacked the courage and integrity to confront white racism.

Richard Wright depicts no middle-class blacks in *Native Son*, which suggests that he regarded them as politically irrelevant. We see Wright's hostility toward middle-class blacks in the comments he made about their reactions to literary depictions of lower-class blacks like Bigger. "I knew from long and painful experience," Wright observed shortly after he published *Native Son*, "that the Negro middle and professional classes were the people of my race who were more than others ashamed of Bigger and what he meant. Having narrowly escaped the Bigger Thomas reaction pattern themselves—indeed, still retaining traces of it within the confines of their own timid personalities—they would not relish being publicly reminded of the lowly, shameful depths of life above which they enjoyed their bourgeois lives. Never did they want people, especially white people, to think their lives were so much touched by anything so dark and brutal as Bigger" (Wright 1970, 26).

We see a similarly jaundiced view of the black middle class in Chester Himes's *If He Hollers Let Him Go*. The story of a racially frustrated young black man (Robert Jones) who works in a wartime shipyard, this novel, in contrast to *Native Son*, depicts middle-class blacks, represented by Jones's social worker fiancée and her solidly middle-class family. His fiancée's father is a doctor; her mother a genteel black middle-class housewife. Himes depicts these middle-class blacks as not just politically impotent, but psychologically deluded, oblivious to the realities of American racism, as can be seen in the following exchange between Jones and his fiancée's mother.

> "Alice tells me you're going to arrange your work so you can attend the university in the mornings," she informed me.
>
> "Oh, yes, that's right." I didn't want to tell her that was the first I'd heard about it. "Yes, I'm going to join the ranks of the Negro professionals."
>
> "It gives me a feeling of personal triumph, too, to see our young men progress so," she said. "I like to think that the doctor and I have contributed

by setting an example, by showing our young men just what they can accomplish if they try."

That was my cue to say, "Yes indeedy." But she looked so goddamned smug and complacent, sitting there in her two-hundred dollar chair, her feet planted in her three-thousand dollar rug, waving two or three thousand dollars worth of diamonds on her hands, bought with dough her husband had made overcharging poor hardworking colored people for his incompetent services, that I had a crazy impulse to needle her. The scotch had gone to work too. So I said, "Well now, to tell the truth, Mrs. Harrison, what I'm so pleased about today is I've just found out how I can get even with the white folks." She couldn't have looked more startled and horrified if I'd slapped her.

"Bob," she said. "Why I never heard of such a thing!"

Her hands made a fluttery, nervous gesture.

"Why on earth should you feel you have to get even with them?" But before I could reply she went on.

"Bob, you frighten me. You'll never make a success with that attitude. You mustn't think in terms of trying to get even with them, you must accept whatever they do for you and try to prove yourself worthy to be entrusted with more."

Now she was completely agitated.

"I'm really ashamed of you, Bob. How can you expect them to do anything for you if you're going to hate them?" (Himes 1956, 51)

The naturalistic protest school's images of middle-class blacks were rooted in several assumptions: first, that they lived in an insular world of petty bourgeois comfort that isolated them from the black masses; second, that they embraced a bogus ethic of individual achievement that lacked relevance to the black community's problems of racial oppression; and finally, that they supported white-controlled, politically moderate organizations like the NAACP and Urban League, which blocked rather than advanced the radicalization of the black masses. In effect, the black middle class was viewed as a distasteful appendage of the racial caste system.

Images of Black Lower-Class Environment

Environmental forces figured prominently in the naturalist protest school's depictions of black American life, which marked another major difference from the primitivist writers. In the racially oriented primitivist perspective, the black lower-class environment was depicted as a gratifying sanctuary of ethnic conviviality, where blacks could express their uninhibited African sensibility and enjoy life's pleasures, apart from the psychologically repressed white American social world.

In contrast, the naturalistic protest writers viewed the black lower-class environment as a wasteland. The black community's segregation, the feature of the racial caste system the primitivists had relished, the naturalistic writers loathed because, in their view, segregated black urban environments relegated blacks to an outcast and desolate existence. We can see black ghetto life evoked metaphorically in Ann Petry's depiction of a Harlem rooming house in *The Street:*

> Respectable tenants in these houses where colored people were allowed to live included anyone who could pay the rent, so some of them would be drunk and loud mouthed and quarrelsome; given to fits of depression when they would curse and cry violently, given to fits of equally violent elation. And, she thought, because the walls would be flimsy, why the good people, the bad people, the children, the dogs, and the godawful smells would all be wrapped together in one big package. (Petry 1971, 8)

This bleak image of the black urban environment as an entrapped ghetto existence, following the *Native Son* paradigm, supplanted the blithe image of that environment as a hedonistic playground, insulated from the sterility of white civilization. Where the primitivist writers saw reasons for optimism, the naturalistic protest writers saw reasons for despair, despair driven by anger and cynicism. In fact, it was their cynical view of the environment shaping segregated black community life that attracted them to the naturalistic literary form, because it allowed them to highlight the negative impact of urban social forces. That negative view of urban social forces can be seen in Richard Wright's statement about the brutalizing effects of the Chicago environment on lower-class black youth. "The urban environment of Chicago, affording a more stimulating life, made the Negro Bigger Thomases react more violently than even in the South. More than ever I began to see and understand the environmental factors which made for this extreme conduct" (Wright 1970, 20).

By depicting the role of environment, these writers aimed not just to dramatize the effects of social degradation and poverty. They aimed also to universalize the plight of the black masses. The forces shaping lower-class black behavior were no longer conceived in simple racial terms, as the expression of primordial African instincts. In fact, nothing could have been further from these writers' conception of black American life. As Wright pointed out: "I made the discovery that Bigger Thomas was not black all the time; he was white, too, and there were literally millions of him, everywhere. The extension of my sense of the personality of Bigger was the pivot of my life; . . . I became conscious, at first dimly, and then later on with increasing clarity and conviction, of a vast, muddied pool of human life in America" (Wright 1970, 20). That "vast, muddied pool of human life" was, of course, the working class.

Images of Racial Integration

This environmental issue throws light on a closely related matter, namely, the naturalistic protest school's view of racial integration. The primitivist school had ridiculed the integrationist efforts of middle-class blacks, and chided them for their squeamish response to exotic portrayals of lower-class blacks. Though the primitivist school derived from interracial associations, its literary preoccupations did not include propagandizing for racial integration. In the opinion of the black primitivist writers, segregated black community life should be cherished and preserved. While they opposed racial nationalism, they hardly saw any salvation for blacks in racial integration, through being absorbed into mainstream white American society. Rather they arrived at the curious belief, as we noted earlier, that "primitivist" black ethnic culture would be the salvation of white American society, by liberating it from psychological inhibition; black ethnic culture would invigorate white America's emotionally flaccid way of life.

The naturalistic protest writers viewed white American culture and racial integration in an entirely different light. In fact, as we saw in the case of Richard Wright, two important but seldom acknowledged facts about the proletarian school were its positive view of white American culture and its faith in the benefits of racial integration. This subtext, which turned out to be far stronger than its commitment to class revolution, was evidenced in the persistence of the integration theme even after the school dissociated from Marxism. In short, it was the mainstream white society, not the segregated black environment, that was seen as black America's salvation. We see the importance placed on racial integration, for instance, in Richard Wright's personal observations: "When I contemplated the area of No Man's Land into which the Negro mind in America had been shunted, I wondered if there had ever been in all human history a more corroding and devastating attack upon the personalities of men than the idea of racial discrimination" (Wright 1969, 173).

And elsewhere he wrote, "The essence of the irony of the plight of the Negro in America, to me, is that he is doomed to live in isolation." Simply put, the root of Bigger's predicament was racial segregation.

> What made Bigger's social consciousness most complex was the fact that he was hovering unwanted between two worlds—between powerful America and his own stunted place in life—and I took upon myself the task of trying to make the reader feel this No Man's Land. The most I could say of Bigger was that he felt the need for a whole life and acted out of that need; that was all. (Wright 1970, 27)

Thus racial integration, in their view, would solve the problems plaguing lower-class blacks. The overlay of Marxian ideology, however, obscured this message, for few critics commented on this assimilationist message. Yet unless we recognize its importance in the naturalistic protest school's ideological perspective, it is impossible to understand the complexity of their attraction to the white American leftist political movement.

Images of Black Ethnic Culture

Not surprisingly, these writers' attitudes toward racial assimilation and black American ethnic culture were diametrically opposed. Scorning segregated black community life, they ignored the strengths of black ethnic culture, as can be seen in Wright's characterization of talk among young lower-class black males: "I could hear Bigger Thomas on Chicago's South Side saying: 'Man, what we need is a leader like Marcus Garvey. We need a nation, a flag, an army of our own. We colored folks ought to organize into groups and have generals, captains, lieutenants, and so forth. We ought to take Africa and have a nation-home'" (Wright 1970, 23).

Such talk, in Wright's opinion, was symptomatic of black America's cultural deprivation.

> I'd know, while listening to these childish words, that a white man would smile derisively at them. But I could not smile, for I knew the truth of these words from the facts of my own life. The deep hunger in those childish ideas was like a flash of lightning, illuminating the whole dark inner landscape of Bigger's mind. Those words told me that the civilization which had given birth to Bigger contained no spiritual sustenance, had created no culture which could mold and claim his allegiance and faith, had sensitized him and had left him stranded, a free agent to roam the streets of our cities, a hot and whirling vortex of undisciplined and unchanneled impulses. (Wright 1970, 23)

These negative images of black ethnic culture reflected these writers' alienation from the values and rituals of black community life.

In contrast to Wright, Chester Himes did perceive a black middle-class culture, but he rejected it as banal, unworthy of respect. This is revealed in the musings of the protagonist in *If He Hollers Let Him Go*.

> In the three years in L.A. I'd worked up to a good job in a shipyard, bought a new Buick car, and cornered off the finest colored chick west of Chicago— to my way of thinking. All I had to do was marry her and my future was in the bag. If a black boy couldn't be satisfied with that he couldn't be satisfied with anything.
>
> But what I knew about myself was that my desire for such a life was conditional. It only caught up with me on the crest of being black—when I could accept being black, when I could see no other out, such a life looked great. (Himes 1956, 144)

The character (Bob Jones) realizes that this is precisely the kind of success that would please most black Americans, a modest improvement in material comforts, marriage, a family, and a resigned, reasonably contented, black middle-class existence. But for him that is not enough.

> I knew I'd wake up someday and say the hell with it, I didn't want to be the biggest Negro who ever lived, neither Toussaint L'Ouverture nor Walter White. Because deep inside me, where the white folks couldn't see, it didn't mean a thing. If you couldn't swing down Hollywood Boulevard and know that you belonged; if you couldn't make a polite pass at Lana Turner at Ciro's without having the gendarmes beat the black off you for getting out of your place; if you couldn't eat a thirty dollar dinner at a hotel without choking on the insults, being a great big "Mister" nigger didn't mean a thing. (Himes 1956, 144–45)

And then he lets fly an outburst of contempt: "Anyone who wanted could be nigger-rich, nigger-important, have their Jim Crow religion and go to nigger heaven" (Himes 1956, 145)

Given their jaundiced view of black American ethnic culture, it is not surprising that none of the naturalistic protest writers worked within the black community as Communist organizers. Nor is it surprising that they thought Africa was irrelevant to black Americans. In fact, as we saw earlier, Richard Wright regarded talk about Garvey and African nationalism as "childish."

A similar indifference to Africa is revealed in the musings of the protagonist in Himes's novel, specifically in reference to his putative African ancestry:

> They keep thinking about me in connection with Africa. But I wasn't born in Africa. I didn't know anyone who was. I learned in history that my ancestors were slaves brought over from Africa. But I'd forgotten them, just like the aristocratic blue bloods of America have forgotten what they learned in history—that most of their ancestors were the riffraff of Europe—thieves, jailbirds, beggars, and outcasts. (Himes 1956, 143)

The implication here is clear: Africa is hardly a place he looked upon with pride.

Their negative attitudes about Africa must be understood within the historical context. As black Americans who had no direct exposure to Africa, they accepted the prevailing stereotypes of Africans as crude and uncivilized people, the view propagated through school curricula, newspapers, magazines, and movies by the dominant Euro-American culture, when most of Africa—it is important to recall—existed under the yoke of colonialism.

Richard Wright would later become interested in African liberation movements, after he settled in France. But those interests, as we will see, failed to change his view about Africa.

EVERYBODY'S PROTEST NOVEL: SOUNDING THE DEATH KNELL FOR A LITERARY SCHOOL

The naturalistic protest school ended in the late 1940s. While it is impossible to cite the specific date of its demise, its death knell was sounded in 1949 by a brash, talented young black writer named James Baldwin. There was a story behind Baldwin's role as its eulogist and executioner. He had met Richard Wright initially in New York, seeking his help in securing a writing fellowship. As did other young black writers, Baldwin regarded Wright as a mentor and icon, as well as a potential source of support for his fledgling literary career. Of that first meeting, Baldwin recalled: "I was twenty, a carnivorous age; he was then as old as I am now, thirty-six; he had been my idol since high school, and I, as a fledgling Negro writer, was very shortly in the position of his protégé" (Baldwin 1963, 152). "Wright's work," Baldwin confessed, "was an immense liberation and revelation for me. He became my ally and my witness, and alas! my father."

Baldwin—with Wright's assistance—acquired a Eugene Saxton Fellowship in 1945. In 1947, Baldwin also expatriated to Paris, where he occasionally saw Wright. One evening, Baldwin recalled, he, Wright, and Chester Himes went out drinking. Baldwin's and Wright's relationship was cordial on the surface, but the surface was deceiving as Baldwin avoided revealing to Wright his feelings about their relationship. He actually resented Wright, whose manner, especially when they talked about literature, was patronizing and condescending. In those conversations, Wright always took a political point of view because he regarded literature as an instrument for effecting social change; while Baldwin, wary about linking literature to politics, favored an artistic conception of literature, which Wright ridiculed as "that art for art's sake crap." Their divergent views about literature were based not on abstract philosophical principles but on their very different life experiences—Baldwin had not apprenticed in the Depression-era Communist Party.

Their relationship finally ruptured in June 1949, as a result of an article Baldwin wrote for *Partisan Review*—"Everybody's Protest Novel"—which unmercifully attacked the naturalistic protest school. Up to that time, the school had been virtually unassailable among black intellectuals, because it was regarded as advancing the black American struggle for racial

justice. But Baldwin's article changed that. He went for the school's jugu-
lar, attacking its ideological rationale and credibility. Baldwin wrote:

> The protest novel, so far from being disturbing, is an accepted and comfort-
> ing aspect of the American scene, ramifying that framework we believe to be
> so necessary. Whatever unsettling questions are raised are evanescent, titil-
> lating; remote, for this has nothing to do with us, it is safely ensconced in the
> social arena, where, indeed, it has nothing to do with anyone, so that finally
> we receive a very definite thrill of virtue from the fact that we are reading
> such a book at all. (Baldwin 1968, 14)

In short, Baldwin suggested that the school's use of shock provided its
white American audience an emotional catharsis, a ritual exorcism of
guilt that relieved them of the burden of taking action to effect social
change. "This report from the pit reassures us of its reality and its darkness and of our own salvation; and as long as such books are published,
an American liberal said to me, 'everything will be alright'" (Baldwin
1968, 14).

Perhaps if Baldwin had set forth his argument in a detached rather than
a personal tone, his relationship with Wright would have survived the critique. But euphemisms hardly suited Baldwin's purpose: he aimed to destroy Wright's reputation. Hence he turned his attack directly to *Native
Son*. "Bigger's tragedy is not that he is cold or black or hungry, not even
that he has accepted a theology of his being sub-human and feels constrained, therefore, to battle for his humanity according to those brutal criteria bequeathed him at his birth" (Baldwin 1968, 17).

This dehumanized image of black American personality, Baldwin argued, had come to symbolize—to the eyes of white America—black
ghetto youth. "The failure of the protest novel lies in its rejection of life,
the human being, the denial of his beauty, dread, power, in its insistence
that it is his categorization alone which is real and which cannot be transcended" (Baldwin 1968, 17).

Several years later Baldwin wrote an even more penetrating critique of
the naturalistic protest fiction for *Partisan Review*. It is important to note
that Wright had published no book since 1945. Although Baldwin did not
know this, Wright was working on a novel that would depart drastically
from the protest ideology. This shift no doubt resulted from the changed
postwar cultural climate that inspired Baldwin's attack.

In this second article, "Many Thousands Gone," Baldwin tempered his
personal attack by noting Wright's importance as a writer. He then explained how whites had thrust on Wright the role of "spokesman" for
thirteen million black Americans. Writers, Baldwin argued, should reject
such roles. "It is a false responsibility (since writers are not congress-
men)." Nor, he added, should the writer act as an agent of revolutionary

struggle. He then indicated where he thought the naturalistic protest movement had gone astray. "This climate common to most Negro protest novels . . . has led us all to believe that in Negro life there exists no tradition, no field of manners, no possibility of ritual or intercourse, such as may, for example, sustain the Jew even after he has left his father's house" (Baldwin 1968, 28).

In effect, Baldwin was complaining about the absence of black ethnic culture (i.e., the rituals, customs, and values of black community life) as the basis of meaning and order, in the lives of the black protagonists depicted in these literary works. This cultural void in the protest fiction, Baldwin argued, created "its climate of anarchy and unmotivated and unapprehended disaster" (Baldwin 1968, 28). Doubtless he was comparing these protest works with the novel he was then writing, *Go Tell It on the Mountain*, which would situate its protagonist firmly within working-class black American ethnic culture.

But black ethnic culture was not the only void Baldwin noted. He also highlighted the absence of interracial romantic attractions in the protest writers' depictions of black/white relationships. Though several of the black protest writers had married white women, such romantic attractions were seldom dealt with in their literary works. "In most novels written by Negroes until today," observed Baldwin "(with the exception of Chester Himes's *If He Hollers Let Him Go* 1956), there is a great space where sex ought to be; and what fills this space is *violence*."

Though Baldwin did not further analyze that attraction, it derived from that literary school's implicit idealization of white middle-class life. Richard Wright's depiction of the Daltons, for instance, contrasts strikingly with Bigger's existence. They have education, money, a large house, and servants, and apparently—a problem-free existence. The Daltons resembled the early television sitcom caricatures of family life depicted in such programs as *Ozzie and Harriet* and *Father Knows Best*, mythical images of mainstream white America that saturated popular culture.

Such idealized images of white American middle-class life had a large hand in shaping the naturalistic protest writers' social aspirations, reflected in the decisions of many of these writers to marry white women and to expatriate to Europe. Europe allowed them to neutralize—if not altogether to escape—racial ascription and find acceptance in white societies, surely an ironic outcome for a literary movement that had begun with the objective of giving voice to the destitute black masses.

Richard Wright and Chester Himes settled permanently in Europe. Younger writers such as James Baldwin and William Demby also found their way to Europe. Ralph Ellison would live in Europe for several years. Willard Motley expatriated to Mexico. It is hardly surprising that these writers, after leaving the United States, ceased to be preoccupied with the hardships of black ghetto life.

CONCLUSION

The privacy or obscurity of Negro life makes that life capable, in our imaginations, of producing anything at all; and thus the idea of Bigger's monstrosity can be presented without fear of contradiction, since no American (white) has the knowledge or authority to contest it and no Negro the voice.

—James Baldwin 1963, 32–33

As Baldwin suggests in this incisive observation, the naturalistic protest school distorted black American social consciousness. Though it drama- tized the social issues of racial injustice and poverty, its ideological per- spective derived from a white American political movement which—like the bohemian-primitivist movement of the 1920s—both provided oppor- tunities for aspiring young black writers and shaped their outlook on black American life. This resulted in images of black social reality that failed to evoke the life experiences of ordinary black Americans.

Finally, we come to the matter of that school's normative implications. Although it was viewed as a political literature that advocated radical so- cial change, the naturalistic protest school actually embodied both politi- cal and assimilationist implications. As we noted earlier, its protest was, in large measure, premised on an idealized image of middle-class white America and aspirations for racial integration. While most commentators highlighted its radical political message, they overlooked its equally im- portant assimilationist subtext, which constituted a new, significant cul- tural development. Put simply, the hegemonic cultural process, through which the naturalistic protest literature developed, went beyond the ear- lier primitivist literary school, as white American values were now being incorporated into black literary assessments of black American life.

We will elaborate on this hegemonic cultural process in the final chap- ter. But now let's turn to the new dominant black literary school that emerged in the postwar social climate, after the naturalistic protest school's demise.

Claude McKay. Photo courtesy of the Yale Collection of American Literature, Beinecke Rare Book and Manuscript Library.

Jean Toomer. Photo courtesy of the Yale Collection of American Literature, Beinecke Rare Book and Manuscript Library.

Langston Hughes. Photo courtesy of the Yale Collection of American Literature, Beinecke Rare Book and Manuscript Library.

Countee Cullen. The photo is
inscribed to Carl Van Vechten.
Photo courtesy of the Yale
Collection of American
Literature, Beinecke Rare Book
and Manuscript Library.

Carl Van Vechten. This photo
is inscribed "For Langston."
Photo courtesy of the Yale
Collection of American
Literature, Beinecke Rare Book
and Manuscript Library.

Alain Locke. This photo is
inscribed to James Weldon
Johnson. Photo courtesy of the
Yale Collection of American
Literature, Beinecke Rare Book
and Manuscript Library.

James Weldon Johnson.
Photo courtesy of the Yale
Collection of American
Literature, Beinecke Rare Book
and Manuscript Library.

Waldo Frank. This photo was taken by Alfred Stieglitz and is reproduced here courtesy of the Yale Collection of American Literature, Beinecke Rare Book and Manuscript Library.

Charlotte Osgood Mason. This photo was taken by James Weldon Johnson and is reproduced here courtesy of the Yale Collection of American Literature, Beinecke Rare Book and Manuscript Library.

Richard Wright.
Photo courtesy of the Yale
Collection of American
Literature, Beinecke Rare Book
and Manuscript Library.

Chester Himes. This photo was
taken by Carl Van Vechten and
is reproduced here with the
permission of the Van Vechten
Trust. Photo courtesy of the
Yale Collection of American
Literature, Beinecke Rare Book
and Manuscript Library.

Ralph Ellison. The photo is inscribed "To Langston, 'the Dreamkeeper.'"
Photo courtesy of the Yale Collection of American Literature, Beinecke
Rare Book and Manuscript Library.

Leroi Jones (Amiri Baraka) and Larry Neal, New York, 1968. This photo was taken by James Hinton and is reproduced here with his permission. Photo courtesy of the Yale Collection of American Literature, Beinecke Rare Book and Manuscript Library.

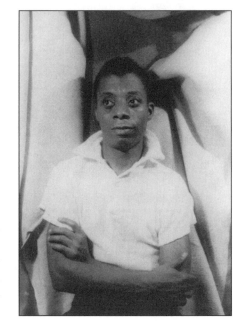

James Baldwin. This photo was taken by Carl Van Vechten and is reproduced here with the permission of the Van Vechten Trust. Photo courtesy of the Yale Collection of American Literature, Beinecke Rare Book and Manuscript Library.

3

※

The Era of the Existentialist School

Political Disillusionment and Retreat into Individualism

> Most of the social realists of the period were concerned less with tragedy than with injustice. I wasn't, and am not, primarily concerned with injustice, but with art.
>
> —Ellison 1966, 170

The advent of a new ideological climate can seldom be neatly demarcated like the founding of a nation or the birth of an individual, for changes in cultural process are too fluid to be assigned such precise chronological markers. Nevertheless, although it is difficult to say when exactly such a change begins, every dominant ideological movement ultimately encounters new social forces that erode its foundation. Like the rising tide of a flood slowly washing away topsoil, new social forces transform perceptions of social reality by shifting the cultural process to different ideological preoccupations. Such were the effects of new social forces on the dominant ideological direction of black American literature during the immediate postwar era.

As noted in chapter 2, the writers of the dominant naturalistic protest school underwent a transition during the war years. They continued to protest racial injustices, but their writings operated in an ideological void—uninspired by a vision of an alternative social order, a vision of social transformation. This was evidenced perhaps most clearly in Richard Wright's *Black Boy* (Wright 1945), where racism was depicted as psychological pathology, rather than as an inherent feature of capitalist society. Thus while the black protest school during this transitional period continued to emphasize the problems of racism and poverty, it was now bereft of its previous Marxist faith, its optimistic anticipation of interracial unity and social change. Also, and equally important, it was no longer linked to the opposition white intelligentsia. In light of these developments, it is hardly surprising that after the mid-1940s the black protest school disintegrated. The former black protest writers were searching for a new ideological direction.

THE NATIONAL SCENE: THE BEGINNING OF THE COLD WAR

Perhaps nothing is of more importance, both as cause and effect, to the conservative mood than . . . the intellectual and political collapse of American liberalism. . . . [In] the economic boom and military terror of this era, a small group of political primitives, on the middle levels of power, have emptied domestic politics of rational content, and decisively lowered the level of public sensibility.

—Mills 1963, 219

Following the economic and social dislocations of the Depression and World War II, most observers assumed American society was entering a period of political normalcy. But those assumptions were soon dispelled. With the Soviet Union's sudden emergence as a superpower, a conservative political reaction swept across the United States in response to what many perceived as a threat of Communist world domination. This Soviet threat, in contrast to previous American international conflicts, was viewed as being not just military but also, indeed most important, ideological. That was because of the large international network of Communist parties, which were thought to be instruments for the expansion of Soviet power. In consequence, the climate of American domestic politics drastically changed. Proponents of leftist ideology now became suspect. Not just the American Communist Party but all American leftist political groups, in fact anyone criticizing injustices in American society, fell under a cloud of suspicion. In the eyes of many Americans, throughout the immediate postwar years, domestic radicalism acquired the onus of treason.

That distorted perception was reinforced by news stories revealing lapses in national security. In 1948, in highly publicized testimony before a congressional committee, Whittaker Chambers, a former editor of *Time* magazine, accused Alger Hiss, a state department official, of giving him documents that were intended for a Soviet agent. This allegation hit the nation like a bombshell. Noted one observer, "No other episode in the postwar period did more to convince the public that, after all, treason had reached into high places and was still there" (Matusow 1970, 7). That view seemed to be corroborated by the discovery of several other federal espionage incidents. Judith Coplon, another state department employee, was caught handing FBI documents to a Soviet agent; and a British scientist, Dr. Klaus Fuchs, who had worked in the United States on the highly secret atomic bomb project, was arrested in England after being caught passing atomic secrets to Soviet agents (Matusow 1970, 9). But among those postwar espionage allegations, none aroused more controversy than the case of Julius and Ethel Rosenberg, who were accused of passing to the Soviets key documents that helped them develop the atomic bomb. The Rosenbergs were convicted and executed for treason.

Many Americans thought these and other suspected national security violations were linked to leftist ideology and the expansion of Soviet power, an expansion which was evidenced most dramatically in the postwar emergence of Communist governments in Poland, Hungary, Czechoslovakia, Yugoslavia, and other Eastern European nations. When the Communists seized power in Asia's most populous country, the perceived threat of leftist groups to American national security reached the point of virtual hysteria. As one historian observed, "The event that most frightened the American people in 1949 and opened the way for a witch hunt was the victorious advance of Mao's guerrillas across mainland China" (Matusow 1970, 8).

An anti-Communist crusade swept across the United States, generating a barrage of repressive measures both within and outside of government. For example, "In March 1947, President Truman issued an executive order which set up the Federal Employee Loyalty Program, which called on the FBI to make a 'name check' on each of more than 300,000 persons already on the Federal payroll, from letter carriers to cabinet officers, and the approximately 500,000 who would apply for jobs each year" (Phillips 1966, 361). Shortly afterwards, Congress passed the Internal Security Act, a law requiring Communists to register with the Attorney General, stipulating imprisonment for those who failed to comply. Though Truman vetoed the act because he believed it was unconstitutional, the tide of anti-Communist hysteria in the nation was so strong that Congress easily overrode the veto. Also in reaction to the presumed Communist danger, "several state legislatures, including California, set up un-American activities committees to investigate 'subversives' in their areas. Dozens of school boards and university regents began to demand loyalty oaths and security checks of their teachers and to fire those who resisted. The American Legion and similar organizations in many communities set themselves up as censors of school texts, libraries, and public lecture platforms" (Phillips 1966, 372–73). Simply put, much of American society was seized by fears of

Communism. Complained one author chronicling these right-wing political developments:

> "Loyalty" has become a cult, an obsession, in the United States. But even loyalty itself is now defined relatively. . . . The whole postwar accent is something called un-Americanism—a hyphenated synonym for un-orthodoxy. . . . The term "Disloyalty" as it is used today is nothing more or less than a circumlocution for treason. (Barth 1951, 361)

The most destructive manifestation of that right-wing reaction occurred with the emergence of Senator Joseph McCarthy. A cunning and ambitious demagogue, McCarthy resorted to ruthless and unprincipled tactics as he exploited postwar political anxieties and emerged as the nation's leading anti-Communist crusader. Noted one historian, "He dominated the channels of communication during the early 1950s. Indeed, no senator in American history, even the most famous and powerful, . . . ever approached the sheer quantity of publicity and notice he was to elicit" (Matusow 1970, 8). McCarthy's histrionic innuendo and slander quickly acquired a legion of imitators.

This was revealed in the rapid diffusion of the anti-Communist crusade throughout American popular culture. For example, "in New York four enterprising ex-FBI agents, using files of various Congressional committees published a book called *Red Channels,* in which they detailed the allegedly Communist connections of 150 writers, actors, directors and others in the entertainment industry" (Goldman 1960, 212). Among the victims of "the commercialized blacklisting was the well-known actress Jean Muir, whose contract to star in a popular radio serial . . . was canceled by the National Broadcast Company. . . . Scores of other actors, writers, professors, and figures in public life found themselves similarly stigmatized by *Red Channels* and its sudden spawn of imitators." A Hollywood studio canceled the movie *Hiawatha* because it thought people might view the hero's efforts to stop wars between Indians as "propaganda for the Communist peace offensive." In yet another example, a television network canceled an actress's contract because her name appeared in the Communist Party's newspaper *Daily Worker.* These and other mean-spirited acts such as harassment, blacklisting, character defamation, and job termination became common tactics that right-wing zealots used to demonize and punish suspected leftists.

The conservative reaction in popular culture also was evidenced in the popularity of several anti-Communist books that appeared on national best-seller lists. *Washington Confidential,* a purported exposé of Communists written by two newspapermen, enjoyed best-seller status through most of 1951. Another best-seller that year, Mickey Spillane's *One Lonely Night*, occupied a class unto itself when it came to projecting anti-Communist propaganda. Its professed hatred of Communists bordered on sadism. As we can see in the attitude expressed by its tough guy detective hero Mike Hammer: "I killed more people tonight than I have fingers on my hands. I shot them in cold blood and enjoyed every minute of it. . . . They were Commies Lee. They were red-sons-of bitches who should have died long ago. . . . They never thought there were people like me in this country. They figured us all to be soft as horse manure and just as stupid" (Goldman 1960, 212). That novel's anti-Communist message apparently reflected widespread public sentiments, as it sold more than three million copies.

Although less crudely expressed than Spillane's melodramatic diatribes, the dominant postwar black literary school would manifest similar anti-Communist sentiments.

THE POSTWAR RETREAT OF LIBERAL WHITE AMERICAN INTELLECTUAL CULTURE

The postwar years brought major changes in the American intellectual community. In sharp contrast to its radical political activism of the 1930s, the oppositional white intelligentsia, which had nurtured the naturalistic protest school, abandoned political radicalism. This was manifested initially during the transitional years of the war, in their retreat from Marxism to liberalism; but later, as the Cold War political reaction surfaced, many retreated even further and embraced a conservative ideology.

Citing examples of this reactionary tendency among some former leftist intellectuals, Morris Dickstein in *Gates of Eden* incisively describes the Cold War cultural climate, as he notes that:

> At a low ebb of American civil liberties Mary McCarthy wrote a novel about a faculty Machiavelli who tries to save his job by posing as a victim of political persecution; that Robert Warshow and Leslie Fielder wrote essays attacking the Rosenbergs and their sympathizers rather than the men who had just executed them; that Irving Kristol and others minimized the importance of McCarthy while criticizing liberals and intellectuals who were alarmed by him; that an influential group of social scientists antipathetic to McCarthy tried to blame him, in a sense, on the Left rather than the Right by associating his demagoguery with populism and the presumed dangers of ideology. (Dickstein 1977, 29)

Even more forthright, some openly supported governmental political repression of leftists. Dickstein goes on to observe that:

Sidney Hook supported the firing of supposed Communists from schools and universities on libertarian grounds, since such centers of independent thought had no room for those whose minds were by definition unfree; that many teachers and academics stood quietly while some of their colleagues became unpersons; that Elia Kazan and others went before the House Un-American Activities Committee to beat their breasts, swear fealty, name names, tell all—the "all" being mainly trivial gossip many years old, the detritus of left wing political life of the thirties and early forties. (Dickstein 1971)

Yet another momentous development occurred when the American Congress for Cultural Freedom (ACCF) was formed, comprising right-wing and liberal intellectuals who, in the words of Christopher Lasch, "took quite literally the assertion . . . that the communist issue overrode conventional distinctions between left and right. Right-wingers like (James) Burnham, (James) Farrell, Ralph De Toledano, John Chamberlain, John Dos Passos, and even Whittaker Chambers consorted with (Arthur) Schlesinger, Hook, Irving Kristol, Daniel Bell, and others" (Lasch 1969, 80).

Later investigation revealed that the ACCF was financed by the U.S. Central Intelligence Agency. Though most participants claimed they had been deceived, their involvement in activity funded by the CIA only underscored the extent to which many prominent liberal intellectuals capitulated to the conservative political reaction. "In the early fifties," notes Lasch, "this uneasy alliance worked because the liberals usually took positions that conceded a good deal of ground to the right, if they were not indistinguishable from those of the right" (Lasch 1969, 80–81).

While many postwar political developments within the white American intelligentsia influenced the ascending postwar black literary school, none was more important than the liberal white literati's shift to an apolitical posture. These white writers were turning away from political opposition because they no longer thought of themselves as rebels. This was revealed most emphatically in a symposium titled "Our Country and Culture." Convened in 1950 by Philip Rahv, the editor of the former leftist *Partisan Review,* this symposium sought to explain the changed liberal ideological outlook.

The "reconciliation" of the intellectuals, according to (Philip) Rahv, reflected not merely the collapse of "Utopian illusions and heady expectations" of the thirties but American culture's coming of age. "The passage of time has considerably blunted the edge of the old Jamesian complaint as to the bareness of the native scene." Most of the contributors to "Our Country and Our Culture" agreed with this optimistic assessment of American culture, even though they could provide no convincing reasons for doing so; indeed they all deplored "mass culture." Rahv himself admitted, moreover, that "the rout of the left wing movement has depoliticized literature" and given rise to "a kind of detachment from principle and fragmentation of literary life." (Dickstein 1971, 39)

This new literary outlook had been inspired, in part, by the modernist philosophy of existentialism, as formulated by French thinkers during the war. Reacting to the ideological fanaticism of Nazi Germany, which they believed demonstrated the ultimate absurdity of modern conformist culture, the French existentialists rejected all transcendent meanings. The most influential of these French existentialist thinkers—the philosopher Jean-Paul Sartre—argued that all notions of collective identity were corrupt, because they exempted individuals from moral responsibility for their actions. The myth of an Aryan collective identity, the existentialists argued, lay behind Germany's genocidal murder of Jews, as well as other mindless, dehumanizing forms of mass violence, undertaken in the name of racial salvation.

In the United States, it was not so much the threat of Nazi fanaticism but rather the insidious spread of a sterile, monotonous, postwar mass culture, with its mindless conformity to group think, that seemed, to these former leftist writers, to justify their skepticism about utopian visions of American society. Already disillusioned with Marxism and the prospect of proletarian revolution, they now retreated from all forms of political involvement, and became preoccupied with problems of self-identity, struggles to maintain their individuality. Surfacing within the reactionary political climate of the Cold War, their new literary outlook easily accommodated and coexisted with the conservative political crusade.

We can see a conspicuous indifference to public issues—a detachment from politics—pervading the era's most celebrated novels. In a time pervaded by political tension, such leading novels by white American writers as *The Naked and the Dead* (1948), *The Catcher in the Rye* (1951), *Lie Down in Darkness* (1951), *The Old Man and the Sea* (1952), and *The Adventures of Augie March* (1952) remained aloof as they exhibited no concern about public issues and political reform. Instead they highlighted, in varying degrees, the struggles of the individual to preserve the integrity of self from group mind, with the result that celebrations of psychological individualism— and heroic personal alienation—emerged as the literary vogue.

This is not to say the new literary outlook lacked a critical posture, only that its critical posture ignored the society's economic and political flaws. As we noted earlier, these writers directed their scorn at American mass culture: the sterile lifestyle of the expanding middle class, the monotonous uniformity of newly constructed suburban communities, and the dull, conformist pressures of the bureaucratized workplace. Seldom did their criticisms go beyond these surface manifestations of postwar American culture, to the elite controlled political economy.

As Morris Dickstein has pointed out, this new outlook, which was termed critical nonconformism, "was lamentably abstract and typically confined to the cultural sphere. . . . Only the smallest handful of independent intellectuals effectively focused their criticisms where it was most needed: on political decisions, on aggregations of social and economic power, on questions of civil liberties which affected many lives" (Dickstein 1971, 40).

These liberal intellectuals were hardly ignorant about such problems as political corruption, corporate domination, lower-class poverty, and pervasive racism; they simply felt skeptical about political solutions. As Dickstein put it:

> The literary intellectuals, while maintaining the cult of alienation, simply abandoned politics to pursue private myths and fantasies, to devote their work to the closet intensities of the isolated self or isolated personal relationships. The concept of alienation lost its social content and took on an increasingly religious and metaphysical cast. European existentialism and crisis theology became an incalculably great influence on the mood of the fifties—shorn, however, of their political matrix. The moral and psychological Sartre of the forties was admitted. The political Sartre of the fifties was ignored or ridiculed. (Dickstein 1971, 40)

It was this intellectual environment of critical nonconformism that fostered the black existentialist literary school. Following the ideological lead of their white American colleagues, these black existentialist writers combined disdain for group conformity and radical politics with celebrations of alienated individualism.

THE IDEOLOGICAL REORIENTATION
OF BLACK AMERICAN LITERATURE

> I have no desire to write propaganda. . . . I felt it important to explore the full range of American Negro humanity and to affirm those qualities which are of value beyond any question of segregation, economics, or previous condition of servitude.
>
> —Ellison 1966, 36

In the wake of the postwar political changes, the dominant ideological preoccupation of black American literature shifted from public issues of racial oppression to private issues of personal identity. Exemplified by Ralph Ellison's *Invisible Man*, this new existentialist black literary consciousness depicted black America from the perspective of a disillusioned, deracinated, and rootless individualism.

Seeing himself as an opponent of literary propaganda, Ellison suggested that his existentialist outlook emanated from his commitment to an artistic conception of literature. While no doubt sincere, his account of how he came to embrace his existentialist literary outlook concealed as much as it revealed, leaving many questions unanswered. Specifically, what social forces influenced the development of his new ideological perspective? Why did it emerge in the conservative postwar political climate—rather than earlier in the Depression era? And why did his commitment to an artistic conception of literature cause him to embrace an individualistic existentialist perspective, as though that were the only possibility, when many ideological perspectives presumably would have been compatible with an artistic mission?

Ellison's defense of his existentialist ideology as the outcome of his artistic mission was intended to thwart sociological explanations of his outlook (which he detested) by suggesting that it was unrelated to the surrounding postwar political environment. But contrary to Ellison's frequent antisociological pronouncements, the Cold War political climate, and particularly the influence of the oppositional white American literati, played a major part in black American literature's ideological transformation.

Those external social forces operated in conjunction with critically important changes within the black community, which must also be taken into account, if we are to understand the social conditions that lay behind the ascent of the black existentialist literary school.

THE POSTWAR BLACK COMMUNITY:
RESTABILIZATION AND MODERATE REFORM

> We have become convinced in the course of this inquiry that the North is prepared for a fundamental redefinition of the Negro's status in America.
>
> —Myrdal 1944

Though few perceived it at the time, the American racial system during the immediate postwar period was undergoing a peculiar structural change, shifting it from rigid caste segregation to token integration, with the result that it fostered the formation of the new black bourgeoisie. The appearance of this group, who were the first black Americans to gain professional employment in mainstream white American institutions, would alter public perceptions of race relations. It was hardly coincidental that their appearance coincided with the ascent of existentialist ideology in black America literature.

As we can see in the above quote, the Swedish sociologist Gunnar Myrdal, who wrote *An American Dilemma*, expected a transformation of American race relations during the postwar period. That transformation, Myrdal noted, would result from both the black community's increased influence in national elections and the United States's growing concern about the effect of racial segregation on its image abroad, especially among the new African and Asian nations emerging from colonialism. Myrdal was at least partly correct. A major sector of the northern white American elite was changing its racial attitudes, but that change hardly resulted in the sweeping racial reforms Myrdal predicted. These northern white elites were prepared to support only piecemeal race relations reforms, by opening some previously segregated professions to a few talented black Americans. This was not what Myrdal expected. Like other optimistic observers of American race relations, he greatly underestimated the resilience of the racial caste system, and in consequence failed to foresee the advent of this token racial integration.

To understand the linkage between the advent of token integration and the formation of the black existentialist literary school, we must examine the postwar changes within the larger black community that encouraged a more conservative outlook on black American life.

The Changed Social Climate within the Postwar Black Community

Perhaps the most conspicuous characteristic of the postwar black community was its political quiescence. This was evidenced in the absence of a major political movement focused on the black community's social problems. No new ideological force—such as the Garvey movement of the 1920s or the leftist movement among black intellectuals during the Depression—surfaced in the immediate postwar era. The tensions in the early 1940s that had produced race riots in Detroit and New York, and A. Philip Randolph's threat to march on Washington, soon dissolved. As postwar economic growth accelerated in response to increased consumer demand, black workers were absorbed in the new industrial expansion, creating a black community, by the mid-1940s, that was enjoying unprecedented economic progress. The black American masses in the northern industrial cities were being transformed into a stable blue collar class. As one observer has noted, this period witnessed "the most dramatic improvement in the economic status of black people that has ever taken place in the urban industrial economy. A million and a half black workers were part of the war-production work force alone, and the income of black workers increased twice as fast as that of whites" (Steinberg 1981, 205).

Hence most working-class blacks felt optimistic during the immediate postwar years, an outlook that helped to stimulate a huge wave of migration as hundreds of thousands of blacks left the South to seek jobs in northern industries. "Between 1940 and 1950 net migration from the South reached an all-time high of 1,600,000" (Steinberg 1981, 205). Blacks were not only becoming one of the largest ethnic groups in northern cities, far exceeding their more modest numbers during the 1920s and 1930s. But also, as a direct result of this unprecedented migration, they were achieving increasing influence in national political elections.

This is hardly to say that urban blacks no longer faced racial barriers. The overwhelming majority were obliged to live within the boundaries of racial caste. In most northern cities, schools, churches, movie theaters, public parks, and residential neighborhoods remained segregated. As the black populations expanded in such cities as Chicago, St. Louis, Detroit, and New York, so too did the borders of the "black belts," the unofficially designated areas of black settlement. Thus, it is important to understand that the black lower class's optimistic outlook was stimulated by their improved economic situation, not their expectations of an end to racial segregation.

The old black bourgeoisie also felt optimistic. But unlike the black lower class, they were optimistic because of their restored faith in black business enterprises, which they saw as the key to the black community's future salvation. Reverting to the black bourgeoisie outlook of the 1920s, they promoted an ethnic conception of the black community's economic development. Despite the absence of evidence that black businesses could employ the steadily increasing flood of black workers, they clung to their faith in black business because of their vested economic interests in preserving segregated black community life. As E. Franklin Frazier observed, they "were the largest beneficiaries of the black community's economic gains" (Frazier 1957, 169). Also important were the attitudes of conservative white political leaders, who encouraged the old black bourgeoisie to believe that black business enterprises eventually would have the resources to solve the black community's problems of unemployment, poverty, and slum housing. As Frazier observed with a note of irony: "The myth of Negro business has . . . been strengthened, by the encouragement which the white community has given the belief of Negroes that the accumulation of wealth through business will solve their problems" (Frazier 1957, 169).

In effect, the postwar social climate restored the old black bourgeoisie's faith in American capitalism. Hence they not only downplayed the problems of racial discrimination; they opposed those black intellectuals who continued to criticize the American government and to advocate radical social changes.

The Black Intellectual Community

Without question, the dominant ideological force within the black intellectual community was the NAACP. Adapting to the Cold War political climate as did liberal white American political groups, the NAACP joined the antileftist crusade, motivated by its desire to protect the credibility of its advocacy for civil rights as a patriotic activity. "The NAACP leaders were disturbed about the communist campaign in the immediate post war period, not because they believed the party had or would secure a significant Negro following, but because the label of 'communist' might be pinned on the Association by its conservative opponents" (Record 1964, 135). The NAACP thus yielded to no group in the vigor of its opposition to the Communist Party as it went beyond public denunciations of leftists to implementing internal organizational controls, with the objective of thwarting Communist infiltration in its branches. "In 1950 the Association adopted a policy of prohibiting membership to communists; it also strengthened the hand of the Executive Board and National Staff in dealing administratively with threatened branches" (Record 1964, 146). The national office was given power to expel any branch that had fallen under the control of the Communist Party, initiating a policy that effectively checked the party's influence. These measures succeeded. As Wilson Record has noted, "after the war (the party's) influence among Negroes generally and in the NAACP specifically hit a new low" (Record 1964, 134).

The black intellectual community's antileftist sentiments were evidenced in not only its opposition to Communists but also its feeble support for the Progressive Party. Most black intellectuals distanced themselves from the Progressive Party because they believed it was backed by Communists. Despite the stronger Progressive Party platform on civil rights, these intellectuals, along with the larger black community, overwhelmingly supported Harry Truman in the 1948 presidential election.

But several maverick black intellectuals deviated from this antileftist trend. Most notable among those who remained committed to leftist ideology throughout the Cold War period were W. E. B. DuBois and Paul Robeson. However, neither wielded much influence in the black community. DuBois, persisting in his attacks against American racial injustices, resigned from the NAACP in 1934 because of a policy dispute. Though he later returned to the association, he was subsequently fired in 1948 for criticizing the NAACP's political moderation. "The break came after the press secured a copy of a memorandum in which DuBois stated that the association was abandoning its efforts to ease the world plight of the Negro in order to serve the interests of the Truman administration" (Broderick 1959, 207). This brought DuBois's long affiliation with the NAACP to an end.

Robeson, having a long track record as a supporter of the Soviet Union, openly expressed leftist sentiments. For example, "in Paris, Robeson was moved to declare before a 'peace' rally that fifteen million American Negroes would not fight against the Soviet Union in the event of war between Jim Crow America and the last stronghold of racial equality" (Record 1964, 125). That statement provoked outrage within the black intellectual community which reflected the anxiety many black intellectuals felt about any alleged links between the black community and radical politics. In the words of Wilson Record, "Robeson was repudiated by practically every American Negro spokesman of national stature, including Walter White of the NAACP, Lester Granger of the National Urban League, and Jackie Robinson, the Negro major leaguer" (Record 1964, 175).

Both Robeson and DuBois were investigated by federal agencies. Robeson appeared before the House Un-American Activities Committee, where he stood his ground and defended his civil liberties. Though he acquitted himself quite well in his testimony before the committee, his theatrical career and public reputation were virtually destroyed. He lost his right to travel abroad, where he remained popular. Stigmatized as a Communist sympathizer and a disloyal American, Robeson never regained his reputation. Following his public degradation, he spent the rest of his life in relative obscurity, shunned by most black and white intellectuals.

DuBois suffered a similar fate. After being indicted for failing to register as "an agent of a foreign principal," and subsequently acquitted because the prosecution failed to prove its case, he, too, was largely shunned within the black community. "He could find some support in the Negro press, but he complained that the Talented Tenth of business and professional men was 'either silent or actually antagonistic.' An attempt . . . to secure the signatures of prominent Negroes to a fairly mild statement of support did not attract enough signers to warrant its publication" (Broderick 1959, 224).

Robeson and DuBois were relegated to a pariah status. By targeting them, the federal government sent black intellectuals an ominous message: the cost of leftist political activity is professional ruin. That message apparently achieved its objective as few black intellectuals during the Cold War period dared to venture beyond moderate political ideology.

DuBois was so disappointed by what he saw as the black community's political cowardice that he began to express serious misgivings about the recent minor civil rights gains. In fact, he stood almost alone in voicing concerns about the perils of token integration, which he believed was weakening the black community's ethnic solidarity and rendering it politically impotent. "The relaxation of discriminatory pressures had left the Negro free to move in the wrong direction," complained DuBois. "More freedom had not led Negroes into a cemented cultural group helping to create a new haven in America. . . . It had freed them to ape the worst chauvinism and 'social climbing' of the Anglo Saxons" (Broderick 1959, 224).

DuBois's observations turned out to be prescient, as both the incipient new black bourgeoisie and the black existentialist literary school would manifest strong assimilationist tendencies.

EMERGENCE OF THE NEW BLACK BOURGEOISIE

To understand the linkage of the individualistic ideology of the existentialist literary school to the postwar black community, we must take into account the latter's political quiescence and moderation, which conduced to a more privatized perspective on black American experiences. We must also understand the formation of the new black bourgeoisie, because this development awakened public perceptions to a new black American personality type, which the protagonists in the ascending black literary works seemed to confirm.

In contrast to the old black bourgeoisie, which was based in the racially segregated black social world, this new black bourgeoisie moved beyond the boundaries of ghetto life. E. Franklin Frazier apprehended aspects of this development in 1947, when he noted that "the barriers in the North, where nearly a third of the Negroes lived, have tended to be lowered in all phases of public life." Yet Frazier, like other postwar sociological observers, failed to perceive the most important impact of those changes. He thought those changes were similarly affecting all northern blacks. But he was mistaken. In fact, as we noted earlier, the great majority of black Americans continued to exist behind the walls of racial caste. Those blacks most affected by the changes Frazier described constituted a tiny fraction, an elite group of black Americans with exceptional talents. This was the new black bourgeoisie. Scaling the walls of racial caste, these blacks were gaining employment in previously all-white professions, in such fields as athletics, international diplomacy, higher education, law, medicine, entertainment, and the arts. Which is to say, a few black individuals were now entering white professional domains.

To cite some notable examples of this postwar development: Charles Johnson became the first black American to serve as a member of a national commission representing the United States at UNESCO in Paris; Jackie Robinson became the first black American major league baseball player; Ralph Bunche became the first black American United Nations mediator and, subsequently, in 1950, the first black American recipient of the Nobel Peace Prize; William Hinton, a serologist, became the first black American professor at Harvard Medical School; William Hastie became the first black U.S. Circuit Court of Appeals judge; Wesley A. Brown became the first black American graduate of the U.S. Naval Academy; the American Medical Association seated its first black American delegate; Althea Gibson became the first black American player in the National Tennis Championship at Forest Hills, New York; the professional basketball league hired its first black American player; the American Sociological Association elected its first black American president—E. Franklin Frazier; and a major symphony orchestra hired its first black American conductor—Dean Dixon. These are only a few examples of new black bourgeois triumphs, triumphs that marked the onset of token racial integration.

Token integration not only initiated a new structural pattern of race relations. It set in motion changed cultural images of blacks that altered white American perceptions, drawing attention to variations of personality, education, and lifestyle among blacks that conventional racial stereotypes of blacks ignored. Most members of this new black bourgeoisie viewed these changes as evidence that the United States was undergoing an evolution in race relations and opening doors of opportunity to talented black individuals, a perception reinforced by the fact that none of their breakthroughs had resulted from political protest. Individual merit appeared to be the only requirement, and this perception actually contained some truth. The blacks who were breaking through the racial caste barriers into the mainstream professions were exceptionally talented. But like most optimistic postwar readings of race relations reform, this one was exaggerated.

The new black bourgeoisie derived less from endemic changes in white American society than from the latter's efforts to neutralize the mounting strains resulting from its practices of racial apartheid. The United States and the Soviet Union, it is important to recall, were engaged in intense ideological competition. Both nations were vying to influence the Asian and African societies emerging from colonialism. The United States was handicapped in this competition, because its practice of racial segregation constituted an obvious and embarrassing contradiction of its democratic values. Communism's image as a racially egalitarian movement was attracting colored peoples throughout the Third World. If the United States was going to successfully counteract that influence, one thing seemed clear: it could no longer afford the *appearance* of being a racist society.

In addition to this growing awareness of the racial caste system's international repercussions, an important sector of the white American elite, comprising a relatively small but increasing number of business, educational, and governmental leaders, were beginning to manifest more liberal racial attitudes. This change was reflected in such acts as the Brooklyn Dodgers' decision to sign the first black major league baseball player, Truman's executive order to desegregate the Armed Forces, and the Carnegie Foundation's decision to commission a large scale study of American race relations, which resulted in Gunnar Myrdal's *An American Dilemma.*

Spurred by these international and domestic changes, the racial caste system shifted from rigid segregation to modified segregation in the form of token integration. Perhaps the most important effect of this development on the black community was that of weakening its ethnic solidarity. Among the assimilated black professional class, token integration encouraged an apolitical, individualistic approach to racial reforms. For example, members of this new black bourgeoisie such as Ralph Bunche, the internationally acclaimed black American diplomat, began to take an aloof posture and sidestep American racial problems. Jackie Robinson, the man who pioneered racial integration in the nation's most popular professional sport, avoided collective black political action and protest as the means to achieve racial reform. His moderate political outlook was evidenced in his membership in the Republican party and his public denunciation of radical black political activists such as Paul Robeson. Nat King Cole, the singer, the first black celebrity to emerge in American popular culture, assumed residence in Beverly Hills and shunned involvement in the black community's social and political life. Simply put, the new black bourgeoisie embraced assimilation.

Token integration created an illusion of major race relations reform. By admitting this small but highly visible group of blacks into mainstream professional careers, it fostered the impression—particularly in the eyes of the still-ghettoized black masses—that racial barriers were collapsing. The success of blacks like Ralph Bunche, Nat King Cole, and Jackie Robinson suggested not only that the doors of opportunity were now opening but also, and equally important, that the responsibility for success in life now lay in the hands of each black individual. Deflecting attention from the persistence of institutionalized racial apartheid, this message of opportunity, which became commonplace during the Cold War era, constituted the racial system's Big Lie.

It was hardly coincidental that token integration's message of psychological individualism was celebrated by the ascending black existentialist literary school. This is not to say the new black bourgeoisie reflected all aspects of that literary school's ideology. That school's existentialist ideology, particularly as represented in Ralph Ellison's *Invisible Man*, embraced two contradictory conceptions of individualism, as we will see later. The broader and more moderate of those two conceptions constituted a virtual hymn celebrating the ethos of the assimilationist black bourgeoisie.

In effect, both the ascending new black bourgeoisie and the black existentialist literary school helped to foster illusions about black American experiences.

RALPH ELLISON AND *INVISIBLE MAN*

People who want to write sociology should not write novels.
—Ralph Ellison, quoted in Bone 1958, 153

Ralph Waldo Ellison emerged in the conservative postwar era as not only the leading black American writer, but also the foremost black intellectual proponent of psychological individualism. Ellison's intellectual development provides important insights into the intersection of personal experiences and social forces that attracted black writers to the existentialist ideology. He attributed his intellectual development to influences emanating from his childhood and college experiences, but his account failed to explain his post-Depression-era shift to the existentialist perspective.

The son of a construction foreman, Ellison was born in Oklahoma City, Oklahoma, in 1914. Though his parents were not college-educated professionals, they strongly identified with middle-class values, as did many stable black working-class families at the time, because middle-class values defined the ideal of respectability. Stressing the importance of education and the arts, the Ellisons reared their son within the traditions of mainstream American culture. Thus, though Ralph Ellison grew up in a working-class household in a segregated black community, it is important to note, his background hardly resembled working-class black life in either the rural South or the urban ghettos of the North. This was a fact Ellison repeatedly emphasized.

In a sense, Ralph Ellison's first and most enigmatic existentialist creation was not *Invisible Man* but himself—or rather the public personae he cultivated. This is revealed particularly in his reminiscences about his Oklahoma childhood, which he felt obliged to stress in his attempts to explain his more moderate outlook on race relations. "On the level of race relations," he recalled, "my father had many white friends who came to the house when I was quite small, so that any feelings of distrust I was to develop toward whites later on were modified by those with whom I had warm relations. Oklahoma offered many opportunities for such friendships" (O'Meally 1980, 8). Oklahoma was a newly settled frontier region that lacked both a history of slavery and the rigid racial segregation of the deep South. As one commentator has observed: "Breaks in the pattern of segregation contributed to the relatively free atmosphere of Oklahoma. Indians and blacks lived side by side for generations. . . . The Ellisons had many white friends, and black-white integration on a cultural level, at least, was widespread" (O'Meally 1980, 30).

Oklahoma certainly differed from the deep South. But Ellison's account of Oklahoma's race relations was much too rosy. During his youth in the 1920s, Oklahoma's racial climate deteriorated with the arrival of waves of southern white migrants. Blacks began to encounter rigid caste restrictions in downtown movie theaters and other public facilities as well as in education and employment. Reflecting Oklahoma's strained race relations, a major race riot erupted in Tulsa in 1921—sparked by a rumor that a black man had attacked a white girl. Whites destroyed a ten-block section of the black residential area, left three thousand blacks homeless, and twenty-one dead. Oklahoma, in short, was hardly an oasis of liberal race relations. But why did Ellison exaggerate Oklahoma's racial tolerance? This apparently resulted from the controversy *Invisible Man* provoked— many critics, particularly on the political left, charged that Ellison's moderate race relations perspective capitulated to the postwar political reaction. To defend the integrity of his moderate perspective on race relations, Ellison typically responded by recounting his youthful experiences in Oklahoma, and in particular his family's friendly relations with whites. But this explanation left much room for skepticism.

If Ellison had begun his literary career writing from an existentialist ideological perspective, his denial of the Cold War political influences on his writing would be plausible; the question about the origins of his existentialist perspective would hardly arise. But the question does arise— because Ellison began his literary career as a proponent not of existentialist individualism but of Marxist ideology.

The Early Years of Ellison's Literary Career

In 1933, at the age of nineteen, Ellison left Oklahoma to attend college at Tuskegee Institute in Alabama, where he was to remain for three years. Though Ellison had positive intellectual experiences at Tuskegee, chiefly through his exposure to several inspiring teachers, none of those experiences apparently had a significant role in shaping his later existentialist perspective. He found southern black life disappointing, particularly the southern black leaders who presided over southern black colleges and community affairs.

At the end of his junior year in the summer of 1936, he left Tuskegee prompted by disillusionment with southern black life, financial hardships, and the stirrings of wanderlust. Though he expected to return and resume his studies after he earned money from summer employment, he never returned to college.

New York's black Harlem was his destination. Like the earlier generation of aspiring black writers he had read about in Locke's *New Negro,* he settled in Harlem with the objective of experiencing its vibrant cultural life. But Harlem was then experiencing the worst years of the Depression, with severe problems of unemployment and poverty. The naturalistic protest literary school was then forming and Ellison was drawn almost immediately into the orbit of that literary movement, as we noted earlier, through the friendship he developed with Richard Wright (Fabre 1973, 145–46). As one commentator has noted: "Ellison had met Langston Hughes quite by chance on his second day in Harlem. Through Hughes he met Richard Wright, and a friendship between them blossomed" (O'Meally 1980, 30).

His friendship with Richard Wright constituted his first significant literary association and marked the beginning of his apprenticeship under Wright's tutelage:

> Though Wright was older and more secure in his identity as an artist, the two men were basically in the same predicament: they were radically inclined black intellectuals with southern backgrounds trying to survive in New York and struggling to make art in the midst of the Great Depression. They talked endlessly about politics and art, and exchanged jokes and stories. (O'Meally 1980, 30)

Through this friendship, Ellison was exposed to Marxist ideology and drawn into leftist political circles, where he met leading white leftist writers of the era such as Granville Hicks, Isador Schneider, Kenneth Fearing, Clifford Odets, Williams Rollings Jr., and Malcolm Cowley. In fact, throughout this apprentice phase of his literary career, Ellison operated as a radical writer. "From 1937 to 1944 Ellison wrote over twenty book reviews for such radical periodicals as *New Challenge, Direction, Negro Quarterly,* and *New Masses.* Most of these were done for *New Masses,* which, in 1940, printed at least one of Ellison's reviews every month. These leftist reviews reflect a leftist persuasion, which becomes, at points, explicitly Marxist" (O'Meally 1980). Ellison's leftist perspective was hardly hidden or restrained. "Mirroring the Communist Party position of the day, Ellison's criticisms often described black Americans as citizens of a state or nation (like a Russian Soviet) within the United States" (O'Meally 1980). In fact, as O'Meally indicates, Ellison's writings about black American literature virtually parroted the Party's line:

> The literature of black Americans . . . was, Ellison believed, an emerging national literature that should serve to heighten the revolutionary consciousness

of the black populace. The black writer should not instill in his audience mere "race consciousness," however, but awareness of class. Ideally the revolutionary black writer inspires black working people to unite with workers of other "nationalities" against the bourgeoisie, white and black. (O'Meally 1980, 38)

This passage echoes Richard Wright's "Blueprint for Black Literature." Yet later, in *Invisible Man* and his later comments on black American literature, Ellison attacks the Communist Party and its conception of collective political solidarity. I note this not to impugn the credibility of Ellison's existentialist ideological perspective, but only to make clear that the Cold War political climate lay behind that perspective's formation.

Despite Ellison's abrupt ideological shift, both the Marxist and the existentialist phases of his literary career remained linked by a single thematic thread. That was the theme of black assimilation. This theme operates in Ellison's Marxist writings as a subtext, revealed in his emphasis on interracial solidarity and his disparagement of racial consciousness. Assimilation was promoted in the early years of the naturalistic protest school—albeit through seeking working-class solidarity—as an avenue to black salvation. We see a recurrence of this assimilation theme in *Invisible Man*'s existentialist perspective on black American life, again as a subtext, but now linked to moderate bourgeois liberalism and the American democratic creed.

The shift in Ellison's ideological outlook occurred following his return to New York after two years in the Merchant Marines. Ellison lived in virtual isolation. Like other black writers during the postwar period, he had no black literary movement. The naturalistic protest school had dissipated. While most of the major black writers were leaving the United States and seeking a new orientation, the remaining black literary community stood in disarray. During this postwar period, Ellison would spend several years in Italy on a fellowship, but continued to make his home in the United States.

The clearest evidence that Ellison had shifted to a new ideological perspective surfaced in his changed attitude to Richard Wright's protest writings. After 1945, he published no favorable comments on Wright's works, yet many years passed before he would openly criticize his former mentor, his silence no doubt prompted by both his gratitude for Wright's generosity and his deference to their continuing friendship. It was not until the early 1960s—following Wright's death—that Ellison, in a bitter debate with Irving Howe, the liberal white literary critic, finally revealed what he thought about Wright's protest writings. Howe had provoked the debate by publishing an article in which he argued that black writers were obliged to protest racial injustices, and then went on to praise Wright for exemplifying political commitment and to chastise Ellison for shrinking from such commitment. The article angered Ellison.

Though this debate erupted roughly a decade after *Invisible Man*'s publication, Ellison's response is noteworthy because it stated his reason for rejecting the protest ideology. Ellison wrote:

Wright believed in the much abused idea that novels are weapons—the counterpart of the dreary notion, common among most minority groups, that novels are instruments of good public relations. But I believe that true novels, even when most pessimistic and bitter, arise out of an impulse to celebrate human life and therefore are ritualistic and ceremonial at their core. (Ellison 1966, 121)

Pointing to Bigger Thomas, the protest school's quintessential image of the racially brutalized black American personality, Ellison went on to observe:

He was designed to shock whites out of their apathy and end the circumstances out of which Wright insisted Bigger emerged. Here environment is all—and interestingly enough, environment conceived solely in terms of the physical, the non-conscious. . . . Wright could imagine Bigger, but Bigger could not possibly imagine Richard Wright. Wright saw to that. (Ellison 1966)

Here was the voice of the new black bourgeoisie affirming the cosmopolitan and apolitical consciousness of black American individualism, which *Invisible Man* transmuted into artistic form.

Ralph Ellison's literary career up to the publication of *Invisible Man* had evidenced continuous progress, but no distinguished achievement. Having received only one fellowship and endured much financial hardship, Ellison was merely one of several minor protest school black writers who had undergone his literary apprenticeship producing leftist tracts. He had attained no literary recognition. But in 1952, with the publication of *Invisible Man*, his life dramatically changed, as he emerged in the mainstream public arena as the new black American literary star.

Let's now turn to the black existentialist school and then examine the novel that established Ralph Ellison's fame and that literary school's postwar dominance.

THE EXISTENTIALIST LITERARY SCHOOL: MAJOR BLACK WRITERS AND LITERARY WORKS

Of the three major existentialist novels produced by black writers during this era—two were written by black writers who had expatriated to Europe. As we noted earlier, many black writers during the postwar period left the United States. Richard Wright, Chester Himes, and James

Baldwin settled in Paris, and William Demby in Rome. Also, although moving to a different part of the world, Willard Motley settled in Mexico. Of these writers, only Demby would return to live in the United States. Baldwin would journey back and forth, but continue to make his home in France.

The three major black existentialist novels produced during the period were *Beetle Creek* (Demby 1950), *Invisible Man* (Ellison 1952), and *The Outsider* (Wright 1953). Although each of these novels attracted attention in the public arena, only Ellison's *Invisible Man* achieved near unanimous acclaim. Most critics regarded it as one of the postwar period's superior literary achievements.

Before examining that novel, we must first clarify the major features of the black existentialist school's ideological perspective.

Ideal Type of Black Existentialist Literature

1. protagonist who lacks close social relationships
2. view of social alienation as a virtue
3. equation of social alienation with personal freedom
4. dissociation from black community and rejection of black ethnic culture
5. disregard of black community's social problems
6. condemnation of leftist radicalism and black nationalism
7. ignore threat to freedom posed by conservative political reaction
8. affirmation of the American political order and its democratic creed

The elements constituting this ideal type do not constitute a logically coherent system. We can see contradictions, for instance, between the ideology's view of social alienation as a virtue and its affirmation of the American political order; its condemnation of leftist radicalism and its disregard of the dangers to freedom posed by the conservative political reaction. Ellison's *Invisible Man*, the paradigmatic black existentialist novel, embodied all of these elements. Wright's *The Outsider* embodies most of the elements, followed by Demby's *Beetle Creek* which embodied only elements one through five. Traces of this existentialist ideology, reflecting the era's strong conservative climate, appeared in other postwar black American literary works, but these three novels will be the focus of our attention, because they constituted the dominant school's most important works.

Now we can turn to Ralph Ellison's *Invisible Man*, the leading novel of the postwar black existentialist literary school.

Invisible Man

Projected through the highly subjective existentialist ideology, *Invisible Man* draws heavily on Ellison's autobiographical experiences, specifically, his personal struggle as a black American to attain a cosmopolitan identity. At the simplest level, the novel narrates a young man's odyssey of social mobility and disillusionment, followed by his quest for a self-identity. At the more complex level, directly linked to this quest, the novel fires acid condemnations at individuals and groups who presume to possess the true meaning of black American identity. In reaction to those presumptions, it suggests that the primary struggle confronting black Americans is not political but existential, that is, the battle to realize their individuality, and to prevail over the stereotypes and abstracted categories that violate their humanity. This is the central normative message *Invisible Man* aims to affirm.

In pursuit of that objective, it dismisses sociological determinism, the view featured by the naturalistic protest school, which is what Ellison means in his reference to "overemphasis on the sociological approach." In contrast to this determinism, *Invisible Man* regards environment as a rich, multifaceted, fluid, deceptive, and magical arena of possibilities. This allows the novel to depict black America as a pluralistic montage of personalities and lifestyles, constituting social worlds far more varied and complex than previous black American literary works had revealed.

Illuminating and complementing this pluralistic vista, *Invisible Man* spans some four decades of black American history, achieving an epic scope. Narrating the picaresque journey of its nameless hero, a deracinated young black man, it envelopes the historical experiences and patterns of social consciousness that characterized black American life between World War I and the mid-1940s. Like *Tom Jones, Huckleberry Finn, The Confessions of Felix Krull, The Adventures of Augie March,* and other picaresque novels that depict socially mobile, rootless characters, *Invisible Man* is steeped in irony emanating from its exploration of a landscape strewn with contradictory social realities. In the most immediate sense, this irony arises as the nameless hero wanders innocently across the minefields of America's racial illusions. Paralleling this ironic journey, the novel reveals subsidiary journeys by individuals and groups who venture into alien terrain: a northern white philanthropist trespassing into the alien terrain of black southern life; the Communist Party trespassing into the alien terrain of Harlem; black intellectuals trespassing into the alien terrain of the Communist Party; and, more broadly, blacks trespassing into the alien terrain of a white society—as evidenced by their degradation in the South and their desperate quests for mass salvation, through black nationalism, as well as other seductive mass delusions, in the urban North.

Though each terrain affects the nameless hero as he moves across it, none ultimately contain or possess his identity, because he refuses to grant them the prerogative of defining his blackness. Which is to say, the nameless hero always bounces back up and embraces his existential freedom despite the various persons and groups seeking to bend him to their purposes. His tenacious commitment to his freedom, namely, his commitment to the realization of his individuality, emerges as the novel's idealistic theme.

But the novel embraces two conceptions of individuality, a radical deracinated version and a cosmopolitan bourgeois version, which are—at best—only loosely linked. The radical deracinated conception of the nameless hero's individuality, which is developed through the narrative, suggests that black self-realization can be achieved only through social isolation. But this conclusion contradicts the political agenda Ellison wanted to advance. So he was obliged at the end of the novel to place the nameless hero outside the narrative, in the epilogue. Here he presented the cosmopolitan bourgeois conception of individuality, resonating the more pedestrian individualism of the new black bourgeois, and its commitment to American democratic ideals. This conveyed the novel's optimistic take on race relations.

Now we can turn to the novel's depictions of black American social reality. Beginning at his journey's end, in a hole underground, where the nameless hero has retreated, the novel opens as he reflects on past events. Setting the tone for what is to follow, he declares:

> I am invisible, understand, simply because people refuse to see me. Like the bodiless heads you see sometimes in circus sideshows, it is as though I have been surrounded by mirrors of hard, distorting glass when they approach me they see only my surroundings, themselves, or figments of their imagination—indeed, everything and anything except me. (Ellison 1952, 7)

He then reveals that he is involved in a battle; but it soon becomes clear that this battle departs from the familiar strategies of warfare. Rather he suggests that the strategy of this battle is more subtle. "I learned in time . . . that it is possible to carry out a fight against them without their realizing it" (Ellison 1952, 9).

This implies a commitment to subterfuge in dealing with the American racial scene. While he was still quite young, he had been taught this lesson by his grandfather, who on his deathbed told him:

Son, after I'm gone I want you to keep up the good fight. I never told you, but our life is a war and I have been a traitor all my born days, a spy in the enemy's country ever since I gave up my gun back in the Reconstruction. Live with your head in the lion's mouth. I want you to overcome 'em with yeses, undermine 'em with grins, agree 'em to death and destruction, let 'em swallow you till they vomit or burst wide open. (Ellison 1952, 19–20)

We are being warned: this novel is not a retreat from the racial struggle but a continuation of that struggle through a disingenuous, more devious means of resistance. This is revealed as the nameless hero recalls that "his grandfather had been a quiet old man who never made any trouble, yet on his deathbed he had called himself a traitor and a spy, and he had spoken of his meekness as a dangerous activity."

Meekness as a dangerous activity? This suggests that the narrator aims to redirect the black political struggle. Presumably, resistance to racial oppression would operate through shrewder means. That redirection must be viewed within the context of the new black bourgeoisie's cosmopolitan ethos. For those few blacks who had gained entry into the mainstream white American social world, the struggle for black social advancement was no longer perceived in terms of political action; nor were antagonists perceived as being exclusively white. The black struggle now consisted of a struggle for self-definition, the struggle to assert and preserve one's individuality. Thus from this standpoint, any person or group who sought to smother one's individuality beneath some category or stereotype constituted an adversary.

The action of the novel opens with a scene that highlights provincial white racism. It is a ceremonial occasion. The nameless hero, shortly after successfully delivering the valedictorian oration for his high school graduation, has been invited to give the speech to a group of the town's leading white citizens. Following his speech, he and nine other young black males are invited to participate in the "battle royal." But he soon discovers that he has been deceived as the contest degenerates into a spectacle of racial degradation.

First the boys are presented with a naked white woman and threatened with punishment for both looking and not looking. Next the boys are blindfolded and placed in a boxing ring where they are forced to slug one another; and, finally, they are obliged to collect their prize money on an electrically wired rug. This spectacle has been staged to entertain the white male audience. Aside from representing the malevolence of provincial white racism, this scene reveals the paradox posed for blacks by the American Dream. As one commentator has aptly noted, "All of the prizes of white society (women, money) are thus held out to them, only to be denied" (Bone 1958, 203).

Although the nameless hero eventually comprehends the game's pathology, he never resolves the paradox of the American Dream, a point I will return to later in assessing *Invisible Man*'s normative implications. The second setting, one of the most complex in the novel, reveals the serpentine guile of the southern black bourgeoisie and the racial paternalism of northern white philanthropists. These are evidenced when the nameless hero enters the social world of a black college. Not coincidentally, this college resembles Booker T. Washington's Tuskegee Institute, the college Ellison attended. Here the nameless hero encounters Dr. Bledsoe, president of the college, and Mr. Norton, one of the college's white New England benefactors.

Still oblivious to the land mines beneath the surface of the South's racial order, the nameless hero commits the inexcusable blunder of being honest and forthright in dealing with whites, in this particular case, the New England philanthropist Mr. Norton.

Assigned to escort Norton on a tour of the town, he unwittingly accedes to Norton's request to see the surrounding rural areas. This results in him inadvertently exposing Norton to the pathology of black rural backwardness in the form of an incestuous family. Norton nearly suffers a heart attack. In a desperate attempt to relieve the badly shaken Norton, who suddenly had recalled erotic thoughts about his own daughter, the boy drives him to a local bar which turns out to have an upstairs brothel being visited by a group of deranged black mental patients.

This encounter is important not only because it introduces, in the novel's image of American race relations, the Freudian theme of psychological repression; but also because it portrays the predicament of the black middle class through these psychologically deranged mental patients. They are under the charge of an orderly named Super-Cargo (or: superego). One of these patients, a former surgeon who had studied medicine in France, gives the following account of his downfall.

> These hands so loving trained to master a scalpel yearn to caress a trigger. I returned to save life and I was refused. . . . Ten men in masks drove out from the city at midnight and beat me with whips for saving a human life. And I was forced to the utmost degradation because I possessed skilled hands and the belief that my knowledge could bring me dignity—not wealth, only dignity—and other men's health. (Ellison 1952, 86)

This surgeon symbolizes the psychological casualties of racism, those members of the new black bourgeoisie who failed to come to terms with their invisibility until it was too late. Being unprepared to wage psychological warfare to preserve their individuality, they took refuge in mental illness—alcoholism, drug addiction, and even suicide. Like the metaphorical "battle royal," this suggests yet other failed black American quests for the American Dream. However, the novel neglects to elaborate the implications of that failure. And that, as we will see, weakens its normative message about American race relations. Nevertheless, the plight of these disabled veterans of psychological warfare is viewed sympathetically; the novel avoids subjecting them to ridicule.

But no similar sympathy is directed toward the old southern black bourgeoisie, those blacks—like Booker T. Washington— designated by whites to run southern black institutions. They are depicted as being egomaniacal and sinister parasites, feeding on the South's racial system like vultures feasting on road kill. The novel depicts one such individual in the character of Dr. Bledsoe. After learning that the nameless hero had taken Norton to see the incestuous black family, Bledsoe, the crafty president of the college, is furious:

> "Boy!" he exploded. "Are you serious? Why were you out here on that road in the first place? Weren't you behind the wheel?"
>
> "Yes, sir. . . ."
>
> "Then haven't we bowed and scraped and begged and lied enough decent homes and drives for you to show him? Did you think that white man had come a thousand miles—all the way from New York and Boston and Philadelphia just to show him a slum? Don't just stand there, say something!"
>
> "But I was only driving him, sir. I only stopped there after he ordered me to. . . ."
>
> "Ordered you?" he said. "He *ordered* you. Damit, white folks are always giving orders, it's a habit with them. Why didn't you make an excuse? Couldn't you say they had sickness—smallpox—or picked another cabin? Why that Trueblood shack? My God, boy! You're black and living in the South—did you forget to lie?"
>
> "But I was only trying to please him. . . ."
>
> "*Please* him? And here you are a junior in college! Why, the dumbest black bastard in the cotton patch knows that the only way to please a white man is to tell him a lie! What kind of education are you getting here?" (Ellison 1952, 124)

Through Bledsoe the novel reveals the southern black bourgeoisie's moral corruption. Ruthless power games, not moral principles, constituted the ugly terms of its survival. Betraying a promise he had made to Norton, Bledsoe informs the boy that he must be punished.

> "Tell anyone you like," he said. "I don't care. I wouldn't raise my little finger to stop you Because I don't owe anyone a thing son. Who, Negroes? Negroes don't control this school or much of anything else—haven't you learned even that? No, sir, they don't control this school, nor white folk either. True they

support it, but I control it. . . . Power doesn't have to show off. Power is confident, self-assuring, self-starting and self-stopping, self-warming and self-justifying. . . . Those are the facts, son. The only ones I even pretend to please are *big* white folk, and even those I control more than they control me. This is a power set-up, son, and I'm at the controls. . . . When you buck against me, you're bucking against power, rich white folk's power, the nation's power—which means government power!" (Ellison 1952, 127)

After delivering this stern lecture on the realities of power, Bledsoe tells the boy he will be suspended for a short time. But he promises to give him letters of reference to some of the school's friends in New York to assist him in finding employment. Bledsoe, of course, is lying; he has no intention of writing positive letters of reference. But still innocent, the nameless hero accepts Bledsoe's word.

Thus, still under the veil of identity illusion, the nameless hero prepares to journey north. The South he leaves behind, it should be noted, is represented as a racial world of repressed impulses. Going to the North, which symbolizes the mass black migration, marks the nameless hero's movement into a world not only of unrestrained impulses and wilder, more dangerous illusions. But also, and perhaps most important, it marks his entry into a world of possibilities for psychological awakening and freedom.

New York is the destination. New York's meaning to the upwardly mobile postwar new black bourgeoisie is revealed in the words of the mentally ill black surgeon, whom the nameless hero encounters at the bus station, shortly before his departure.

"New York!" he said. " That's not a place, it's a dream. When I was young it was Chicago. Now all the little black boys run away to New York. Out of the fire and into the melting pot. I can see you after you've lived in Harlem three months. Your speech will change, you'll talk a lot about 'college,' you'll attend lectures at the Men's House. . . . You might even meet a few white folks. And listen," he said, leaning closer to whisper, "you might even dance with a white girl." (Ellison 1952, 136)

More than Chicago, Boston, or any other American city, New York with its cosmopolitan culture and more tolerant atmosphere of race relations symbolized freedom and possibility. In the eyes of the fledgling new black bourgeoisie, New York was special. Most chose to live in or near New York. Only Paris surpassed New York's appeal. However, only a few blacks in such arts as jazz, dance, and writing could afford to live in Paris. For most upwardly mobile blacks, including the new black bourgeoisie, relocating to Paris was simply impossible.

New York's appeal is enhanced by the presence of Harlem, which corresponds to neither the 1920s literary image of a primitive jungle nor the

1930s literary image a desolate black ghetto. Rather *Invisible Man*'s Harlem constitutes a rich and varied universe of black lifestyles—black America's new, vibrant, pulsating epicenter. As the astonished nameless hero observes:

> I had never seen so many black people against a background of brick build-ings, neon signs, plate glass and roaming traffic. . . . They were everywhere. So many, and moving along with so much tension and noise that I wasn't sure whether they were about to celebrate a holiday or join in a street fight. There were even black girls behind the counters of the Five and Ten as I passed. Then at the street intersection I had the shock of seeing a black po-liceman directing traffic—and there were white drivers in the traffic who obeyed his signals as though it was the most natural thing in the world. Sure I had heard of it, but this was *real*. . . . The vet had been right: For me this was not a city of realities, but of dreams. (Ellison 1952, 141–42)

Though his New York experiences will seduce him into deeper identity illusions, the stage is now being set for his gradual psychological awak-ening. This begins with his discovery of Dr. Bledsoe's deceit. After re-peated failures to locate employment through the reference given him by Bledsoe, he discovers the content of the letter. Contrary to the recommen-dation he had expected, Dr. Bledsoe had written:

> The bearer of this letter is a former student of ours (I say *former* because he shall never, under any circumstances, be enrolled as a student here again) who has been expelled for a most serious defection from our strictest rules of deportment. . . . I beg of you, sir, to help him continue in the direction of that promise which, like the horizon, recedes ever more brightly and distantly be-yond the hopeful traveler. (Ellison 1952, 167–68)

After this discovery, the nameless hero seeks to start a new life in New York as he ventures into various disappointing experiences: residence in a Harlem boarding house; a job with a paint company where he is given a bizarre (symbolically potent) assignment of mixing white and black paints; conflict with a racist white labor union; an accident at the paint factory which results in a stay at a hospital where he apparently receives a prefrontal lobotomy; encounter with a Garvey-style black nationalist group; and membership in the Brotherhood (a thinly disguised replica of the Communist Party).

Image of Black Folk Culture as Depicted in *Invisible Man*

The novel conveys its image of black American urban folk culture prima-rily through the character of Mary, the black landlady from whom the nameless hero rents a room shortly after he arrives in Harlem. Mary represents transplanted black southern folk culture's protective warmth and wisdom. This can be seen in her admonition to the young man: "'And you have to take care of yourself, son. Don't let this Harlem git you. I'm in New York but New York ain't in me, understand what I mean. Don't git corrupted'" (Ellison 1952, 222).

Mary's values contrast sharply with those of Dr. Bledsoe, revealing the novel's very different views of members of black lower-class folk culture and the old black bourgeoisie. "Other than Mary I had no friends and desired none. Nor did I think of Mary as a 'friend'; she was something more—a force, a stable, familiar force like something out of my past which kept me from whirling off into some unknown which I dared not face" (Ellison 1952, 225).

Yet he feels obliged to maintain his distance from even Mary. We see here the existential imperative of personal freedom conflicting with the communal bonds of black ethnic culture. "I might as well admit it right now, I thought, there are many things about people like Mary I dislike. For one thing they seldom know where their personalities end and yours begins; they usually think in terms of 'we' while I have always tended to think in terms of 'me'—and that has caused some friction, even with my family" (Ellison 1952, 225). The Invisible Man thus rejects attachment to New York's black ethnic community.

Images of Black Nationalism in *Invisible Man*

Here we encounter a Garvey-type movement, one of the two major radical political forces the novel torpedoes. That movement is depicted as a bizarre eruption on the Harlem landscape, which the nameless hero encounters the first afternoon of his arrival.

> It was ahead of me, angry and shrill, and upon hearing it I had a sensation of shock and fear such as I had felt as a child when surprised by my father's voice. An emptiness widened in my stomach. . . . Before me a gathering of people were almost blocking the walk, while above them a short squat man shouted angrily from a ladder to which were attached a collection of small American flags.
> "We gine chase 'em out," the man cried. "Out."
> "Tell 'em about it Ras, mahn," a voice called. (Ellison 1952, 142)

The nameless hero goes on:

> And I saw the squat man shake his fist angrily over the uplifted faces, yelling something in a staccato West Indian accent, at which the crowd yelled threateningly. It was as though a riot would break out any minute, against whom I didn't know. . . .

The clash between the calm of the rest of the street and the passion of the voice gave the scene a strange out-of-joint quality, and I was careful not to look lest I see a riot flare. (Ellison 1952, 142–43)

A riot does eventually erupt, as we will see; it plays a crucial part in the novel's climax.

While taking black nationalism more seriously than did either the primitivist writings of Claude McKay or the Marxist writings of Richard Wright, *Invisible Man*—nevertheless—views that movement with similar disdain. In the eyes of the individualistic new black bourgeois, racial nationalists constitute a frustrated and fanatical fringe, an angry and deluded group driven by an absurd notion of freedom. Even more distressing, the nameless hero soon discovers that Ras and the black nationalists threaten his own survival, because their conception of black identity leaves no room for his individuality. "And that I, a little black man with an assumed name should die because a big black man in his hatred and confusion over the nature of reality that seemed controlled by white men whom I knew to be as blind as he, was too much, too outrageously absurd" (Ellison 1952, 484).

This phrase "confusion over the nature of reality that seemed controlled by white men" suggests not only that black nationalism amounts to a dangerous ideological fantasy, but also, and even more significant, that white power over black American social reality was merely an illusion. This reveals *Invisible Man*'s more conservative perspective on race relations.

Here we see Ellison, who professes an apolitical conception of literature, veering onto a political terrain with a personalistic notion of power. But if white men did not control the racial system, as well as the government, the economy, the laws, the military, and the media—then who did?

Invisible Man and the Image of Radical Leftist Party

More complex is the novel's denunciation of the Brotherhood, an organization modeled on the Communist Party, for it is here that *Invisible Man* becomes even more explicitly political, as it joins, in full throat, the Cold War antileftist crusade. Being among the disillusioned black intellectuals formerly influenced by the Communist Party, Ellison seeks in this depiction of the Brotherhood to "settle old accounts." However, unlike former white leftist Communist denunciations, which highlighted the evils of Stalinist policies, *Invisible Man* focused on the party's threat to the black American's personal identity. We can see this as Brother Jack, a white party leader, initiates the nameless hero by giving him a new identity:

"You must realize immediately that much of our work is opposed. Our discipline demands therefore that we talk to no one and that we avoid situations

in which information might be given away unwittingly. So you must put
aside your past. Do you have a family?" . . .
"This is your new identity," Brother Jack said.
"Open it."
Inside I found a name written on a slip of paper.
"That is your new name," Brother Jack said. "Start thinking of yourself
by that name for the moment. Get it down so that even if you are called in
the middle of the night you will respond. Very soon you shall be known by
it all over the country. You are to respond to no other, understand!" (Ellison
1952, 268)

Aside from its image of crude paternalism, this depiction distorts the
features of the Communist Party that attracted black intellectuals,
namely, its moral idealism (however misguided it may have been in practice), its antiracism, and its anticolonialism. These are simply ignored in
the novel's depiction of the black Communists' motives for joining. Instead the Brotherhood is represented as merely a cynical and dictatorial
clique, which offers the friendless and socially isolated nameless hero a
supportive community. But the novel fails to reveal why he chooses that
community rather than his own black community. Was he seeking to as-
similate? The desire to be absorbed into a white American social world—
which actually attracted some blacks to the Communist Party—is ignored. And for good reason: assimilation was closely linked to the new
black individuality. Not surprisingly, this is an issue *Invisible Man* is unprepared to explore.

Alienated and adrift before joining the Brotherhood, the nameless hero
now proclaims: "I was dominated by the all embracing idea of Brotherhood. The organization had given the world a new shape, and me a vital
role. We recognized no loose ends, everything could be controlled by our
science. Life was all pattern and discipline; and the beauty of discipline is
when it works. And it was working" (Ellison 1952, 331).

Such images suggesting that Communist Party recruits were seeking to
"escape from freedom," as the social theorist Erich Fromm had argued in
his book with that title, became a common postwar line of attack against
Communist movements. Images of Communism as a cult bent on brainwashing were internalized by the emerging black bourgeoisie who, having
gained entry into mainstream American institutional life, shared mainstream American anxieties about the prospect of radical political revolution.
In denouncing the political left, *Invisible Man* is affirming the new black
bourgeoisie's patriotism—its loyalty to the United States—in an era when
many Americans viewed anti-Communism as a prerequisite of citizenship.
In this connection, it is important to recall that leading members of the new
black bourgeoisie such as Jackie Robinson, William Hastie, and Channing
Tobias led the way in publicly denouncing leftist black intellectuals.

Image of a Black Hustler

Despite its individualistic existentialist ideology, *Invisible Man* has been often praised as a celebration of black American ethnic culture. It certainly depicts urban black ethnic culture in greater depth, and with more subtlety and richness of detail than did any previous major black American literary work, except the writings of Langston Hughes. At first, this might seem paradoxical—a novel reputed for its celebration of both black American individualism and black American ethnic culture—since ethnic cultures tend to consist of communal, or group-centered, behavior patterns that attenuate individual proclivities. The apparent inconsistency is resolved once we realize that the novel's depiction of black ethnic culture, although skillfully elaborated, exists as only a backdrop to the narrative, to which it provides a contrast of detached romanticism. For example, the nameless hero expresses wonder, and even fascination, as he encounters the deviant urban black social worlds; but his identity remains unclaimed by their values and lifestyles. Which is to say, his relationship to that culture is reminiscent of the assimilated black professional's weekend forays into a nearby black community to hear blues and consume soul food.

The novel's romantic view of this deviant urban black ethnic culture is revealed most clearly in its depiction of Rinehart, the Harlem hustler. "Rine the runner and Rine the gambler and Rine the briber and Rine the lover and Rine the reverend? . . . A vast seething world of fluidity, and Rine the rascal was at home. Perhaps *only* Rine the rascal was at home in it" (Ellison 1952, 430).

Significantly, this image departs sharply from the naturalistic protest school's depiction of lower-class blacks. Here we see the image of a Harlem street hustler, not as a criminal or a social parasite spawned by a disorganized community life and an oppressive racial system. Rather we see the hustler as the romanticized expression of existential freedom—as the source of insight into life's true meaning. This romantic aura is clearly exhibited as the nameless hero reflects on Rine's life. "His world was possibility and he knew it. He was years ahead of me and I was a fool. I must have been crazy and blind. The world in which we lived was without boundaries" (Ellison 1952, 430).

A world without boundaries? Perhaps no phrase better captures *Invisible Man*'s postwar existentialist illusions. Is it actually a world without boundaries—or a world whose boundaries blacks like Rinehart had been obliged to subvert, to finesse into a deviant lifestyle to achieve a modicum of autonomy and dignity? The actual possibilities of Rinehart's existence are definitely constrained. He lives in a society that is indifferent to his existence. When he and tens of thousands of other blacks are obliged to live in dilapidated dwellings, to attend substandard schools, and to endure long periods of unemployment, it constitutes no societal crisis. Their well being is not regarded as a measure of the society's health. People like Rinehart, thus, live on the margins, superfluous to white America's concerns. His world was not possibility; it was desperation.

It should be noted that Rinehart is depicted from a distance—like Van Vechten's portrait of the Scarlet Peeper—nothing about his social consciousness, and the experiences that shaped it, is revealed. He exists as only a one-dimensional character, hastily moved across the stage, to suggest that Harlem street life is a fun-filled social world of existential freedom.

Though this depiction of Harlem street life surpasses *Nigger Heaven*'s banal street scene, which served as simply exotic ornamentation, it is hardly serious. Despite the flash and allure of Rinehart's appearance, his lifestyle fails to claim the nameless hero's identity. As the nameless hero later confesses: "And sitting there trembling I caught a glimpse of the possibilities posed by Rinehart's multiple personalities and turned away. It was too vast and confusing to contemplate" (Ellison 1952, 431).

So much for the romantic black street hustler. Used to support Ellison's antisociological view of black ghetto life which operates as a major premise of his existentialist outlook, Rinehart could hardly serve to define the new black bourgeoisie's identity. There romanticization ends. For not only is Rinehart's lifestyle "too vast and confusing," as the nameless hero observes. It is also dangerous and—ultimately—a dead end. The prisons, drug clinics, hospitals, and cemeteries absorbed daily those who discovered too late that the hustler's magical possibilities had tragic limits. This the nameless hero fails to point out. Books such as *The Autobiography of Malcolm X*, Claude Brown's *Manchild in the Promised Land*, and Piri Thomas's *Down These Mean Streets* would later reveal that postwar Harlem's deviant social world was no school picnic. But *Invisible Man* could not deal with those harsh realities without being ensnared in a sociological discourse on black ghetto life. That is why Rinehart's life was depicted from a distance.

Now we can pick up the final episodes of the narrative. Following a series of frustrating experiences and his retreat from the Brotherhood, the nameless hero awakens, disillusioned with all relationships. He observes:

And now I looked around a corner of my mind and saw Jack and Norton and Emerson merge into a single white figure. They were very much the same, each attempting to force his picture of reality on me and neither giving a hoot in hell for how things looked to me. I was simply a material, a natural resource to be used. I had simply switched from the arrogant absurdity of Norton and Emerson to that of Jack and the Brotherhood, and it all came out the same—except now I recognized my invisibility. (Ellison 1952, 439)

He thus awakens to the reality of his individuality, the existential birth of his personal identity, only to discover himself caught in the middle of a riot. Ras's black nationalists and the Brotherhood are at war. Narrowly escaping from Ras's nationalists and later the police, he takes refuge in a hole underground, an abandoned cellar, from which his retrospection begins. Although he considers returning to Mary's, the social world of black folk culture, he decides against it.

In the epilogue, Ellison appends a conventional social philosophy that negates the novel's anarchistic implications. Through presenting the nameless hero's reflections on his experiences, Ellison informs the audience how to "read" the novel's social relevance. But this is disappointing, as one critic aptly observes: "It must be said that Ellison is to be seen at the very last moment trying to take back the book he has written, or at the very least muffling its severities, and that is unfortunate. But then it should be said that lacking some such attempt, there will be nothing more for Ellison ever to say" (Klein 1966, 264).

Actually, Ellison in the epilogue transforms *Invisible Man*'s existentialism into the more pedestrian new black bourgeoisie social consciousness. This he does in several steps. First, the epilogue presents a clear statement of the postwar new black bourgeoisie's optimism, as the nameless hero declares: "I assign myself no rank or any limit, and such an attitude is very much against the trend of the times. But my world has become one of infinite possibilities. . . . Until some gang succeeds putting the world in a straitjacket, its definition is possibility" (Ellison 1952, 498). The nameless hero here ignores the fact that possibility, if it is to be something more than a banal abstraction, can scarcely be realized without *opportunity*, a word he never uses. Nevertheless, it is clear from his oblique reference to totalitarian regimes that he believes American society affords (or will afford) the opportunity to achieve that possibility.

Second, and closely linked to his optimistic outlook, the nameless hero affirms the principles of American democracy. Those principles resemble Gunnar Myrdal's notion of the "democratic creed" rather than the actual American social reality. The nameless hero, through recalling his own experiences, suddenly becomes aware of the discrepancy. This revelation appears as he unravels the meaning of his grandfather's deathbed utterances.

> Could he have meant—hell, he must have meant the principle, that we are to affirm the principle on which the country was built and not the men, or at least not the men who did violence. Did he mean to say "yes" because he knew that the principle was greater than the numbers and the vicious power and all the methods used to corrupt its name? . . .
>
> Or did he mean that we had to take the responsibility for all of it, for the men as well as the principle, because we were the heirs who must use the

principle because no other fitted our needs? Not for the power or for vindication, but because we, with the given circumstances of our origin, could
only thus find transcendence. (Ellison 1952, 496–97)

The principle apparently will come to fruition through a gradual evolution.
Also noteworthy in his statement is the ambiguous word *transcendence*.
This suggests the possibility of black social mobility and individuation—
that is, that blacks will overcome the barriers of both racial discrimination
and racial categorization. In the optimistic worldview of the emerging
new black bourgeoisie, only American democratic ideals offer this possibility. Never mind that the narrative reveals no basis for that hope, that
the nameless hero had encountered a life of bitter disappointment, and
that he had realized his identity only through social alienation. Readers
are now being informed that blacks are climbing aboard the bandwagon
of faith in American democracy—because it alone offers them prospect of
individuality and freedom.

This is a rather curious insight for a man dwelling in a hole underground. Which brings us to the third major point made in the epilogue:
the nameless hero's decision to abandon his underground refuge.

And, as I said before, a decision has been made. I'm shaking off the old skin
and I'll leave it here in the hole. I'm coming out nevertheless. And I suppose
it's damn well. Even hibernation can be overdone, come to think of it. Perhaps that's my greatest social crime. I've overstayed my hibernation, since
there's a possibility that even an invisible man has a socially responsible role
to play. (Ellison 1952, 503)

For a writer who decries the intrusion into literature of sociological
concerns, Ellison seems oddly preoccupied with this novel's social repercussions. The nameless hero's statement that he is "coming out" should
be seen as affirmation of the new black bourgeoisie's spirit. He has arrived in American society. He is moving beyond his old defensiveness. He
is shedding his racial identity. Although the social situation looks far from
propitious, as he acknowledges that he remains an "invisible man" whose
individuality still tends to be ignored, the time, nevertheless, has come for
change—"since there's a possibility that even an invisible man . . . can
play a socially responsible role" (Ellison 1952, 503).

A curious conclusion. This suggests not only that the new black bourgeoisie are committed to participating in the mainstream society; but that
they must to do so from a position of marginality—as invisible men. Simply stated, they are prepared to accept that others may continue to define
them with stereotypes that smother their individuality.

Invisible Man's existentialist ideology thus embraced an assimilationist
agenda that went beyond the ideologies of the previous dominant black

literary schools. As we can see in the epilogue's final point, the novel attempts to universalize black American experience by suggesting that invisibility is likely to be experienced by anyone seeking a life of existential authenticity: "Who knows but that, on the lower frequencies, I speak for you?" (Ellison 1952, 503).

This is aimed at the novel's white American readers. They are being invited to see their own lives, at least in part, as a struggle against stereotyped social expectations, and the conformist demands of group norms. The novel thus concludes by linking the issue of black American individuality to the then intellectually fashionable critique of conformist mass culture. This point was hardly lost on Ellison's liberal white literary peers, as we will see in the comments of Saul Bellow. Such popular books as *The Organization Man, Man in a Gray Flannel Suit, The Status Seekers, Rebel without a Cause, The Catcher in the Rye,* and other apolitical attacks on the emerging postwar middle-class American culture also embraced this theme.

Responses to *Invisible Man*

To say *Invisible Man* was well received by the liberal white American literati would be an understatement. In the opinion of most critics, it surpassed the achievements of not only *Native Son* but all previous black American literary works. Winning the National Book Award as the best novel published in 1952, it eventually was ranked as one of the best American novels. In a poll of two hundred prominent authors, critics, and editors conducted by *Book Week* in 1965 to determine "which works of fiction between 1945 and 1965 are most likely to endure," *Invisible Man* was voted number one.

But not all of the responses to *Invisible Man* were laudatory. As we observed in reference to the primitivist and the naturalistic protest schools, critical responses to literary works typically reflect the ideological perspective of the critic's social base. To gain further insight into both the social base of *Invisible Man*'s existentialist ideology and its relationship to the social bases of competing postwar ideological perspectives, let's now examine briefly some characteristic critical responses to the novel.

The Liberal White Literary Community

The existentialist ideology derived from the postwar liberal white literary community which, though now fragmented, continued to operate as the social base of the ideologies projected by the dominant black literary schools. Not surprisingly, these liberal white literary intellectuals, who made up a major sector of the literary establishment, praised *Invisible Man*. Orville Prescott of the *New York Times*, for example, declared that *Invisible Man* was "the most impressive work of fiction by an American Negro that I have ever read" (Prescott 1952). What these liberal critics found especially pleasing was the novel's transcendence of race, its assimilationist implications. As Webster Schott of the *Kansas City Star* observed: "It's a paradox but the quality which classifies Ralph Ellison's *Invisible Man* as one of the best novels yet written by an American Negro is that it's concerned with themes which are . . . universal rather than racial" (Schott 1952).

An even more generous liberal assessment of the novel was written by Saul Bellow in *Commentary*: "But what a great thing it is when a brilliant individual victory occurs, like Mr. Ellison's, proving that a truly heroic quality can exist among our contemporaries" (Bellow 1952). Bellow, too, was impressed by *Invisible Man*'s universalism, its nonethnic consciousness: "I was keenly aware, as I read this book, of a very significant kind of independence in the writing. For there is a 'way' for Negro novelists to go at their problems, just as there are Jewish and Italian 'ways.' Mr. Ellison has not adopted a minority tone. If he had done so, he would have failed to establish a truly middle-of-consciousness for everyone."

Echoing the liberal literati's apolitical critiques of American mass culture, Bellow goes on to praise the novel's conception of a marginalized individualism: "In our society man—himself—is idolized and publicly worshipped, but the single individual must hide himself underground and try to save his desires, his thoughts, his soul, in invisibility. He must return to himself . . . rejecting all that threaten his manhood."

The liberal white literati, in showering praise on *Invisible Man*'s antipolitical existentialist ideology, were simply affirming their own worldview.

The Conservative White Response

Sharply contrasted to the liberal white literati, conservative white commentators denounced the novel. Reflecting Cold War conservative ideological preoccupations with patriotism and positive images of American life, they were repulsed by the novel's depiction of racial conflicts, which they saw as an attack on American society. Indicative of this type of response was the review by Sterling North in the conservative *New York World Telegram and Sun*. Characterizing *Invisible Man* as less a novel than a "flaming manifesto," North wrote, "The white man has much on his conscience. But his respect and affection will never be won by such novels as this one, which is virtually a battle cry to civil war" (North 1952). Expressing a similarly jaundiced view, a reviewer in the *Columbus* (Ohio) *Sunday Dispatch*, saw the novel as a protest against black subordination in American society, and concluded, "Mr. Ellison's novel will shed considerable heat but little light."

Most conservative commentators, it seems accurate to conclude, failed to understand the implications of the novel's social critique. Their attention was riveted to its depictions of racial strife. As supporters of racial segregation, they simply were oblivious to the novel's message about black identity, the feature that stirred many leftist and black critical responses.

Non-Communist White Leftist Literary Community

One of the most jarring critiques of *Invisible Man* came from the democratic socialist community. This article, which was mentioned earlier, was written by Irving Howe for *Dissent* magazine. Although the democratic socialists opposed the Communist Party, because of their disdain for what they saw as its doctrinal orthodoxy and authoritarian tactics, they nevertheless continued to advocate a progressive political conception of literature. Viewing *Invisible Man* from this progressive political standpoint, Howe attacked its existentialist ideology: "What astonishes one most about *Invisible Man* is the apparent freedom it displays from the ideological and emotional penalties suffered by Negroes in this country—I say 'apparent' because the freedom is not so complete as the book's admirers like to suppose" (Howe 1963, 256).

Disturbed by the novel's effort to affirm a mythical view of American society, which he saw as the product of the postwar cultural climate, Howe went on to add:

> Still more troublesome, both as it breaks the coherence of the novel and reveals Ellison's dependence on the postwar *Zeitgeist*, is the sudden, unprepared and implausible assertion of unconditional freedom with which the novel ends. . . .
> If *Native Son* is marred by the ideological delusions of the thirties, *Invisible Man* is marred, less grossly, by those of the fifties. (Howe 1963, 265)

Howe, like other critics of *Invisible Man*'s existentialist optimism, failed to perceive its link to the new black bourgeois consciousness. Rather he saw the novel's ideology as merely the product of the apolitical postwar white liberal community, its cowardly retreat from the struggle for social justice. But in fact, as suggested in our earlier discussion, that hegemonic ideology enveloped not only black writers but also the newly forming sector of the black bourgeoisie. Both were seduced by the co-optive hegemony of token integration, the critically important subtext, which Howe failed to perceive. Nevertheless, his sociological insights into the flaws of the postwar existentialist ideology were so penetrating they deserve to be quoted at length.

Though the unqualified assertion of self liberation was a favorite strategy among American literary people in the fifties, it is also vapid and insubstantial. It violates the reality of social life, the interplay between external conditions and personal will, quite as much as the determinism of the thirties. The unfortunate fact remains [that] to define one's individuality is to stumble upon social barriers which stand in the way, all too much in the way, of infinite possibilities. Freedom can be fought for, but it cannot always be willed or asserted into existence. (Howe 1963, 266)

Not just Ellison but all of the postwar black existentialist writers glossed over the sociological barriers of race and class, as they abandoned Marxist illusions of socialist revolution for metaphysical fantasies of self-determination. Though Howe and the democratic left subjected those existentialist fantasies to blistering critiques, they had little influence in altering the cultural climate, because they occupied the periphery of the postwar literary establishment.

Responses of the Black Literary Community

The postwar black community, as we noted earlier, evidenced a mood of quiescence and moderation. Most black Americans had shifted away from political and economic preoccupations. In consequence, the fanfare that greeted *Invisible Man* in the mainstream public arena failed to stir strong reactions in the black community as had *Native Son*. Responses to *Invisible Man* derived from two literary groups within the black community: the ethnically oriented black literati and the leftist-oriented black literati. While differing sharply in their assessments of the novel, neither group embraced *Invisible Man*'s existentialist ideology. Ellison and the other black existentialist writers, it should be noted, existed apart from both groups as well as the institutional bases of the larger black community.

Characteristic of the ethnically oriented responses, Henry F. Winslow (in *Crisis*), Alain Locke (in *Phylon*), and Langston Hughes (in *New York Age*) applauded *Invisible Man*. Sharing the apolitical outlook of the times, they ignored its politics. What most impressed them was Ellison's skillful depiction of black ethnic culture, which they saw as affirming black America's humanity, though they tended to interpret this in communal rather than individualistic terms. Put simply, they welcomed the novel's rich array of black ethnic depictions.

Far different—indeed resembling, in many ways, the Depression-era outlook of the naturalistic protest school—were the responses of the black leftist literary community. Few in number and lacking access to the mainstream media, their reviews appeared in relatively obscure small circulation publications. Written by alienated and beleaguered black political radicals in an era dominated by conservative reaction, these reviews expressed the most bitter opposition to *Invisible Man*. Abner Berry, for example, reviewing the novel in the Communist Party's *Daily Worker*, declared that it was "in effect . . . 439 pages of contempt for humanity, written in an affected, pretentious and otherworldly style to suit the king-pins of world white supremacy" (Berry 1952).

Aware of Ellison's earlier involvement with the political left, Berry accused him of having "sold out" to white racism in writing the novel. Similarly vitriolic, but not linked ideologically to the Communist Party, was the leftist commentary of John O. Killens in *Freedom:* "The Negro people need Ralph Ellison's *Invisible Man* like we need a hole in the head or a stab in the back. It is a vicious distortion of Negro life" (Killens 1952).

The bitterness of these leftist responses derived as much from professional envy as ideological pique. They resented the fact that *Invisible Man* was receiving critical acclaim and awards denied their own writings, which—they believed—provided far more truthful depictions of black American life.

Undeterred by these detractors from the literary fringe, *Invisible Man* soared in notoriety as it inscribed new—politically disillusioned—images of postwar black America in the public culture. Only time would determine the significance of those images for the future direction of race relations.

Ralph Ellison's Celebrity Status

Following *Invisible Man*'s successful critical reception, Ralph Ellison was elevated to the status of an intellectual celebrity, becoming the recipient of the most generous outpouring of patronage ever bestowed on a black American writer. He was hired for visiting lectureships at more than a dozen elite universities, including Columbia, Princeton, Chicago, UCLA, and Yale. He was appointed to the Carnegie Commission Study of Educational Television, the American Academy of Arts and Sciences, the National Council of Arts, the Institute of Jazz Studies, and the Century Club—an elite male private social club in New York City. Also among the generous patronage bestowed on him, he was selected to occupy the Albert Schweitzer Chair of Humanities at New York University, a position, funded by the state of New York, for which he was paid one of the highest academic salaries in the country. In short, *Invisible Man* catapulted Ellison into America's intellectual elite, as a token black representative, where he operated as the leading black spokesman for moderate bourgeois liberalism.

In light of Ellison's scant literary output, the generous support that came his way was rather curious. He had published only one novel, which was followed some fourteen years later by a collection of essays (*Shadow and Act* 1966). Yet other black writers such as Langston Hughes, Zora Neale Hurston, and Richard Wright, who had produced far more literary works than Ellison, were largely ignored by the postwar white literary establishment. Ellison occupied a unique niche, because his novel delivered a powerful message about black American experiences that transcended the usual antagonisms of race relations discourse.

Though criticized frequently for his lack of political involvement, Ellison—voicing a typical new black bourgeois outlook—argued that his moderate stance was a more rational way to deal with the country's racial problems than was militant political protest, as can be seen in his response to an interviewer's question in 1963:

> What do I do? I belong to the Committee of One Hundred which is an arm of the legal defense committee of the NAACP. I vote. I try to vote responsibly. I contribute whenever I can to efforts to improve things. Right now one of the things I am trying to do is point out it's [political action's] a more complex problem than that of simply thrusting out your chin and saying "I'm defiant." (Geller 1969, 167)

These words, it is important to note, were uttered in 1963, on the eve of the largest political mobilization of black Americans in the nation's history.

Lionized for his attacks on black political radicalism in an era of political reaction, Ralph Ellison would continue to defend his silence about America's racial problems—as a commitment to a more moderate, reasonable, means to their solution.

RICHARD WRIGHT AND *THE OUTSIDER*

Perhaps no development evidenced the impact of the postwar political climate on black American literature more than did Richard Wright's changed outlook. The leader of the naturalistic protest school, who played such a key role in shaping black American literature's most controversial ideological perspective, now also embraced the apolitical outlook.

Wright's redirection occurred while he was living in Paris. As noted in the previous chapter, he became acquainted with Gertrude Stein shortly after he wrote a favorable review of her book, and this led to an invitation, from the French government, for him to visit Paris. He accepted the invitation, and visited Paris (at the expense of the French government) where he was feted and honored by some of France's most famous intellectuals. Returning to the United States and its political climate of anti-Communist hysteria, Wright longed for the more cosmopolitan, racially tolerant

Parisian atmosphere—as he became convinced that he could no longer feel comfortable living in the United States. He decided, in 1947, to move to France.

As an intellectual who needed to feel passionately committed to a cause to spur his creative energy, Wright was now seeking a new ideological worldview. The most significant influence on Wright's intellectual outlook during his early years in Paris derived from his friendship with the French existentialist philosophers Jean-Paul Sartre and Simone de Beauvoir, who had a large hand in steering him to French existentialism.

In Paris, far removed from black America, Wright altered not only his ideological worldview but also his conception of the black writer's social role. Though he continued to write about black American characters in the United States, he no longer believed that environmental forces shaped their fate. He no longer saw himself as speaking on behalf of a monolithic and oppressed black community. He no longer envisioned a future in which black and white workers would become united. Rather he now felt inclined to a more complex, ego-centered outlook as his literary focus shifted from racially oppressed lower-class blacks to politically disillusioned—and socially marginalized—middle-class blacks like himself. In short, like other black writers during the Cold War era, he latched on to the fashionable postwar vogue of alienated individualism.

The Outsider, Wright's literary venture into existentialism, appeared after an eight-year hiatus. During that period of adaptation to a new country, a new intellectual network, and a new worldview, he enjoyed the status of an international intellectual celebrity. Although he ceased to present himself as the spokesman for black America, he continued to perform that role—or rather it was thrust upon him—in the Parisian intellectual community, where he was absorbed in a swirl of activities—giving press interviews, writing articles for French publications, participating in book signings, attending honorary luncheons, and traveling on lecture tours throughout Western Europe—befitting an intellectual celebrity. Small wonder his new novel sharply diverged from *Native Son*—he was now a different man.

The Outsider: Richard Wright's Entry into the Existentialist School

Cross Damon, the novel's protagonist, is a socially alienated black man, who lives on Chicago's South Side and works for the post office. Better educated (several years of college) and more psychologically complex than Bigger Thomas, Cross clearly comprehends his predicament, which is fostered not by racial oppression but by marital infidelity. Though it looms large in Cross's mind, his predicament actually resembles more a soap opera than a existential crisis. Cross, who is a married man with children, but now separated from his wife, learns that his girlfriend is pregnant with his child. Burdened by this domestic problem, Cross feels isolated, cut off from ordinary human discourse. For example, in his relationship to this mother, a conventional black woman steeped in black religious morality, we can see his feelings of estrangement. "But to whom could he talk? To his mother? No, she would only assure him he was reaping the wages of sin and his sense of dread would only deepen" (Wright 1965, 23).

Similar to *Invisible Man*'s rejection of Mary's folk culture, Cross's low regard for his mother's black religious sensibility suggests that he is alienated from the social world of black culture. This alienated attitude is echoed and further underscored by his feelings toward his fellow black postal workers: "He knew that they liked him, but he felt that they were outside of his life, that there was nothing that that they could do that could make any difference. Now more than ever he knew that he was alone and that his problem was one of the relationship of himself to himself" (Wright 1965).

As the problems generated by his girlfriend's pregnancy mount—her threat to inform his wife, his wife's demand for child support money, and racial insults from his white postal supervisor about black sexual morality—Cross feels a need to escape. This escape is set in motion by a melodramatic contrivance. While traveling to his wife's apartment to deliver the child support money, Cross is involved in a subway train wreck. He survives the wreck with the money still securely in his pocket—but loses his topcoat, which contains all of his identification cards. Reading about the wreck in the newspaper the following day, he discovers that the authorities, having found his topcoat and identification cards, mistakenly listed him among the dead. The train wreck thus is suddenly transformed from a minor misfortune into a life-altering epiphany—a sudden revelation—marking the birth of his existential freedom: "He was dead. . . . Alright. . . . Okay. . . . Why the hell not? . . . He, of all the people on earth, had a million reasons for being dead and staying dead! An intuitive sense of freedom flashed through his mind" (Wright 1965, 82–83).

Compared with the *Invisible Man*'s hard-earned awakening to his existentialist freedom, this seems shallow and unconvincing. Cross's interpretations of his experiences are too formulaic, too self-consciously philosophical, to be plausible depictions of a postal worker's thinking. In this respect, *The Outsider* resembles the dry philosophical novels written by Sartre. We can see this Sartreian influence in the wooden descriptions of Cross' feelings. "Anxiety now drove a sharp sense of distance between him and his environment. Already the world around him seemed to be withdrawing" (Wright 1965, 86).

Through focusing on the psychological meaning of Cross's escape, Wright aims to highlight the novel's central theme—Cross's transcendence of racial identity: "There was no racial tone to his reactions; he was a man, any *man* who had an opportunity to flee and had seized upon it" (Wright 1965, 86).

This existential image of a black American man fleeing into his individuality, abandoning his social identity, and moving beyond racial categorization suggests that there exists a social world where such individuality can prevail. No previous black American literary works could have produced that image of black American personality. It would have seemed not just implausible—but ludicrous. The only way to escape black identity encountered in previous black literary works was through racial "passing," a recourse pursued by some fair complexioned African Americans to acquire white racial privileges. But in the postwar world, with the advent of the new black bourgeoisie and token racial integration, Cross's deracinated black individuality seemed plausible. At least in reference to the experiences of such black Americans as Richard Wright, Josephine Baker, Ralph Bunche, and Nat King Cole—it seemed more than an illusion.

Shortly after Cross gains his existential freedom, he confronts several threats to his new identity. The first surfaces when he accidentally encounters one of his fellow black postal workers, who is astonished to discover that Cross is alive. Rather than risk losing his new freedom, Cross kills the postal worker—a symbol of his black social world, the racial identity baggage, he aims to discard.

The second, and more serious, threat to his freedom arises while he is riding a passenger train to New York. A black waiter accidentally spills coffee on a white female passenger, who angrily raises a pitcher to strike the waiter, but Cross steps in between them. Indignant with rage, the woman declares that she is going to report the incident to the railroad. The waiter turns to the other white passengers seeking witnesses to testify on his behalf that it was an accident. But the other white passengers refuse to serve as his witnesses. He then turns to Cross.

Aside from depicting racial bigotry and conflict, this scene represents a failed appeal to black racial solidarity. Cross seems willing to support the waiter, but the name and address in Harlem he gives the waiter, to contact him, turn out to be false. He refuses to risk losing his new existential freedom.

Though the issue of black racial solidarity receives much less attention in *The Outsider* than *Invisible Man*, the message of Cross's gesture is as emphatic as the nameless hero's rejection of Ras the Destroyer—black solidarity is dead. Even in the face of white racial oppression, Cross feels no obligation to sacrifice his personal freedom for another black person: "The insistent claims on his own inner life had made him too concerned with himself to cast his lot wholeheartedly with Negroes in terms of racial struggle. *Practically he was with them, but emotionally he was not of them* [emphasis added]" (Wright 1965, 142).

Cross thus opts for an individual rather than a collective identity. "His decisive struggle was a personal fight for the realization of himself." But this turns out to be paradoxical, because his retreat from blacks is paralleled by his gravitation to whites. As in *Invisible Man*, Cross's alienation is contradicted by an assimilationist subtext. The most important consequence of his escape from blacks turns out to be his involvement in the middle-class white social world. From the moment he abandons his old identity, both the range and the depth of Cross's involvement with whites increase.

Cross enters this social world of middle-class whites through the Communist Party. Reflecting the postwar cultural climate as well as his own political disillusionment, Wright uses Cross's encounter with the party to denounce its mission, which—throughout the course of Cross's involvement—is represented as that of cynically manipulating blacks to promote its petty struggles. In fact, *The Outsider*'s depictions of the Communist Party and *Invisible Man*'s depictions of the Brotherhood bear striking similarities.

With the assistance of the black waiter, Bob Hunter, whom Cross locates following his arrival in New York, he meets several white Communists: Gil and Eva Blount and Jack Hilton. Gil invites Cross to live with him and his wife in their seven-room Greenwich Village apartment, because the Communists are about to stage a struggle with landlords, and they need a black to generate a confrontation. Cross accepts the invitation. Though intended to depict the party as cynically manipulative of blacks, this episode fails to pose the crucially important question: why did rootless blacks like Cross submit? The apparent answer to this question is that Cross—and other deracinated blacks—desired not existential freedom, but entry into the white social world. Wright aims to present a different account of Cross's motives for joining the party. "He had no desire to join the Communist Party, but he knew that he would feel somewhat at home with communists, for they, like he, were outsiders. To be with them was not at all a bad way of ending his isolation and loneliness" (Wright 1965, 164).

If avoiding self-negating social bonds motivated Cross's desire for existential freedom, as is suggested in the earlier account of his escape from the black social milieu, then his decision to join the Communist Party seems implausible. Wright can resolve this apparent contradiction only by acknowledging Cross's desire to become part of a white social world, but this he is unwilling to do. For the motives underlying his own attraction to both Communism and existentialism were, if anything, equally assimilationist. But to admit that would mean admitting that Cross's quest for identity was, in fact, a quest for assimilation.

Wright's apparent aim in depicting Cross's encounter with the Communist Party is to reveal the party's ruthless, authoritarian methods. Like many anti-Communist attacks during the Cold War, which emphasized the party's ruthless tactics to discredit its professed commitment to humanitarian ideals, Wright does this in *The Outsider* by depicting the party as racially insensitive and paternalistic.

At a dinner party given by the Hunters with Cross and the Blounts present, Jack Hilton shows up with a message from the party, instructing Bob Hunter to cease his efforts at organizing the black waiters. Hunter is furious, and demands an explanation. Hilton merely tells him, "You don't discuss party decisions. You *obey* them." Though Hunter submits without complaint, his wife, Sarah, explodes. Seeing the conflict not in political, but racial terms, she rebukes her husband: "A white man held out a stick to you and said, 'Jump!' and, by God, you jumped just like any nigger. . . . Listen, woman! This is the Party! This. . . . But it's a white *man's* Party, ain't it, Sarah demanded" (Wright 1965, 181).

This suggests that black experiences in the party are doubly humiliating, because not only are they obliged to take orders from whites; they also are refused explanations of the reasons for those orders. Cross's disenchantment with the party's authoritarian practices is revealed in his reflections as he leaves the Hunters' house. "But why had the party chose that procedure? Had they found that men would *not* obey otherwise? Did communists prefer fear?" (Wright 1965).

If Cross feels such skepticism, the question arises: why is he going to move in with the Blounts in Greenwich Village? What is he seeking? What became of his desire for existential freedom? Why didn't he affiliate with black Communists? These questions call attention to Wright's failure to deal with Cross's motives.

Shortly after he moves in with the Blounts, Cross is used as a pawn by the Communists to provoke a confrontation, which results in a violent fight between Gil and the fascist landlord. "Both men were oblivious to Cross, who stood in the doorway with a bitter smile on his face. Cross could barely contain himself as he watched the battle. Which man did he hate more?" (Wright 1965, 223). While the two men lay exhausted and gasping for breath from the fight, Cross—in a supreme gesture of contempt for communism and fascism—murders both of them.

However unlike *Invisible Man*, *The Outsider* ends without an epilogue— or a reassuring afterword affirming the ideals of American democracy. Rather it concludes on a pessimistic note, as Cross is hunted down and killed by Communists.

That *The Outsider* depicts a bleaker fate for black individuality than does *Invisible Man* no doubt derived from Richard Wright's more hostile view of the United States. While he shared the new black bourgeoisie's disillusionment with radical politics, he never embraced their bland optimism. In clear contrast to Ellison, he never compromised or muted his novel's pessimistic implications. He never became a voice of the new black bourgeoisie consciousness as did Ellison. Rather he continued to live in Europe, socially isolated from the United States. His pessimistic outlook about the fate of black individuality reflected his feelings of rootlessness, his sense of dislocation and despair, which he clearly expressed in 1957:

> I am a rootless man, but I'm neither psychologically distraught nor in any wise particularly perturbed because of it. . . .
> I declare unabashedly that I like and even cherish the state of abandonment, of aloneness: it does not bother me; indeed, to me it seems the natural, inevitable condition of man, and I welcome it.

THE LAST PHASE OF RICHARD WRIGHT'S LITERARY CAREER

The Outsider was more philosophically ambitious than *Native Son*, but it failed to measure up to the latter's sociological and literary impact. If Wright's efforts to project a perspective that resonated his personal experiences as an alienated black intellectual fell short of his earlier works, it was because his talents were more suited to the genre of naturalistic fiction. As an astute observer of the corrosive effects of poverty and racism on black American youth living in the nation's ghettos, he towered above all other black writers of his generation.

However, during the 1950s as Ralph Ellison's literary reputation grew, Richard Wright's declined, as a result of several factors. First, *The Outsider* constituted less of an artistic accomplishment than did *Invisible Man*. Second, Wright's name remained linked, in the minds of many white Americans, to political radicalism, which was now viewed as unpatriotic. Finally, and perhaps most important, Wright was no longer an active participant in the American intellectual scene. Seven years after the publication of *The Outsider*—at the young age of fifty-two—Richard Wright died of a heart attack in Paris.

CONCLUSION

The dominant existentialist ideology, which prevailed until the mid-1950s, was also manifested in another major black American novel published during the period of postwar political reaction—William Demby's *Beetle Creek*. Though *Beetle Creek* lacked the fashionable denunciation of the Communist Party, which Demby was too young to have experienced, it projected the existentialist theme of social isolation and, in the words of one critic, "a robust rejection of American culture and Negro life in particular" (Bone 1958, 191). Written while Demby was living in Europe, *Beetle Creek* embraced a more abstract metaphysical conception of bourgeois individualism. Also, in contrast to Ellison's and Wright's existentialist novels, Demby's protagonist, through whom *Beetle Creek* symbolized existentialist consciousness, was white.

There were other manifestations of the deracialized, assimilationist conceptions of social reality in black American novels during this postwar period, as many depicted all—or mainly—white characters: Ann Petry's *Country Place;* Willard Motley's *Knock on any Door;* Chester Himes's *Cast the First Stone;* and James Baldwin's *Giovanni's Room.* This tendency was by no means restricted to black literary artists. Other black intellectuals manifested it as well. One especially revealing expression of this postwar new black bourgeois consciousness was expressed by the black American literary scholar J. S. Redding in his book *On Being Negro in America.* Declaring his desire to move beyond concerns with race in his future work, Redding wrote:

> I hope this piece will stand as the epilogue to whatever contribution I have made to the "literature of race." I want to get on to other things. . . . The obligations imposed by race on the average educated or talented Negro (if it sounds immodest, it must) are too vast and become at last onerous. I am tired of giving up my creative initiative to these demands. (Redding 1951, 26)

This curious declaration, reflecting Cold War-era bourgeois individualism, was made by a black English professor teaching in a black college, in racially segregated Virginia, three years before the Supreme Court school desegregation decision and some five years prior to the civil rights movement. Redding was merely echoing the fashionable ideological posture of the period.

Thus the dominant postwar black existentialist literary school, paralleling the experiences of the primitivist and naturalistic protest schools, developed through the cultural process of co-optive ideological hegemony, as once again the leading black American literary school depicted black American life through an ideological lens drawn from the liberal white intellectual community.

In highlighting the theme of black disillusionment with political protests, the existentialist literary school marked an important—if short-lived—turn to a more conservative outlook on American race relations. Valorizing token racial integration in the name of individualism, it accommodated the illusion of black American freedom within a social order still dominated by racial caste. No other dominant black literary school would manifest such faith in the transformative powers of individualism.

4

✳

The Era of the
Moral Suasion School

Political Re-Engagement
through Protest for Civil Rights

This is the crime of which I accuse my country and my countrymen, and
for which neither I nor time nor history will ever forgive them, that they
are destroying hundreds of thousands of lives and do not know it and
do not want to know it.

—James Baldwin 1963, 19

Despite the unprecedented critical acclaim that greeted Ralph Ellison's
Invisible Man, the dominance of the existentialist school was short-lived.
Beginning in the mid-1950s, a new climate of race relations was dawning
and this was soon evidenced in black American literature by the ascent of
a new ideological perspective, spearheaded by James Baldwin. This new
ideological perspective, projected through Baldwin's angry and eloquent
essays, rejected existentialist individualism and revived images of a cohe-
sive black community, rooted in shared experiences of racial outcast.
Highlighting the black community's experiences of racial oppression, and
its increasing impatience, it sought to awaken the nation's moral conscience. Which is to say, it revived the protest tradition. But in contrast to
the Depression-era naturalistic protest school, it did so by promoting a
moral rather than a Marxist rationale for racial relations reform.

Hence in less than a decade, black American literature's dominant ideological perspective changed and, once again, a dominant black literary
outlook depicted the United States as a racist society, relations between
blacks and whites as hateful, the black community as a desolate ghetto,
and the black American masses as dehumanized, dispirited, and desperate.

233

But why such an abrupt turn? What social conditions lay behind this new perspective on black American life?

As we observed in the developments of the earlier dominant black literary schools, their ideological perspectives did not emerge from a sociological vacuum—but rather from social and political changes in American society mediated through the hegemonic influence of the liberal white intelligentsia. While also manifested in the development of the moral suasion literary school, this liberal white hegemonic influence now was linked more closely to social dynamics within the black community, as the moral suasion literary school surfaced against the backdrop of a major black political movement—and was widely thought to be that movement's literary voice.

To understand the broader social context which facilitated the ascent of the moral suasion school, we first must take into account the national political climate, particularly the shift from conservative reaction to liberal reform, which set in motion a tumultuous period in American race relations.

THE NATIONAL SCENE: EMERGING CONTRADICTIONS AND DISCONTENTS OF AN AFFLUENT SOCIETY

> It is clear now the years of the cold war consensus were only an interlude, a period of brief political quiescence marking the end of one stage of capitalist development and the beginning of another
>
> —Lasch 1969, 173

By the mid-1950s, new social and political developments restored the nation's confidence and stability. Especially important among these new developments was the general trend of economic prosperity. As one historian put it, "the great waves of prosperity kept rolling in, overwhelming any concerns about the world. In 1957 the government could issue figures establishing that despite the slowly continuing inflation, most Americans were enjoying more real income than ever before" (Goldman 1960, 301). Accompanying this improving standard of living were the expanding opportunities for upward social mobility from blue collar to white collar jobs, which reflected the first signs that the national economy was undergoing structural changes as the United States was being transformed into an affluent postindustrial society.

> The government issued figures indicating that the number employed in the worker's job of producing things was now less than the number making their livings from largely middle-class occupations. More than half the population

had reached or was just about to reach the cherished status of the white collar. Other signs of the social upsurge were less statistical, more satisfying. Ivy League colleges were scouting the secondary schools to enroll able students regardless of family background. (Goldman 1960, 301)

The economic transformation also produced dramatic changes in American lifestyles as tens of thousands of families abandoned the cities. "More miles of suburbia were stretching out, inhabited not only by the $25,000-a-year old-stock American but by the automobile worker, the man who ran the pharmacy in the city, and the children of immigrants" (Goldman 1960, 298).

But perhaps most encouraging, as the background to this new mood of national stability, was the demise of Joseph McCarthy. The anti-Communist crusade had run aground. In the words of one observer, "The decline of the cold war consensus in the cultural sphere in the late fifties runs parallel to a gradual dismantling of the cold war itself. The heyday of McCarthyism in the United States coincided with the Korean War and the last psychotic phase of Stalinism in the Soviet Union. But Stalin died in 1953, the war ended in 1954, and by December of that year McCarthy was censured by his colleagues in the Senate" (Dickstein 1977, 55). In the wake of Stalin's death, the Soviet Union shifted to the more moderate leadership style of Nikita Khrushchev which, along with the calm, and more temperate, demeanor of Dwight Eisenhower, helped to dissipate the American anti-Communist hysteria. While Cold War tensions persisted beyond the mid-1950s as was evidenced in the expansion of the arms race and the United States' large military presence in Germany, the American public no longer felt threatened by Soviet-sponsored subversion of American institutions and, consequently, the nation soon returned to political normalcy.

But on the domestic political front this hardly resulted in the demise of conflict. Despite the popularity of the sociologist Daniel Bell's *The End of Ideology* (Bell 1960), which argued that Western societies were witnessing the end of political divisions and moving into an era of political consensus, new voices of liberal political opposition were stirring on the periphery of mainstream political discourse, voices that marked "the beginnings of a new critical outlook among intellectuals, who had in the early fifties succumbed to the pro-American, anti-Communist, antipolitical attitudes" (Dickstein 1977, 156). Calling attention to the flaws in American society, liberal proponents of this new critical outlook, by the late 1950s, were "warning . . . that a nation dedicated to lifting endlessly the standard of living and to a longtime coexistence with a powerful enemy could easily turn into a militarized, overfat, numb civilization" (Goldman 1960, 303).

Projected by such intellectuals as Paul Goodman (*Growing Up Absurd*), C. Wright Mills (*The Power Elite*), John Kenneth Galbraith (*The Affluent Society*), and Michael Harrington (*The Other America*), this new liberal critical outlook attacked the persisting problems of social inequality, political manipulation, and corporate power in American society. Even more caustic were the critiques launched by Beat writers such as Jack Kerouac (*On the Road*), Allen Ginsberg (*Howl*), Norman Mailer (*The White Negro*), and Lawrence Ferlinghetti (*Coney Island of the Mind*), who advocated an antimaterialist, sexually liberated, bohemian ethos as they ridiculed mainstream American society and its emerging consumption-driven middle-class lifestyles. Joining this chorus of critics advocating cultural liberalization were several major Freudian-oriented writers—such as Herbert Marcuse (*Eros and Civilization*), Erich Fromm (*Escape from Freedom*), and Norman Brown (*Life against Death*)—who highlighted the problems of alienation in modern life, which they attributed not simply to American society but also to Western civilization, and particularly its legacy of psychosexual repression.

The impact of this changing cultural climate was soon evidenced in new attitudes toward sexuality and obscenity. For example, publication of the Kinsey Report , a comprehensive survey of American sexual behavior, suggested that American sexual practices were more varied and unconventional than had been suggested by the movies, magazines, and music of the conservative popular culture. New court rulings broke down the walls of censorship and permitted the publication of previously banned books, such as James Joyce's *Ulysses,* D. H. Lawrence's *Lady Chatterley's Lover,* and Henry Miller's *Tropic of Cancer* which opened the floodgates to literary works exhibiting graphic sexual content. Hollywood movies featured new screen icons such as James Dean and Marlon Brando, who depicted youth alienation and rebellion in a manner that would have been inconceivable in earlier decades. And a new breed of comedian, led by Lenny Bruce and Mort Sahl, began to appear regularly in hip nightclubs, where they found sympathetic audiences for their irreverent, and often obscene, assaults on conventional American morality.

This new critical outlook, giving voice to a liberal social consciousness, soon gained a sympathetic response from educated middle-class Americans, causing many to question the conservative morality, the hollow materialism, and the political complacency of the Eisenhower years.

Perhaps the first major effect of that changing social climate was the election of President John F. Kennedy in 1960. Shifting the direction of federal policy, the election aroused optimistic expectations among liberals that the government would now complete the unfinished business of the New Deal, and transform the nation into a liberal welfare state.

As for the black community, the most important effects of this emerging liberal social climate were evidenced in the changing black American outlook on race relations. The moral suasion literary school, which grew out of that climate, presented itself as the voice of the new black American outlook. By focusing on the black community's experiences of racial oppression and its growing impatience with the racial caste system in 1950s America, the moral suasion school had a large hand in changing public perceptions of black America. But to what extent did its ideological construction of black America—and particularly its conception of the solution for the nation's racial problem—reflect the black community's social consciousness?

The Black Community: Rising Expectations amid Socioeconomic Deterioration

> I can conceive of no Negro native to this country who has not, by the age of puberty, been irreparably scarred by the conditions of his life. All over Harlem, Negro boys and girls are growing into stunted maturity trying desperately to find a place to stand; and the wonder is not that so many are ruined but that so many survive. The Negro's outlets are desperately constricted.
>
> —Baldwin 1963, 59

The moral suasion school, with its new politicized images of black America, emerged against the background of a black community that was experiencing dramatic changes. Those changes, particularly as evidenced in the black community's new expectations of race relations reforms, aroused both curiosity and concern among white Americans. Not since the era of the Civil War and Reconstruction had the United States experienced such a tumultuous period in race relations, and even that period, important though it was, hardly witnessed the large scale black American political mobilization of the 1960s. To comprehend fully the social forces that lay behind that change and the appeal of the new moral suasion literary school, we must view the black community within a developmental perspective.

CHANGING SOCIAL AND ECONOMIC CONDITIONS WITHIN THE BLACK AMERICAN COMMUNITY

The black community's mass urbanization and entry into the industrial economy marked the onset—but hardly the fulfillment—of its quest for modernization as blacks continued to be hobbled by the barriers of racial caste. If by modernization we mean the point at which most members of a group attain educational, occupational, and income levels conducive to a middle-class standard of living, then the 1950s black community remained underdeveloped, existing as a virtual backwash, within an increasingly affluent white society. Despite the increasing migration of blacks from the rural South to northern cities and their employment in the urban economy, most fruits of the nation's postwar economic prosperity eluded their grasp. Scholars and journalists disagreed about the causes, but about one thing all seemed certain: black Americans lagged far behind white American ethnic groups—Irish, Italian, Jewish, and Polish Americans—who had immigrated from Europe during the past century. Those groups now were experiencing upward social mobility into the American middle class, whereas the black community remained marginalized. By almost every social and economic indicator, from education, home ownership, and income to infant mortality, health and life expectancy, black Americans occupied the bottom rungs of the ladder.

This is not to say the black community failed to make any social and economic progress. Beginning with World War I, the first two generations of blacks who migrated from the South had been fortunate. Coming north at a time the United States was experiencing industrial expansion and a shortage of unskilled labor, those early migrants found stable jobs. In fact, except for the Depression years, urbanization brought significant social and economic developments in the black community. Those developments, which stood in sharp contrast to the conditions blacks left behind in the South, nurtured the black community's optimism during both the 1920s and the immediate post–World War II years when, not coincidentally, the dominant black literary schools were apolitical.

This trend of relative improvements halted in the mid-1950s as the link between black urbanization and economic progress snapped, marking the onset of deteriorating economic conditions caused by structural changes in the American economy. Those changes, which were transforming the United States into a high-technology postindustrial society, brought economic dislocations and hardships in the black community.

Exacerbating those economic hardships was the increasing ghettoization of black Americans, relegating them to houses in decaying central city slums. This trend, which accelerated in the immediate post–World War II years, became glaringly obvious during the decade of the 1950s. "From 1950 to 1960, the black population in the inner cities grew by 3,300,000 and the white population dropped by 2,000,000. . . . In only two of the nation's ten largest cities—Los Angeles and Houston—did the white population rise during the 1950s" (Klebanow et al. 1977, 317–18).

The human landscape of urban America was being permanently altered, as one major demographic study of the period concluded:

> A high degree of residential segregation is universal in American cities. Whether a city is a neighborhood center or a suburb; whether it is in the North or South; whether the Negro population is large or small—in every case, white and Negro households are highly segregated from each other. . . . Negroes are by far the most residentially segregated minority in recent American history. (Klebanow et al. 1977, 321–22)

But what was the sociological significance of this development? In the narrowest sense, it meant that white Americans were abandoning cities at virtually the same rate as blacks were entering. But more broadly, seen from a longer historical perspective, it meant that the structural changes in the American economy, now combined with racial caste barriers, were threatening to relegate black America to a state of permanent destitution. This was perhaps nowhere more dramatically manifested than in the increasing rate of black unemployment. Whereas during the decade of the 1940s, the nonwhite unemployment rate had dropped from 14.1 percent to 4.5 percent, by 1955 it shot up to 8.8 percent—more than twice the rate of white unemployment—peaking at almost 13 percent in 1961 (Klebanow et al. 1977, 329). Though a recession hit the national economy in the early 1950s, this hardly accounted for the increased rate of black joblessness. That rate was also affected by the changing occupational structure of the American economy, changes that placed the caste subordinated black labor force at a distinct disadvantage. With a note of irony, Daniel Patrick Moynihan and Nathan Glaser, referring to this structural displacement of black workers in their study of the changing urban scene, wrote, "Just as the Negro Southern agricultural laborer has been displaced by machinery, so too the Negro urban unskilled laborer is being displaced" (Moynihan and Glaser 1963, 38–39). The demand for unskilled labor in northern industries, the anchor that had stabilized northern black community's economic foundation, was slipping away. Moynihan and Glaser (1963) warned: "This is the 'social dynamite' that so shocked James Conant in the Negro slums of the great Northern cities in the late fifties, and that reduces social workers to despair in Bedford-Stuyvesant in Brooklyn and Harlem in Manhattan" (39).

Yet another manifestation of the black community's economic deterioration was the increasing gap between white and black incomes—and the resulting contrasts in the lifestyles of the two racial groups. Whereas in 1951 the average black income was 62 percent of the average white income, by 1962 blacks had dropped to only 55 percent of the incomes received by whites.

Structural changes in the American economy clearly played an important part, but the black community's economic deterioration was hardly the simple result of blind market forces. As noted earlier, the racial caste system contributed substantially to that deterioration, primarily through persisting racial discrimination against blacks seeking employment. Among the most formidable of these obstacles confronting blacks in the labor market were the racist white unions. Observed Moynihan and Glaser in reference to New York City:

> There are jobs that involve relatively little training but are likewise restricted by a union-employer network. The State Commission Against Discrimination (SCAD) and the Urban League have made intensive efforts to get Negro jobs in breweries, as truck-drivers, and as bakery driver-salesmen. These efforts have brought small results. (Moynihan and Glaser 1963, 43)

The black community's economic decline was hardly restricted to problems of unemployment. It was also linked to a racially biased educational system, where blacks were increasingly isolated in substandard public schools. "In Manhattan 75% of the elementary school population was Negro and Puerto Rican," noted one study, which went on to add that "the situation is aggravated by the large number of (white) children attending parochial and other private schools" (Moynihan and Glaser 1963, 48). Similar, equally disappointing examples of segregated and substandard schools for blacks prevailed in other American cities.

While all of the above conditions contributed to black American discontents, even more worrying—if not to say, alarming—was the dramatic spread of social disorganization which was corroding the black community's social fabric. Noted one urban historical account: "As the ghetto was perpetuating itself rather than dispersing it became associated with problems like drugs, crime, broken families, and juvenile delinquency. Indeed, the statistics for most black ghettos are staggering when measured against the rest of the community" (Klebanow et al. 1977, 322).

All of the above problems made one thing clear: the token integration of the immediate postwar years, celebrated by the bourgeois individualism of Ellison's *Invisible Man*, hardly forecast progressive race relations reform. Not only were the conditions of blacks in northern cities worsening. In the South, where most black Americans continued to live in wretched rural poverty, the racial situation remained largely unchanged since the postreconstruction period in the 1880s.

It was thus primarily the confluence of two developments—the black community's economic deterioration and the upsurge of liberal political ideology—that fostered a social climate receptive to black protest, creating an opening for a black civil rights movement.

THE CHANGING OUTLOOK ON AMERICAN RACE RELATIONS AND THE EMERGENCE OF THE CIVIL RIGHTS MOVEMENT

What America is constantly reaching for is democracy at home and abroad. The main trend in its history is the gradual realization of the American Creed.

—Myrdal 1944, 1021

Intellectual thinking about American race relations was changing. Following the Marxist influences of the Depression years, as earlier noted, black intellectuals tended to retreat from radical approaches to the problem of race relations. This was evidenced in the outlooks of both the existentialist literary school and the NAACP. But equally important, a change occurred in the function of black literary works. Beginning in the 1940s, white American leaders and the educated white American public turned increasingly to social science research as the basis for understanding the nation's racial problems. And in consequence, sociological studies of both black community life and race relations begin to achieve influence.

Probably the most influential of these studies was a Carnegie Foundation sponsored study undertaken by the Swedish sociologist Gunnar Myrdal in the early 1940s, published under the title *An American Dilemma*. This study, as well as other social science investigations of American racial problems, gradually supplanted black American literature's long-standing "sociological function" of informing public opinion about the conditions of black American life, a function that reached its high point in the naturalistic protest school. Social science research rendered literary naturalism passé. By providing controlled observations and systematic empirical accounts of American race relations, social science produced what many perceived as more credible information. But this stronger claim to credibility was not the only reason for social science's increased influence. That increased influence also derived from social science's more optimistic liberal worldview, which suggested that the nation's racial problem could be resolved within the existing framework of American society. Thus, in the eyes of many mainstream white leaders, liberal social science offered the prospect of a more pragmatic solution to the race problem than did either the political left with its apocalyptic vision of revolution or the political right with its obtuse denial of the problem.

Myrdal's study, in particular, exemplified those qualities of liberal pragmatism. Sponsored by the liberal Carnegie Foundation, that study amassed an unprecedented body of data on American race relations. While noting white America's past failure to uphold the nation's democratic creed, the study concluded with an optimistic prognosis, which predicted both changed white American attitudes and significant racial reform. The impact of Myrdal's and other liberal social science studies of race relations were soon evidenced.

Without question, the most momentous vindication of that optimistic liberal worldview on American race relations occurred in April 1954, when the U.S. Supreme Court unanimously voted to desegregate the nation's public schools. Jolting the national political landscape like a colliding asteroid from outer space, that court decision shattered a major pillar of the racial caste system: legally mandated racial segregation in public schools. That change, which was legitimized by expert social science testimony documenting the psychological damage black children suffered in segregated schools, inadvertently opened the door for other challenges to racial discrimination. As one historian has aptly observed: "The Brown decision was immediately recognized as a revolutionary step in American race relations" (Quarles 1969, 238). Marking a historic watershed, that decision meant that racial segregation could never again be justified, in the American legal system, as a manifestation of natural law.

By affirming black Americans' claims to civic equality, that decision flashed an ominous message to the white American South, that the racial hierarchy on which it had built its way of life by monopolizing political power was doomed. Not since the Emancipation Proclamation had the federal government taken such bold action on behalf of black American citizenship rights. And in consequence, many black Americans felt a new confidence, which was soon expressed in expectations of even larger racial reforms.

Alain Locke had heralded the 1920s as the era of the "New Negro," but like most boasts associated with the Harlem Renaissance, this turned out to be yet another example of that era's hyperbolic rhetoric. If any period of black American history deserved to be designated as the era of the "New Negro," marking the beginning revolt against the racial caste system, it was the late 1950s and 1960s, following the Supreme Court school desegregation decision. As one historian insightfully noted: "In fine, the Brown decision meant that America would have to look anew at its colored citizens. . . . And as the nation came to grips with this historic decision, it would come face to face with a Negro who seemed to have grown taller" (Quarles 1969, 238).

The nation soon witnessed the repercussions of the Brown decision as the first rumblings of a black protest movement stirred in the South. The Brown decision delivered a major victory to the moderate integrationist strategy of the NAACP, whose legal defense arm had successfully challenged and reversed the constitutional legality of racially segregated schools. But if that decision handed the NAACP a sweet victory, it also

brought unanticipated consequences, as the organization watched its influence decline because its moderate strategy of court litigation to effect
change proved too slow, too cautious, to suit the impatient mood of
many blacks, who now wanted to pursue bolder, more dramatic political
initiatives.

Hence a few months after the school desegregation victory, as the focus
of racial reform shifted from the North to the South, the NAACP's litigation strategy was displaced by a strategy of direct action. Under the leadership of Dr. Martin Luther King Jr., a charismatic young black minister in
Montgomery, Alabama, black civil rights activists targeted racist laws in
the South by practicing nonviolent resistance. King, who had adapted this
strategy from the teachings of Mahatma Ghandi, the Indian independence
leader, expressed clearly his uncompromising commitment to this Ghan-
dian philosophy: "We believe that the American dilemma in race relations
can be best and most quickly resolved through the action of thousands of
people, committed to the philosophy of nonviolence, who will physically
identify themselves in a just and moral struggle" (Meier and Rudwick
1966, 270).

Using that nonviolent strategy in 1955, King launched a successful
black boycott of the city bus service in Montgomery, Alabama, and afterwards moved from one southern setting of racial conflict to another, extending the movement of nonviolent resistance throughout the South. He
eventually consolidated the movement in 1957, roughly three years after
the Brown decision, by creating the Southern Christian Leadership Conference (SCLC), an organization composed of activist southern black cler-
gymen. But by 1960, several years after King launched SCLC, yet another
new direction in racial protest surfaced as black college students appeared
on the political stage, committed to even bolder acts of nonviolent resistance. The students began by staging sit-ins to protest racially segregated
southern restaurants, but soon expanded their political activity to community organizing, voter registration campaigns, and other political initiatives as they sought to mobilize black political participation by democ-
ratizing local southern governments. All of these new black protest
activities were by-products of the Brown court decision and the changed
national political climate.

White America was no longer in denial about the nation's racial injustices. Racial segregation, which had seemed, for several centuries, a perfectly reasonable way to organize American society, was beginning to be
perceived as a social problem. This changing political climate of race relations fostered the development of the moral suasion literary school, which
would cause many conventional white Americans to re-examine their
thinking about race relations.

THE EMERGENCE OF JAMES BALDWIN AND THE MORAL SUASION IDEOLOGY

James Baldwin was too exceptional to be wholly the black spokesman that many whites took him to be.

—Kinnamon 1974, 1

In the late 1950s, the mantle of leadership in black American literature passed to James Baldwin, a writer some twenty years younger than Richard Wright and ten years younger than Ralph Ellison. Baldwin—like Ellison—underwent a major shift in ideological perspective before he emerged as the leader of a black literary school. In his early writings, when he was relatively unknown, he embraced a conception of his social role that scorned politics. As we noted in our discussion of the naturalistic protest school's demise, Baldwin had been one of that school's most severe critics, a stance that was clearly evidenced in his first major critical essays.

But those critical essays were written during the period of the Cold War reaction, when antipolitical conceptions of literature were in vogue, and Baldwin, as a young writer in the formative phase of his literary career, was still groping for a professional identity. His views of protest literature would later change.

Baldwin's moral suasion career was very much a product of the cultural process of co-optive hegemony. In this regard he and Ellison were in some ways comparable. Notwithstanding their very different conceptions of the black writer's social role, both writers—in the most acclaimed phases of their literary careers—embraced the prevailing liberal white ideological outlook of their time. For Ellison, it was the liberal retreat from politics during the reactionary Cold War period; for Baldwin it was the liberal social activism of the late 1950s and the 1960s. If Baldwin is now remembered as having been a more sociologically significant black writer than Ellison, it is because his writings were linked to major political developments in American race relations.

Before we discuss Baldwin's social role as the leader of the moral suasion literary school, we must first examine his unusual social background, the life of poverty, family strains, and religious fundamentalism, to understand how his childhood environment shaped his sensibility and aspirations, and predisposed his attraction to the liberal white intellectual world.

Childhood Experiences in Harlem

James Baldwin was born out of wedlock in Harlem in 1925 and grew up in a hostile household. The source of that hostility was his stepfather, the minister of a small storefront Harlem church. Baldwin's stepfather belonged to that group of southern black migrants who had successfully negotiated the transition from rural to urban life by resisting the debilitating vices of black ghetto life, by finding a spiritual sanctuary in fundamentalist Christianity and its rigid puritanical moral code. The social world of his stepfather's storefront church, which resembled the church Baldwin would later depict in his novel *Go Tell It on the Mountain* (1953), was essentially a rural southern black church that had been transplanted to the Harlem ghetto, where it was sustained by authoritarian black religious traditions.

Those authoritarian traditions cast a shadow over Baldwin's childhood. As a sensitive and precocious boy, he was intimidated by his stepfather's unrelenting, and pitiless, Old Testament morality that never forgave his illegitimate birth. This hostility was exacerbated by the hardships of poverty, which often caused lower-class black men to view their stepchildren with ambivalence, if not outright hostility, because dependents—particularly those sired by another man—were regarded as an unwelcome burden. It was because of these and other strains of black lower-class family life that Baldwin's relationship to his stepfather remained cold, tense, and bitter.

While still quite young, and no doubt motivated by the desire to defend his self esteem, Baldwin began to resist his stepfather's authority, setting in motion a pattern of defiance that continued into his adulthood, until finally, after his stepfather's death, he openly confessed his hatred for this man who had tyrannized his childhood. In one of the essays he published in *Notes of a Native Son,* Baldwin recalled his stepfather's funeral and how he had resisted viewing his corpse, because he wanted to avoid feeling any compassion for him. Though he later tempered that hatred with stoical detachment, the psychological scars from the abuses of his childhood endured.

One way Baldwin had resisted his stepfather's authority was by refusing to join his church. In Baldwin's words: "I did not join the church of which my father was a member and in which he preached" (Baldwin 1963, 41–42).

During this stage of his childhood, before he perceived an alternative to his life in Harlem, Baldwin sought personal salvation in religion. He joined the church attended by his best friend. His reason, aside from defying his stepfather's control, derived from his fear of falling into the wayward life of Harlem's streets. "Many of my comrades were clearly headed for the Avenue, and my father said that I was headed that way too," Baldwin recalled. "My friends began to drink and smoke, and embarked—at first avid, then groaning—on their sexual careers" (Baldwin 1963, 30).

Like other poor black males who grew up in dysfunctional families in ghetto environments, Baldwin knew street life—"the Avenue," as he called it—provided a readily accessible social world to which he could turn for the friendship and support he did not find at home. But he also knew street life—with its pleasures of hustling, alcohol, drugs, and casual sex—often led to disease, physical debilitation, prison, even violent death. Baldwin thus managed to avoid the Avenue by taking refuge in the church, where he underwent the life altering experience of "being saved."

> I became more guilty and more frightened, and kept all this bottled up inside me, and naturally, inescapably, one night, when this woman had finished preaching, everything came roaring, screaming, crying out, and I fell to the ground before the altar. It was the strangest sensation that I have had in my life—up to that time, or since. . . . It moved in me like one of those floods that devastated countries, tearing everything down, tearing children from their parents and lovers from each other, and making everything an unrecognizable waste. (Baldwin 1963, 43–44)

This religious conversion changed Baldwin's life, by awakening and nurturing his spiritual sensibility; it left a deep and lasting imprint on his personality.

His childhood involvement with the church soon went beyond his conversion. Acting out of what he termed "adolescent cunning," Baldwin recalled, "I realized immediately that I could not remain in the church merely as another worshipper. I would have to give myself something to do in order not to be bored and find myself among all the wretched unsaved of the avenue" (Baldwin 1963, 48). Baldwin was actually understating his ego needs for the spotlight. For that "something" he gave himself to do turned out to be preaching the gospel, a choice, he readily conceded, that was influenced by his desire to outshine his stepfather.

> I don't doubt that I also intended to best my father on his own ground. Anyway, very shortly after I joined the church, I became a preacher—a young minister—and I remained in the pulpit for more than three years. My youth quickly made me a much bigger drawing card than my father. I pushed the advantage ruthlessly, for it was the most effective means I had found of breaking his hold over me. (Baldwin 1963, 46)

However, his involvement with the church did not last. After a series of personal experiences, beginning with his awakening intellectual curiosity, his habit of voracious reading, and his gradual encounter with the complex social world beyond Harlem through (predominately white) DeWitt Clinton High School, his religious faith waned. Yet, despite the intellectual reservations he later felt about religion, he remained committed to Christian ethics, which had a large hand in shaping his social role as a writer.

This awakening intellectual curiosity not only supplanted his involvement in the church; it also provided a more enchanting alternative to the Avenue. Through the life of the mind, and, particularly, his new network of liberal white friends at high school, he discovered a different and more compelling path to personal salvation. Signs of this potential direction in his life had surfaced earlier, when he was just ten years old. He had written a play in the class of a white teacher, who immediately recognized his exceptional talents and took an active interest in fostering his intellectual development. On one occasion, Baldwin recalled, she came to his home to get permission to take him to see a play at a downtown theater (Baldwin 1968, 76). His stepfather, looming like a prison sentry separating Baldwin from the beckoning outside world, responded suspiciously. Because he routinely prohibited the family from indulging in popular entertainments, it was only with much reluctance—after interrogating the teacher at length—that he finally consented to let Baldwin attend the Broadway play. The older man's reluctance, Baldwin later noted, was prompted probably as much by his dislike of whites as of the theater. Nevertheless, Baldwin's intellectual identity was slowly being molded. Through relationships with liberal middle-class whites like his teacher and his high school friends, he would find a way out of Harlem.

Baldwin's Formative Intellectual Experiences

DeWitt Clinton High School—a predominately Jewish school noted for its high academic standards—played a crucial part in shaping this new direction of Baldwin's life and identity. It was there that Baldwin's simple faith in the veracity of the Bible was shattered. After he learned that the Gospels had been composed after Jesus' death, he recalled, "I was forced, reluctantly to realize that the Bible itself had been written by men" (Baldwin 1963, 49).

His more skeptical view of the Bible precipitated a collapse of his religious faith. It was hardly coincidental that this development paralleled his increasing estrangement from his Harlem social world. His closest companions now were Jewish and his interests turned more and more to writing. "Lately, I had been taking fewer engagements and preached as rarely as possible. It was said in church, quite truthfully, that I was 'cooling off'" (Baldwin, 1968, 90).

His stepfather was one of the first to notice his waning interests in religion. "My father asked me abruptly, 'You'd rather write than preach, wouldn't you?' I was astonished at his question—because it was a real question. I answered, 'Yes.' That was all we said. It was awful to remember that was all we ever said" (Baldwin 1968, 90).

Baldwin's life became increasingly centered on his high school activities as he became editor of the school magazine and devoted most of his energies to writing. But the transition was hardly painless. A huge cultural void separated the social world of his religiously conservative home life from that of his cosmopolitan high school, as was poignantly revealed in a traumatic incident of conflict Baldwin later recalled. One day he brought home his best high school friend, who was Jewish. After his friend left, Baldwin was interrogated by his stepfather.

"Is he a Christian?" by which he meant "Is he saved." I do not know whether my answer came out of innocence or venom, but I said coldly, "No. He's Jewish." My father slammed me across the face with his great palm, and in that moment everything flooded back—all the hatred and all the fear, and the depth of a merciless resolve to kill my father rather than allow my father to kill me—and I knew that all those sermons and tears and all that repentance and rejoicing had changed nothing. (Baldwin 1963, 51)

The major reason Baldwin gave for his decision to stop preaching was the moral hypocrisy of Christians he had observed. "When we were told to love everybody, I had thought that meant everybody. But no. It applied only to those who believed as we did, and it did not apply to white people at all. . . . But what was the purpose of my salvation if it did not permit me to behave with love toward others?" (Baldwin 1963, 54).

This explanation amounted to little more than a retrospective rationalization which, though stated in religious terms, grew out of Baldwin's increasing allegiance to the liberal white world he experienced in high school, a world that eventually became the basis of his intellectual identity and social consciousness.

It should also be noted that Baldwin was a homosexual, an additional factor that caused him to dissociate from Harlem. Having found the black community abusive toward homosexuals, he was also drawn to the liberal white intellectual community because of its greater tolerance of unconventional sexual orientations. In a very real sense, this liberal white intellectual community, with its values stressing tolerance and racial integration, became Baldwin's reference group, a fact that few of his readers perceived, because most assumed that he was firmly rooted in the black community. Baldwin's high school friends included young liberal whites such as Emile Capouya, Richard Avedon, and Sam Shulman, who would remain close to him through much of his adult life.

Attracted by the values of this liberal white social world, Baldwin left Harlem after graduating from high school, and moved to Greenwich Village, the center of the New York's bohemian liberal white community. Had he come from a black middle-class family background, he no doubt would have taken a different path—attending college and pursuing a professional career in education, medicine, or law. But the circumstances of poverty, and the conflicts with his stepfather, forced him out on his own at an early age.

In 1943, shortly after his stepfather's death, Baldwin sought assistance from Richard Wright. He had read Wright's works and looked upon him as a spiritual father. Their meeting marked the beginning of a stormy relationship. Though Wright read the stories Baldwin brought to his apartment and in 1945 helped him get a writing fellowship, he tended to treat his youthful protege with playful condescension. It is impossible to say whether that was because Wright failed to recognize Baldwin's literary talents or simply disliked his personality, but he never befriended and mentored Baldwin as he had Ralph Ellison.

Baldwin avoided openly expressing his feelings to Wright, but he resented Wright's condescending manner, and this no doubt contributed to the hostility he later expressed toward the naturalistic protest school. In "Everybody's Protest Novel"—the essay in which Baldwin launched his initial attack—he revealed little of his own ideological perspective on black American life, but rather focused on the type of social role he thought the black writer should avoid. Earlier, when Baldwin and Wright had a more cordial relationship, they often engaged in friendly debates about the black writer's social role. However, after Baldwin published his critical essays on the naturalistic protest school, their relationship was permanently ruptured; Wright never forgave Baldwin for what he considered a personal assault on his reputation.

Baldwin was able to assume this role of dragon-slayer because he did not need Richard Wright to advance his literary career. The apprenticeship phase of his career was supported by a liberal white New York intellectual network, which included editors such as Robert Warshaw of *Commentary* and Philip Rahv of *Partisan Review* who published his writings. Between April 12, 1947, and November 11, 1948, Baldwin wrote seventeen articles, mostly reviews, that appeared in *Commentary* and *Partisan Review* as well as *The Nation* and *The New Leader* (Kinnamon 1974, 4).

Despite this promising start, Baldwin felt dissatisfied living in repressive postwar America, and sailed to France on a one-way ticket in 1948, vowing never to return. Baldwin's exile, like most literary exiles, turned out to be more physical than cultural as he remained tied to the United States, particularly his social base within New York's liberal white intelligentsia, which was evidenced by both his dependence on their periodicals to publish his writings and his allegiance to their apolitical postwar conception of literature.

That apolitical posture obscured major contradictions in Baldwin's thinking. Though he said he left the United States because he felt repelled by American racism, no hint of those sentiments appeared in his two novels, *Go Tell It on the Mountain* and *Giovanni's Room* (1956), which he published while living in Paris. He apparently suppressed his disgust with American racism while writing those two novels. In light of his feelings about American racism, his defense of the apolitical conception of the writer's role in his debates with Richard Wright was actually ironic. For in a very real sense, he was debating with himself, arguing against using his literary works to protest social problems. Yet he left the country of his birth because of its social problem of racism. The conspicuous absence of references to racism in his early published fiction suggests not that he was oblivious to racism in the United States but that he acquiesced to the postwar political climate to find an outlet for his writings.

But Baldwin's avoidance of American racism in his writings did not last. His ideological perspective began to change twelve years after he expatriated to France, following the Supreme Court's momentous desegregation decision and the resurgence of liberal political activism in the United States in the late 1950s. James Baldwin returned home a very different writer.

James Baldwin's Ascent to Leadership

Baldwin ascended to notoriety in the public arena projecting an image of himself as an angry and politically committed advocate for racial reform. Having redefined his intellectual identity, he now sought to reconstruct public images of black America in terms of the new activist liberal political ideology, and thereby transform mainstream white America's perceptions of American race relations.

To understand how and why Baldwin came to perform this role, and ultimately to dominate the black literary discourse in the public arena, it is necessary to take into account several important factors. The first, alluded to earlier, was Baldwin's religious background, which nurtured his moral sensibility. Obliquely expressed during the early phase of his literary career (e.g., in his quasi-autobiographical novel, *Go Tell It on the Mountain*), this moral sensibility, derived from his early religious experiences, remained a major force in his personality. As he put it, "The church was very exciting. It took a long time for me to disengage myself from this excitement, and *on the blindest most visceral level, I never really have, and never will* [emphasis added]" (Baldwin 1963, 49).

Elsewhere, in responding to a question about the major influences on his life, Baldwin said, "I hazard to say that the King James Bible, the rhetoric of the storefront church, something ironic and violent and perpetually understated in Negro speech." In fact, Baldwin's writings, much like Martin Luther King's speeches, used biblical images and precepts that reflected the nation's Judeo-Christian moral heritage. In contrast to earlier black literary works of protest, and, in particular, the naturalistic protest school, Baldwin's moral suasion writings did not present a sociological discourse, premised on abstract theoretical arguments, to account for black America's predicament. Rather his writings operated as a liberal moral rhetoric, an emotionally driven appeal, that sought to arouse white Americans' conscience by expanding their awareness of the nation's racial injustices.

Baldwin's unshakable conviction that racial discrimination was evil gave enormous emotional force to his writings. Combining the eloquence of lyrical poetry and the ferocity of evangelical sermons, his writings addressed his white audience as if they were wayward but potentially repentant sinners, who needed to be instructed about the evil nature of their actions. Baldwin's rhetorical strategy, crafted in some of the most passionate essays ever produced by an American writer, promised them moral redemption through racial reform.

Which brings us to the second factor contributing to his role, his public. Baldwin wrote for a white American audience, particularly his reference group, the liberal white New York Jewish community. As noted earlier, Baldwin underwent his initial intellectual socialization at DeWitt Clinton High School, which marked his first encounter with liberal intellectual culture. The influence of that liberal intellectual culture on Baldwin would increase after he left Harlem and moved to downtown Manhattan. Though most of his writings would focus on the black American social world, his prose style was drawn from the culture of educated whites not black ethnic culture, a point that becomes glaringly evident when his prose is compared with that of the 1960s black nationalist literary school.

Ironically this aspect of Baldwin's work was first highlighted by Ralph Ellison. When asked about Baldwin's tendency to stress his black identity, whereas he (Ellison) referred to himself simply as an American writer, Ellison—obviously piqued by this implicit criticism of his intellectual posture—declared, "But when you actually look at Mr. Baldwin's prose you see that he is not writing in the Negro idiom, even, not as much as I do. He's writing a mandarin prose, a Jamesian prose, which tips you off to where he really comes from" (Geller 1969, 165). Ellison's observation was astute. Actually neither he nor Baldwin nor, for that matter, any leading writer in the earlier dominant black literary schools (except Langston Hughes) wrote in black American idiom. This was a consequence of not just their ideological outlooks—but also their audience orientation.

If Baldwin's prose possessed a singular distinction, it was its surpassing eloquence, the rich, supple, and nuanced rhythms of his style, that echoed cadences of the King James Bible, Henry James, and romantic poets, as well as other high cultural traditions of English literature. As an expression of elite culture, Baldwin's prose style constituted cultural capital, an emblem of high social status, with enormous prestige and appeal. By skillfully deploying the high cultural tradition of English prose with which his educated white audience identified, he effectively appropriated their sensibility, and—thereby—achieved a deep level of psychological intimacy, which bridged the chasm of social distance that ordinarily separated the black and white American social worlds—albeit on white cultural terms.

The third factor underlying Baldwin's social role was his literary personae as a black American spokesman-informant. We can see this clearly in his second book of essays, *Nobody Knows My Name*, in which he projects himself as the voice of black aspirations for racial justice. His spokesman-informant personae is revealed in the titles of such essays as:

"Fifth Avenue, Uptown: A Letter from Harlem"
"East River, Downtown: Postscript from Harlem"
"Nobody Knows My Name: A Letter from the South" (Baldwin 1961)

These titles suggest that he is writing as an inhabitant of an alien territory, distant from the social world of his audience. In "Fifth Avenue, Uptown: A Letter from Harlem," for example, we see that personae manifested in his bleak description of the Harlem social world for his white readers.

> When we reach the end of this long block, we find ourselves on wide, filthy, hostile Fifth Avenue, facing that project which hangs over the avenue like a monument to the folly, and the cowardice, of good intentions. All along the block, for anyone who knows it, are immense human gaps, like craters. These gaps are created merely by those who have moved away, inevitably into some other ghetto; or by those who have risen, almost always into a greater capacity for self-loathing and self-delusion; or yet by those who, by whatever means—World War II, the Korean War, a policeman's gun or billy, a gang war, a brawl, madness, an overdose of heroin, or, simply, unnatural exhaustion—are dead. (Baldwin 1961, 56)

And then a bit later in the essay, he skillfully, subtly, reveals the destructive effects of poverty and racism on the lives of ordinary Harlem residents.

> And the others, who have avoided all these deaths, get up in the morning and go downtown to meet "the man." They work in the white man's world all day and come home in the evening to this fetid block. They struggle to instill in their children some private sense of honor or dignity which will help the child to survive. This means, of course, that they must struggle, stolidly, incessantly, to keep this sense alive in themselves, in spite of the insults, the

indifference, the cruelty they are certain to encounter in their working day. They patiently browbeat the landlord into fixing the heat, the plaster, the plumbing; this demands prodigious patience; nor is patience usually enough. In trying to make their hovels habitable, they are perpetually throwing good money after bad. Such frustration, so long endured, is driving many strong, admirable men and women, whose only crime is color to the very gates of paranoia. (Baldwin 1961, 57)

This was not a voice addressed to a black Harlem audience, as was, say, the oratory of Elijah Muhammad and Malcolm X. Rather it was the voice of a Harlem insider addressing a white American audience about black ghetto life.

The fourth and final factor that distinguished Baldwin's role was his attitude toward his white audience, and whites in general. Though born in the wretched world of racial outcast and poverty, Baldwin professed no ill will toward whites. This was a crucially important feature of his personae: a racial attitude of moral compassion. This suggested that a black could grow up in an inner-city ghetto, suffer the deprivations of poverty and racism, and end with a feeling of empathy for whites. It implied heroic forbearance (as indeed did the other noble images of blacks during the nonviolent phase of racial protest). In none of his many exhortations to whites did Baldwin express or encourage racial hostility. "I don't think I hate anybody anymore. It's too expensive. I stopped trying to be white. It's a law that if I hate white people I have to hate black people" (Baldwin 1961).

Though the logic of Baldwin's rhetoric was suspect, this statement revealed the moral suasion ideology's central premise: humane and lasting racial reform can be achieved only by means of compassion. It was this outlook that accounted for much of the civil rights movement's success in mobilizing northern white support.

Baldwin's moral suasion ideology appeared in *Nobody Knows My Name*. With eloquent descriptions of black American experiences, the book elevated him to the status of the nation's leading black writer as its essays broke new ground in race relations discourse. Its impact was soon evidenced in the lavish praise of critics and reviewers.

The voice of a new generation . . . a major literary talent . . . passionate, probing, controversial . . . a searing commentary. (*Atlantic Monthly*)

A vastly important book. If it can't arouse the American conscience, then there isn't much hope for America—white or black. (*Kansas City Star*)

He writes wisely . . . the most effective spokesman between the races in America. He makes you answer questions in your heart, instead of aloud. (*Dallas Times-Herald*)

With the book's publication, Baldwin achieved celebrity. Like Wright and Ellison before him, he soon found himself inundated by requests for lectures, conferences, magazine articles, television interviews, and sundry other inducements routinely directed toward the reigning black literary Caesar. Ellison, who unhappily observed Baldwin's ascent as a protest writer, chose to remain detached from the civil rights struggle. He had fallen from the throne of leadership, as the white liberal intellectual community turned from existentialist retreatism to progressive social reform. Baldwin's morally engaged social role suited ideally this emerging political culture, whereas Ellison's ironic and skeptical individualism did not. This was revealed in a statement Ellison made in 1963, obliquely berating Baldwin's role:

> I prefer his essays to his novels as well as his pronouncements about the situation, but that isn't for me to decide. If there are people who are moved and who are moved toward changing their view of themselves and the world, I think that is to the good. *The one thing I do know is that this is not the role for me.* I'm not that kind of speaker and I think I can serve my people and my nation by trying to write as well as I can [emphasis added]. (Geller 1969, 165)

What was most noteworthy about this statement was what it did not say—namely, that Baldwin had usurped Ellison's leadership position within the liberal white intellectual community. While both Baldwin and Ellison embraced a liberal outlook, Ellison remained more a moderate liberal, committed to bourgeois ideals of individual mobility, wary of collective notions of black identity and collective black political action. Ellison, in short, clung to an outlook that recent events had rendered historically obsolete. It was now Baldwin's era because his rhetorical talents and moral sensibility were more relevant to the emerging climate of crisis in racial relations.

Impending Signs of Dissonance

The South was the primary arena of the civil rights movement which made the initial issues of the race relations crisis relatively simple. As the movement's chief antagonist, the white South possessed little national power or prestige. What potential sympathy it might have aroused among northern whites was eroded by media images of southern white police brutally attacking nonviolent black civil rights protesters.

Given the white South's pariah status, blacks and northern white supporters of the civil rights movement had little difficulty forming a liberal interracial alliance. The forces of good and evil appeared to stand in stark contrast and the solution to the nation's racial problems never seemed simpler nor more imminent than in the early 1960s. Though James Baldwin attempted to call attention to the other, more complex, story of racial discrimination and despair in northern black ghettos, most northern whites chose to ignore those problems. The southern civil rights struggle seized the nation's imagination. Conforming to the script of an uplifting moral narrative, it created the confident expectation, at least among most northern whites, that a solution to the nation's racial problem was at hand.

That expectation of racial reform was strengthened by the election of John F. Kennedy to the presidency in 1960. A northeastern liberal, Kennedy had voiced strong support for civil rights reforms during the election campaign, and most liberals now expected him to initiate a new era of progressive reform in race relations. But Kennedy turned out to be a disappointment. After narrowly defeating Richard Nixon with strong support from the white South, he decided to avoid alienating his southern white supporters in the Democratic Party by steering a moderate course on civil rights. In truth, Kennedy never had a strong emotional commitment to black civil rights.

But Kennedy's weak support for civil rights was only part of the problem. There were also the increasing strains on race relations in the North, which threatened to erupt into a major conflict that could destroy the liberal interracial alliance. The most visible sign of that potential conflict was evidenced in the nascent Black Muslim movement. Advocating an anti-white, racial separatist ideology, the Muslims were expanding in northern black ghettos of Chicago, New York, Detroit, and other major northern cities. Though the actual number of the movement's followers was a matter of dispute, some observers estimated that the group might have as many as 100,000 members, and ten times that number of sympathizers.

Reflecting the anxiety aroused by the specter of this anti-white mass movement gaining influence in the black community, the mainstream media began to scrutinize the Black Muslims. As early as the summer of 1959, two journalists, Mike Wallace and Louis Lomax (a black reporter), produced a special television documentary on the Black Muslims in which they concluded that the movement had only 10,000 fully committed members. Though this figure fell far below the claims made by Muslim leaders, one thing seemed indisputably clear: Black Muslim influence in northern black ghettos was rapidly expanding.

Most followers of the Black Muslims came from the dispossessed urban black working class, especially those experiencing the shock of economic dislocation, living without hope of attaining a stable job and income within the changing urban labor market. This growing northern black ghetto underclass was largely unaffected by the civil rights reforms. As the historians Meier and Rudwick have noted, linking the underclass's economic hardships to the Black Muslim's expansion: "The first real spurt in the membership ranks of the Black Muslims seems to have occurred during the recession of 1953–54" (Meier and Rudwick 1966, 265). Which is to say, the Muslim movement fed on the economic frustrations festering within urban black ghettos.

James Baldwin found this development disturbing, particularly in light of the Muslims' promotion of a racial separatist ideology. As a black American who achieved his intellectual development within a liberal white social world and felt strongly committed to eradicating racial segregation, he regarded the Muslims and other black nationalists as retrograde forces of racial division, bent on polarizing race relations and derailing prospective racial reforms.

The Black Muslims' impact remained limited, in part, because they had failed to attract prominent black intellectuals. They had nurtured a formidable black intellectual of their own in the person of Malcolm X. An ex-convict whose life had been transformed by the Muslim movement while he was in prison, Malcolm X commanded a razor sharp intellect and daunting debating skills, which quickly earned him a reputation, particularly within inner-city black ghettos, as a visionary thinker. Even so, despite his growing national and international notoriety, Malcolm X's influence was restricted; he bore the stigma of a racial extremist. In light of that fact, the Muslim leader Elijah Muhammad felt the movement needed to attract an established black intellectual to gain legitimacy in the larger black community. Hence his pursuit of James Baldwin.

Baldwin's meeting with Elijah Muhammad at the latter's Chicago residence, which was recounted in one of his most poignant essays, we will return to momentarily. But first, to comprehend the mounting political pressures that surrounded Baldwin as he pursued his literary mission of moral suasion, we must examine briefly the deepening crisis within the civil rights movement.

THE EMERGING CRISIS
WITHIN THE CIVIL RIGHTS MOVEMENT

By 1960, as earlier noted, the liberal civil rights movement was threatened by college students committed to radical action. The United States lacked a history of significant student involvement in politics. But that changed in 1960. The appearance of these activist students created problems for the leadership of Martin Luther King and the Southern Christian Leadership Conference (SCLC). Cognizant of both the enormous energy and the potential dangers the student activists brought to the movement, King succeeded in co-opting them within SCLC's organization framework by forming an auxiliary student organization, Student Nonviolent Coordinating Committee (SNCC). The guiding influence of the parent SCLC was clearly revealed in SNCC's original mandate, which stated:

> We affirm the philosophical or religious ideal of nonviolence as the foundation of our purpose, the presupposition of our faith, and the manner of our action. Nonviolence as it grows from Judeo-Christian traditions seeks a social order of justice permeated by love. Integration of human endeavor represents the crucial step toward such a society. (Meier and Rudwick 1966, 273)

SNCC, however, abandoned this cautious strategy when, several years later, it joined forces with the Congress of Racial Equality (CORE), led by James Farmer, and shifted to a more confrontational strategy. Moving beyond such symbolic gestures as the "freedom rides" and demonstrations to desegregate lunchrooms to the more difficult work of voter registration drives in the rural South, they forged ahead to new, more dangerous political terrain.

Meanwhile, in this atmosphere of a mounting race relations crisis, James Baldwin published his third novel in an attempt to consolidate his literary reputation.

Another Country: Baldwin's 1960s Novel

In 1962, James Baldwin published *Another Country*, which—due in large part to his celebrity status as the nation's leading black writer—became an instant best-seller. As his first major fictional work since he shifted to a protest ideology, this was the book his admirers had long awaited.

Set in the interracial social worlds of Greenwich Village and Paris, *Another Country* depicted the narrow milieu of Baldwin's personal life rather than the larger public struggle for race relations reform. Put simply, the novel possessed neither the scope nor the moral force of his essays. And many people, having expected him to seize the mantle of creative innovation by producing a major novel comparable in significance and scale to Ellison's *Invisible Man* and Wright's *Native Son*, were disappointed. *Another Country* failed to launch a new literary paradigm for understanding black American experiences.

The novel begins depicting the ordeal of a dissipated black man, who symbolizes a racially degraded personality, echoing the grim images of black American racial oppression so frequently invoked by Baldwin in his moral suasion essays. Unlike Wright's Bigger Thomas, this black character appears to be a complex individual—a jazz musician, living in the liberal social world of downtown Manhattan, a place very different from Bigger Thomas's bleak South Side Chicago ghetto. This is not a life that can be reduced to the simple calculus of naturalism. Nor is it a life like that of the invisible man, that can be comprehended as confrontation with political demons in a struggle for individual identity. No politics of the cold war figure in this character's fate. There are no denouncements of communists or any other political group, because not only did these concerns lack relevance to Baldwin's life experiences; they ceased—by the late 1950s—to preoccupy white liberal political consciousness.

   Another Country attempts to come to terms with a largely neglected aspect of black American experiences: New York's cosmopolitan interracial milieu. That is, the marginalized social world inhabited by many black writers, jazz musicians, artists, and actors. Baldwin apparently had aimed to reveal this interracial world of parties, friendships, romances, and marriages, which constituted an important—though largely closeted—aspect of American race relations. Other black American literary works had avoided writing about it. As Baldwin several years earlier had observed in reference to the peculiar way Richard Wright and other black writers had ignored black-white romantic relationships: "In most of the novels written by Negroes until today (with the exception of Chester Himes's *If He Hollers Let Him Go*) there is a great space where sex ought to be; and what usually fills the void is violence" (Baldwin 1961, 151). In effect, Baldwin was calling attention to their failure to deal with this rich and complex interracial subculture that constituted a major part of their lives, as evidenced by their friendship networks and romantic involvements.

   Another Country thus seeks to redress that neglect. By focusing on this marginalized interracial world, the social world of downtown Manhattan, it seeks to tell a story about another, very different, country of American race relations. But the novel is flawed by incoherent black anger. No doubt from some points of view that black anger is justified. But in the context of the narrative, it fails to make sense of the motives (like Wright's and Ellison's depictions of blacks in the Communist Party) that attracted blacks to those interracial relationships. In short, that black anger seems to be contradictory and illogical, because it fails to reveal *why* the black characters are drawn emotionally to people they profess to hate. This mystery *Another Country* fails to explain.

   The novel opens on sleazy Forty-Second Street—amidst the blight of tourist bars, sex shops, and adult movie theaters—symbolizing human degradation. Rufus, the jazz musician, is standing on the street.

He was facing Seventh Avenue, at Times Square. It was past midnight and he had been sitting in the movies, in the top row of the balcony, since two o'clock in the afternoon. Twice he had been awakened by the violent accents of the Italian film, once the usher had awakened him, and twice he had been awakened by caterpillar fingers between his thighs. He was so tired, he had

fallen so low, that he scarcely had the energy to be angry; nothing of his belonged to him anymore . . . but he had growled in his sleep and bared his
white teeth in his dark face and crossed his legs. (Baldwin 1962, 3)

Rufus has hit the bottom, the final phase of a swift and brutal decline.
His life, which is depicted in a series of flashbacks, first of his Harlem
childhood, and later of his lifestyle as a celebrated jazz musician, now—
after a series of misfortunes—hovers on the edge of an abyss.

Racism, we gather from another flashback, played a major part in his
downfall. We see a poignant expression of his racial hatred of whites in a
description of Rufus having sexual intercourse with a southern white
woman shortly after they met.

Her breath came with moaning and short cries, with words he couldn't understand, and in spite of himself he began moving faster and thrusting
deeper. He wanted her to remember him the longest day she lived. And,
shortly, nothing could have stopped him, not the white God himself nor a
lynch mob arriving on wings. Under his breath he cursed the milk-white
bitch and groaned and rode his weapon between her thighs. . . . A moan and
a curse tore through him while he beat her with all the strength he had and
felt the venom shoot out of him, enough for a hundred black-white babies.
(Baldwin 1962, 22)

For Rufus, this sexual encounter is a means to vent his racial rage as it
marks the beginning of an abusive relationship rent by racial tensions.

By far the novel's most intriguing feature, Rufus's troubled adult life,
centered in New York's bohemian interracial milieu, echoed the magical
success and tragic decline which resembled the lives of such marginalized
black creative artists as Charlie Parker, Billie Holiday, Dorothy Dan-
dridge, and Bud Powell, who were taken down by the delusions and dis-
sipations of fast living—the result of lonely, anomic experiences of
celebrity in a society that stigmatized them as pariahs. Baldwin apparently aims to explain how racial oppression produces this dissipation, but
he fails to make a convincing case through his depiction of Rufus, whose
actions seem to be more the product of a personality disorder than of
racial abuse. That message about American racism is further diluted
because Rufus is eliminated early in the novel, driven by a fit of
depression—he leaps off the George Washington bridge to his death.

The remainder of the novel shifts from a serious effort to depict this interracial world of black American experience. Except for Rufus's sister,
who implausibly becomes part of Rufus's downtown interracial circle following his death, the novel ceases to deal with black Americans, but
rather stumbles along, depicting the personal torments of its white characters. Echoing *Giovanni's Room*, the theme of homosexuality reappears in

Baldwin's writing. *Another Country* failed to provide a new vision of black American experiences in the restive 1960s because it was flawed by incoherence, revealing contradictions in Baldwin's liberal worldview, particularly in reference to intimate interracial relationships, which enfeebled its ideological message.

Responses to *Another Country* by the Liberal White American Intelligentsia

Not surprisingly, most liberal white reviewers expressed bewilderment and disappointment in response to *Another Country.* For example, Sam Maloff wrote in *The Nation:*

> Baldwin loses control almost immediately, and never recovers it: and the manner in which he fails lies at the heart of the novel's totally disabling flaws. . . . It is the full measure of Baldwin's confessions that he should insist that Rufus is the very symbol of suffering humanity, our kind of saint, when he is—on the creator's own overwhelming evidence—nothing other than a sadist and a swine. (*The Nation,* 14 July 1962, 15)

Similarly underwhelmed was Paul Goodman's assessment of the novel in the *New York Times Book Review:*

> It is mediocre. It is unworthy of its author's lovely abilities. (*New York Times Book Review,* 24 June 1962, 5)

As a leading member of New York's liberal intelligentsia, as well as one of the nation's most radical and visionary social critics, Goodman felt particularly dismayed by the book's emotional irrationality. As did *New Yorker* reviewer Whitney Balliett, who found the motivations of the characters implausible:

> Baldwin's novel is primarily a turbid melodrama. . . . The lovemaking, graphically and frequently presented, seems far larger than life because it is generally between males (Negro and white or white and white) or between Negroes and whites (males and females). . . . Many of the relationships are halting, and not because they happen between Negroes and whites. They just don't make sense; they don't ring properly. (*New Yorker,* 4 August 1962, 69)

The review in *Time* magazine, the moderately liberal news weekly, presented a conventional middle-class reaction to the novel:

> Much was expected of Baldwin's new novel. Now out—it proves a failure—doubly disappointing not only because it does not live up to advance hopes, but also because it so clearly has tried to be an important book. In one fictional fling, Baldwin has tried to unburden himself of all his feelings about

racism and homosexuality, about the cacophony of despair and misunderstanding that he believes America to be. But in *Another Country* this is projected on a wholly inadequate fictional frame: six characters in search of love and self-knowledge in a Dostoyevskian substratum of Greenwich Village. (*Time*, 29 June 1962, 76)

That "substratum of Greenwich Village," though no doubt alien to *Time*'s mainstream readers, constituted familiar terrain to the marginalized New York cultural intelligentsia, who viewed Baldwin as not simply a writer, but one of their own. Hence they felt betrayed, because, in their opinion, *Another Country* distorted their social world, particularly its race relations.

Notwithstanding *Another Country*'s failure, the liberal interracial social world remained the source of Baldwin's worldview, the vision of enlightened and compassionate race relations, that he projected through his moral suasion writings. That liberal worldview, as we will see, embodied a complex and controversial conception of race relations, which went beyond the outlook of the black civil rights movement. We will return to this issue when we assess Baldwin's social role.

THE ERUPTING STORM OF RACIAL VIOLENCE AND THE CULMINATION OF THE MORAL SUASION LITERARY SCHOOL

A civilization is not destroyed by wicked people; it is not necessary that people be wicked but only that they be spineless.

—Baldwin 1963, 69

The year 1963 turned out to be a pivotal one. Marking the high point of the civil rights movement, several hundred thousand people descended on the nation's capital on August 15 for the March on Washington, the largest political demonstration in American history. That event also marked Martin Luther King's finest hour as he delivered his most eloquent and forceful plea for black civil rights in the keynote speech.

But off-stage, all was not well as several new strains were threatening to disrupt the harmony of the March and radically alter the direction of the civil rights movement. Young militant activists from SNCC, who had grown impatient with the King's moderate strategy, argued for tougher speeches. Several older civil rights leaders managed to resolve the dispute through a hasty compromise, but these SNCC complaints were only the first rumblings of an approaching storm. According to one historical account:

The March was more than a summation of the past years of struggle and aspiration. It symbolized certain new directions: a deeper concern for the economic problem of the masses; more involvement of white moderates; and a new radicalism among the most militant, as suggested by the address of the SNCC chairman, John Lewis, who implied that only a revolutionary change in American institutions would permit blacks to achieve the dignity of human beings and citizens. (Meier and Rudwick 1966, 270–71)

These SNCC activists, along with other young black militants, would soon succeed in derailing both the civil rights movement and James Baldwin's social role.

Several events lay behind the developing crisis. First was the November 1963 assassination of President John F. Kennedy in Dallas, Texas. Though he had provided only lukewarm support for southern civil rights reforms, Kennedy had used his superb public relations skills to gain considerable popularity among black Americans. Hence most black Americans regarded his death as a tragic setback for black civil rights, a feeling that was reinforced by the ascent of Lyndon Johnson, a white southerner whom most blacks distrusted, to the presidency. These developments intensified the difficulties King and other civil rights moderates confronted as they tried to maintain the strategy of nonviolent protest and to counter the growing influence of the young black militants, who expressed cynicism about the federal government's commitment to racial justice.

The storm clouds hovering over the civil rights movement grew even more ominous when, shortly after Kennedy's assassination, the Black Muslims suspended Malcolm X. According to the Muslims, he was suspended because he made insulting remarks about Kennedy's death. But Malcolm X disputed that account, saying that he was suspended after he had questioned Elijah Muhammad about rumors that the Muslim leader had fathered several children born to women in the organization. Whatever the truth of the Muslims' and Malcolm X's accounts of the suspension, that event had significant repercussions for the black nationalist movement; Malcolm X was now free to organize a secular nationalist movement, unfettered by the Nation of Islam's religious doctrines.

It was during this period of Malcolm X's growing influence as an independent and militant black nationalist, in 1964 and 1965, that the black ghettos in New York and Los Angeles erupted in riots, which further strained the liberal interracial alliance behind the black civil rights movement.

Distressed by the growing influence of black nationalism and the mounting crisis threatening the civil rights movement, Baldwin published his third and most powerful book, *The Fire Next Time*. In this book, which attempts to explain the psychological scars black Americans suffered living in racist society (an undertaking he had failed to achieve in his novel), he implored his white audience to support race relations reforms. Evoking an atmosphere of danger as he drew on the symbolism of Old Testament prophecy, he forecast a gathering storm of black rage that would soon explode in massive violence, if white America failed to heed his warning.

Although committed to racial integration, Baldwin's attitude to the rising tide of black militancy was oddly ambiguous. Reluctant to criticize the militancy, he sought instead to explain the social conditions from which it sprang. This tactic allowed him both to appeal to his white audience's moral conscience and to maintain his cordial relations with the militant nationalists. Having witnessed such moderate black leaders as Whitney Young and Roy Wilkins berated as "lackeys" and "Uncle Toms" for criticizing black militant nationalism, Baldwin chose to steer clear of that fate. This was not simply because he feared being labeled a proponent of white interests, but also, and more important, because he needed to preserve the credibility of his public personae as a spokesman for black political aspirations—the sine qua non of his literary role. But now, as the threat of racial polarization intensified, he was obliged to achieve this balancing act by walking an increasingly slippery tight rope. Any misstep could topple his literary reputation.

As an integrationist and a homosexual, Baldwin apparently found black nationalist ideology distasteful, because it aimed to create a society within which cosmopolitan blacks like himself would have no place. The fact that he did not choose to live in a black neighborhood after he returned to the United States suggests that his childhood experiences in Harlem soured him on segregated black community life. His cosmopolitan lifestyle hardly predisposed him to embrace a racial separatist ideology. Yet curiously, despite his personal reservations about black nationalism, he never actually said what he thought about that ideology in his essays but rather sought to avert its growth, to undermine its appeal to blacks, by exhorting white America to repudiate racism. Let's now turn to *The Fire Next Time* and examine the strategy he used in pursuit of his mission.

Baldwin's Final Plea: *The Fire Next Time*

Baldwin opens the first section of *The Fire Next Time* by employing the rhetorical device of a personal letter, in this instance, written to his nephew. Invoking the wise tone of an elder counseling an innocent black child, he informs the boy about racial practices of the society into which he was born. By using this device, Baldwin obliged his white audience to see American racial injustices through the fresh, hopeful eyes of a black child. Baldwin began: "This innocent country set you down in a ghetto in which, in fact, it intended that you should perish. . . . You were born and faced the future that you faced because you were black and for no other reason. The limits of your ambition were, thus, expected to be set forever" (Baldwin 1963, 17–18).

Though Baldwin had gained his initial notoriety by attacking Richard Wright's bleak depiction of Bigger's black environment, his moral suasion images of black ghetto life, as an "entrapped existence," ironically resembled Bigger's desolate slum life. It contained no cultural heritage, no social order, no rituals and humor, nor even spiritual meaning. Only oblivion and despair. At least as constructed for his white audience, black ghetto life seemed a cold and gloomy dungeon where blacks were condemned to exist, a dungeon from which only a lucky few managed to escape. For this wholesale destruction of black lives Baldwin blamed white racism, yet he avoided concluding his argument with hostility, as one might expect. Rather he concluded by urging his nephew to feel compassion for white Americans: "You must accept them and accept them with love" (Baldwin 1963, 22).

Here again Baldwin invoked the rhetoric of Christian moral compassion as he suggests one must overcome his adversary through love, not hatred. This departed sharply from the message he projected in *Another Country*, where there was no hint of black moral compassion toward whites. This essay, by contrast, assumes the tone of a virtual hymn to interracial fraternity as it summons the spirit that inspired and energized the interracial alliance behind the civil rights movement. "These men [whites] are your brothers—your lost, younger brothers. And if the word integration means anything, this is what it means: that we with love, shall force our brothers to see themselves as they are, to cease fleeing from reality and begin to change it" (Baldwin 1963, 21).

The book's second section, "Down at the Cross," which appeared initially in the cosmopolitan *New Yorker* magazine, made an obvious allusion to Jesus and the crucifixion as Baldwin now perceived his social role as that of a prophet about to be sacrificed (how right he was). Baldwin was now reverting to his earlier pulpit experience as a preacher. The structure of this essay resembled a black religious sermon, beginning in a slow, measured, and meditative tone, and then gradually shifting and rising to a loud, angry crescendo of moral indignation. While the gospel still derived from Christianity, the hoped-for salvation was no longer located in heaven, but in interracial community.

Baldwin begins the essay by offering his readers yet another biographical sketch, a review of his early years in Harlem and elsewhere, that recounts his experiences of home life, high school, and racial insults, and then, suddenly, he shifts to the essay's chief concern: to warn his white audience about the growing attraction of black Americans to the Black Muslim movement.

Baldwin described a meeting he had with Elijah Muhammad at the latter's South Side Chicago mansion. The Muslims, who were seeking to recruit prominent black intellectuals to add legitimacy to their movement, regarded Baldwin as a especially attractive prize. Baldwin was invited to meet Elijah Muhammad after he had appeared on a television program with Malcolm X (who was still then in the Muslim movement), where he had responded to a question about violence by defending—or so it seemed—the Muslim position on violence. Actually Baldwin did not agree with the Muslim position on violence but, as was often his habit in public debate, he had resorted to hyperbole to score debating points. Malcolm X was impressed by Baldwin's performance, and informed his superior. Shortly afterwards, Baldwin was invited to meet Elijah Muhammad in Chicago. Baldwin realized he had been invited to the Muslim headquarters for some unspecified political purpose, and confessed to feeling frightened.

He was hardly alone in feeling frightened by the Black Muslims. Many whites were frightened by the Muslims as well. Frequent media reports highlighting the Muslims' hatred of whites (who were referred to as "devils") and their advocacy of violence had convinced white American authorities that the group was dangerous and warranted close scrutiny. If Baldwin's *New Yorker* essay attracted great interest, it was because it presented the first intimate depiction of that strange movement—for a white American audience—by a distinguished liberal black writer.

After dinner got under way, Baldwin recalled, the real intent of the meeting began to surface as Elijah Muhammad asked about his religious affiliation. Baldwin responded that he saw himself as a writer, not an organization man, and then went on to state his views about race relations. "I told Elijah that I did not care if white and black people married, and that I had many white friends. I would have no choice, if it came to it, but to perish with them, for (I said to myself, but not to Elijah), 'I love a few people and they love me and some of them are white and *isn't love more important than color* [emphasis added]'" (Baldwin 1963, 98).

Perhaps nowhere else did Baldwin express his racial worldview more clearly than in this response. What is especially revealing about the essay was the way Baldwin used the occasion of reporting on a conversation with Elijah Muhammad to inform his white readers how he felt about whites, much of which he apparently failed to tell the Muslim leader. By using this device to set forth his integrationist sentiments, Baldwin established an emotional bond with his white readers, an emotional bond, he implied, he did not feel toward the Black Muslims.

To accept the Muslim ideology, he would have to abandon his predominantly white social network, which he candidly admitted were the most important friendships in his life. It was this liberal white social network that had nurtured his intellectual aspirations, given him a sense of self-worth, provided him an outlet for his writings, and—perhaps most important—enabled him to escape the bleak and impoverished ghetto environment of his childhood. In short, this social network was the social base of his intellectual identity and worldview.

Although he did not say this to Elijah Muhammad, Baldwin realized that he could not oppose racial integration without simultaneously destroying his social role as a writer. His literary career as a Black Muslim was simply inconceivable.

In reporting his rejection of Elijah Muhammad's overture, Baldwin avoided criticizing him as he described the Muslim leader as warm and sincere. In taking this uncritical public posture toward black nationalists, Baldwin manifested his characteristic tendency to attribute the power to change the racial situation to whites. In his view, white America's intransigence was the problem. The violence being advocated by black nationalists was simply a natural reaction to that intransigence, a temper tantrum generated by frustrations blacks could no longer contain. Though he thought the black nationalist reaction was irrational, he could not bring himself to say so publicly. Instead, he appealed to whites to recognize their power to effect racial reform. This was indeed ironic. For Baldwin's moral suasion ideology ended up depicting blacks as politically impotent, even when they were advocating aggressive action. We see Baldwin's emphasis on white agency in his attempt to explain frustrations that lead black Americans to hate whites.

A Negro just cannot believe that white people are treating him as they do; he does not know what he has done to merit it. And when he realizes that the treatment accorded him has nothing to do with anything he has done, that the attempt of white people to destroy him—for that is what it is—is utterly gratuitous, *it is not hard for him to think of white people as devils* [emphasis added]. (Baldwin 1963, 95)

The dubious validity of Baldwin's armchair black psychology notwithstanding, he was rhetorically constructing a black American image of whites for his white readers—in effect, an inverted mirror—that rendered the irrational hatred of the Black Muslims reasonable. Insofar as his white readers accepted the plausibility of this image of themselves, they were obliged to feel some responsibility for the Muslim development. Such was the power of moral suasion ideology. After weaving this intricate web of white culpability, Baldwin ended the book by expressing fear, because he felt that time was running out. The potential explosive violence in northern black ghettos, lurking beneath the surface, he believed, would soon erupt and plunge the nation into racial purgatory—if white America failed to heed his warning.

Everything now, we must assume, is in our hands; we have no right to assume otherwise. If we—and now I mean the relatively conscious whites and the relatively conscious blacks, who must, like lovers, insist on, or create the consciousness of the others—do not falter in our duty now, we may be able, handful that we are, to end the racial nightmare, and achieve our country, and change the history of the world. If we do not now dare everything, the fulfillment of that prophecy, recreated from the Bible in song by a slave, is upon us: God gave Noah the rainbow sign, No more water, the fire next time. (Baldwin 1963, 141)

In these essays, Baldwin not only recaptured his earlier moral force, he soared to new heights of eloquence. And the impact was soon evidenced in reviews of *The Fire Next Time*, which, in stark contrast to *Another Country*, provoked raves and instantly ascended to the *New York Times'* bestseller list. Indicative of those favorable comments, a reviewer in *Harper's* magazine wrote: "If ever there was a compassionate and eloquent sermon for our time, demanding the most agonizing self-examining from anyone who reads, this is it. . . . Great." Similarly enthusiastic was the review that appeared in the liberal *New York Post*: "These pages burn their way through our mind with a tortuous feline grace. If there is a better writer today than Baldwin, I don't know his name." The reviewer for *Atlantic Monthly* described Baldwin's book as being "so eloquent in its passion and so scorching in its candor that it is bound to unsettle any reader. As a novelist and writer of uncommon talent, James Baldwin plunges to the human heart of the matter." The *New York Times* reviewer described the book with such words as "searing . . . brilliant . . . masterful." And *Newsweek* proclaimed it: "Anguished. . . . Stabbing. . . . A final plea and warning . . . to end the racial nightmare."

Despite arousing this near-universal acclaim in the public arena, the essays failed to achieve their mission. White America did not demand sweeping race relations reforms as both the civil rights movement and Baldwin's literary reputation peaked in 1963–1964.

Following *The Fire Next Time*, Baldwin's popularity waned. He wrote a play for the Broadway stage titled *Blues for Mr. Charlie*, based on the Emmet Till murder, in yet another effort to stir white America's moral conscience. But the negative critical responses to the play signaled a changing climate of race relations as the play garnered scant public support and closed shortly after opening.

In 1965, soon after the play was produced, Baldwin published a book of short stories, *Going to Meet the Man*, and in 1967, a novel, *Tell Me How Long the Train's Been Gone*. But like his play, these books failed to arouse the enthusiastic critical acclaim that had greeted *The Fire Next Time*. Although he continued to write, Baldwin realized that he had fallen into disfavor.

His reputation was a casualty of the nation's increasingly polarized race relations. Following the mid-1960s ghetto riots in New York, Los Angeles, Newark, and Detroit, as thousands of northern black youth (as noted earlier) gravitated to the black nationalist movement and many northern whites, in angry reaction, stopped supporting racial reform, the nation found itself mired in its worst racial crisis of the twentieth century. While it is impossible to specify precisely the moment of that historical turn, SNCC's and CORE's conversion to black nationalist ideology in the summer of 1966 and Martin Luther King's assassination approximately a year later, in the spring of 1967, marked the breakdown of the interracial alliance for integration and deepening antagonism between blacks and whites.

This changed climate of race relations profoundly affected Baldwin. By the late 1960s, after witnessing ghetto racial violence erupt and spread from one city to another, creating the racial nightmare he had worked so hard to avert, Baldwin's faith in his liberal worldview collapsed and he fell into a state of psychological despair. He retreated once again to Europe, where, shortly after arriving, he experienced a nervous breakdown. This marked the end of his journey as the leading literary proponent of the moral suasion literary ideology.

Though he continued to write after his recovery, he was no longer the same writer. He now expressed distrust of white America and cynicism about American race relations. This was evidenced clearly in an interview he gave in a June 1972, when he responded to a question about the effect of the civil rights movement on his life by saying:

> The most tangible thing that happened to me—and to blacks in America—during that whole terrible time was the realization that our destinies are in our hands, black hands, and no one else's.
> I do not believe in the promises of America in the same ways. *There will be no moral appeals on my part to this country's moral conscience. It has none* [emphasis added]. (Bigsby 1969)

Equally revealing was his changed attitude toward Christianity, the source of the moral ideals that had suffused his earlier arguments for racial reforms. Asked about the black intellectual's disenchantment with that religion, Baldwin responded acidly: "We have begun to see the nature of the hoax." Which is to say, he now viewed Christianity as part of the moral hypocrisy that sustained American racism. It is important to understand that his disengagement from Christianity resulted from his disillusionment with white America's capacity to act in terms of moral conscience, which he had believed was the only hope for the nation's achievement of racial justice. He no longer saw Christianity as the bridge linking black and white Americans in a shared moral universe.

Seen from a sociological perspective, Baldwin lost his white audience because the social conditions that had generated support for progressive race relations reform dissipated. Though it was not then obvious, the entire national political climate, not just the white attitudes about race relations reform, was shifting toward political conservatism, marking the descent of the 1960s liberalism.

In light of the enormous influence Baldwin enjoyed in the early 1960s, we must now briefly assess his ideological perspective on race relations and ask, To what extent did his outlook actually represent black civil rights aspirations?

BALDWIN'S MORAL SUASION IDEOLOGY: A FAILED QUEST FOR RACIAL AMALGAMATION

As we noted earlier, Baldwin's worldview and social base were largely misperceived by his white audience. That misperception was hardly accidental, for Baldwin carefully constructed his personae as literary spokesman of the black community. Though he performed that personae superbly, his views on American race relations diverged, in significant aspects, from those embraced by Martin Luther King and other black civil rights activists.

As a product of the predominately white New York cultural intelligentsia, Baldwin rejected not just America's racial caste system; he also rejected much of its mainstream culture. Though he seldom revealed his broader critical view of American society in his moral suasion essays, he had long felt alienated from the commercialism, corporate careerism, and political conformity that suffused the American institutional order, and shaped its conventional middle-class lifestyles. Baldwin's critical view, it is important to note, diverged sharply from the views on American society expressed by *Native Son* and *Invisible Man*. Both of those novels, while objecting to white racism, exhibited an almost idealized view of mainstream white American society.

Baldwin's writings, by contrast, suggested that white American society, not just its race relations, needed to be transformed. As can be seen in the following passage, his critical take on mainstream American culture, echoing the adversarial style of the New York cultural intelligentsia, was hardly sympathetic.

How can one respect, let alone adopt, the values of a people who do not, on any level whatever, live the way they say they do, or the way they say they should? I cannot accept the proposition that the four-hundred-year travail of the American Negro should result merely in his attainment of the present level of the American civilization. I am far from convinced that being released from the African witch doctor was worthwhile if I am now—in order to support the moral contradictions and spiritual aridity of my life— expected to become dependent on the American psychiatrist. It is a bargain I refuse. (Baldwin 1963, 110)

Such comments coming from Richard Wright or Ralph Ellison would have been inconceivable. Actually those comments resembled some of the caustic bohemian pronouncements of the 1920s black primitivist writers Claude McKay, Langston Hughes, and Jean Toomer. But unlike those writers, Baldwin did not see salvation in lower-class black American ethnic culture. He was too cosmopolitan to succumb to primitive romanticism.

Which brings us to the differences between Baldwin's outlook on racial reform and that of the civil rights leaders.. Those differences can be perhaps best illustrated by noting the distinction E. Franklin Frazier drew between integration and assimilation. "Integration," wrote Frazier, denotes "the acceptance of Negroes as individuals into the economic and social organization of American life," and as such, it "involves . . . the organized life of the Negro community vis a vis the organized white community." By contrast, Frazier suggested, "assimilation involves integration into the most intimate phases of the organized social life of a country" which "leads to complete identification with the people and culture of the community in which the social heritages of different people become merged or fused" (Frasier 1968, 268).

The civil rights movement, in this sense, sought integration, which as envisioned by Martin Luther King and other black civil rights activists, as well as their white supporters, aimed to open access for blacks to mainstream American institutional life, including such previously segregated domains as political elections, public schools, public transportation, governmental and private sector employment, and public recreational facilities. In effect, they embraced a pluralistic model of race relations, which would allow blacks to participate in the mainstream social order, while preserving their ethnic institutions. Though the civil rights proponents failed to make clear which black institutions would be preserved in this new racially integrated America, the black church was certainly one institution that most blacks wanted to preserve. But when it came to other black institutions such as black professional associations, black political organizations, black labor unions, black athletic associations, black branches of the YMCA, black radio stations, and black entertainment facilities such as New York's Apollo Theater, there was scarcely a consensus.

Even so, it is hardly surprising that King and his SCLC cohorts appeared to favor a mixture of ethnic community institutions and racially integrated public institutions. As black ministers, they had vested interests in the survival of the black church.

In contrast, the cosmopolitan Baldwin looked beyond ethnicity in his conception of racial reform. Reflecting the social consciousness of his liberal white social circle, he envisioned racial and ethnic amalgamation, in effect, a society in which blacks and whites ceased to exist as distinct social categories. To his mind, race was an artifact of social construction. As he put it: "Color is not a human or a personal reality; it is a political reality" (Baldwin 1963, 118).

Though he avoided making it the central issue in his writings, he wanted to see a melding of the races. "We, the black and the white, deeply need each other here if we are to become a nation—if we are really, that is, to achieve our identity, our maturity, as men and women" (Baldwin 1963, 111).

Baldwin's amalgamationist outlook should not be confused with the assimilationist views of the black existentialist writers. Not only were the latter's views largely uncritical of mainstream white American society, they never honestly owned up to their assimilationist values. Instead, they masked those values in abstracted celebrations of black individuality.

Baldwin, in contrast, addressed directly the issue of black and white amalgamation, even though he felt less than sanguine about the prospect of its realization. He rejected the prevailing conventional wisdom which suggested that the nation's racial problems derived from whites' aversion to dark skin. Instead he offered an alternative, psychoanalytic explanation. White racism, he argued, derived from white America's psychological repression, repression stemming from its hypocritical mainstream culture, which caused whites to project their frustrated sexual and emotional impulses—that is, what they saw as, their sinful proclivities—onto blacks. In consequence, blacks came to symbolize white America's repressed id. As Baldwin's put it:

> The racial tensions that menace Americans today have little to do with real antipathy—on the contrary, indeed—and are involved only symbolically with color. These tensions are rooted in the very same depths as those from which springs love, or murder. The white man's unadmitted—and apparently, to him, unspeakable—private fears are projected onto the Negro. The only way he can be released from the Negro's tyrannical power over him is to consent, in effect, to become black himself, to become a part of that suffering and dancing country he now watches wistfully from the heights of his lonely power and, . . . visits surreptitiously after dark. (Baldwin 1963, 109)

Again, we see Baldwin expressing a conception of racial reform that resembled the 1920s primitivist views of such writers as Claude McKay and

Langston Hughes: the notion that whites first must acquire black America's uninhibited emotionality, and achieve psychological health, if they were to overcome their Afrophobia. Though Baldwin's explanation of white Afrophobia was more sophisticated than that of the primitivists, it amounted to essentially the same thing, the notion that whites must get in touch with their repressed feelings ("that suffering and dancing country inside themselves") to overcome their emotionally stunted lives. Then there would be no need to fear and dislike blacks. But in contrast to the black primitivist writers, Baldwin hardly thought that whites could get to that place by slumming in black ghettos or by being exposed to sensational images of black American sexuality. He knew better than that. Even so, his formulation was flawed because it not only ignored the white economic and political interests implicated in American racism, but it failed to suggest a process through which white Americans could achieve racial healing. Exhortations were insufficient. Certainly his novel *Another Country* had failed to point the way for mainstream white Americans who wished to get to that "place of emotional liberation" he deemed essential to racial reform. One could perhaps argue that the enormous influence of black music in American popular culture, beginning in the 1960s, has helped to change American culture. However, Baldwin apparently never considered the implications of that development for the unfolding dynamics of race relations.

THE END OF MORAL ENGAGEMENT: A BLACK MILITANT ASSAULT ON BALDWIN'S SOCIAL ROLE

Although Baldwin's white readers perceived him as the quintessential black community spokesman, both his social base and worldview during the period of the early 1960s as earlier noted, were dissociated from the black community. And this led to problems for Baldwin as the 1960s racial antagonisms intensified. He became the target of brutal black critical attacks. In much the same way that he earlier had attacked and helped to dethrone Richard Wright, a relatively unknown young black writer set out to undermine his achievements.

That writer was Eldridge Cleaver, an ex-convict and leader of the Black Panther Party. In a highly acclaimed examination of the American racial crisis, *Soul on Ice* (1970), Cleaver argued that Baldwin's amalgamationist views stemmed from ethnic self-hatred, the desire to escape his identity as a black man. "Self-hatred," Cleaver wrote, "takes many forms. . . . Ethnic self-hatred is even more difficult to detect. But in American Negroes, this ethnic self-hatred often takes the bizarre form of a racial death-wish, with many and elusive manifestations. Ironically, it provides much of the impetus behind the motivations of integration" (Cleaver 1970, 99).

As a product of the new generation of ghetto-based militant black writers who identified with black ethnic culture and third world revolutionaries like Fidel Castro, Che Guevara, and Frantz Fanon, Cleaver responded to Baldwin's stance on racial integration with rage. Reflecting the disdain young ghetto blacks increasingly felt toward the assimilationist-oriented black intellectuals, he wrote: "In this land of dichotomies and disunited opposites, those truly concerned with the resurrection of black Americans have had eternally to deal with black intellectuals who have become their own opposites, taking on all of the behavior patterns of their enemy, vices and virtues, in an effort to aspire to alien standards in all aspects" (Cleaver 1968, 343).

With a meanness eerily reminiscent of Baldwin's earlier attack on Richard Wright, Cleaver declared: "The racial death-wish is the driving force in James Baldwin. His hatred for blacks, even as he pleads what he conceives as their cause, makes him the apotheosis of the dilemma in the ethos of the black bourgeois" (Cleaver 1970, 101).

Cleaver thus sounded the death-knell on moral suasion ideology. This and other bare-knuckled attacks by young black militants on Baldwin's integrity had a large hand in precipitating his psychological breakdown. But beyond its destructive impact on Baldwin and the moral suasion ideology, Cleaver's attack also can be viewed—in a broader sense—as the epitaph for the 1960s liberal interracial alliance.

> A grave danger faces this nation, of which we are as yet unaware. And it is precisely this danger Baldwin's work conceals; indeed, leads us away from. We are engaged in the deepest, the most fundamental revolution and reconstruction which men have ever been called upon to make in their lives, and which they absolutely cannot escape or avoid except at . . . (their) peril . . . . The time of the sham is over, and the cheek of the suffering saint must no longer be turned to the brute. The titillation of the guilt complexes of bored white liberals leads to doom. (Cleaver 1970, 106–7)

A new and more radical era was dawning. Baldwin's decline marked the end of the liberal white hegemony over black literary discourse. Cooptive hegemony had run its course. A more alienated and angry generation of black writers was moving onto the cultural stage, expressing a radical black nationalist ideology that questioned not only the credibility of earlier white acclaimed black literary achievements—but the very basis of white cultural authority.

It is this story we turn to in the next chapter.

5

Amiri Baraka and the Rise of the Counterhegemonic Black Cultural Nationalist School

> This cultural revolution will be the journey to our rediscovery of ourselves.
>
> —Malcolm X 1972, 563

Perhaps no events signaled more clearly the impending demise of James Baldwin's reputation than did the responses of the white critics to his play *Blues for Mister Charlie*. Those responses prefigured a passing of the mantle of leadership—or so it seemed. Recalling the reaction to Baldwin's play, Amiri Baraka later provided the following intriguing account of Baldwin's literary fate.

> In February 1964, James Baldwin's *Blues for Mister Charlie* opened up on Broadway . . . and, while it had mixed reviews, it was one of the great theater experiences of my life. A deeply touching "dangerous" play for Jimmy, it not only questioned nonviolence, it had a gutsy (but doomed) black hero and his father go at each other's values, echoing the class struggle that raged between Dr. King and Malcolm X. . . . Jimmy . . . (questioned even) "God in his heaven" for his part in the conspiracy that leaves us powerless and our young men killed. (Baraka 1984, 187)

And then with chilling insight Baraka added: "It was an extremely powerful work, so powerful I believe that the bourgeois (mainly white) critics at that point read Jimmy out of the big-time U.S. literary scene. He had gone too far" (Baraka 1984, 187).

Interestingly, Baraka stood to gain from Baldwin's demise. Though still a relatively unknown black writer, Baraka had written a play—*The Dutchman*—that was soon to be produced off-Broadway. In his words:

> *Dutchman* opened the next month, downtown, at the Cherry Lane. . . . I went out late that night after the opening, up to the corner of St. Marks and Second Avenue, and read the reviews. They were mixed too, but there seemed to me a kind of overwhelming sense from them that something explosive had gone down. I had a strange sensation standing there like that. I could tell from the reviews that now my life would change again. . . . I walked home slowly, looking at my name in the newspapers, and felt very weird indeed. (Baraka 1984, 187)

We see here yet another manifestation of the cultural process of co-optive hegemony as the liberal white intelligentsia was about to designate a new black writer to the throne of leadership. Baraka soon realized that he was being courted.

> Suddenly I got offers to write for the *Herald Tribune* and *New York Times*. One magazine wanted me to go down South and be a civil rights reporter. I got offers to rewrite Broadway plays in tryout, . . . with the producer flying me down from Buffalo, where I'd gone as a visiting lecturer in American poetry, to eat breakfast in his well-appointed brownstone on the upper East Side. There was all kinds of interest and requests and offers and propositions. It was as if the door to the American Dream had just swung open, and despite accounts that I was wild and crazy, I could look directly inside and—there—money bags stacked up high as the eye could fly! (Baraka 1984, 188)

The liberal white intelligentsia was definitely correct in identifying Amiri Baraka (then Leroi Jones) as an emerging major literary talent, but they were mistaken in believing that he could be ideologically co-opted. Baraka not only rejected their lures, he eventually spearheaded the first dominant black literary school outside the white-controlled system of co-optive cultural hegemony. The black cultural nationalist literary school surfaced in the late 1960s, following Baldwin's decline.

To understand Baraka's leadership role, we must take into account the social and historical context of race relations that fostered the spread of black nationalist sentiments, because his intellectual development was intertwined with the 1960s racial strife.

RACIAL POLARIZATION AND GROWTH OF THE BLACK NATIONALIST MOVEMENT

> How are you going to be nonviolent in Mississippi, as violent as you were in Korea? How can you justify being nonviolent in Mississippi and

Alabama, when your churches are bombed, and your little girls murdered and at the same time you are going to get violent with Hitler, and
Tōjō, and somebody else you don't even know. . . . If it is wrong to be violent defending black women and black children and black babies and
black men, then it is wrong for America to draft us and make us violent
in defense of her.

—Malcolm X 1963, "Message to the Grass Roots"

The black nationalist movement grew out of the failures and frustrations
of the civil rights movement. King had attracted hundreds of college students to the movement with his appeals for racial justice, as we noted earlier, but the students soon became impatient with the movement's moderate tactics and slow pace of change. King, in response to these signs of
discontent, convened the students in a meeting with the objective of chan-
neling their more radical proclivities into SCLC's strategy of nonviolent
action. This resulted in the founding of the Student Nonviolent Coordinating Committee (SNCC) and a period of relative harmony.

But strains between SCLC and SNCC eventually resurfaced. As the
struggle for black civil rights passed beyond the relatively easy victories
of integrating public transportation and lunchroom counters to the more
difficult tasks of registering voters and running blacks for political office,
the students found themselves confronting the mounting dangers of
white vigilante violence. This was highlighted by the murder of three student civil rights workers, James Chaney, Andrew Goodman, and Michael
Schwerner, in rural Mississippi.

Following the 1963 March on Washington—as we noted in chapter 4—
the students' disillusionment with King's strategy deepened, evidenced
by the fact that SNCC and CORE began to outflank the moderate SCLC
just as the latter had outflanked the more moderate NAACP. Thus by the
summer of 1963, SNCC's chairman, John Lewis, bitterly complained:

> There has been little progress in terms of getting a significant number of Ne-
> groes actually registered to vote. In some areas here we've been involved
> since the fall of '61, it's been like pressing against a stone wall. . . . Personally,
> . . . I now accept the philosophy of nonviolence . . . but I think that when we
> accept nonviolence, *we don't say that it is the absence of violence* [emphasis
> added]. (Lewis 1965)

Attempting to add moral legitimacy to this controversial stance, Lewis
quoted an obscure statement by Ghandi: "If I had the personal choice to
make between no movement and a violent movement, I would choose a
violent movement" (Lewis 1965).

Less than a year after this speech, race relations were strained so severely by the increasing disillusionment among young black militants

that John Lewis was toppled from SNCC leadership for being "too moderate" and a new black nationalist faction took control of the organization.

This swift change was generated by the spread of black nationalist sentiments, along with the growing attraction to violence, among many young black militants who now saw racial separation and armed struggle as the only realistic options left to black Americans.

If Malcolm X's angry speeches set forth the intellectual vision for this new black nationalist consciousness, it was the ghetto riots, the burned-out buildings, the smashed glass windows, the looted stores, and the sniper shots at police—in short, violent expressions of urban black alienation, which seemed to affirm the need for radical change.

Further exacerbating this atmosphere of crisis was the worsening relationship between black militants and white liberals. As black protest shifted its focus from southern white racism to northern white racism, black militants increasingly targeted white liberals for verbal abuse. Noted the historians Meier and Rudwick: "White liberal joined 'black bourgeoisie' and 'Uncle Tom' as epithets of opprobrium in the vocabulary of many black militants" (Meier and Rudwick 1966, 263).

Angered by those attacks, many white liberals slackened their support for racial reform, and, in some cases, simply abandoned liberalism and embraced a conservative political agenda that opposed new government initiatives on behalf of blacks. Hence as the civil rights movement stumbled, black nationalism surged forward, gaining ground in the eyes of many young black Americans. Examples of the spread of these black nationalist sentiments were numerous. As early as 1959, Robert Williams, the head of the NAACP local chapter in Monroe, North Carolina, was dismissed by the NAACP for advocating armed struggle. Alleged to have held several whites as hostages during a riot in Monroe, Williams fled the country while being pursued by the FBI. In the early 1960s, a group of college-educated blacks organized RAM (Revolutionary Action Movement) and were shortly afterward arrested for planning to assassinate the moderate civil rights leaders Whitney Young and Roy Wilkins. In 1964, the Deacons for Defense, a group of blacks pledged to retaliatory violence, was formed in Louisiana with the objective of providing protection for black civil rights workers. A short time later in Oakland, California, two black junior college students formed the Black Panther Party—ostensibly to protect the local black community from police brutality; but they soon shifted from that defensive strategy to a revolutionary ideology. That same year in Detroit, the Republic of New Africa was founded by a group of local blacks, who advocated a separatist position.

Third World political developments also influenced the growth of black nationalist sentiments. For example, Fidel Castro's Cuba played an important, though indirect, role because its revolution symbolized successful defiance of American power. Fidel Castro supported the black nationalist racial struggle in the United States, which he perceived as a revolt against capitalist oppression. Robert Williams, the former NAACP official, assumed residence in Cuba, where he broadcast a radio program ("Radio Free Dixie") beamed at the American South. Other fugitive black radicals also took refuge in Cuba during the 1960s.

But among Third World developments that stimulated the growth of black nationalism in the United States, none were as important as the African independence movements, the images of black Africans casting off the yoke of colonial domination, and taking control of newly created nation-states. The film clips of Mau Mau freedom fighters in Kenya violently resisting British colonial authority; television newscasts showing elegantly dressed African diplomats at the United Nations and in Washington, D.C., being treated as official representatives of black nations; and the speeches of radical African leaders like Patrice Lumumba in the Congo: all these developments quickened the pulse of black Americans, deepening their discontent with American race relations, and awakening their desire for a separate black American nation. Reflecting those feelings, tens of thousands of black Americans began to embrace an African cultural identity, which was manifested in such things as their adoption of African names, African clothing, and African hairstyles and their growing interest in studying African history and visiting African nations.

Ghana played an especially important role in the formation of this new Africanized American black identity because its president, Kwame Nkrumah, the leading proponent of Pan-Africanism, symbolized the new black consciousness. Nkrumah attracted a small group of black American intellectuals to Ghana, shortly after he assumed power, to assist in modernizing that nation. The most famous of those black American expatriates was W. E. B. DuBois, the former NAACP official and irrepressible black political activist, who renounced his American citizenship and lived the remainder of his life on Ghanaian soil.

Yet another important Third World influence on the black nationalist movement was Frantz Fanon, the French-educated black West Indian psychiatrist, whose books—*Black Skin, White Masks* (1967) and *The Wretched of the Earth* (1968)—highlighted the psychological violence of colonial racial domination. Blending ideas from such theorists as Karl Marx, Sigmund Freud, and Antonio Gramsci, as well as drawing on his personal experiences growing up in the French colony of Martinique and later working as a psychiatrist in Algeria, Fanon's images of the racial psychopathology and suffering engendered by colonialism helped to inspire the counter-hegemonic black cultural nationalist literary school.

While this black nationalist consciousness was spreading rapidly in urban black ghettos, mainstream white America remained largely unaware of its development. But that soon changed. The event that seized the white public's attention was a dramatic speech, during the summer of 1966 in Mississippi, by Stokely Carmichael, the former civil rights worker, who now was the head of SNCC. Standing before a crowd of blacks in Greenwood, Mississippi, Carmichael declared:

> The only way we gonna stop them white men from whuppin us is to take over. We been saying freedom for six years and we ain't got nothin'. What we gonna start saying now is black power. . . . Ain't nothing wrong with anything all black because I'm all black and I'm all good. Now don't you be afraid. And from now on when they ask you what you want, you know what you want, you know what to tell them. (The crowd replied in unison) "Black Power! Black Power! Black Power!" (Meier and Rudwick 1966, 289)

That speech exploded on the national political landscape like a volcano. Major newspaper and television journalists scrambled for reactions from black and white leaders to what they perceived as a dangerous turn in the nation's race relations. Unlike the earlier 1950s reports on the Black Muslims that dismissed it as a fringe movement, these media reports suggested that a greatly expanded black nationalist movement, preaching hatred of whites, was stirring in black ghetto communities. Further reinforcing that perception, shortly after Carmichael's speech, two of the stalwart organizations in the civil rights movement—SNCC and CORE—adopted a black separatist ideology and expelled their white members. The specter of racial warfare James Baldwin had warned his white readers about seemed at hand.

Not since Marcus Garvey's ill-fated UNIA had the United States witnessed such an upsurge of black racial nationalism. This movement, however, differed from the Garvey movement in several significant aspects. First, it had broader appeal. In contrast to the Garvey movement, it attracted not only working-class blacks but also black college students and middle-class intellectuals, two groups that greatly strengthened its cultural impact.

> Cultural nationalism . . . enjoyed an enormous popularity among all social classes. There was more interest in Negro history than ever before; countless local groups devoted to black art, literature, and drama sprang up, and a national magazine like *Ebony*, heretofore devoted largely to chronicling the achievements and social life of the black bourgeoisie, became a leading popularizer of "black consciousness." (Meier and Rudwick 1966, 292)

Garvey's movement never achieved this range of influence, particularly among the black middle-class and black intellectuals. Moreover, and equally significant, the Garvey movement never produced a black literary school. Despite the movement's efforts to attract such major black writers as Claude McKay and Langston Hughes, those writers, feeling optimistic about the direction of race relations, regarded separatism as a simple-minded—if not to say, an absurd—idea.

By contrast, the 1960s black nationalist movement had a much greater impact. Emerging after the black community had undergone significant social and political development, that movement spawned a black literary school, which became the cutting edge of black nationalist ideological consciousness. It also broke the liberal white cultural hegemony that had long dominated black American literary discourse.

Standing at the head of this revolt was Amiri Baraka, the black writer mentioned at the outset of this chapter. We will examine first the personal and intellectual experiences that transformed Baraka's racial consciousness, and second, the pivotal role he played in transfusing that consciousness into his literary works, launching black nationalism as the dominant ideological force in black literature in the late 1960s.

AMIRI BARAKA AND THE EMERGENCE OF THE DOMINANT CULTURAL NATIONALIST LITERARY SCHOOL

The Black artist's role in America is to aid in the destruction of America as he knows it. His role is to report and reflect so precisely the nature of the society, and of himself in that society, that other men will be moved by the exactness of his rendering and, if they are black men, grow strong through this moving, having seen their own strength, and weakness; and if they are white men, tremble, curse, and go mad, because they will be drenched with the filth of their evil.

—Baraka 1966, 251

Emerging as arguably the most talented and versatile black writer of the young generation, Amiri Baraka sustained a rate and range of productivity that was surpassed in black literary history by only the works of Langston Hughes. Though primarily committed to poetry, Baraka published works also included notable achievements in drama, short stories, and cultural history.

For the purpose of our discussion, Baraka's literary career can be divided into three periods: the Beat period (1957–1961); the Transition period (1961–1965); and the Cultural Nationalist period (1965–1975). The latter period, which followed Baraka's conversion to Islam and black nationalism, had such a profound effect on his identity that he changed his name, replacing his Anglo-Saxon "slave" name of Leroi Jones with the Islamic name of Amiri Baraka. Although this name change occurred in the late 1960s, we will refer to him throughout this discussion as Amiri Baraka to avoid confusion.

Born in Newark, New Jersey, in 1934, the son of a postal employee (father) and a social worker (mother), Baraka grew up in a black middle-class family. But this hardly deterred him, as it did some middle-class blacks, from developing a strong black ethnic identity. As he put it:

> Inside our house my sister and I were readied for brown stars. . . . Yet outside under the invisible white tarpaulin of held-down obstructed life called oppression there was black life and it was strongest every day where we lived. And no matter the brown inside game plan your mama hammered out with piano lessons, drum lessons, art lessons, singing and dancing in summer school and at the Y in choruses of yellow and brown folks. Or ballet and tap lessons for my sister and pink shoes and tutus or our trips down South where we lived out in the suburbs of Columbia, S.C., between two rich yellow doctors . . . when you came out that house it was black people whose lives spelled out the direction and tenor of our day-to-day being. (Baraka 1984, 44–45)

He attended predominantly white Barringer High School, where his literary interests were exhibited in his work on the school magazine. However, this interracial educational experience failed to attract him to mainstream white culture; he simply learned to negotiate living in black and white social worlds. In his words: "I ran the streets and walked the streets every day hooked up to black life. And it builded, however, despite the cold white shot of my daily Barringer trip that taught me to lust after abstract white life abstractly. . . . But you come back from white Barringer, bam, it was blues and black people everywhere" (Baraka 1984, 45).

Although he enrolled initially in Rutgers University in Newark planning to major in religion, he soon changed his mind, and transferred to Howard University. His Howard experiences scarcely turned out to be any more pleasant. If Howard left a lasting impact on Baraka, it was a feeling of disdain, revulsion, for what he saw as black bourgeois pretensions: "Howard University shocked me into realizing how desperately sick the Negro could be, how he could be led into self-destruction and how he would not realize that it was the society that had forced him into a great sickness" (Baraka 1984, 51).

To illustrate this point, Baraka recounted an incident in which he was reprimanded by the dean for eating watermelon on a campus lawn. Citing this incident and another in which Howard refused to permit a jazz concert in its auditorium because the administration did not consider jazz respectable music, he observed that "these are all examples of how American society convinces the Negro he is inferior" (Baraka 1984, 52).

These incidents, it should be noted, took place during the conservative years of the early 1950s, the period when Ellison's *Invisible Man* was being hailed for its detached, existentialist depiction of black American personality; and when the black bourgeoisie, for whom a Howard education constituted the pinnacle of black achievement, still discouraged its offspring from exhibiting "ethnic traits," because those behaviors might cause whites to mistake them for lower-class blacks. Black ethnic culture was embarrassing to the black bourgeoisie. They lived in what E. Franklin Frazier termed "a world of make-believe," a world in which they pretended to possess an elite status and culture, even though they lacked the power and influence ordinarily associated with elite groups.

Baraka's Howard experiences had a large hand in permanently alienating him from the black middle class. His bitterness toward the black middle class was revealed clearly in his later reflections on his Howard experiences:

> We were not even being taught to pile up, like the common petty capitalist of the xenophobically abused South and East Europeans. All we were being readied for was to get in, to be part of the big ugly which was that ugly because it would never admit us in the first motherfucking place! We were being taught integration and nothing of the kind existed. If so, why were we here in the second motherfucking place? We were readied for a lie as a lie. . . . We were not taught to think but readied for super-domestic service. . . . The school was an employment agency at best, at worst a kind of church. (Baraka 1984, 92–93)

It was his contempt for both the black bourgeoisie and the mainstream white society that prefigured his attraction to a bohemian lifestyle.

After being suspended from Howard in 1954 for poor academic work, Baraka joined the U.S. Air Force, thinking that military service would help him find a new direction for his life. This decision, however, turned out to be another mistake as he soon discovered that his irreverent and sarcastic temperament was incompatible with the authoritarian discipline of military life. In 1957, after many conflicts with his Air Force superiors, he was dishonorably discharged. This was a major watershed in his life.

With the failures of college and military service behind him, he returned home to Newark, and shortly afterward moved to New York's Greenwich Village. This move marked the beginning of his most important formative years as a writer.

The Beat Period (1957–1961)

Baraka arrived in Greenwich in 1957 when the national political climate was changing. As he put it, it was a time of transition "from the cooled-out reactionary '50s, the '50s of the Cold War and McCarthyism and HUAC, to the late '50s of the surging civil rights movement." Largely indifferent to both developments, Baraka latched on to the Beat literary movement in Greenwich Village.

The social world of Greenwich Village, where he was to live for the next seven years, consisted of bohemian artists, theater people, jazz musicians, painters, homosexuals, and intellectuals, an odd assortment of mavericks from varied ethnic backgrounds, who were drawn to the Village's free-spirited, antibourgeois lifestyle.

> At this time the Village was the scene of the kind of intellectual and artistic ferment that lent itself readily to a genuine and substantive rebelliousness regarding the middle-class mainstream. The social atmosphere was decidedly liberal, racially integrated to a degree, and decidedly permissive. And it attracted considerable numbers of the politically alienated and the just plain disaffected, usually from affluent white families in the greater New York and surrounding areas. (Brown 1980, 19)

Baraka found the Village a pleasant sanctuary. Shortly after settling there, in 1958, he married a young Jewish woman—Hettie Cohen—with whom he had two children, and collaborated on many writing and editing ventures. They "founded and co-edited *Yugen,* a literary magazine that they launched in 1958" (Brown 1980, 20). Also in collaborating with his wife, Baraka worked as an editor for Totem press, an avant garde publisher, and organized jazz workshops.

Anchoring his life during this formative period of his literary career, Baraka's marriage figured importantly in his Beat lifestyle and writings. As one commentator has noted, his circle of Beat "friends and associates developed after the marriage—largely as a result of the biracial couple's activities as writers and editors between 1958 and 1965" (Brown 1980, 19). He edited the writings of such Beat authors as Allen Ginsberg, Jack Kerouac, and Diane Wakosi. Over time his home became a center of Beat social gatherings that attracted, among others, such luminaries as Ginsberg, Gregory Corso, and Diane DiPrima, as well as Black Mountain poet Claude Olsen (Brown 1980, 20).

As a black literary rebel who regarded the black community with skepticism and the mainstream white society with contempt, Baraka found in the Beat movement kindred antinomian spirits, proponents of a bohemian worldview that influenced virtually every aspect of his life. Describing the outlook of the Beats, Kimberly Benston noted:

> They are wary of commitment to any sort of "otherness." By and large they are disengaged. They have moved from the liberal sentiments and political optimism of the prewar years to a recognition of the ambiguities and the pos-

sibly irremediable nature of man's moral condition. They deny that man, in the ideal center of his mind, is a prelapsarian innocent who is coerced into evil by circumstances and institutions that can be changed by collective action. (Bentson 1976, 7)

In fact, the Beats shared the postwar liberal white literati's pessimistic view of revolutionary politics and ideologies of group salvation. Perhaps no literary work expressed the Beat outlook more profoundly than did Allen Ginsberg's *Howl*, which many observers regarded as the defining manifesto of the Beat movement. As Bentson observed: "Allen Ginsberg's *Howl* set the tone of their concern, with its keen sense of satire and pathos, of the conflict between man's ideals and his actions, between his creative life and imminent death, between his being and the encroachment of the material nonlife around him" (Bentson 1976, 7).

But the Beats hardly embraced alienated individualism of the sort projected by Ellison's *Invisible Man;* they were too absorbed in hedonistic indulgence, living on the razor's edge between artistic exploration and psychic pleasure, to find comfort or meaning in isolation. They valued community, albeit community rooted in personal freedom and artistic sensibility, apart from bourgeois conventions.

The Beat's antinomian ideology figured importantly in their acceptance of Baraka. Like the leftist writers of the 1930s, they rejected mainstream white American taboos of racial caste. Being bohemian writers who defined themselves in cultural rather than racial terms, they welcomed Baraka and encouraged his rebellious proclivities. His presence, as a black American, underscored the depth of their estrangement from the mainstream white society.

While the Beats felt socially alienated like the 1930s leftist writers, they lacked the latter's political consciousness. Because they scarcely cared about politics, they never developed a radical political ideology. They had no interest in the plight of workers, minorities, or the poor. They had no interest in mobilizing people for social change. They had no interest in the controversy over McCarthyism. They had no interest in thwarting American imperialism and the emerging postwar American national security state. Rather they were interested in establishing a sanctuary, a place of refuge, from—what they regarded as—the preoccupations of "the square world." These were the conservative Eisenhower years, the period of intellectual disillusionment with radical political ideology. Reflecting the temper of the time, the Beats shared that disillusionment.

Instead of a radical political ideology, they cultivated a defensive subcultural ideology which rejected mainstream American values of ambition and success for the "hip world" of free-form poetry, jazz, experimental painting, adventurous travel, exotic experiences, marijuana, and free love. These prevailed as Beat culture's chief preoccupations in 1950s America.

This was the world Baraka entered. As he recalled, reflecting on Ginsberg's *Howl* and other Beat influences:

> I'd come to the Village *looking*, trying to "check," being open to all flags. Allen Ginsberg's *Howl* was the first thing to open my nose. . . . I dug *Howl* myself, in fact many of the people I'd known at the time warned me off it and thought the whole Beat phenomenon a passing fad of little relevance. I'd investigated further because I was looking for something. I was precisely open to its force as the statement of a new generation. . . . I took up with the Beats because that's what I saw taking off and flying and somewhat resembling myself. The open and implied rebellion—of form and content. . . . I could see the young white boys and girls in their pronouncement of disillusion with and "removal" from society as being related to the black experience. That made us colleagues of the spirit. (Baraka 1984, 156)

Indeed, Baraka soon absorbed the Beat worldview and polemical style, which can be seen in his comments about the 1950s era: "We saw 'the man in the gray flannel suit' as an enemy, an agent of Dwight Eisenhower whose baby-food mentality we made fun of. We could feel, perhaps, the changes that were in motion throughout the whole society. We reflected some of that change. Though, in those days, I was not political in any conscious way, or formally political at any rate" (Baraka 1984, 152).

That Beat worldview surfaced clearly in Baraka's first book of poetry, *Preface to a Twenty-Volume Suicide Note,* which displays his new-found bohemian irreverence. For instance, in "Hymn for Lanie POO" he castigates his sister's bourgeois lifestyle:

> my sister drives a green jaguar
> my sister has her hair done twice a month
> my sister is a school teacher
> my sister took ballet lessons
> my sister has a fine figure; never diets
> my sister doesn't like to teach in Newark
> because there are too many colored
>   in her classes
> my sister hates loud shades
> my sister's boy friend is a faggot music teacher
> who digs Tchaikovsky
> my sister digs Tchaikovsky also
> it is because of this similarity of interests
> that they will probably get married.
> Smiling & glad/in the huge & loveless white-anglo sun/of
> benevolent step mother America. (Baraka 1961, 11–12)

This penchant to ridicule mainstream America takes a different direction in *In Memory of Radio*, in which he targets American media icons:

Who has ever stopped to think of the divinity of Lamont Cranston?
(Only Jack Kerouac, that I know of: & me.
The rest of you probably had on WCBS and Kate Smith,
Or something equally unattractive.)
What can I say?
It is better to have loved and lost
Than to put linoleum in your living rooms?
Am I a sage or something?
Mandrake's a hypnotic gesture of the week?
(Remember, I do not have the healing powers of Oral Roberts. . .
I cannot, like F. J. Sheen, tell you how to get saved & rich!
I cannot even order you to gas chamber satroi like Hitler or Goody Knight.
(Baraka 1961, 12)

The sarcastic style of these poems reflect a defining feature of the Beat literary sensibility.

Though Baraka, during this period, took graduate courses at the New School for Social Research and Columbia University, the main intellectual influences on his literary work derived from his white bohemian peers. Their disdain for the affectations and mechanics of genteel literature, their rejection of poetic meter for free verse and their penchant for poetic expression that exhibited the loose, supple cadences of conversational speech, as was evidenced in such Beat classics as Allen Ginsberg's *Howl* and Lawrence Ferlinghetti's *Coney Island of the Mind*, formed an important legacy of his Beat literary socialization.

Transition Period (1961–1965)

If Baraka's Beat period exhibited alienation and irreverence, his transition exhibited increased ambivalence and contradictions, growing discontent with his existence as a Beat writer, that gradually led him to a more political outlook. This metamorphosis was set in motion by his 1960 trip to Cuba. Though he had accepted the invitation to visit Cuba assuming that he would be joined by several other well-known black writers (James Baldwin, John Killens, and Langston Hughes), he was disappointed to discover on reaching the airport that only one other black writer—Julian Mayfield—was making the trip. Nevertheless, he decided to stick with his initial plan to visit Cuba. The group of twelve assembled at the airport included Mayfield; Harold Cruse, the historian; Robert Williams, the militant former NAACP leader; and John Henrik Clark, the publisher of *Freedomways*, a black nationalist magazine, marking Baraka's first contact with a network of radical black American intellectuals. This opportunity to visit revolutionary Cuban society with this group turned out to be a momentous life experience.

Because the Cuban government was paying their expenses, Baraka—still comprehending the world through his cynical Beat worldview—admitted to being initially skeptical. Thinking of himself exclusively as a "writer," he distrusted politics, and was on guard. "From the outset of the trip, " he noted, "I was determined 'not to be taken.'"

Much to his surprise, he found Cuba to be deeply moving. He and the other black American intellectuals were accorded the respect of visiting dignitaries and were briefed by Cuban officials on the revolution's economic and educational achievements. What touched Baraka most, however, were the thousands of excited Cubans he saw alongside the road, celebrating the anniversary of the revolution, as his group traveled to Castro's former mountain hideout to attend a commemoration ceremony. After arriving at the old hideout, he briefly met Castro.

Baraka found the trip especially rewarding because he spoke Spanish and was able to interact directly with Cubans in informal conversations and elicit their comments about the revolution. He was also struck by the political consciousness displayed by the young visitors to Cuba from other Latin America countries. The stark contrast between what he saw in Cuba and what the American press wrote about Cuba jolted him, and deepened his distrust of American foreign policy. At the end of his journey, shortly before returning to the United States, he reflected on what he had experienced in Cuba.

> The new ideas that were being shoved at me, some of which I knew would be painful when I eventually got to New York. The idea of "a revolution" had been foreign to me. It was one of those inconceivably "romantic" and/or hopeless ideas that we Norteamericano have been taught since public school to hold up to the cold light of "reason." That reason being whatever repugnant lie our usurious "ruling class" had paid their journalists to disseminate. (Baraka 1966, 61)

The Beat movement began to disintegrate in 1960 as many of its writers and artists left the United States for exotic sanctuaries in such places as Mexico and Morocco. Baraka already had begun to feel troubled by his Beat friends' antipolitical outlook, such as the comment one of them made when Baraka had informed him about his plans to visit Cuba. Unimpressed, his friend replied that he distrusted people in uniforms. Though Baraka still lacked a coherent political outlook, by the end of his Cuban visit he began to see his bohemian social circle in a more negative light.

> The rebels among us have become merely people like myself who grow beards and will not participate in politics. Drugs, juvenile delinquency, com-

plete isolation from the vapid mores of the country, offer a few current ways out. But name an alternative here. Something not inextricably bound up in a lie. Something not part of liberal stupidity or the actual filth of vested interest. There is none. It's much too late. We are old people already. Even the vitality of our art is like bright flowers growing through a rotting carcass. (Baraka 1961, 61–62)

By 1963, we see Baraka openly attacking the civil rights movement. In an article he wrote for *Midstream*, "What Does Non-Violence Mean," he dissociated himself from Martin Luther King's redemptive liberalism, assailing King's nonviolent approach. He suggested that King was a modern-day Booker T. Washington, who was asking blacks to assume the onus for past racial wrongs. "Booker T. Washington prepared the way for such utilization of Negroes. Martin Luther King, as a faceless social factor, is the same man." To Baraka the civil rights movement seemed to be merely another welfare state effort to deny the existence of the black lower class ("which is like a rotten blimp attached to the sleek new airline"). That movement, he suggested, merely expanded token integration rather than achieved genuine racial justice. There was no effective black movement, in Baraka's view. "The Negro's real problem remained in finding some actual goal to work toward." This was also Baraka's problem as a writer.

In another article written in 1963, his growing contempt for liberalism took a different turn. This time he attacked the assimilationist stance of James Baldwin (this was before Baldwin's *Blues for Mister Charlie*, which Baraka liked) and Peter Abrams, a black South African writer exiled in Jamaica, for proclaiming themselves individualists. Baraka saw this stance as an outgrowth of the moral suasion strategy. "Again the *cry*, the spavined whine and plea of these Baldwins and Abrams is sickening beyond past belief . . . (they) want the hopeless filth of enforced ignorance to be stopped only because they are sometimes confused with sufferers." That is—lower-class black masses.

Baraka was now edging toward a new ideological outlook, although the context of the article's production indicated that he was addressing a largely white audience. The article appeared in the Beat publication *Kulchur*, which he apparently continued to use out of sheer convenience. Despite the place of the article's publication, he seemed enraged by white culture oriented racial integration—as he accused Baldwin and Abrams of wanting to be white. "Their color is the only obstruction I can see to this state they seek, and I see no reason they should be denied it for so paltry a thing as heavy pigmentation. Somebody turn them! And then perhaps the rest of us can get down to the work at hand. Cutting throats" (Baraka 1964, 120).

His shift in focus from Beat irreverence to black concerns was also re- vealed in the pioneering sociological study of black music he published in 1963. There he highlighted black culture's positive achievements, and suggested that black music constituted black America's most authentic cultural institution. The research he did on this book helped to alter his thinking about American race relations, foreshadowing even more radical ideas and feelings he soon would incorporate into a new perspective on black American literature.

The Dutchman

Baraka's first major literary achievement during this transitional period— *The Dutchman*—became an instant success, and won the prestigious Obie Award as the best off-Broadway play in 1964. Its success catapulted Baraka into the spotlight, marking a turning point in his literary career. *The Dutchman* appeared shortly after Baldwin's ill-fated *Blues for Mister Charlie*, revealing not only Baraka's considerable talents as a playwright, but also his evolution as a black intellectual.

The play depicts a racial confrontation on a subway train between a big- oted white woman (Lula) and a young middle-class black man (Clay) who has a white self-image. The play opens as the attractive Lula takes a seat beside Clay, and starts a conversation. But the tone of the conversa- tion abruptly changes as Lula begins to tease and taunt Clay.

> *Lula:* What do you think you're doing?
>
> *Clay:* What?
>
> *Lula:* You think I want to pick you up, get you to take me somewhere and screw me, huh?
>
> *Clay:* Is that the way I look?
>
> *Lula:* You look like you been trying to grow a beard. That's exactly what you look like. You look like you live in New Jersey with your parents and are try- ing to grow a beard. That's what. You look like you've been reading Chinese poetry and drinking lukewarm sugarless tea. (Baraka 1964, 8)

In addition to stereotyping Clay as an assimilated middle-class black, Lula in turn racially berates, and flirts with, him. Reminiscent of the "bat- tle royal" scene in Ellison's *Invisible Man*, this encounter echoed main- stream white America's contradictory signals to middle-class black males: act white and enjoy moderate material success with the risks of losing your racial identity or act black and preserve your racial identity with the risks of social outcast. Through her crude taunts and insults, Lula man- ages to shatter the shallow facade of Clay's assimilated self-image, a development that echoes the collapse of the racial integration movement. The encounter quickly degenerates into raw racial antagonism.

Lula: And why're you wearing a jacket and tie like that? Did your people ever burn witches or start revolutions over the price of tea? Boy, those narrow shoulder clothes come from a tradition you ought to feel oppressed by. . . . Your grandfather was a slave, he didn't go to Harvard.

Clay: My grandfather was a night watchman.

Lula: And you went to a colored college where everybody thought they were Averell Harriman.

Clay: All except me.

Lula: And who did you think you were? Who do you think you are now?

Clay: Well, in college I thought I was Baudelaire. But I've slowed down since.

Lula: I'll bet you never once thought you were a black nigger. (Baraka 1964, 18–19)

Baraka's point of view in the play revolves around two equally repugnant images: a dehumanized white bigot and an deluded middle-class black. These images allowed him to attack both white racism and black bourgeois delusions of assimilation. In effect, he was suggesting that white racial bigotry was so deeply rooted in American life that change could come only through brutal confrontation that exposed its cancerous malignancy. No doubt an element of personal exorcism was involved in Baraka's choice of characters, for he also seemed to be venting anger accumulated from his youthful experiences as a middle-class black. Lula was apparently modeled on a neurotic white woman with whom he had a brief romantic affair shortly after he moved to the Village.

Lula: You middle-class black bastard. Forget your social-working mother for a few seconds and let's knock stomachs. Clay, you liver-lipped white man. You would be Christian. You ain't no nigger, you're just a dirty white man. . . . Screw yourself. Uncle Tom. Uncle Thomas. Wooley-headed. . . . Let the white man hump his ol' mama, and he jes' shuffle off in the woods and hide his gentle gray head (Some of the riders are laughing . . .). (Baraka 1964, 31–32)

Clay reacts by slapping Lula across the mouth so hard that her head bangs against the seat. Stripped of his assimilated self-image, Clay now seems to be a man possessed by demons as he delivers an angry speech. This speech reveals what Baraka regards as the psychic time bomb lurking inside the middle-class black psyche, repressed beneath the facade of an assimilated identity but subject to explode suddenly under stress. The bomb apparently goes off inside Clay's head. With his white personae now shredded by racist insults, he turns on Lula and erupts in rage:

I'll rip your lousy breasts off! Let me be who I feel like being. Uncle Tom. Thomas. Whoever. It's none of your business. You don't know anything except what's there for you to see. An act. Lies. Device. Not the pure heart, the pumping black heart. You don't ever know that. And I sit here, in this buttoned-up suit, to keep myself from cutting all your throats. I mean wantonly. You great liberated whore. You fuck some black man, and right away you're an expert on black people. What a lotta shit that is. (Baraka 1964, 34)

Clay proceeds to strike even deeper as he slips into black vernacular and insults Lula's capacity for sexual performance; ridiculing the very notion of white sexuality, he tells her:

The only thing you know is that you come if he bangs you hard enough. And that's all. The belly rub? You wanted to do the belly rub? Shit, you don't even know how. You don't know how. That ol' dipty-dip shit you do, rolling your ass like an elephant. That's not my kind of belly rub. Belly rub is not Queens. Belly rub is dark places, with big hats and overcoats held up with one arm. Belly rub hates you. Old bald-headed four-eyed ofays popping their fingers . . . and don't know yet what they're doing. (Baraka 1964, 34)

He then shifts to the aesthetic of black music, mocking liberal whites who profess to understand black American blues and jazz: "They say, 'I love Bessie Smith.' And don't even understand that Bessie Smith is saying, 'Kiss my ass, kiss my black unruly ass.' Before love, suffering, desire, anything you can explain, she's saying, and very plainly, 'Kiss my black ass.' And if you don't know that, it's you that's doing the kissing" (Baraka 1964, 34–35).

This attack hardly amounts to a standard declamation against racism, for the people he is attacking are not the southern bigots who stand in doorways impeding black access to public schools or voting booths. Rather Clay is declaiming against the liberal white cognoscenti, those liberal whites who identified with black musical culture, and the liberal white hipster, the new breed of rebel Norman Mailer had termed "the white Negro," who modeled their lifestyle after black jazz musicians.

Charlie Parker? Charlie Parker. All the hip white boys scream for Bird. And Bird saying, "Up your ass, feeble minded ofay! Up your ass." And they sit there talking about the tortured genius of Charlie Parker. Bird would've played not a note of music if he just walked up to East Sixty-seventh Street and killed the first ten white people he saw. Not a note! (Baraka 1964, 35)

Clay is proffering a theory that black musical sensibility derives from displaced rage, a rage nurtured by racial oppression, which liberal whites who profess to love black music are too blinded by racial privilege to see.

> And I'm the great would be poet. Yes. That's right! Poet. Some kind of bastard literature . . . all it needs is a simple knife thrust. Just let it bleed you, loud whore, and one poem vanished. A whole people of neurotics, struggling to keep from being sane. And the only thing that would cure the neurosis would be your murder. Simple as that. I mean if I murdered you, then other white people would begin to understand me. You understand? No. I guess not. If Bessie Smith had killed some white people she wouldn't have needed that music. She could have talked very straight and plain about the world. No metaphors. No grunts. No wiggles in the dark of her soul. Just straight two and two are four. Money. Power. Luxury. Like that. All of them. Crazy niggers turning their backs on sanity. When all it needs is that simple act. Murder. Just murder! Would make us all sane. (Baraka 1964, 35)

After this neurotic rant about black creativity, Clay ends his speech with a most peculiar argument: Whites should avoid assimilating blacks into Western culture, because once blacks acquire its cold rationalism they will revolt and kill whites.

> Tell him not to preach so much rationalism and cold logic to these niggers. Let them alone. Let them sing curses at you in code and see your filth as simply lack of style. Don't make the mistake, through some irresponsible surge of Christian charity, of talking too much about the advantages of Western rationalism, or the great intellectual legacy of the white man, or maybe they'll begin to listen. And then, maybe one day, you'll find they actually do understand exactly what you are talking about, all these fantasy people. All these blues people. And on that day, as sure as shit, when you really believe you can "accept" them into your fold, as half-white trusties late of the subject peoples. With no more blues, except the very old ones, and not a watermelon in sight, the great missionary heart will have triumphed, and all of those ex-cons will be stand up Western men, with eyes for clean hard useful lives, sober, pious and sane, and they'll murder you. They'll murder you and have very rational explanations. Very much like your own. (Baraka 1964, 36)

In short, racial assimilation resembled the ironic logic of the Marxian dialectic, a force created by the ruling class to consolidate its rule that would turn inevitably into its antithesis, a hostile force destined to destroy that rule. We will see this ironic message later echoed in other Baraka literary works.

After delivering this message, the play ends on an unresolved note. Clay is gathering his belongings to get off the train when Lula suddenly plunges a knife into his chest (was she heeding the message's warning?), apparently killing him. She orders the other passengers to push his body onto the subway platform; and then, at the next subway stop, she orders them to get off. Just before the door closes, another innocent-looking young black man steps inside the train. Lula looks up and smiles.

Baraka had clearly moved beyond the Beat disdain for politics and social problems. With the appearance of this play, he transcended Beat cultural rebellion, and gave his anger a sharper, more serious, sociological focus than the middle-class hypocrisies that preoccupied the Beats. Nevertheless, his outlook remained constricted because it was essentially negative. As yet, he exhibited no sign of a perspective that affirmed an alternative, more positive direction of race relations.

How relevant was the play's message to working-class blacks living in such places as New York's Harlem or Chicago's South Side? What were its normative implications for resolving their problems of unemployment, menial jobs, decrepit housing, substandard schools, and political powerlessness? The Clay-Lula confrontation hardly touched those problems. Baraka had not yet defined his social role in terms of a black political agenda. The play addressed a largely white liberal audience off-Broadway. Though angry, Baraka was apparently also still ambivalent, still engaged in a dialogue with liberal whites, still seeking to arouse their guilt, and still suggesting—at least by implication—that they could effect the needed change. In this sense, the play embodied strong elements of moral suasion. It is noteworthy that this play derived from Baraka's involvement with a drama workshop for playwrights that had been started by the white Jewish playwright Edward Albee and his producers at the Cheery Lane Theater in the Village (Baraka 1984, 187).

Most critics praised the play and hailed Baraka as a major talent. As one critic put it, "*The Dutchman* may be the most important imaginative literary document of the American race war since *Native Son*." That depended on what he meant by "most important." Though emotionally charged, the play hardly approached *Native Son*'s explosive sociological impact. As a literary narrative that centered on the bleak realities that confronted poor ghetto blacks and that seemingly justified black violence against whites, *Native Son* shocked and tormented liberal white America's moral conscience. Baraka's *The Dutchman* failed to achieve that effect. Few liberal whites could identify with either Lula or Clay. At this point in his intellectual evolution, Baraka was still groping for a political perspective that went beyond the black protest literary tradition and their efforts to provoke white guilt.

The Dutchman nevertheless marked a crucial moment in the regimen of co-optive ideological hegemony. As we noted earlier, that play gave Baraka an opportunity to acquire the mantle of leadership as the reigning black literary Caesar in the public arena. The white liberal intelligentsia was prepared to bestow that honor on him and recruit him into the liberal ideological camp. Baraka certainly could have used the money celebrity status generated, but he resisted the lure. The white liberal intellectual establishment had misread his political stance, as he later recalled:

> I can see now, it was just my confusion that allowed so much of the Great White Way to flow in my direction. It was the contradictions in my life and thinking, the unresolved zigzags of my being that permitted them to hoist me up the flagpole to wave, for them. . . .
>
> What "fame" *The Dutchman* brought me and raised up in me was this absolutely authentic and heartfelt desire to speak what should be spoken for all of us. I knew the bullshit of my own life, its twists and flip-outs, yet I felt, now, some heavy responsibility. If these bastards were going to raise me up, for any reason, then they would have to pay for it. (Baraka 1984, 189)

That is, "they would have to pay for it" by accepting his commitment to a radical black-oriented worldview. This they refused to do. But the white liberal intelligentsia were hardly alone in seeking to co-opt Baraka. The Communist Party tried to hire him to edit their literary magazine. He admitted that he felt flattered by the offer, but he refused to re-travel the ideological road of the Depression-era black writers (Baraka 1984, 183). He was seeking a more phenomenologically grounded black worldview than the culturally misguided black protest works of the 1940s.

The Slave

If *The Dead Lecturer*—the collection of poems he published in 1964—revealed Baraka's continuing quest for a radical black political perspective, *The Slave*, his second play, signaled another major turning in that quest. A play produced off-Broadway in December 1964, eight months after *The Dutchman*, *The Slave* showed unmistakable signs of Baraka's emerging black nationalist political consciousness, though he still lacked a coherent black aesthetic ideology. This play, which resonated the turmoil in his personal life, defined a new moment in not just his literary career but also black literature.

Heavily influenced by the racially polarized atmosphere of the mid-1960s, the action of the play takes place in the living room of a house, while outdoors, mirroring the unfolding drama inside the house on a larger scale, a race war rages in the streets, where a black American liberation army is battling white American troops. Three characters occupy the living room on stage: Walker, a black poet and leader in the black liberation army; Grace, a liberal white woman who is Walker's ex-wife; and Easley, a liberal white professor of literature who is Grace's husband. Walker has a gun and is holding Grace and Easley hostage.

The play revolves around two themes: Walker's relationship to Grace, which conflates marital and racial conflict; and the debate between liberalism and black nationalism, as represented by the white professor (Easley) and the black revolutionary poet (Walker).

First, the marital and racial conflict. The play's fusion of these two issues was undoubtedly influenced by Baraka's personal life as he and his wife (Hettie Cohen Jones) were then experiencing marital strains caused by Baraka's changing political outlook (Baraka 1964, 196). Though Walker and Grace are divorced, their dispute over the custody of their two children ensnare them in a web of mutual interest, which reopens the wounds of their failed marriage. Grace for her part regards Walker's request for custody as merely a political ploy. "You don't want those children. You just want to think you want them for the moment . . . to excite one of those obscure pathological instruments you've got growing in your head. Today, you want to feel like you want the girls. Just like you wanted to feel hurt and martyred by your misdirected cause, when you first drove us away" (Baraka 1964, 60).

Their marriage collapsed when Walker adopted a radical black political agenda, a development that alienated Grace and the other whites who had been close to him. As Easley points out: "Even I know you pushed Grace until she couldn't retain her sanity and stay with you in that madness. All the bigoted racist imbeciles you started to cultivate. Every white friend you had knows that story" (Baraka 1964, 61).

Grace then tells Walker she left him after he embraced an antiwhite ideology, because she had no other alternative as a white person. "Walker, you were preaching the murder of all white people. Walker, I was, am, white. What do you think was going through my mind every time you were at some rally or meeting whose sole purpose was to bring about the destruction of white people?" (Baraka 1964, 72).

Walker, in defense of the feelings he once had for Grace, tries to explain that he had told her how he felt about whites because he had wanted to preserve the intimacy of their marriage. He pointed out that he simply had tried to be honest, and that his views had not been directed at her as an individual. "Oh, goddamn it, Grace, are you so stupid? You were my wife . . . I loved you. You mean because I loved you and was married to you . . . had children by you, I wasn't supposed to say things I felt. I was crying out against three hundred years of oppression; not against individuals" (Baraka 1964, 72).

The play, through depicting this tortuous conflict, highlights the problem the new black political consciousness created for interracial relationships. Though Walker suggests that the personal and the political could remain separate, he does not actually believe it. He is simply trying to defend himself against the charge of having betrayed his marriage and friends. He pursues this tactic as a face-saving gesture, even though he believes that his new political outlook represents a higher standard of morality that obliges him to cast aside his white associates. He knew Grace and Easley would reject that moral argument. Much like the civil rights movement, his interracial marriage becomes a casualty of the society's widening racial divide, and it eventually degenerates into ugly verbal exchanges. We see this in Grace's racially charged verbal attack on Walker after he struck her husband, Easley.

> *Grace:* Ohh! Get away from him, Walker! Get away from him, (*hysterically*) you nigger murderer!
>
> *Walker:* (*Has started to tilt the bottle again, after he slaps Easley, and when Grace shouts at him, he chokes on the liquor, spitting it out, and begins laughing with a kind of hysterical amusement*) Oh! Ha, ha, ha . . . you mean. . . . Wow! (*Trying to control laughter, but it is an extreme kind of release.*) No kidding? Grace, Gracie! Wow! I wonder how long you had that stored up. (Baraka 1964, 54)

The question—how long you had that stored up—raises a critically important issue from the standpoint of Walker's black political perspective, which views liberal whites like Grace as bigots who routinely hide their true feelings about blacks until they are caught in stressful situations, when those feelings inadvertently tend to surface. Reflecting the mid-1960s radical black consciousness, he believes that liberal whites differ from conservative whites only in degree of their hypocrisy.

Which brings us to the play's focus on the conflict between liberalism and black nationalism, represented by Easley and Walker respectively. This conflict encircles and amplifies the private marital conflict, by situating black-white racial antagonism within a more public discourse. The issue of liberal hypocrisy arises when Walker accuses Easley of betrayal, because Easley threatens to call white soldiers to arrest him—if the opportunity occurs.

> *Walker:* Yeah, yeah, I know. That's your job. A liberal education, and a long history of concern for minorities and charitable organizations can do that for you.
>
> *Easley:* No! I mean this, friend! Really! If I get the slightest advantage, some cracker soldier will be bayoneting you before the night is finished. (Baraka 1964, 52)

Angered by this threat to have him killed by a racist white soldier, Walker strikes Easley, and then insults and berates him.

Walker: (*Slaps Easley across the face with the back of his left hand, pulling the gun out with his right and shoving it as hard as he can against Easley's stomach. Easley slumps, and the cruelty in Walker's face at this moment also frightens Grace.*) "My country, 'tis of theee. Sweet land of libert-ty." (*Screams off-key like drunken opera singer*)

   Well, let's say liberty and ignorant vomiting faggot professors. (Baraka 1964, 52)

It is noteworthy that throughout the play Walker insults Easley's manhood, characterizing him as both homosexual and impotent. Baraka is here invoking the black male street corner sexual ethos, with its homophobic and anti-intellectual attitudes. From this black point of view, Easley's alleged lack of integrity reflects his flawed masculinity, his effete liberal intellectualism.

   Closely related to this issue of liberal integrity, the play raises the issue of white responsibility for past racial injustices against blacks. Which whites should bear responsibility? This question echoed yet another conflict that sharply divided liberals and black nationalists. Walker, reflecting the outlook of black militants in the 1960s, lumps all whites into a single category. Easley, however, challenges this categorical condemnation of whites, arguing that it victimizes individuals. But Walker scoffs at such subtle distinctions, as he tells Easley, "It was individuals who were doing the oppressing. It was individuals who were being oppressed. The horror is that oppression is not a concept that can be specifically transferable. From the oppressed, down on the oppressor" (Baraka 1964, 72).

   This prompts a bitter exchange about utopian political ideals as Easley, personifying the postwar liberal intellectual community, opposes revolutionary idealism of the sort the black nationalists espouse. Like Ellison's politically disillusioned Invisible Man, he views racial revolution as no more appealing than class revolution.

Easley: You're so wrong about everything. So terribly, sickeningly wrong. What can you change? What do you hope to change? Do you think Negroes are better people than whites . . . that they can govern a society better than whites? That they'll be more judicious or more tolerant? Do you think they'll make fewer mistakes? I mean really, if the Western white man has proved one thing . . . it's the futility of modern society. So the have-not peoples become the haves. Even so, will that change the essential functions of the world? Will there be more love or beauty in the world . . . more knowledge . . . because of it? (Baraka 1964, 73)

This politically jaded liberal modernist outlook, which Baraka himself only recently had abandoned, fails to impress Walker. By setting up this exchange, Baraka answers liberal modernists who cynically dismiss revolutionary movements among Third World peoples. Walker thus responds to Easley's question about whether the new rulers would produce more love, more beauty, or more knowledge in the world:

Walker: Probably. Probably there will be more . . . if more people have a chance to understand what it is. But that's not even the point. It comes down to baser human endeavor than any social-political thinking. What does it matter if there's more love or beauty? Who the fuck cares? Is that what the Western ofay thought while he was ruling . . . that his rule somehow brought more love and beauty into the world? Oh, he might have thought that concomitantly, while sipping a gin rickey and scratching his ass . . . but that was not the point. Not even on the Crusades. The point is that you had your chance, darling, now these folks have theirs. (*Quietly*) Now they have theirs.

Easley: God, what an ugly idea. (Baraka 1964, 73)

Walker, who elsewhere refers to Easley's views as "horseshit liberal definitions of the impossibility of romanticism or idealism," is not about to be deterred. He sees liberal modernism as being afflicted with cancerous inaction, as he tells Easley:

You never did anything concrete to avoid what's going on now. Your sick liberal lip service to whatever was the least filth. Your high aesthetic disapproval of the political. Letting the sick ghosts of the thirties strangle whatever chance we had. (Baraka 1964, 74)

In short, Walker is saying that the only chance the country had for racial justice died with the failure of the Depression-era leftist movement. Blacks and other Third World peoples have no choice now except to go it alone. He does not say why the white working class is excluded, but one can surmise that he sees them as part of the problem, because they are inured to white privilege.

Further elaborating on this problem of liberal inaction, Walker turns to the issue of his earlier commitment to the modernist aesthetic, with its notion that art and politics occupied incompatible domains. Here Baraka seems to be explaining, at least in part, his own transformation as an writer:

The aesthete came long after all the things that really formed me. It was the easiest weight to shed. And I couldn't be merely a journalist . . . a social critic. No social protest . . . right is in the act! And the act itself has some place in the world . . . it makes some place for itself. Right? But you all accuse me, not understanding that what you represent, you, my wife, all our intellectual cutthroats, was something that was going to die anyway. One way or another.

You'd been used too often, backed off from reality too many times. (Baraka 1964, 75)

Walker then proceeds to argue that liberal academics like Easley lack the ability to write poetry because of their liberal inaction—their liberal retreat from the real world. "Yeah, well, I know I thought then that none of you would write any poetry either. I knew that you had moved too far away from the actual meaning of life . . . into some lifeless cocoon of pretended intellectual and emotional achievement, to really be able to see the world again" (Baraka 1964, 75–76). Liberal white academics, in Walker's view, are afflicted with artistic impotence, because only politically engaged writing possesses artistic vitality.

Finally, in this connection, Walker defends black political violence. By arguing that blacks are forced into it by the country's racial oppression, he seeks to exonerate blacks who physically assault whites. But neither Easley nor Grace are swayed by Walker's argument.

> *Easley: (Taking very cautious step toward Walker, still talking)* The politics of self-pity. *(Indicates to Grace that she is to talk)*
>
> *Walker: (Head down)* Yeah. Yeah.
>
> *Easley:* The politics of self-pity.
>
> *Grace: (Raising her head slowly to watch, almost petrified)* A murderous self-pity. An extraordinarily murderous self-pity. (Baraka 1964, 77)

The play thus reaches an impasse: white liberals and black nationalists simply have nothing else to say to one another. This conclusion is underscored emphatically as Walker, fed up with Easley's liberal opposition, fires several bullets into his chest killing him. Grace tells Walker that he is crazy.

> *Grace:* You're out of your mind. *(Slow, matter-of-fact)*
>
> *Walker:* Meaning?
>
> *Grace:* You're out of your mind.
>
> *Walker: (Wearily)* Turn to another station.
>
> *Grace:* You're out of your mind.
>
> *Walker:* The way things are, being out of your mind is the only thing that qualifies you to stay alive. The only thing. Easley was in his right mind. Pitiful as he was. That's the reason he's dead. (Baraka 1964, 82)

The play ends as an explosion hits the house. Grace and the two children (in the bedroom off-stage) are killed, but Walker survives.

In writing this play, Baraka reveals why he abandoned his earlier bohemian liberal stance. Though he had not yet formulated a cultural nationalist literary ideology, this play indicated that he had come to the end of his dialogue with the liberal white American audience.

The Toilet

The Toilet, the companion play presented with *The Slave*, expressed hatred of whites rather than intellectual arguments in defense of black nationalism (Baraka 1964). A one-act drama set in a high school toilet, the play's unseemly setting symbolized Baraka's bleak view of America's race relations.

If this play can be said to have achieved any distinction, it was the dubious one of being perhaps the most artistically accomplished depiction of black ghetto street profanity ever presented on an American stage. The play reveals both Baraka's superb ear for black vernacular and his intimate knowledge of the black male ghetto subculture. This was no doubt a product of his youthful experiences in Newark's working-class black ghetto. In his words: "And though I came striding out of a brown house with plenty of bullshit packed between my eyes. There was nowhere to go but the black streets and the people who ran those streets and set the standards of our being were black" (Baraka 1984, 47).

The main characters in the play are young black ghetto males, whom Baraka refers to as "4th Street toughs." Baraka depicts these characters positively, as exemplars of black American manhood. In contrast to Wright's Bigger Thomas, they are not defeated by American racism. Though racially oppressed, they create and control a cultural space from which they comprehend their predicament, develop alternative values, and fight back. Again, like *The Dutchman* and *The Slave*, the play highlights a racial confrontation, this time between these tough black ghetto teenagers and a white teenager, who is apparently a homosexual. We see here yet another example of Baraka's tendency to link issues of sexuality and race. In the case of this play, the white teenager, who is depicted as being effeminate, is subjected to racial degradation, retaliatory symbolic violence. That seems the whole point of the play.

Although produced off-Broadway, *The Toilet* seems to have been written for a black rather than a white audience. In fact, it attracted sizable crowds of blacks, who were unaccustomed to attending plays, as evidenced by their frequent eruption into cheers—resembling fan behavior at an athletic contest—in response to the racial violence on the stage. Unlike *The Slave*'s enactment of arguments between white liberals and black nationalists, this play simply vents black rage. Baraka no longer seemed interested in a dialogue with whites. He continued, however, to operate through Village publishing outlets. *The Toilet* was published in *Kulchur,* the Beat magazine. This was due less to his lingering allegiance to the Beat worldview than to his lack of an alternative black-oriented publishing outlet. The counterhegemonic black nationalist literary school was hampered by the lack of an infrastructure of publishing and distribution facilities.

Paralleling the increasingly strident tone of his plays, Baraka's relationships to his white associates in New York were becoming more and more strained. This marked the end of the liberal white intelligentsia's flirtation with Baraka. As he later put it: "I guess, during this period, I got the reputation of being a snarling, white-hating madman. There was some truth to it, because I was struggling to be born, to break out from the shell I could instinctively sense surrounded my dash for freedom. I was in a frenzy, trying to get my feet solidly on the ground of reality" (Baraka 1984, 194).

His attitude toward white liberals had turned caustic, alienating most of his white friends. For instance, Baraka and Jules Feiffer, the *Village Voice* political cartoonist, became embroiled in a bitter controversy that was played out through a public exchange of letters. The controversy, which apparently started when Feiffer criticized another black writer for appealing to black unity, ended their friendship.

A similar ugly controversy flared through a public exchange of letters in *The New York Review of Books* between Baraka and Philip Roth, the white Jewish writer who had also grown up in Newark. This controversy centered on the issue of whether Newark should retain its public library in the face of a declining city budget. Roth, recalling his valuable experiences of visiting the library as a child, argued that it should be retained. Baraka, in contrast, argued that the library had little relevance to a predominately black Newark, whose residents lacked many basic necessities of life. The exchange soon degenerated into personal attacks, which ruptured their friendship.

Ironically Roth, in his novel *Letting Go,* had depicted a black youth who became obsessed with visiting the Newark library after he discovered a book with nude female pictures. But *Letting Go* appeared several years before the black cultural movement, so that image of a black youth dutifully visiting the library to ogle pictures of naked women failed to provoke controversy.

Baraka's most serious confrontation with white liberals occurred during a meeting at the Village Gate, the famous jazz nightclub in Greenwich Village, that catered to liberal avant garde patrons. At that meeting one Sunday afternoon, Baraka became the center of a controversy because he allegedly made anti-Semitic remarks. In a discussion of the black predicament in the United States, someone had mentioned the murder of six million Jews in Germany to indicate that Jews were different from other whites. What precisely Baraka said in response is not clear; however, his reported response was perceived by many Jews as an insult. According to a *New York Times* account Baraka responded, "You're like other (whites), except for the cover story"; "the cover story" being the Jewish experience under Hitler. Other accounts attributed even harsher remarks to Baraka. The role of Jews in the black struggle for racial justice became a contentious issue in the mid-1960s. With the expulsion of whites—many of them Jews—from SNCC and CORE, the questions arose: Did Jews have a special relationship to blacks or were they like other whites? Were Jewish attitudes toward progressive social reform changing? Were Jewish and black experiences of oppression similar? These issues were hotly debated, especially in New York, where most liberal Jews had supported the black struggle for civil rights until the movement took a militant antiwhite turn. The Baraka Village Gate incident simply revealed another conflict in the late 1960s that aggravated the already fragile black-Jewish alliance (Cruse 1967, 486).

Despite his ideological drift to black nationalism, Baraka continued, in some ways, to straddle the white bohemian and the black social worlds. One thing that caused him to remain in the Village was his family situation. As he recalled, "I had said outright that the black and white thing was over, but I did not think I could act. For one thing, the little girls, now, were walking around and there was certainly both a deep love and a sense of pressing responsibility there. It seemed to me that I was caught, frozen between two worlds" (Baraka 1984, 197).

The strains in his marriage soon surfaced. As Hettie Jones recalled:

Dutchman was to be performed at Howard University's homecoming weekend. Bored with typing, as I wrote Helene, "twelve copies of everything in the world" for Roi's latest grant application, I thought it might be fun to go.
Memory's so tricky. All I can see is the open door behind his back. "I can't take you," he said. "I don't want to."
I could feel it coming, like an awful tide. I said "Why?" and then there it was:
"Because you are white."
"As if the tragic world around our 'free zone' had finally swept in and frozen us to the spot," was the way he told it later. My eyes, he said, showed such pain he almost covered his face. (Jones 1990, 218)

Also, he felt troubled by the prospect of abandoning his two closest white friends, Allen Ginsberg and Lew Olsen, the Black Mountain poet. "It was Olsen, because of his intellectual example, and Ginsberg, because of his artistic model and graciousness as a teacher, whom I thought most about in terms of the road I was moving along. Where would they be in all this?"

Nevertheless, he felt the need to the break with the Village world because he was troubled by the contradictions between his racial identity
and his daily existence, contradictions which could not be resolved unless
he severed ties to these white friends, as he later noted: "These white men
saw I was moving away from them in so many ways and there was some
concern, because it wasn't that I didn't like them any longer, but that
where I was going they could not come along. Where that was, I couldn't
even articulate" (Baraka 1984, 192).

Around the time of his move to Harlem in 1965, Baraka divorced Hettie Jones. If there was any event that signaled the end of his ties to the
white bohemian social world, it was this divorce. Hettie had played a pivotal part in his Beat literary career. Even during the period of Transition,
she and he continued to collaborate on his literary work. But now in an
era rent by black and white antagonism, he no longer regarded his marriage as being tenable. In the words of one observer:

> His interracial marriage coincided with a period in his life when radicalism
> was not defined entirely in terms of black protest or black culture. The di-
> vorce took place at a time when he entered into the black separatist phase. As
> black nationalist spokesman. And this black nationalist commitment coin-
> cided, in turn, with his marriage (1966) to a black woman, Sylvia Robinson.
> (Brown 1980, 22)

The political and the personal had finally come together in Baraka's life.

The Black Nationalist Period

Malcolm X's assassination and the mid-1960s ghetto riots completed
Baraka's ideological transformation. In the ensuing maelstrom of racial
violence, he publicly declared his commitment to black nationalism,
moved to Harlem, and plunged into the work of creating a revolutionary
black theater.

This was the racial climate in which Stokely Carmichael made his explosive "black power" speech, the climate in which tens of thousands of
young black Americans rejected the goals of racial integration and gravitated to racial nationalism. Observed Kimberly Benston:

> LeRoi Jones's journey from the hell of an alien tradition to home in blackness
> was not carried out in a historical vacuum. His search for identity, while in-
> tensely personal, coincided with the dramatic changes in Afro-American sen-
> sibility which have been variously described as the Black Power, black con-
> sciousness, or Neo-Black movement. By whatever appellation, there did
> occur in the 1960s a profound process of revaluation, redefinition, and re-
> grouping, primarily among young black intellectuals and artists, which has

irrevocably affected the shape of Afro-American culture. (Benston 1976, 30–31)

Now located in Harlem, Baraka produced agit-prop plays for the Black Arts Theater Project from 1965 to early 1966. The mainstream media regarded him as an intellectual pariah. Symptomatic of that media disdain, the *Los Angeles Times* banned all advertisements of his plays. Aside from being mentioned in occasional news reports that labeled him a "black political extremist," Baraka was ostracized by the mainstream media. His plays and poetry were ignored by reviewers. But despite this opprobrium, he emerged as the leader of a new dominant black literary school. Such a development would have been impossible prior to the mid-1960s. No dominant black literary school could have formed outside of liberal white intelligentsia's ideological hegemony.

As the United States entered its most dangerous period of racial conflict since the civil war, Baraka's Harlem agit-prop theater sought to fuel black ghetto insurrections: "We begin by being nationalist. But a nation is land, and wars are fought over land. The sovereignty of nations, the sovereignty of culture, the sovereignty of race, the sovereignty of ideas and ways 'into the world'" (Baraka 1966, 240).

In an effort to effect this new vision, Baraka's writings shifted from producing symbolic racial confrontations for white audiences to staging consciousness raising political dramas—agit-prop theater—for black audiences. This new black theater, he declared, "must be food for all those who need food, and daring propaganda for the beauty of the Human Mind. It is a political theater, a weapon to help in the slaughter of those dim-witted fat bellied white guys who somehow believe that the rest of the world is here for them to slobber on" (Baraka 1966, 211–12).

Despite its vigorous beginning, Baraka's Harlem theater project abruptly closed in March 1966. New York City police raided and subsequently shut down the theater after they discovered a stockpile of guns in the building. This discovery generated an outraged political reaction from mainstream politicians, because the theater had been funded by a federal government antipoverty program.

Shortly after the theater was closed Baraka became embroiled in another public controversy, this time involving police violence. On the evening of 13 July 1967, hearing that a riot had erupted in his hometown, he left Harlem and headed for Newark in an automobile, accompanied by several friends and armed with guns. The car was stopped by white New Jersey policemen, who attempted to search the car. An argument and scuffle ensued, with the result that Baraka was severely beaten by several policemen.

Embittered by this experience, Baraka announced that he was cutting all ties to whites. His commitment to racial separatism was now apparently total. Soon after this incident, he moved back to Newark, and organized a new theater group—Spirit House Movers and Players—to carry out his nationalist literary mission.

THE CULTURAL NATIONALIST LITERARY SCHOOL

> We have always said, and continue to say, that the battle we are waging is for the minds of Black people.
>
> —Karenga 1972, 477

Background

Born between the mid-1930s and the mid-1940s, the writers of the cultural nationalist school came of age during the period that witnessed the most far-reaching changes in American race relations since the Civil War. Most had grown up in the caste-segregated black communities of the urban North. Belonging to the expanding postwar black middle class which, in the 1960s, experienced both the rising expectations sparked by African liberation movements and the frustrating barriers imposed by the white American racial discrimination, these writers turned to black nationalism because they believed it was the only black movement that challenged white domination.

In contrast to previous leading black literary schools, however, the black nationalist school literary school was decentered, dispersed throughout the country. Noted one observer:

> With the closing of the Black Arts Theater, the implications of what Brother Jones and his colleagues were trying to do took on even more significance. Black Arts groups sprang up on the West Coast. And the idea spread to Detroit, Philadelphia, Jersey City, New Orleans, and Washington, D.C. Black Arts movements began on the campuses of San Francisco State College, Fisk University, Lincoln University, Hunter College in the Bronx, Columbia University, and Oberlin College. (Neal 1972b, 262)

This geographical dispersion resulted from the school's being based in a mass black political movement, which operated in black communities throughout the urban north. No previous dominant black literary school had grown out of a black political movement. Instead, most of the earlier dominant black literary schools had been centered in New York where they were attached to the liberal white social networks and publishers. But unlike those dominant black literary schools, the black cultural nationalist literary school turned its back on the liberal white intelligentsia and, hence, had less need to be located in New York. To publish their works, these writers created their own local publishing outlets, outlets that attracted an unprecedented level of black literary productivity.

Also different from the four earlier dominant black literary schools, which never comprised more than six or seven major writers, the cultural nationalist school consisted of some fifty recognized writers. Most of these writers, however, were poets, who earned their livelihoods through teaching or related occupations rather than from the sales of their literary works. Significantly, no major novelist surfaced in the cultural nationalist school.

If any characteristic distinguished the cultural nationalists from earlier black literary schools, it was their cultural radicalism, their departure from white American conceptions of literature, evidenced in their desire to articulate a distinctive black aesthetic. In the words of the black literary critic Hoyt Fuller: "The young writers of the black ghetto have set out in search of a black aesthetic, a system of isolating and evaluating the artistic works of black people which reflect the special character and imperatives of black experience" (Fuller 1969, 268).

They thus sought to define the black writer's social role in terms of black ethnic culture. That aesthetic outlook can be discerned perhaps most clearly by contrasting it to the outlook of the 1920s primitivist school, its most relevant parallel. The primitivists claimed to be creating literary works rooted in a black aesthetic (e.g., Langston Hughes's pronouncement, "We intend to express our individual dark skinned selves") but they failed to realize that such a literature needed to shun white critical validation and establish its own critical precepts. The cultural nationalist school's repudiation of white critical validation set it apart from the primitivists; for it is inconceivable that a white literary impresario like Carl Van Vechten could have shaped the ideological direction of this literary school. Fuller describes that new black aesthetic, in the black nationalist poetry, produced by the Chicago Organization of Black American Culture as "deliberately striving to invest their work with the distinctive styles and rhythms and colors of the ghetto, with those peculiar qualities which, for example, characterize the music of a John Coltrane or a Charlie Parker or a Ray Charles" (Fuller 1972, 269).

This was hardly a literature providing spectacles of black exoticism, highlighting images of black sensuality, and jungle antics, designed to attract and titillate a white audience. Put simply, it was a literature not of public exhibition, but of affirmation and renewal.

But why no major novels? The black cultural nationalist aesthetic emanated from a populist vision of black American unity, which favored literary forms that were accessible to the black American masses. "The Black Arts movement is radically opposed to any concept of the artist that alienates him from the community," noted Larry Neal, one of the school's leading poets. "Black Art is the aesthetic and spiritual sister of the Black Power concept. As such, it envisions an art that speaks directly to the needs and aspirations of Black America" (1972b, 257).

Poetry and plays, because they operated through oral expression, conduced to this mission of communicating black nationalist consciousness through black vernacular, making it appropriate for theaters, meetings halls, and even street corners where black people could collectively share literary expression as ritual experiences of identity affirmation. This remained close to the black American tradition of religious worship. Novels, by contrast, did not; they demanded isolation and a solitary engagement of the reader with the text, experiences alien to communally oriented black ethnic culture.

BLACK NATIONALIST IMAGES OF REALITY

We will now turn to cultural nationalist poetry to illustrate some of that school's representative images and themes. First we have a poem by Amiri Baraka—*Afrikan Revolution*—which projects images of European imperialism and African liberation. The appearance of African nationalist movements and the demise of European colonialism, as we noted earlier, had a large hand in galvanizing black nationalist sentiments. The black cultural nationalists embraced a global perspective which, in sharp contrast to the perspectives of the earlier politically oriented black literary schools (e.g., naturalistic protest and moral suasion), viewed the black American struggle as part of the larger revolutionary struggle of Third World peoples, particularly Africans, fighting to overthrow white domination. Baraka's *Afrikan Revolution* expresses this global perspective.

> Afrikan People all over the world
> Suffering from white domination
> Afrikan People all over the world
> Trying to liberate their African nation(s)
> Afrikan People all over the world
> Under the yoke, the gun, the hammer, the lash
> Afrikan People all over the world
> being killed & stifled melted down for the Imperialist cash. . . .
> The world must be changed, split open and changed
> All poverty sickness ignorance racism must be eradicated
> All capitalists, racists, liars, Imperialists. All who can not change
> they also must be eradicated, their lifestyle, philosophies
> habits, flunkies, pleasures, wiped out—eliminated. (Baraka 1979, 230)

If their identification with Third World liberation struggles against European colonialism gave the black nationalists a larger global perspective, the 1960s Vietnam War brought that global reality home and dramatically reinforced its meaning by revealing the absurd spectacle of black Americans dying in the service of white America's imperialist ambitions. We see these sentiments expressed in Clarence Major's poem *Vietnam #4*:

> a cat said
> on the corner
> the other day
> dig man
> how come so many
> of us
> niggers
> are dying over there
> in that white
> man's war
> they say more of us
> are dying
> than them peckerwoods
> & it just
> don't make sense
> unless it's true
> that the honkeys
> are trying to kill us out
> with the same stone
> they killing them other cats
> with
> you know, he said
> two birds with one stone. (Major 1972, 299)

Such a poem by a major black writer during World War II or the Korean War would have been unthinkable, because the dominant black American literary schools during those earlier wars were subjugated by white liberal leftist ideological hegemony

It is especially noteworthy that two black women—Nikki Giovanni and Sonia Sanchez—emerged as major writers in the black nationalist literary school. Both women, as we can see in the following poems, shared the new revolutionary spirit. Projecting an image of defiance in the face of governmental efforts to repress the black movement, Giovanni—in *My Poem*—writes:

> my phone is tapped
> my mail is opened
> they've caused me to turn

on all my old friends
and all my new lovers
if I hate all black
people and all negroes
it won't stop
the revolution. (Giovanni 1972, 251)

Expressing a similar, but tougher, image of defiance, Sonia Sanchez in *liberation/poem* uses street vernacular to declare blues music a form of resistance.

blues ain't culture
        they sounds of
oppression
        against the white man's
shit/
        game he's run on us all
these blue/yrs.
        blues is a struggle
        strangulation
of our people
        cuz we cudn't off the
white motha/fucka
        soc/king it to us
but. now.
        when i hear billie's soft
soul / ful / sighs
        of "am i blue"
                i say
no. sweet/ billie.
no mo
blue/ trains running on this track
        they all been de / railed.
am i blue?
        sweet / baby / blue /
        billie.
no. i'm blk/
        & ready. (Sanchez 1972, 337)

Black cultural nationalists also frequently highlighted the beauty of blackness theme. Counteracting centuries of white American cultural conditioning that revered Caucasian physical features as the society's beauty standard, this new black aesthetic celebrated African physical features. We see a poignant example in Rockie D. Taylor's poem *Black Henry*.

When Henry was a baby
Folks'd tell his momma, "My, but
Your son is Black"

his momma just smiled
like she knew something
they didn't
When Henry went to school
It was always, "Git back
Too big,
Too Black
smut colored Henry." . . .
Then something happened
Came a man
Named X
and Rap
and Stoke taught blk/ ppl how to love
themselves
Now when you see Henry
Comin down the street
the folks he'd meet would say
after he walked away
"Ain't That BLACKMUTHAFUKKA BEAUTIFUL"
he'd kinda
hold his head up
with the beginning of a smile
like he know something
they *know*. (Taylor 1972, 311–12)

Accepting the precept "black is beautiful" often entailed rejecting that self-image the individual had acquired prior to his/her black consciousness, that self-image rooted in a white aesthetic, that self-image that desired fair skin, straight hair, and a pointed nose. The poet Don Lee gives expression to this personal transformation in the poem *The Self Hatred of Don L. Lee:*

after painfully
struggling
thru DuBois,
Rogers, Locke,
Wright & others,
my blindness
was vanished
by pitchblack
paragraphs of
"us, we, me, i"
awareness.
i
began
to love
only a
part of

                    me—
                    my inner
                    self which
                    is all
                    black—
                    &
                    developed a
                    vehement
                    hatred of
                    my light
                    brown
                    outer. (Lee 1971, 298)

As writers committed to forging a counter-hegemonic ideology, the cultural nationalists could hardly be satisfied occupying a niche in the prevailing white liberal Euro-American worldview. Rather they challenged virtually every conception of American reality (i.e., historical, political, psychological, philosophical, literary) that passed for knowledge in mainstream American media and schools. A major target of their reconstruction focused on the history of slavery, which white America had appropriated, sanitized, and reduced to a minor episode in its triumphalist narrative of the nation's past. An example of the black nationalist revaluation that slavery history can be seen in Larry Neal's poem *Middle Passage and After:*

                    Decked, stacked, pillaged from
                    Their homes
                    packed bodies on bodies in the belly
                    of death
                    sea blood, sea blood churns
                    production for the West's dying
                    machine: commodities for profit—
                    stuffed empires with spices;
                    moved history closer to our truth—
                    death's prophecy—in the sea their
                    screams and the salt smell on our
                    faces pressed against one another,
                    hands push stiffward, push for air. (Neal 1972a, 305–06)

THE DEMISE OF THE CULTURAL NATIONALIST SCHOOL

If the cultural nationalist school emerged in an era of political turmoil, it dissolved in an era of political quiescence, with its aims to transform black America unfulfilled. By the early 1970s most black Americans drifted toward political moderation, and away from the separatist aspirations of racial nationalism.

The cultural nationalist school's decline resulted from a confluence of unfavorable developments: the nation's shift to a conservative political climate, the doctrinal schisms between black nationalist leaders, the disintegration of the larger black nationalist movement, the employment of many black nationalist leaders in university based black studies programs, and the expansion of the black middle-class. All combined to extinguish the fires of racial polarization.

Perhaps the most revealing sign of that literary school's impending decline was Amiri Baraka's ideological transformation. Although it had begun earlier with his gradually accumulating doubts about black nationalism, that transformation crystallized in 1974 when he attended the Sixth Pan-African Congress in Tanzania. "After the Congress Baraka's career as black nationalist is comparable with the black nationalist movement itself in the 1970s. Both went into swift decline. The black movement lost its impact as an explosive, potentially revolutionary force. America, specifically the white majority, was increasingly preoccupied with other crises" (Brown 1980, 25).

It was at that conference, Baraka later recalled, that he decided to voice his allegiance to socialism. That decision was influenced by the examples of Julius Nyerere and Sekou Toure, two respected African leaders, who had articulated socialist and anti-imperialist ideological views at the conference. Both men had participated in their nations' struggles against European colonialism, and both opposed racial nationalism as a reactionary ideology. Hearing their speeches moved Baraka. "I was convinced I was moving in the right direction," Baraka noted. Being in Africa and interacting with Africans caused him to question the black nationalist ideas about Africa he had acquired in the United States. As he put it: "How great a trek to go from the never-never-land of Africa of nationalist invention to the real thing" (Baraka 1984, 311).

Baraka's disillusionment with black nationalism was also prompted by his perception of its political flaws. First was what he perceived as its neocolonial tendencies, the ease with which black nationalist leaders were willing to sell out to white economic and political power, particularly disturbed him. In his words:

> When I returned to the U.S. . . . . I was no longer a nationalist, I knew clearly that just black faces in high places could never bring the changes we seek. . . . I could see my own life and those tasks I had declared for myself with new light. I had seen Gibson [Newark's black mayor] and domestic "neocolonialism." I had been to Africa and seen that same boy at work over there holding the people down. It was clearer to me that only socialism could transform society. (Baraka 1984, 311)

Second was what he perceived as black nationalism's effect in encouraging a form of integration that bypassed poor blacks and benefited bourgeois blacks. "Despite its avowedly separatist, antiestablishment rhetoric, the movement's real accomplishment was to create a political atmosphere of tension and confrontation which pressured white society into making concessions; but these concessions actually encouraged integration rather than separation by opening up opportunities to blacks, to those whom Baraka attacks as the 'black petite bourgeoisie' who had grown fat off the gains made by the struggle of the people." In short, he viewed the new expanded black middle class as one unfortunate consequence of the movement's failure to develop a critical class analysis of American race relations (Brown 1980, 43).

Third, and particularly crucial, was his disavowal of racial hatred. He now viewed the movement's racial hostility toward whites as misguided.

> The old sickness of religion—all the traps we can understand. Crying blackness and from all the strength and goodness of that, not understanding the normal contradictions and the specific foolishness of white-hating black nationalism. The solution is not to become the enemy in black-face, that's one of the black intellectuals' problems. . . . Hating whites, being the white-baiting black nationalist is, it might seem, justifiable but it is still a supremacy game. The solution is revolution. . . . We thought it meant killing white folks. But it is a system that's got to be killed and it's even twisted some blacks. It's hurt all of us. (Baraka 1984, 323)

Thus the leading figure in the quest for a black aesthetic, a driving force behind the emergence of the cultural nationalist literary school, left the movement. The struggle, in Baraka's view, now consisted of opposition to capitalism and bourgeois class domination. In a sense, Baraka had come full circle as he returned to the racial universalism of his earlier bohemian days, albeit now with an explicit political agenda.

To say that Baraka turned away from black nationalism is not to say that he viewed his earlier black nationalist activities as wholly negative. Despite emphasizing shortcomings of the nationalist literary works, he pointed to their positive effects on black Americans. "In that thralldom, that dumb thrall, we built some actual things, we laid out a process of learning. For the close readers. We did step through madness and bullshit" (Baraka 1984, 326). Put simply, Baraka believed the black nationalist writers had had a large hand in fostering a new black ethnic consciousness.

But Baraka failed to foresee the ways in which that legacy would affect black Americans. The "process of learning" he alluded to nurtured an attraction not to socialism but to a more Afrocentric conception of black ethnic identity. Exhibited in such things as advertising, music, clothing fashions, sports, movies, and demands for black-oriented courses in school curriculums, this new more Afrocentric conception of black ethnicity ironically accommodated black Americans to a reformed, but still racially unjust, American society.

6

A Theoretical Overview

The Negro as a writer was always a social object whether glorifying the concept of white superiority, as a great many early Negro writers did, or in crying out against it, as exemplified by the stock "protest" literature of the thirties. He never moved into the position where he could propose his own symbols, erect his own personal myths, as any great literature must. . . . The literary and artistic models were always those that could be socially acceptable to the white middle class, which automatically limited them to the most spiritually debilitated imitations of literature available.

—Baraka 1966, 112, 108

I have argued in this study that the dominant black American literary schools, from 1920 to the mid-1960s, transmitted white liberal ideological perspectives on black American life. But as indicated by the above quote from Amiri Baraka, this argument, at least in its most cursory form, is hardly new. Following the example of Malcolm X, many black political activists in the early 1960s began calling attention to black intellectuals' subjugation to white influence. Black literary intellectuals simply extended that criticism to black American literature, charging that black writers had been duped by liberal white American brainwashing. Perhaps the most detailed and influential assertion of this view, with specific reference to black writers, was set forth by Harold Cruse, author of *Crisis of the Negro Intellectual*.

In American Negro history there has been a collaboration going on between the black and white literary scene and the whites have been predominant, have been the ones who set the tone for writing about Negroes. This has influenced the black writer's perception of what the black experience is, because craftwise, formwise, he has imitated the white writer's imitation of himself and this has worked, I think, to the detriment of the black writer. (Cruse 1967, 229)

Cruse's argument moved beyond the others in one crucial respect: he called attention to the heretofore unexamined personal relationships, namely, the friendships and other associations between white and black writers, that had served as conduits for patronage and ideological influence. But if Cruse's reference to those relationships embarked on new ground, he failed to till the terrain. This was revealed by several flaws in his discussion. First, he provided scant information about those relationships. Second, he said nothing about that literature's successive dominant ideologies and the varied sociohistorical contexts of race relations from which they emerged. In short, he provided no analysis of the primitivist ideology, the naturalistic protest ideology, the existentialist ideology, or the moral suasion ideology—or of why each prevailed when it did. Rather he conceived ideology in narrow racial terms, reducing it to a simplistic black versus white dichotomy, which ignored that literature's historically complex and changing functions. Though Cruse presented his book as a sociological analysis, he actually set forth a polemical history of black intellectual life that aimed not so much to explain black American literature's ideological functions as to advance a black nationalist political agenda.

Above all, Cruse's and the other nationalist criticisms of the earlier black literature were crippled by one key analytical weakness: they ignored the institutional complex—the structures of power, economic resources, and racial relations—that created and sustained that literature's ideological dependency. Rather than place that literature in a broader analytical perspective, and thereby examine it in relationship to other black cultural institutions, they resorted to simplistic ad hominem attacks on the black writers' alleged character flaws (e.g., excessive ambition, gullibility, identity confusion) to account for their submission to liberal white influence.

To avoid that pitfall, we need an analytical perspective that highlights the constraints of the racial caste system that lay behind that literature's cultural dependency. This chapter addresses those theoretical concerns.

THE CULTURAL FUNCTIONS OF
BLACK AMERICAN LITERATURE COMPARED WITH
OTHER BLACK AMERICAN CULTURAL INSTITUTIONS

We must begin this theoretical quest by asking if the major black literary schools' cultural dependency constituted a unique phenomenon. That is, were they the only black American cultural institutions that manifested

liberal white ideological outlooks? The answer is no. Though the dominant black literary schools experienced the most severe cultural dependency, they were hardly unique. Other black American cultural institutions also experienced cultural dependency, as we will see later in this
discussion.

But before turning to that issue, we must identify the different types of
cultural institutions related to the black American community. These are
indicated in figure 6.1.

First, we encounter *ethnic black cultural institutions*, such as black newspapers, black religion, black radio networks, and much of black music. These
had the distinction of being produced within a black community social base
and oriented to a black American constituency, from which they derived
financial support. Few white Americans were familiar with these black cultural institutions, just as few black Americans were familiar with the ethnic
cultural institutions of Jewish Americans or Italian Americans. These black
American cultural institutions produced the ideas, customs, and beliefs that
distinguished black America as an ethnic community.

Second, we encounter *mass cultural institutions*, such as the mainstream
television and radio networks, movie studios, magazines and newspaper
publishers, and public schools, which reproduced American popular culture. Reaching virtually all groups in the society, these institutions constituted the cultural adhesive that bound the people of the United States into
a national society.

And finally, we encounter what I term *esoteric cultural institutions*, those
that were neither oriented to nor supported by the black community.
These esoteric cultural institutions, consisting of such artistic enterprises
as European-American opera, classical music, ballet, and painting, had no
role in producing representations of black American life. Though they
may have included individual black American practitioners—such as
Leontyne Price and Jessye Norman in opera, Henry Tanner in art, and
Dean Dixon in classical music—black American experiences hardly oriented their traditions, outlooks, or social functions.

However, we find exceptions to this larger pattern in *esoteric black American cultural institutions*, a sector that deserves special emphasis. These in-

	Audience Orientation	
	Black American	*White American*
Black American	Ethnic	Mass
White American	—	Esoteric

Source or Support (row label spanning the left of the two source rows)

Figure 6.1. Typology of Cultural Institutions Based on Their Relationship to the Black Community

stitutions (e.g., black American jazz, black American dance, black American painting, and the dominant black literary schools) consisted of black American cultural producers who created ideas and images representing black American social reality for cosmopolitan audiences. Despite their considerable aesthetic achievements, these esoteric cultural enterprises hardly exerted equal influence on public perceptions of black American life. In fact, among these esoteric black cultural institutions, only the dominant black American literary schools operated as substantial ideological forces in American race relations. Though some observers regarded the musical works of such jazz greats as Duke Ellington, Count Basie, Charlie Parker, and John Coltrane as major ideological forces, jazz musical symbols are ideologically ambiguous. Because their public meanings derive from the interpretations of jazz critics and jazz historians, who are often in disagreement, rather than from messages discerned directly from the music, jazz performances rarely constituted an ideological discourse. Which is not to say that black American jazz transcended the cultural conflicts of race relations. Black jazz has occupied a peculiar cultural space since the 1940s when black jazz musicians, partly in reaction to the theft of their work by white musicians, shifted from the popular dance-band orientation to a small-group format that emphasized improvisation. Repelled by the racially subservient images associated with jazz's earlier entertainment functions, these young black musicians demanded that their audiences sit and quietly listen to their music as an art form. Black jazz thus was transformed into an esoteric art performed for a small and devoted cosmopolitan constituency—located outside the black American community (Watson 1972; Spellman 1970). Some post–World War II critics celebrated jazz's new aloof posture as a rebellion against conventional white bourgeois values, but that impression derived more from observations of the musicians' unconventional lifestyles than from ostensible ideological messages projected by the music. Bebop, the jazz musical style associated with this transition, advanced no discernible sociopolitical ideology.

In contrast, black American literary works—specifically the dominant black literary schools—projected robust sociopolitical ideologies that influenced white American perceptions of black American life, ranging from black experiences of community life, work, and racism to struggles for political change. Claude McKay's Jake, Richard Wright's Bigger, Ralph Ellison's Invisible Man, James Baldwin's Rufus, and Amiri Baraka's Walker, to cite only the paradigmatic characters of the dominant black literary schools, conveyed powerful messages about being black in America.

Yet these literary schools occupied an odd position. Though regarded by most of their white American readers as barometers of black American social consciousness—they never constituted a black ethnic cultural institution in the strict sense of the term. In contrast to the stoical blues melodies of Muddy Waters and B. B. King, the mournful gospels of Mahalia Jackson, the ecstatic rhythms of James Brown, or the poetic ballads of Smokey Robinson, this literature was sustained by neither black cultural traditions nor black audiences. Its perspectives on black American life, its financial support, and its cultural validation derived from liberal white Americans. Put simply, this literature functioned as a liberal white American cultural institution.

This, however, conveys only part of the story—a static description of cultural subjugation. To account for the changes that literature experienced as a cultural institution, we need an analytical typology that allows us to identify the developmental phases of cultural institutions linked to the black community. We identify four such phases in figure 6.2.

The *paternalistic* phase refers to situations in which the dominant group creates and controls the subgroup's cultural institutions. In these situations, writers, journalists, historians, and social scientists from the dominant group virtually monopolize the production of discourse depicting the subgroup in the public arena. This pattern was evidenced in the dominant literary depictions of black Americans prior to the 1920s.

The *co-optive* phase usually follows the paternalistic pattern. It appears when subgroup writers and intellectuals are recruited into the mainstream cultural process, replacing the dominant group's writers and intellectuals as the leading producers of the subgroup's images, but continuing their hegemonic role. Subgroup writers and intellectuals now operate as agents of the dominant group's cultural hegemony as they depict the subgroup's life in terms of the dominant group's ideological perspectives. Many observers of this change mistake it for the subgroup's breakthrough to cultural independence, because it marks the point when the works of subgroup cultural producers gain recognition and acclaim in the mainstream culture. The excitement aroused by the so-called Harlem Renaissance in the 1920s evidenced this confusion, as we observed earlier

Producers

		White American	Black American
Intellectual Perspectives or Cultural Styles	*White American*	Paternalistic	Co-optive
	Black American	Expropriated	Segregated/Separatist

Figure 6.2. Developmental Phases of Cultural Institutions Linked to the Black American Community

in this study. Black writers and critics, deluded by the mainstream white culture's recognition of black literary works, believed they were spearheading a cultural revolution. Remarkably similar delusions of cultural liberation were expressed by the culturally co-opted first generation writers in neo-colonial African societies.

The *segregated* and *separatist* phases share certain characteristics. Unlike the paternalistic and the co-optive phases, both consist of subgroup cultural producers whose ideological perspectives derive from the social consciousness of the subgroup community. However, in the case of cultural producers operating in segregated cultural institutions (e.g., black American newspapers, radio stations, churches), this allegiance tends to result from custom—sometimes assisted by legal constraints—rather than from ideological opposition to the dominant culture. In contrast, the cultural producers operating in separatist cultural institutions have revolted against the dominant culture, and redirected their ideological allegiance, usually under the impetus of a nationalist ideology, to struggles for subgroup cultural autonomy. This revolt tends to follow earlier historical phases of paternalistic or co-optive subjugation. The cultural movement of Afrikaners in South Africa, French Canadians in Canada, Catholics in Northern Ireland, and Kurds in Turkey, as well as a variety of ethnic group cultural revolts in postcolonial Third World nations, proceeded to this separatist institutional phase. In this study, we witnessed this separatist phase in the late 1960s ascent of the black cultural nationalist literary school.

The *expropriated* phase has less relevance to the current discussion. It appears when dominant group cultural producers commercially exploit a subgroup cultural perspective or style, usually by presenting themselves as its creators. The expropriation of black American musical styles by white American musicians (e.g., Elvis Presley, Jerry Lee Lewis, Bobby Darin, Righteous Brothers, Peggy Lee) fit this pattern, which flourishes in societal situations where the subgroup is excluded from celebrity, hence allowing lesser talented artists and entertainers from the dominant group to exploit the subgroup's creative products (Dates and Barlow 1990, 57–121). Though expropriation has operated as a major historical feature of black America's cultural subjugation, we need not elaborate on that development here because those expropriated cultural forms ceased to function as cultural discourse representing black America after they were detached from the black community and given a white cultural identity. Our concern here is with the developmental phases of those cultural institutions that represented black America.

It should be noted that a subgroup's cultural institutions need not occupy the same phase of development. A paternalistic pattern in one cultural institution may coexist with a segregated or co-opted pattern in another cultural institution. Thus, for example, the segregated pattern of black American religion and newspapers coexisted with the co-opted pattern of black American literary discourse. Such divergences in a group's cultural institutions often lead to conflicts, especially between co-opted and separatist subgroup cultural producers, as bitter antagonisms are likely to arise over the issue of cultural authenticity: whose perspective actually represents the subgroup's culture? Who has the moral authority to represent its culture to the outside world? The relations between assimilationists and black nationalists in the 1960s were rent by such conflicts, derived from their contradictory social functions.

HISTORICAL OVERVIEW OF BLACK CULTURAL INSTITUTIONS

Figure 6.3 allows us to take a more comprehensive view of this process by denoting the functions of the developmental phases of cultural institutions that produced images or symbolic representations of black American life.

Using figure 6.3, we can trace more clearly the historical changes of black cultural institutions. During the period from the 1920s to 1970, the black American community was characterized by three patterns of cultural production: ethnic cultural segregation, mass cultural paternalism, and high cultural co-optation. Ethnically segregated black American cultural institutions, though they have the longest history, extending back to the isolation of slave quarters, played a decreasing role after the 1920s. This segregated pattern at one time pervaded the black community's cultural life: religion, religious music, folklore, entertainment enterprises, newspapers, and magazines. But this situation was not to last. With the migration of increasing numbers of blacks to

		Phases			
		Paternalistic	*Co-opted*	*Segregated*	*Separatist*
Type of Cultural Institution	*Ethnic*	—	—	Ethnic Cultural Segregation	Ethnic Cultural Separatism
	Mass	Mass Cultural Paternalism	Mass Cultural Co-optation	—	—
	Esoteric	High Cultural Paternalism	High Cultural Co-optation	—	Cultural Dislocation

Figure 6.3. Phases of Institutional Development

the industrial North—which coincided with the emergence of the technology of American mass culture, especially in the form of movies, radio, and later television—many ethnically segregated black American cultural enterprises began to decline. This marked the encroachment into the black community of American mass cultural enterprises, namely, cultural paternalism. These capitalistically driven American mass cultural enterprises, which required a maximum mass audience to grow their profits, enveloped black America, as well as other American ethnic communities, within their expanding tentacles. The only black American ethnic cultural enterprises to survive this encroachment were the churches, the rhythm and blues music performed in black nightclubs and on black radio stations, and a few black newspapers and magazines, in large part, shrunken to parochial concerns with sports, crimes, local black politics, and the activities of black celebrities.

Thus the perspectives of both ethnically segregated cultural institutions and American mass cultural institutions coexisted in the black American community, the former controlled by black Americans and the latter by white Americans. These American mass cultural enterprises, spanning roughly from their inception in the 1920s to the mid-1960s, produced images of black Americans in the forms of "Amos 'n' Andy," "Buckwheat," "Beulah," and "Roscoe"—stereotypes of blacks as shuffling, docile, comical, ignorant, and affectionate simpletons—while presenting no contrasting images of black American professional men and women, nor of even the stable core of the black American working class, to counterbalance those stereotypes. In fact, it was commonplace until the late 1950s to see white American comedians such as Al Jolson and Eddie Cantor in blackface, portraying black Americans as charlatans, buffoons, and cretins. Those paternalistic mass cultural institutions reinforced racist beliefs about black inferiority during the critically important historical period of black mass migration to the urban North, when the old racial caste system was being challenged by the emergence of an urban black working class.

Corresponding to these ethnic and paternalistic mass cultural institutions, other cultural institutions depicting black Americans operated under the thrall of high cultural co-optation. It was here that the dominant black literary schools were located, along with most areas of black American intellectual culture, within the social networks of the liberal white American intelligentsia. Projecting images of black American life shaped by those liberal white perspectives, these co-opted cultural enterprises performed two key functions: first, they helped to socialize their audience into liberal ideological conceptions of black American experiences; and second, they absorbed talented, ambitious black American intellectuals into racially integrated social milieu. Hence many who might have devoted their talents to building and strengthening black ethnic cultural institutions, spent their intellectual careers consumed by liberal white American ideological preoccupations.

The co-opted social role embraced by the dominant black literary schools characterized much of black American intellectual culture: the works of E. Franklin Frazier, Horace Cayton and Sinclair Drake, Benjamin Quarles, Charles Johnson, Abraham Harris, Robert Weaver, and Ralph Bunche. What set the dominant black American literary discourse apart was not its co-opted role but its notoriety, its greater visibility and impact in the public arena. No black American scholarly works even approximated the notoriety achieved by such black literary works as Richard Wright's *Native Son*, Ralph Ellison's *Invisible Man*, James Baldwin's *The Fire Next Time*, or Amiri Baraka's *The Dutchman*. Because those literary works were discussed in the mainstream media and reached a larger and more diverse white audience, they occupied a higher, more influential, plane in American public culture.

Nevertheless, we must bear in mind that the history of cultural relations between the black community and mainstream American society was hardly static. As the black community's capacity for mobilization increased, so too did the dominant culture's ideological penetration into the cultural domains of black American life. The first shift occurred in the 1920s. Shortly after the beginning of mass black migration and the emergence of the radical Garvey movement, the black American community experienced the encroachment of white-controlled cultural enterprises. This marked a critical turning point in the cultural relations between the black community and the mainstream society which was characterized by two new phases of cultural subjugation: the penetration of American mass culture into black American popular culture and the co-optation by liberal white American intelligentsia of the newly formed black American intelligentsia.

This white American cultural encroachment not only undermined many ethnic black cultural enterprises by subjecting the black masses to the cultural conditioning of American mass culture. It also, and perhaps most importantly, dissociated much of the black American intelligentsia from the cultural life of the black community. Hence increasingly the black American masses consumed white American mass culture, and the black American intelligentsia absorbed and reproduced liberal white American ideological perspectives. This trend of paternalizing black American mass culture and co-opting black American intellectual culture, which prevailed during the half century of black American mass urbanization, had a large hand in culturally thwarting the black community's potential radicalization.

A caveat must be added along with this account—if this analysis is to avoid implying that those developments occurred within a vacuum. We

must recognize that they were facilitated by favorable economic conditions, which, except for the 1930s Depression, allowed the increasing
black American working class to locate jobs on the lower levels of the expanding urban labor market. These urban jobs, especially for recent black
migrants, constituted substantial life improvements, a welcome contrast
to the grueling agriculture labor they left in the South. This relative economic progress prevented severe hardships that might have politically
alienated the black community and sparked a rebellion against the encroachment of white American culture.

But this changed in the late 1960s. As economic dislocations within the
black working class and political frustrations within the black middle
class spawned the black nationalist cultural revolt, the cultural practices
that had buttressed the racial caste system broke down. We need not elaborate that development here since we have discussed it in chapter 5.

Now we come to the final task: to provide a theoretical explanation of
black America's cultural subjugation.

THEORETICAL MODELS FOR EXPLAINING
BLACK AMERICA'S CULTURAL SUBJUGATION:
ASSIMILATION VERSUS HEGEMONY

Assimilation theory was formulated initially to explain the absorption of
immigrants into the culture of American society and later extended, into
a more general model, to explain the enculturation of varied subgroups
into a dominant group culture. But assimilation theory possessed several
weaknesses. First, it ignored the effects of enculturation for debilitating
the subgroup's capacity to mobilize and advance its interests. Second, it
failed to consider situations where only the subgroup's intelligentsia was
absorbed into the dominant group's culture, while its masses remained
provincial and marginalized. Third, and perhaps most important, it ob-
fuscated the underlying power dynamics of a subgroup's enculturation.
These weaknesses resulted from the tendency of assimilation theorists to
view enculturation as a benign social evolution rather than a process of
social control, that is, the outcome of power relations in society.

To comprehend those power relations, we must remove the rose-tinted
spectacles of assimilation theory and seek a more adequate model for explaining cultural process in racially stratified societies. We begin this
quest with the writings of Karl Marx. In his book *German Ideology*, Marx
set forth the following bold proposition:

The ideas of the ruling class are, in every age, the ruling ideas: i.e., the class
which is the dominant *material force* in society is at the same time the domi-

nant *intellectual force*. The class which has the means of material production at its disposal, has control at the same time over the means of mental production, so that in consequence the ideas of those who lack the means of mental production are, in general, subject to them [emphasis added]. (Bottomore and Rubel 1963, 93)

The Marxist theoretical model, unlike the assimilationist model, focuses on cultural process from the standpoint of class relations in society. The dominant ideological perspectives and images of reality propagated by the cultural enterprises of literature, art, popular music, movies, and so on, according to this Marxian argument, are not autonomous but sociologically conditioned developments, rooted in—or at least congenial to—the worldview of the dominant class. This is not as far-fetched as it might seem. One needs only to consider the status of Nazi or Communist ideology in American society. Sympathetic dramatizations of those ideologies, no matter how artistically accomplished, are unlikely to appear on American television networks or in public school literature classes, to say nothing of achieving dominance in American culture.

As an explanation of black American literature's cultural subjugation, the Marxist theoretical model is not so much inaccurate as too narrow, too constricted by its social class premise. The notion that dominant cultural products in capitalist society necessarily reflect the bourgeois class's worldview is too simplistic to explain black America's cultural subjugation.

American society certainly possesses a formidable social class order, but bourgeois class interests hardly shape the totality of its complex cultural processes. To deal with that complexity, we need a theoretical model that can encompass the many manifestations of cultural power in civil society. This we find in Antonio Gramsci's theory of cultural hegemony (Gramsci 1971). Gramsci developed this theory to explain the domination of one class over another class by cultural rather than coercive means. According to Gramsci, the state controlled the means of coercive force (political hegemony), whereas the institutions of civil society controlled the means of ideological domination (cultural hegemony). Although the balance between these two means of achieving compliance tends to vary over time, Gramsci suggested, in modern capitalist societies, cultural hegemony would be the key means of control.

Gramsci thus conceived culture as a manipulated system of values, beliefs, and morality, reproduced by the major institutions of civil society (i.e., schools, trade unions, churches, mass media), to support the established order. This hegemonic culture, Gramsci argued, is internalized by the masses as "common sense," which is evidenced by their compliant attitudes toward the society's prevailing institutional arrangements.

To respond to the issues posed by the present study, we must extend Gramsci's theory beyond its Marxian preoccupation with social class. This revised Gramscian hegemonic model gives us a broader conception of cultural process that highlights the links between dominant cultural representations and structures of social power. Hence this model suggests that not just the class structure but every institutionalized sphere of social domination—such as the racial structure, the gender structure, the sex-orientation structure, the religious structure—in society is reproduced through a hegemonic culture that conditions people to perceive its social arrangements, its distribution of privileges and resources, as a natural process.

Thus in the sphere of racial domination in American society we find a hegemonic racial culture, projected through subtle and not so subtle cultural messages, that naturalizes white superiority (e.g., in history texts, monuments, movies, music, art, the names of cities, museums, and airports); in the sphere of gender domination we find a hegemonic gender culture that naturalizes male superiority (e.g., in business, science, sports, art, literature, and architecture); in the sphere of class domination we find a hegemonic class culture that naturalizes bourgeois privileges (e.g., in education, history books, popular entertainment, fashion, and laws); in the sphere of sex-orientation domination, a hegemonic culture that naturalizes heterosexuality (e.g., in advertising, literature, art, law, movies, and television shows); in the sphere of language, a hegemonic bourgeois form of English; in the sphere of religion, a hegemonic religious culture; and so on.

To note the existence of these patterns of cultural domination is not to suggest that they are static; quite the contrary, hegemonic cultural spheres change in response to changes in the structures of social power, which is precisely what happened to the liberal white cultural hegemony that pervaded the dominant black literary schools.

This notion that American society is characterized by racial cultural hegemony is hardly new. Writing in the early 1970s, Robert Blauner used this concept to describe the white culture that sustained white racial domination in American society.

The United States was founded on the principle, that it was and would be a white man's country. Nowhere was this insistence expressed more clearly than in the hegemony of Western European values in the national consciousness and in the symbolic forms that have expressed this cultural hegemony—institutionalized rituals (such as ceremonies of patriotism and holidays, written history, the curriculum of the schools, and today the mass media). (Blauner 1972, 31)

Blauner not only describes that pervasive racial cultural hegemony; he also points to the pitfalls of assimilation: "Even the promise of assimilation to those individuals whose adaptations were deemed successful was at bottom a control device, since assimilation weakened the communities of the oppressed and implicitly sanctioned the idea of white cultural superiority" (Blauner 1972, 32).

Also, in perhaps the most penetrating part of his essay, he discusses the intellectual manifestations of white cultural hegemony and the specific ways in which that hegemony affected representations of nonwhite minorities. "Cultural control over third world minorities has been particularly significant in intellectual life. The very characterization of their existence and group realities and the interpretation of their history and social experience have been dominated by the analyses of white thinkers and writers" (Blauner 1972, 32).

While Blauner clearly delineated the racial cultural hegemony that shaped perceptions of black America, he failed to focus on its manifestations in black American intellectual life. This omission was actually ironic—given his analytical aims to unmask the white cultural hegemony and reveal its role in maintaining the racial caste system. Blauner also failed to explore the complex dynamics of that hegemony; rather he regarded it as a fixed, static cultural regimen. Put somewhat differently, he seemed to suggest that hegemony developed and persisted in what I have termed a paternalistic form.

But as we noted earlier in this study, the paternalistic pattern, consisting of white writers who monopolized the production of literary images of black America in the public arena prior to World War I, gave way to a co-optive pattern, during the 1920s, in response to mass black migration. That co-optive pattern of hegemony absorbed the leading young black writers as black America was becoming a significant urban presence.

While Blauner made an invaluable contribution by calling attention to the cultural dimension of American racial stratification, he seemed unaware of this change. This is clearly evidenced in his allusion to the Harlem Renaissance, echoing the popular misconceptions of that black literary ferment, as an autonomous black cultural awakening (Blauner 1972, 149). Blauner, like other sociologists of race relations, overlooked the important role of co-optive cultural hegemony in stabilizing the social structure of racially and ethnically stratified societies.

To comprehend the workings of racial cultural hegemony in American society, we must take into account not just its changes in form; we must also understand its differential impact. While that cultural hegemony negatively affected all black Americans, its impact on the black American masses was attenuated by the pervasive countervailing influence of black

American ethnic culture. This was evidenced in such things as language, black music, folklore, vernacular, food, clothing styles, family organization, religious customs and the like, which occupied a distinct ethnic cultural space, apart from the hegemonic white culture. By contrast, its impact on the major black American intellectuals was far more profound, more extensive and more lasting, as it dominated their ideological perspectives on black American life for roughly a half-century. Since we demonstrated that impact in our discussions of the leading black literary schools, this point needs no further elaboration.

Which brings us to this study's final concern, the role of the liberal white intelligentsia in the dominant black literary schools' cultural subjugation.

THE IRONIC ROLE OF THE
LIBERAL WHITE AMERICAN INTELLIGENTSIA

The aspect of this study that seems most likely to provoke heated debate is its argument that the liberal-left white American intelligentsia both fostered and culturally subjugated the dominant black literary schools. Because this argument flies in the face of conventional wisdom, particularly given the liberal-left white intelligentsia's long involvement in the struggle for black American rights, it demands further elaboration.

To explain how the liberal white intelligentsia moved into that controlling role, we must briefly recapitulate the history of black literary production in terms of the hegemonic theoretical perspective. As earlier noted, production of the dominant literary images of black American life shifted from a paternalistic to a co-optive pattern of hegemony during the 1920s. This shift resulted from changed power relations in the American racial system brought about by the mass black migration to the urban North. While this mass black migration hardly posed a threat of revolution, the urban race riots and the Garvey movement that followed in their wake signaled potential dangers of social instability. The migrants to northern cities constituted a nascent urban black working class. Unlike in the South where blacks were dispersed and relatively isolated on rural farms, in the North they lived in close proximity to one another in densely populated ghetto neighborhoods, and had community leaders independent of white control. Urbanization, thus, enhanced the black community's capacity for radical political action, which threatened to destabilize the racial caste system and plunge the nation into racial strife. Hegemonic co-optation of black literary expression, as well as other areas of black intellectual life, thus constituted the dominant white culture's adaptive response to this new and more volatile environment of urban race relations. Which brings us to the role of the liberal-left white intelligentsia.

The liberal-left white intelligentsia emerged as a major force in American cultural life during the tumultuous post–World War I period, when American society was undergoing severe cultural strains engendered by its transformation into an urban-industrial society. In response to those strains, the liberal-left intelligentsia not only led the way in adapting American culture to the secular and cosmopolitan values of modernity. It also—as a direct result of its role in promoting those new values—had a large hand in stabilizing the new urban environment of race relations. This stabilizing function it performed by transforming the cultural process of race relations from the old paternalistic hegemony into a new, more tolerant, and inclusive co-optive hegemony—which absorbed the most talented black writers into their social networks and altered drastically the dominant literary images of black American life. It was thus in the spirit not of racism and repression but of cultural liberalization and inclusion that the liberal-left intelligentsia subjugated black literary culture.

Which brings us to what might strike some readers as a paradox entailed by this argument: the liberal-left white intelligentsia's lack of conspiratorial motives. This paradox is more apparent than real, for hegemony need not derive from conspiratorial motives; it needs only to create attitudes and beliefs that sustain the dominant group's power. Indeed, the agents implementing the hegemony may be unconscious, if not to say misguided, about its larger sociological repercussions. The fact that many Christian missionaries in colonized African societies were unconscious about the effects of their teachings for helping to sustain European colonial domination hardly made those teachings any the less hegemonic. As Michael Burawoy has so aptly put it:

> Dominant classes are shaped by ideology more than they shape it. To the extent that they engage in active deception , they disseminate propaganda, not ideology. As the first approximation, it is lived experience that produces ideology, not the other way around. Ideology is rooted in and expresses the activities out of which it emerges. (Burawoy 1979, 18)

In short, the agents of hegemony often may mean well but lack the capacity to see beyond their ethnocentric life experiences.

The liberal-left white intelligentsia's co-optation of black American literary culture was encouraged by the assumptions of the ethnocentric liberal worldview that shaped their perceptions of black-white relations. First, that liberal worldview assumed the superiority of white Euro-American culture, not because of superior racial ancestry but because of fortuitous historical circumstances that had favored Western cultural development. These white intellectuals took for granted the notion of a hierarchy differentiating advanced from lower cultures, and viewed blacks, because of the oppressed, isolated conditions of their lives, as possessing a lower (i.e., deprived) culture. Except for the brief challenge launched by the primitivist movement in the 1920s, which turned out to be more a bohemian flirtation with black exoticism than a serious critique of white Euro-American cultural arrogance, the liberal-left intelligentsia, for the most part, ignored black American culture. The black Marxist-oriented naturalistic protest school, the black existentialist school, and the black moral suasion school shared this one characteristic: all disregarded any distinctive black American worldview in the perspectives they projected on black American life.

Second, and directly linked to the notion of black cultural backwardness, the white liberal worldview assumed that integration meant assimilating blacks into white Euro-American culture, and, more specifically, into white liberal-left ideological perspectives. Hence perceptions of black American literary achievement were determined by liberal-left criteria of cultural validation.

Third, that liberal worldview assumed that whites, in their interracial alliances with blacks, would retain power and control. This expectation was hardly surprising. Given the white intelligentsia's assumptions about their cultural superiority *and their control of the resources*—it seemed logical and natural that they would lead and blacks would follow. Between 1920 and the mid-1960s, very few blacks gained positions of authority in the liberal-left cultural establishment. The fields of publishing, foundations, and literary criticism, despite the liberal-left intelligentsia's attitude of racial tolerance and inclusion, remained almost exclusively white, arrangements that reflected the deeply rooted norms of caste subordination that pervaded race relations. Black writers were scarcely unique in this regard; very few black intellectuals in academic disciplines such as sociology, psychology, history, and English literature held posts at liberal white universities prior to the 1960s. While many of these black intellectuals criticized racism in their professional works, they failed to criticize the racial structures, and the white liberal-left worldview, that shaped their intellectual socialization.

Though the values promoted by the new co-optive hegemony scarcely resembled the crude racial bigotry of the earlier paternalistic hegemony, both shared the pernicious assumption of white cultural superiority. If the conservative worldview of the earlier paternalistic racial hegemony openly proclaimed that belief in timeworn racist dogma, the liberal racial hegemony expressed it tacitly, by omission and implication, rather than direct assertion.

But how do we explain the black writers' compliance? Hegemony, it is important to recall, succeeds only if the subordinate group consents to its domination. What seems at first glance to be an inexplicable, if not to say absurd, submission of black writers to liberal white ideological influence turns out to be less so, if we take into account the conditions of black American literary life.

First, the marginalized plight of black writers hardly disposed them to refuse the benefits of participating in liberal-left white intellectual networks: financial support, access to publishers, and publicity. Whites possessed the resources black writers needed to pursue successful literary careers. Second, and equally significant, these black writers were strongly committed to racial integration. Integration was the value rationale that justified their attachment to liberal white social networks. To comprehend their perception of racial integration, it is important to recall the social and political context of the times, for racial integration then seemed to be the inevitable direction of a rational evolution in race relations. Myrdal's conclusions in his monumental *An American Dilemma* appeared to confirm that perception. Not just to black writers but to black intellectuals in general, racial integration seemed to be synonymous with social progress. Unlike the black nationalist writers who emerged in the late 1960s and 1970s, the writers of the dominant black literary schools up to the mid-1960s were resolute integrationists. To state the matter somewhat differently, these black writers and intellectuals hardly perceived liberalism in racial terms. It seemed to be a universalistic worldview, rooted in rational and scientific knowledge that exploded past racial myths. Jesse Owens's triumphs at the 1936 Olympics in Munich, the performance of black soldiers in World War II, the defeat of Nazi Germany, the integration of the armed forces, Jackie Robinson's spectacular achievements as the first black major league baseball player, the Supreme Court's school desegregation decision, the removal of racial barriers to public accommodations and voting rights, plus hundreds of other successful assaults on racial discrimination, all seemed to attest to the progressive—inexorable—advance of rationality over bigotry and ignorance in black-white relations. That was their frame of reference for understanding liberalism's meaning.

But that faith in liberalism was jolted in the mid-1960s, when the movement for racial integration ran into a stone wall of white resistance, manifested most dramatically in such developments as the northern white opposition to school desegregation, the persistence of segregated black ghetto housing patterns, the increase in black ghetto poverty, and the significant northern white support George Wallace garnered in his bid for the presidency. In the face of these chilling developments and the fading euphoria of the southern civil rights victories, many black writers and intellectuals abandoned their commitment to liberalism. No longer seeing liberalism as a universalistic worldview devoted to promoting rational social policy, they now regarded it as the doctrine of devious northern white intellectuals, who retreated from the struggle for racial justice when it began to impose sacrifices on northern whites. It was this atmosphere of racial antagonism and distrust that spawned the counter-hegemonic black cultural nationalist movement.

If black writers and intellectuals made any mistake in that counter-hegemonic quest for autonomy, it was their tendency to conflate the moral failings of liberal white intellectuals and liberal social philosophy. Because they now saw the earlier interracial alliances as hoaxes through which they had been manipulated and controlled by white intellectuals, many black writers and intellectuals cynically dismissed liberal values of tolerance and pluralism, and resorted to authoritarian tactics of coercion and defamation to protest racial injustices, thereby undermining the democratic ideals they sought to effect. Those authoritarian proclivities were fortunately short-lived.

By the late 1970s, after roughly a decade, American society moved into a new era of race relations that was characterized by a transformed black literary culture.

Epilogue

The New Postpolitical Black Literary Culture

The mid-1960s witnessed the end of not just the moral suasion school; but also—and even more far-reaching—the racial caste era of black literary culture. As was demonstrated in this study, the dominant black literary images of black American life, up to the emergence of the black nationalist school, derived from white liberal ideological perspectives, a hegemonic cultural process of literary production that was rooted in the racial caste system. One consequence of this was the strong preoccupation of black literary culture with themes of racial conflict.

But this changed. Following the brief interlude of racial polarization and the black nationalist school in the late 1960s and early 1970s, the impact of civil rights reforms shifted American race relations to a loose quasi-caste system, in which racial barriers were attenuated by class status. In broad outline, this loose quasi-caste system resembles the Brazilian racial order, where higher class status decreases the stigma of African racial ancestry. However, the United States' loose quasi-caste system is more advanced and complex than Brazil's because it possesses a much larger black middle class.

This is hardly to say that the racial stigma of African ancestry has disappeared in the United States, but only that it has weakened—such that these middle and upper middle-class blacks (a group of roughly ten million or one-third of the black American population) increasingly work and reside in racially integrated environments and share most consumption and leisure patterns of their white American counterparts. In contrast, lower-class blacks, who make up roughly two-thirds of the black population, still encounter many constraints of racial caste as they continue to live in racially segregated neighborhoods and manifest black ethnic cultural traits that are stigmatized by the mainstream society. Thus the post-1960s black community has undergone a deep status-class division, which shows little evidence of dissolving within the foreseeable future (Wilson 1978).

Most important for our purposes, the shift to the loose quasi-caste system significantly altered black American literary culture. While an in-depth analysis of that post-1960s black literary culture is beyond the scope of this study, I have been asked so often to comment on the aftermath of the black nationalist school that I will briefly note several of the most important changes. First, black literary culture, over the past several decades, has evidenced a conspicuous absence of protest oriented works. A staple genre of the rigid caste era of race relations, black protest literature has virtually disappeared. In fact, if the new black literary culture has any one distinguishing feature, it is its postpolitical orientation, which is revealed in its tendency to focus on black communal experiences rather than black-white racial conflicts—as can be seen in such leading black literary works as Alice Walker's *The Color Purple*, Toni Morrison's *Song of Solomon*, Terry McMillan's *Waiting to Exhale*, and Gloria Naylor's *The Women of Brewster Place*. This postpolitical orientation of black literary culture is linked to a second significant tendency, its preoccupation with defining and illuminating new—more complex—meanings of black identity. Influenced by the identity movements and celebrations of cultural diversity fostered by American Third World minorities, (e.g., black Americans, Asian Americans, Hispanic Americans, and Native Americans), as well as women and homosexuals, black literary culture has assumed the functions of an identity discourse, seeking to explore, to define, and to affirm a distinctive black American ethnicity.

This preoccupation with affirming black ethnicity is related to a third tendency, the sharp decline in black literary works oriented to a white audience. The result of both the decreased black literary emphasis on racial conflicts and the greatly expanded black middle-class audience for black literary works, this new black literary culture speaks to black American readers who are seeking images of black experiences that not only inspire cultural pride but also provide normative orientation to the uncharted, ambiguous terrain of race relations in contemporary American society.

It is perhaps not coincidental that black women writers have played a major part in this development, which brings us to the final tendency manifested by the postpolitical black literary culture: the emergence of black women as the leading black American literary artists. Stimulated in part by the women's movement and the increased interests it has aroused in black women's experiences and concerns—areas that were largely neglected in earlier dominant black literary schools—personal and communal themes have superceded political themes in the new black literary culture.

In light of all these developments—the changed racial caste system, the expanded black middle class, the increased but largely depoliticized black ethnic consciousness, and the transformed cultural process of black literary production—it seems likely that black American literary culture will continue to function, at least for the foreseeable future, as an identity discourse.

References

Aaron, Daniel. *Writers on the Left*. New York: Harcourt Brace, 1961.

Abcarian, Richard. *Richard Wright's* Native Son. Belmont, Calif.: Wadsworth, 1970.

Algren, Nelson. "Remembering Richard Wright." *The Nation*, 28 January 1961.

Allen, Frederick Lewis. "The Revolution in Manners and Morals." In *The 1920s: Problems and Paradoxes*, edited by Milton Plesur. Boston: Allyn and Bacon, 1969.

Ammermann, N. T. *Meaning and Moral Order: Explorations of Cultural Analysis in the Modern World*. New Brunswick, N.J.: Rutgers University Press, 1987.

Arden, Eugene. "The Early Harlem Novel." In *Images of the Negro in American Literature*, edited by Seymour L. Goss and James Edward Hardy, 106–114. Chicago: University of Chicago Press, 1966.

Baldwin, James. *Nobody Knows My Name*. New York: Dell, 1961.

———. *Another Country*. New York: Dial Press, 1962.

———. *The Fire Next Time*. New York: Dial Press, 1963.

———. *Notes of a Native Son*. New York: Bantam Books, 1968. Originally published by Beacon Press, 1955.

Balliet, Whitney. *The New Yorker*, 4 August 1962.

Baltzell, Digby. "Introduction." In *Philadelphia Negro*, by W. E. B. DuBois. New York: Schocken Books, 1967.

Baraka, Amiri (Leroi Jones). *Preface to a Twenty-Volume Suicide Note*. New York: Totem Press/Corinth Books, 1961.

———. *Autobiography of Leroi Jones/Amiri Baraka*. New York: Freunlich Books, 1984.

———. *Home: Social Essays*. New York: William Morrow, Appollo Paperback edition, 1966.

———. *Selected Poetry of Amiri Baraka/Leroi Jones*. New York: William Morrow, Quill Paperback edition, 1979.

———. *The Dutchman* and *The Slave*. New York: William Morrow, Appollo Paperback edition, 1964.

Barth, Alan. *The Loyalty of Free Men.* New York: Viking, 1951.

Becker, Howard. *Art Worlds.* Berkeley: University of California Press, 1982.

Bell, Daniel. *The End of Ideology.* Glencoe, Ill.: Free Press, 1960.

Bellow, Saul. *Commentary* xiii, no. 6 (June 1952): 608–10.

Benson, Brian Joseph, and Mabel M. Dillard. *Jean Toomer.* Boston: Twayne, 1980.

Bentley, Eric. *Thirty Years of Treason.* New York: Viking, 1971.

Bentson, Kimberly. *Baraka: The Renegade and the Mask.* New Haven: Yale University Press, 1976.

Berry, Abner. *Daily Worker,* 1 June 1952.

Berry, Faith. *Langston Hughes: Before and Beyond Harlem.* Westport, Conn.: Lawrence Hill, 1983.

Bigsby, C. W. E. *The Black American Writer.* Baltimore: Penguin, 1969.

———, ed., "Harold Cruse: An Interview." In *The Black Writer vol. II: Poetry and Drama.* Baltimore: Penguin, 1969.

Blauner, Robert. *Racial Oppression in America.* New York: Harper and Row, 1972.

Bone, Robert. *The Negro Novel in America.* New Haven, Conn.: Yale University Press, 1958.

Bottomore, Tom, and Maximilien Rubel. *Karl Marx: Selected Writings in Sociology and Social Philosophy.* Middlesex, England: Pelican Books, 1963.

Bourdieu, Pierre. *Distinction.* Cambridge, Mass.: Harvard University Press, 1984.

Breitman, George, ed. *Malcolm X Speaks.* New York: Evergreen Black Cat Edition, 1966.

Broderick, Francis L. *W. E. B. DuBois.* Palo Alto, Calif.: Stanford University Press, 1959.

Brooks, Van Wyck. "The Literary Life." In *Civilization in the United States,* edited by Harold Stearns. New York: Harcourt Brace, 1922.

Brown, Lloyd. *Amiri Baraka.* Boston: Twayne, 1980.

Brown, Sterling. "Negro Characters as Seen by White Authors." In *Dark Symphony,* edited by James Emmanuel and Theodore Gross, 139–71. New York: Free Press, 1968.

Burawoy, Michael. *Manufacturing Consent.* Chicago: University of Chicago Press, 1979.

Burgurn, Edwin Percy. "The Promise of Democracy in Richard Wright's *Native Son.*" In *Richard Wright's* Native Son, edited by Richard Abarcian. Belmont, Calif.: Wadsworth, 1970.

Campbell, James. *Talking at the Gates.* London and Boston: Faber and Faber, 1961.

Cantor, Muriel. *Prime-Time Television Content and Control.* Beverly Hills, Calif.: Sage, 1980.

Cayton, Horace, and Sinclair Drake. *Black Metropolis.* New York: Harper and Row, 1945.

Chapman, Abraham. *New Black Voices.* New York: New American Library, 1972.

Cleaver, Eldridge. *Soul on Ice.* New York: Dell, 1970.

Cooper, Wayne F. "Foreword to 1987 Edition." *Home to Harlem.* Boston: Northeastern University Press, 1987.

Coser, Lewis, Charles Kadushin, and Walter Powell. *Books: The Culture and Commerce of Publishing.* New York: Basic Books, 1982.

Crane, Diana, "The Transformation of the Avant-Garde." *The New York Art World, 1940–1985*. Chicago: University of Chicago Press, 1987.

Cronon, Edward David. *Marcus Garvey*. Madison: University of Wisconsin Press, 1955.

Crossman, Richard. *The God Who Failed*. New York: Bantam Books, 1950. Reprinted from "I Tried to Be a Communist," by Richard Wright, *Atlantic Monthly*, August 1944.

Cruse, Harold. *Crisis of the Negro Intellectual*. New York: Morrow, 1967.

Cunard, Nancy. "Harlem Reviewed." In *Voices from the Harlem Renaissance*, edited by Nathan Huggins. New York: Oxford University Press, 1976.

Dates, Jannette, and William Barlow, eds. *Split Image*. Washington, D.C.: Howard University Press, 1990.

Davis, Charles. "Jean Toomer and the South: Region and Race as Elements within a Literary Imagination." In *The Harlem Renaissance Re-examined*, edited by Victor A. Kramer. New York: AMS Press, 1987.

DeVault, M. L. "Novel Readings: The Social Organization of Interpretation." *American Journal of Sociology* 95 (1990): 887–921.

DeVoto, Bernard. *The Literary Fallacy*. Boston: Little Brown, 1944.

Dickstein, Morris. *Gates of Eden*. New York: Basic Books, 1977.

DiMaggio, Paul. "Classification in Art." *American Sociological Review* 52 (1987): 440–55.

Drass, K. A., and E. Kiser. "Structural Roots of Visions of the Future: World System Crisis and Stability and the Production of Utopian Literature in the United States, 1883–1975." *International Studies Quarterly* 32 (1988): 421–38.

DuBois, W. E. B. *Crisis*, December 1926.

———. "The Browsing Reader." *Crisis*, June 1928.

———. *The Philadelphia Negro*. New York: Schocken Books, 1967. Originally published in 1899.

Eagleton, Terry. *Literary Theory*. Minneapolis: University of Minnesota Press, 1983.

Edwards, Franklin G. *The Negro Professional Class*. Glencoe, Ill.: Free Press, 1959.

Ellison, Ralph. *Invisible Man*. New York: New American Library, 1952.

———. *Shadow and Act*. New York: New American Library, 1966.

———. Public lecture at conference on Richard Wright, University of Iowa, June 1971.

Emmanuel, James. *Langston Hughes*. New York: Twayne, 1967.

Emmanuel, James, and Theodore Gross, eds. *Dark Symphony*. New York: Free Press, 1968.

Fabre, Michel. *The Unfinished Quest of Richard Wright*. New York: William Morrow, 1973.

Fanon, Frantz. *Black Skin, White Masks*. New York: Grove Press, 1967.

———. *The Wretched of the Earth*. New York: Grove Press, 1968.

Ferguson, Blanche. *Countee Cullen and the Negro Renaissance*. New York: Dodd and Mead, 1966.

Fischer, Rudolph. "The Caucasian Storms Harlem." Reprinted in *Voices from the Harlem Renaissance*, edited by Nathan Huggins. New York: Oxford University Press, 1976.

Fiske, J. *Understanding Popular Culture*. Boston: Unwin Hyman, 1989.

Foucault, Michel. *Discipline and Punish*. New York: Vintage, 1977.

Frank, Waldo. Foreword to *Cane*, by Jean Toomer. New York: Boni and Liveright, 1923.

Frazier, E. Franklin. *Black Bourgeosie*. New York: Free Press, 1957.

———. *Negro Churches in America*. New York: Schocken Books, 1964.

———. "The Failure of the Negro Intellectual." In *E. Franklin Frazier on Race Relations*, edited by G. Franklin Edwards. Chicago: University of Chicago Press, 1968.

Fuller, Hoyt. "Towards a Black Aesthetic." In *Black Espressionism*, edited by Addison Gale Jr. New York: Weybright and Talley, 1969.

Fullinwinder, S. P. *The Mind and Mood of Black America*. Homewood, Ill.: Dorsey Press, 1969.

Gale, Addison, Jr., ed. *Black Expressionism*. New York: Weybright and Talley, 1969.

———, ed. *The Black Aesthetic*. New York: Anchor Books, 1972.

Garvey, Amy Jacques. *Garvey and Garveyism*. London: MacMillan, 1963.

Geller, Allen. "An Interview with Ralph Ellison." *The Black American Writer vol. 1*, edited by C. W. E. Bigsby. Baltimore: Penguin Books, 1969.

Giles, James. *Claude McKay*. New York: Twayne, 1972.

Giovanni, Nikki. "My Poem." In *New Black Voices*, edited by Abraham Chapman. New York: New American Library, 1972.

Gitlin, Todd. *The Whole World Is Watching*. Berkeley: University of California Press, 1980.

Gloster, Hugh. *Negro Voices in American Fiction*. Chapel Hill: University of North Carolina Press, 1948.

Goffman, Erving. *Gender Advertisements*. New York: Harper and Row, 1976.

Gold, Michael. "Notes of the Month." *New Masses*, February 1930.

Goldman, Eric. *The Crucial Decade and After: America 1945–1960*. New York: Vintage, 1960.

Goodman, Paul. *New York Times Book Review*. 24 June 1962.

Gosnell, Herbert. *Negro Politics*. Chicago: University of Chicago Press, 1967.

Gottdiener, M. "Hegemony and Mass Culture: Semiotic Approach." *American Journal of Sociology* 90 (1985): 979–1001.

Gramsci, Antonio. *Selections from the Prison Notebooks*, edited by Quentin Hoare and Geoffrey Nowell Smith. New York: International Publishers, 1971.

Griffith, Robert. *The Politics of Fear*. Lexington: University of Kentucky Press, 1970.

Griswold, Wendy. "The Devil's Techniques: Cultural Legitimations and Social Change." *American Sociological Review* 48 (1983): 668–80.

———. *Renaissance Revivals: City Comedy and Revenge Tragedies in London Theater, 1576–1980*. Chicago: University of Chicago Press, 1986.

———. "The Fabrication of Meaning: Literary Interpretation in the United States, Great Britain, and the West Indies." *American Journal of Sociology* 92 (1987): 1077–177.

———. "The Writing on the Mud Wall: Nigerian Novels and the Imaginary Village." *American Sociological Review* 57 (1992): 709–24.

Gross, Seymour L., and John Edward Hardy. *Images of the Negro in American Literature*. Chicago: University of Chicago Press, 1966.

Gusfield, Joseph. *The Culture of Public Problems: Drinking and Driving and the Symbolic Order*. Chicago: University of Chicago Press, 1981.

———. *Symbolic Crusade*. Urbana: University of Illinois Press, 1966.

Gutman, Herbert. *The Black Family in Slavery and Freedom 1750–1925*. New York: Vintage Books, 1977.

Habermas, Jürgen. *The Theory of Communicative Action. Vol. I: Reason and Rationalization of Society*. Boston: Beacon, 1984.

———. *The Theory of Communicative Action. Vol. II: Life World and System: A Critique of Functionalist Reason*. Boston: Beacon, 1987.

Hall, Stuart. "Cultural Studies at the Center: Some Problematics and Problems." In *Culture, Media, Language*, edited by S. Hall, Dorothy Hobson, Andrew Lowe, and Paul Willis. London: Hutchinson, 1984.

Hebdige, Dick. *Subculture: The Meaning of Style*. London: Methuen, 1979.

Hebling, Mark. *Jean Toomer: A Critical Evaluation*, edited by Therman B. O'Daniel. Washington, D.C.: Howard University Press, 1988.

Hill, Herbert. *Anger and Beyond*. New York: Harper and Row, Perennial Paperback edition, 1968.

Himes, Chester. *If He Hollers Let Him Go*. New York: Berkeley Books Paperback edition, 1956.

Hirsch, P. M. "Processing, Fads, Fashions: An Organization-Set Analysis of Cultural Industry Systems." *American Sociological Review* 77 (1972): 639–59.

Horkheimer, M., and T. Adorno. "The Culture Industry: Enlightenment of Mass Deception." In *Dialectic of Enlightenment*, edited by M. Horkheimer and T. Adorno. New York: Seabury Press, 1944.

Horstein, Lillian, et al. *The Reader's Companion to World Literature*. New York: Mentor Books, 1956.

Howard, J. A., and C. Allen. "The Gendered Context of Reading." *Gender and Society* 4 (1990): 534–52.

Howe, Irving. *Literary Modernism*. New York: Fawcett Premier Original, 1967.

———. "Black Boys and Native Sons." In *A World More Attractive: A View of Modern Literature and Politics*. New York: Horizon Press, 1963.

Huggins, Nathan. *The Harlem Renaissance*. New York: Oxford, 1971.

———. *Voices from the Harlem Renaissance*. New York: Oxford, 1976.

Hughes, Carl. *The Negro Novelist*. New York: Citadel, 1953.

Hughes, Langston. "The Negro and the Racial Mountain." *Nation* 122 (1926a): 692–94.

———. *Not without Laughter*. New York: Alfred A. Knopf, 1930.

———. *The Big Sea*. New York: Hill and Wang American Century Series, 1963. Originally published by Alfred A. Knopf, 1940.

———. *The Weary Blues*. New York: Alfred A. Knopf, 1926b.

Inge, Thomas M., et al. *Black American Writers vol. 2*. New York: St. Martin's Press, 1978.

Iser, W. *The Implied Reader: Patterns of Communication in Prose Fiction from Bunyan to Beckett*. Baltimore: John Hopkins University Press, 1974.

Johnson, James W. *Along this Way*. New York: Viking, 1933.

———. *Black Manhattan*. New York: Antheneum, 1969.

Jones, Hettie. *How I Became Hettie Jones*. New York: Penguin, 1990.

Karenga, Ron. "Black Art: Mute Matter Given Force and Function." In *New Black Voices*, edited by Abraham Chapman. New York: New American Library, 1972.

Kellner, Bruce. *Carl Van Vechten and the Irreverent Decades*. Norman: University of Oklahoma Press, 1968.

Killens, John O. *Freedom*, June 1952.

Kinnamon, Kenneth. *Critical Essays*, edited by James Baldwin. Englewood Cliffs, N.J.: Prentice-Hall, 1974.

Kiser, E. "Utopian Literature and the Ideology of Monopoly Capitalism: The Case of Edward Bellamy's *Looking Backward*." *Research in Political Sociology* 1 (1983): 1–26.

Kiser, E., and K. A. Drass. "Changes in the Core of the World System and the Production of Utopian Literature in Great Britain and the United States, 1883–1975." *American Sociological Review* 52 (1987): 286–93.

Klebanow, Diana, et al. *The Urban Legacy*. New York: New American Library, 1977.

Klein, Marcus. "Ralph Ellison's *Invisible Man*." In *Images of the Negro in American Literature*, edited by Seymour Gross and John Hardy. Chicago: University of Chicago Press, 1966.

Kramer, Victor, ed. *The Harlem Renaissance Re-examined*. New York: AMS Press, 1987.

Lamont, Michele, and Robert Wuthnow. "Betwixt and Between: Recent Cultural Sociology in Europe and the United States." In *Frontiers of Social Theory*, edited by George Ritzer. New York: Columbia University Press, 1990.

Lasch, Christopher. *The Agony of the Left*. New York: Vintage, 1969.

Lee, Don (Haki R. Madhubuti). "The Self Hatred of Don Lee." In *The Black Poets*, edited by Dudley Randall. New York: Bantam Books, 1971.

Leuders, Edward. *Carl Van Vechten*. New York: Twayne, 1965.

Levi-Strauss, Claude. *Structural Anthropology*. New York: Basic Books, 1963.

Lewis, John. "A Trend Toward Aggressive Nonviolent Action." In *Negro Protest in the Twentieth Century*, edited by August Meier and Francis Broderick. Indianapolis: Bobbs-Merrill, 1965.

Lewis, Sinclair. *Main Street*. New York: Harcourt and Brace, 1920.

Locke, Alain. *The New Negro*. New York: Albert and Charles Boni, 1925.

———. "This Year of Grace" *Opportunity* ix (1931): 49.

Long, E. *The American Dream and the Popular Novel*. London: Routledge and Kegan Paul, 1985.

Long, Richard. "The Genesis of Locke's *The New Negro*." *Black World* xxv, no. 4 (1976): 14–20.

Luker, Kristin. *Abortion and the Politics of Motherhood*. Berkeley: University of California Press, 1984.

Major, Clarence. "Vietnam #4." In *New Black Voices*, edited by Abraham Chapman. New York: New American Library, 1972.

Malcolm X. "Message to the Grass Roots." In *Malcolm X Speaks*, by George Breitman. New York: Evergreen Black Cat Edition, 1966.

———. "Statement of Basic Aims and Objectives of the Organization of Afro-American Unit." In *New Black Voices*, edited by Abraham Chapman. New York: New American Library, 1972.

Maloff, Saul. *Nation*, 14 July 1962.

Mannheim, Karl. *Ideology and Utopia*. New York: Harcourt and Brace, 1936.

———. *Essays on the Sociology of Culture*. London: Routledge and Kegan Paul, 1956.

———. *Essays on the Sociology of Knowledge.* London: Routledge and Kegan Paul, 1952.

———. *Essays on Sociology and Social Psychology.* London: Routledge and Kegan Paul, 1953.

Margolis, Edward. Quotes from an unpublished letter by Mike Gold. Public lecture at conference on Richard Wright, University of Iowa, June 1971.

Matusow, Allen. *Joseph McCarthy.* Englewood Cliffs, N.J.: Prentice Hall, 1970.

McDowell, Tremaine. "The Negro in the South Novel Prior to 1850." In *Images of the Negro in American Literature,* edited by Seymour L. Gross and John Edward Hardy. Chicago: University of Chicago Press, 1966.

McKay, Claude. *Harlem: Negro Metropolis.* New York: Harpers, 1933.

———. *A Long Way from Home.* New York: Lee Furman, 1937.

———. *Home to Harlem.* Boston: Northeastern University Press, 1987. Originally published by Harpers, 1928.

Meier, August, and Elliot Rudwick. *From Plantation to Ghetto.* New York: Hill and Wang, 1966.

Mencken, H. L. *Mencken,* edited by Alistair Cooke. New York: Vintage Books, 1955.

Meyer, John, and Brian Rowan. "Institutionalized Organizations: Formal Structure as Myth and Community." *American Journal of Sociology* 83 (1977): 340–63.

Mills, C. Wright. *The Marxists.* New York: Penguin, 1963.

Modleski, T. *Loving with a Vengeance: Mass-Produced Fantasies for Women.* New York: Methuen, 1982.

Moynihan, Daniel Patrick, and Nathan Glazer. *Beyond the Melting Pot.* Cambridge, Mass.: MIT Press, 1963.

Myrdal, Gunnar. *An American Dilemma.* New York: McGraw-Hill, 1964.

Neal, Larry. "Middle Passage and After." In *New Black Voices,* edited by Abraham Chapman. New York: New American Library, 1972.

———. "The Black Arts Movement." In *The Black Aesthetic,* edited by Addison Gale Jr. New York: Anchor Books, 1972b.

North, Sterling. *New York World Telegram and Sun,* 16 April 1952.

O'Meally, Robert. *The Craft of Ralph Ellison.* Cambridge, Mass.: Harvard University Press, 1980.

Ogorzaly, Michael. *Waldo Frank: Prophet of Hispanic Regeneration.* Lewisburg, Pa.: Bucknell University Press, 1994.

Osofsky, Gilbert. *Harlem: The Making of a Ghetto 1890–1930.* New York: Harper and Row, 1966.

———. *The Burden of Race.* New York: Harper Torchbook, 1968.

Ottley, Roi. *New World A-Coming.* New York: New York Times, Arno Books Reprint, 1968.

Petersen, R. A. *The Production of Culture.* Beverly Hills, Calif.: Sage, 1976.

Petry, Ann. *The Street.* New York: Pyramid Books, 1971.

Phillips, Cabell. *The Truman Presidency.* New York: Macmillan, 1966, 361.

Popcock, J. G. A. "Texts as Events: Reflections on the History of Political Thought." In *Politics of Discourse,* edited by Kevin Sharpe and Steven N. Zwicker. Berkeley: University of California Press, 1987.

Powell, Walter. *Getting into Print: The Decision-Making Process in Scholarly Publishing.* Chicago: University of Chicago Press, 1985.

Prescott, Orville. *New York Times,* 16 April 1952.

Quarles, Benjamin. *The Negro in the Making of America,* New York: Macmillan, 1969. Originally published in 1964.

Radway, Janice. *Reading the Romance: Women, Patriarchy, and Popular Literature.* Chapel Hill: University of North Carolina Press, 1984.

Rampersad, Arnold. *The Life of Langston Hughes.* New York: Oxford, 1986.

Rampersad, Arnold, and David Roessel. *The Collected Poems of Langston Hughes.* New York: Alfred A. Knopf, 1994.

Randall, Dudley, ed. *The Black Poets.* New York: Bantam Books, 1971.

Record, Wilson. *Race and Radicalism.* Ithaca, N.Y.: Cornell University Press, 1964.

Redding, Saunders J. *On Being Black in America.* Indianapolis: Bobbs Merrill, 1951.

Rideout, Walter. *The Radical Novel in America.* New York: Hill and Wang, 1956.

Rodgers, M. F. *Novels, Novelists, and Readers: Toward a Phenomenological Sociology of Literature.* Albany: State University of New York Press, 1991.

Sanchez, Sonia. "Liberation Poem." In *New Black Voices,* edited by Abraham Chapman. New York: New American Library, 1972.

Schott, Webster. *Kansas City Star,* 31 May 1952.

Schudson, Michael. *Advertising, the Uneasy Persuasion: Its Dubious Impact on American Society.* New York: Basic Books, 1984.

Scott, James. *Domination and the Arts of Resistance.* New Haven, Conn.: Yale University Press, 1990.

Silberman, Charles. *Criminal Violence–Criminal Justice.* New York: Random House, 1978.

Sillen, Samuel. "The Response to *Native Son.*" *New Masses* 35 (23 April 1940).

Singh, Amritjit, William S. Shiver, and Stanley Brodwin. *Harlem Renaissance: Revaluations.* New York: Garland, 1989.

Spellman, A. B. *Black American Music: Four Lives.* New York: Schocken Paperback, 1970.

Spero, Sterling, and Abraham Harris. *The Black Worker.* New York: Atheneum Press, 1969.

Stearns, Harold. *Civilization in America.* New York: Harcourt and Brace, 1922.

Steinberg, Stephen. *The Ethnic Myth.* Boston: Beacon Press, 1981.

Swidler, Ann. "Culture in Action: Symbols and Strategies." *American Sociological Review* 51 (1986): 273–86.

Takaki, Ronald. *Iron Cages: Race and Culture in 19th Century America.* New York: Oxford, 1979.

Taylor, Rockie D. "Black Henry." In *New Black Voices,* edited by Abraham Chapman. New York: New American Library, 1972.

Time. Review of *Another Country,* 29 June 1962.

Toomer, Jean. *Cane.* New York: Harper and Row Perennial Classic, 1969. Originally published by Boni and Liveright, 1923.

Tuchman, G. *Edging Women Out: Victorian Novelists, Publishers, and Social Change.* New Haven, Conn.: Yale University Press, 1978.

Tuttle, William M. *W. E. B. DuBois.* Englewood Cliffs, N.J., 1973. Originally published as "Culture of Negro Art," *Crisis,* xxxii, October 1926, 290–97.

Van Doren, Carl. *Opportunity,* 1924, 93–94.

Van Vechten, Carl. *Nigger Heaven.* New York: Harper Colophon, 1971. Originally published by Alfred A. Knopf, 1926.

Walker, Margaret. Public lecture at Richard Wright conference, University of Iowa, June 1971.

Walton, Oritz. *Music: Black, White, and Blue.* New York: William Morrow, 1972.

Washington, Robert. Interview of Mary Wirth in Chicago, May 1971.

Webb, Constance. *Richard Wright: A Biography.* New York: Putnam, 1968.

White, H., and C. White. *Canvases and Careers.* New York: Wiley, 1965.

White, Walter. *How Far the Promised Land.* New York: Viking, 1955.

———. "Opportunities for Negro Migrants." In *The Negro and The City,* edited by Richard B. Sherman. Englewood Cliffs, N.J.: Prentice Hall, 1970. Originally published as "The Success of Negro Migration" in *Crisis* 19 (January 1920), 112–15.

Wilson, William Julius. *The Declining Significance of Race.* Chicago: University of Chicago Press, 1978.

Wright, Richard. "Joe Louis Uncovers Dynamite." *New Masses,* 8 October 1935.

———. *Uncle Tom's Children: Five Long Stories.* New York: Harper and Row, 1938.

———. *Native Son.* New York: Harper and Row, 1940.

———. *12 Million Black Voices.* New York: Viking Press, 1941.

———. "I Tried to Be a Communist." In *The God Who Failed,* edited by Richard Crossman. New York: Bartram Books, 1950. Originally published in *Atlantic Monthly,* August 1944.

———. *Black Boy.* New York: Harper and Row Perennial Classic, 1945a. Originally published by Harper, 1945.

———. "Introduction to Black Metropolis." In *Black Metropolis,* edited by Horace Cayton and Sinclair Drake. New York: Harcourt Brace, 1945b.

———. *Black Power.* New York: Harper and Row, 1954a.

———. *Savage Holiday.* New York: Avon, 1954b.

———. *The Color Curtain.* Cleveland and New York: World Publishing, 1956.

———. *Pagan Spain.* New York: Harper and Row, 1956b.

———. *White Man, Listen!* Garden City, N.Y.: Doubleday, 1957.

———. *The Long Dream.* Garden City, N.Y.: Doubleday, 1958.

———. *Eight Men.* Cleveland and New York: World Publishing, 1961.

———. *Lawd Today.* New York: Walker and Co., 1963.

———. *The Outsider.* New York: Harper and Row Perennial Paperback, 1965. Originally published by Harper, 1953.

———. "How Bigger Was Born." In *Richard Wright's* Native Son, edited by Richard Abcarian. Belmont, Calif.: Wadsworth, 1970. Originally published in *Saturday Review,* 1 June 1940.

———. "Blue Print or Negro Writing." In *Richard Wright Reader,* edited by Ellen Wright and Michel Fabre. New York: Harper and Row, 1978. Reprinted from *New Challenge II,* Fall 1937.

Wuthnow, Robert. *Meaning and Moral Order: Explorations of Cultural Analysis.* Berkeley: University of California Press, 1987.

Index

349

on, 84–86; ideological forces affecting, 39–41, 40*f*, 44–47; on *Invisible Man*, 222–23; and McKay, 77–79; in postwar period, 194–96; Wright and, 142–43
black lower class: current status of, 335–36; naturalistic protest school on, 174–75
black middle class: Baraka and, 291–92; and black nationalism, 280; Cullen on, 116; current status of, 335; *Home to Harlem* on, 84; Hughes and, 101–3; and McKay, 77; naturalistic protest school on, 173–74; new, emergence of, 196–99; in postwar period, 191–93; in twenties, 45–46; Van Vechten on, 62
black militants, 272–73. *See also* black nationalism
black music, 31, 320; and emancipation of white America, 34–35; *Home to Harlem* on, 81; Sanchez on, 310
Black Muslim movement, 255–56, 262; Baldwin and, 264–65
black nationalism, 268; Baldwin and, 266; growth of, 276–81; Hughes and, 93; as ideological force, 40*f*, 42–44; *Invisible Man* on, 212–13; and literary trends, 275–315; McKay and, 75; versus socialism, 144–45
Black Panthers, 278
Black Power, 280
Black Power (Wright), 128
black publications, on *Native Son*, 167–68
black rage: Baldwin on, 263–69; Baraka on, 292–93, 301–2; Wright on, 160
black unemployment, 239
black working class: and Black Muslim movement, 255–56; McKay and, 76; in postwar period, 192–93
black writers: audiences of, 100; belief in emancipation of white culture, 25–27, 34–35; black ethnic culture and, 307; and Communist Party, 127, 138–39; misguided optimism in twenties, 23–28; roles of, 8; Wright and, 147–51. *See also* friendships

Blauner, Robert, 328–29
Blood on the Forge (Attaway), 172
Blues for Mr. Charlie (Baldwin), 267, 275
Bone, Robert, 18, 80, 87, 149, 172
Bontemps, Arna, 14–15, 23; *God Sends Sunday*, 14; and Wright, 147
Book of American Negro Spirituals (Johnson), 55
Bourdieu, Pierre, 8
Briggs, Cyril, 122
Brooks, Van Wyck, 31
Broun, Heywood, 51
Browder, Earl, 155
Brown, Lawrence, 56
Brown, Norman, 236
Brown v. Board of Education, 242–43
Brown, Wesley A., 197
Brynner, Witter, 52
Bunche, Ralph, 197–98
Burawoy, Michael, 331
Burgess, Ernest, 156
Burke, Kenneth, 107
Burns, Ben, 166
Butcher, Fanny, 170

Caldwell, Erskine, *Tobacco Road*, 101
Calverton, V. F., 103
Canby, Henry Seidel, 168
Cane (Toomer), 14, 105, 109–12
Capouya, Emile, 248
Carmichael, Stokley, 280, 304
Carnegie Foundation, 241
Castro, Fidel, 273, 278–79, 288
Cast the First Stone (Himes), 231
Cather, Willa, 51
Catholicism, 29
Cayton, Horace, 37, 123, 156–57, 162
Cendras, Blaise, 32
Chambers, Whittaker, 184
Chaney, James, 277
Chestnutt, Charles, 18–19
Chicago: Black Muslim movement in, 255; Wright and, 133–36
Chicago School of Sociology, 156–58
The Chinaberry Tree (Fausett), 14
Christianity, Baldwin and, 248, 264, 268–69

Civic Club, 92
Civil Rights intellectuals: and Harlem Renaissance, 47; and McKay, 77; on *Nigger Heaven*, 68–69; parties given by, 50–52
Civil Rights movement: and black nationalism, 43–44; divisions in, 254–62; effects of, 335; emergence of, 241–43; as ideological force, 40*f*, 41–42; and integration, 270–71
Clark, Emily, 52
Clark, John Henrik, 287
Cleaver, Eldridge, *Soul on Ice*, 272–73
Cocteau, Jean, 32
Cohen, Hettie, 284, 296
Cohn, David, 169
Cold War, 184–96, 235
Cole, Nat King, 198
Color (Cullen), 114
The Color Curtain (Wright), 128
The Color Purple (Walker), 336
Colum, Patric, 115
Comedy: American Style (Fausett), 14
Communist Party, 184; and black community, 122–27; black writers and, 127, 138–39; Ellison and, 201–2; *Invisible Man* on, 213–14; on *Native Son*, 166–67; and white American literary community, 136–38; Wright and, 139–51, 154–56, 228–29
Comrade X, 125–26
Comrade Y, 126
Conant, James, 239
Coney Island of the Mind (Ferlinghetti), 236, 287
The Congo (Lindsay), 105
Congress of Racial Equality (CORE), 257, 268, 280
The Conjure Man Dies (Fischer), 14
Conrad, Joseph, 148
co-optive hegemony, 36–38, 329, 331–32
co-optive phase, 321–22, 325
Coplon, Judith, 185
CORE. *See* Congress of Racial Equality
cosmopolitans, 30–31, 52, 271

counterhegemonic black cultural nationalist school, 275–315; emergence of, 281–306; end of, 312–15
Country Place (Petry), 231
Cowley, Malcolm, 136, 168, 201
Crane, Hart, 52, 107
Crime and Punishment (Dostoyevsky), 163
Crisis, 46, 51; and Hughes, 92; and McKay, 77
critical nonconformism, 189–90
Cruse, Harold, 24, 287, 317
Cuba, 278–79; Baraka in, 287–88
Cullen, Countee, 112–16; background of, 113; *Color*, 114; and Hughes, 94–95, 101; and interracial socialization, 51; *One Way to Heaven*, 14, 116; and primitivist school, 71; and Van Vechten, 66
cultural hegemony theory, 8–9, 327–28; and black cultural subjugation, 326–30; on white liberal intellectuals, 330–34
cultural nationalist school, 275–315
culture: power and, 7–8; production of, 7; sociology of, and ideologies of black American literature, 5–9; as symbolic codes, 6
Cunard, Nancy, 47–49; on *Nigger Heaven*, 65
Curtis, Natalie, 95

Daiches, David, 168
Daily Worker, 151, 186
Dali, Salvador, 52
Daniels, Jonathan, 169
Dark Laughter (Anderson), 32–33, 106
Dark Princess (DuBois), 14
Darrow, Clarence, 52, 152, 163
Davis, Ben, 166
Davis, Frank, 168
Deacons for Defense, 278
The Dead Lecturer (Baraka), 295
Debs, Eugene, 90, 121
Demby, William, 181; *Beetle Creek*, 204, 230–31

About the Author

Robert E. Washington received his Ph.D. in sociology from the University of Chicago. He is a professor of sociology at Bryn Mawr College.